BUSINESS LEADERSHIP
IN A CHANGING WORLD

BUSINESS LEADERSHIP IN A CHANGING WORLD

A Report of the International
Industrial Conference at San Francisco
September 11–15, 1961, sponsored by
National Industrial Conference Board
and Stanford Research Institute

Editor: Robert L. Baker
National Industrial Conference Board

McGRAW-HILL BOOK COMPANY, INC.
New York   Toronto   London
1962

BUSINESS LEADERSHIP IN A CHANGING WORLD

PREFACE

The International Industrial Conference held in San Francisco in September, 1961, brought together by special invitation about 500 business leaders from 60 countries of the free world. The purpose of the week-long meeting was to provide a forum in which the senior executives of private enterprise could take stock of the present and exchange experience, philosophies, and information on common problems, opportunities, responsibilities, and goals for the future. Such a meeting, it was believed, could contribute to a more rapid and balanced world economic growth, and would be a significant act of leadership through private initiative for the benefit of peoples everywhere.

Four years had passed since a similar and very successful conference had been held, also in San Francisco. Ever since that historic meeting, business leaders around the world had been expressing interest in a new opportunity to get together. So much was happening, so many changes were taking place, that the need was indisputable. The European Common Market had come of age much more rapidly than was anticipated, other regional economic groups were taking shape, and the Communist bloc was mounting a serious challenge to the free world on the economic front. Perhaps most important of all, twenty new nations had won their political independence. They were making their voices heard at the United Nations and in other international organizations. With few exceptions they had little but their sovereignty, raw materials, unskilled manpower, and a determination to better the way of life of their people. Although desperately in need of assistance, they appeared to be fearful of private enterprise—fearful that they would become a victim of economic colonialism.

Many older countries were still struggling with unbalanced economies, too dependent on the economic vagaries of primary products. Even the highly industrialized and prosperous countries were finding themselves confronted by the necessity for making major adjustments to the changing world economic scene.

What did the leaders of private enterprise have to say—broadly, as to their philosophies and goals, and specifically, as to their experience and proposed solutions? This report answers that question. Of the 57 addresses that follow, 43 are by distinguished business authorities from outside the United States.

Neil H. McElroy, General Chairman of the Conference, stressed the search for facts and unfettered opinion in his opening remarks: "From our meetings will come no proclamations or ringing manifestoes. We shall not leave here agreeing with each other on every matter we discuss. But I am confident that we shall leave better prepared and more deeply inspired to meet successfully the momentous common problems we face."

Co-sponsorship of the International Industrial Conference was undertaken by the National Industrial Conference Board, with headquarters in New York City, and Stanford Research Institute, in Menlo Park, California. Both are nonprofit organizations with long experience in the study of economic and management problems. The costs of the Conference were met by 150 United States and Canadian companies that were convinced of its potential value in strengthening the economies of the free world.

From the hundreds of letters received from participants by the Chairman of the Policy Board of the Conference, an excerpt from that of Dr. Paolo N. Rogers, Director of Foreign Relations of the Olivetti Company of Italy, might be taken as typical:

I am particularly impressed by the fact that the conference has revealed a much wider and deeper acceptance by businessmen all over the world of new challenges and responsibilities. No doubt the conference will have an enduring effect and one can only hope that an opportunity will arise in the not too distant future to resume discussions, assess achievements, and forecast developments.

J. E. Wallace Sterling
Chairman of the Policy Board
International Industrial Conference

CONTENTS

Preface   v

I. A WORLD PERSPECTIVE   1

The Task for Business Leadership
                                        NEIL H. MC ELROY   3
The Call for Leadership   JOHN J. MC CLOY   12
Economic Growth: The Record
                                        MARTIN R. GAINSBRUGH   25
Economic Growth: The Outlook
                                        SIR OLIVER FRANKS   41

II. INTERDEPENDENCE OF THE
FREE WORLD   57

1. *Population Pressures and the
    Consumption Explosion*   59
    The Demographic Outlook   KINGSLEY DAVIS   59
    Developing Human Resources   ALEXANDER KING   67
    Medical and Biochemical Implications
                                        S. CHANDRASEKHAR 76
    The Consumption Explosion
                                        CHARLES H. KELLSTADT 82

2. *The Changing Structure of World Trade*   93
    Primary Commodity Problems
                                        JOSÉ GARRIDO TORRES 93

Competition Among Industrial Nations
HATSUJIRO YOSHIDA 101

The Impact of Regional Groups
LÉON A. BEKAERT 106

*Institutional Arrangements to Advance
World Trade* J. ROYER 114

The OECD and Future World Trade
W. RANDOLPH BURGESS 127

3. *Investment and Financial Policies* 137
*Evaluation of Structures in
International Finance* MARCUS WALLENBERG 137

India's Monetary and Fiscal Disciplines
H. V. R. IENGAR 146

Currencies, Capital, Balance of Payments
HERMANN J. ABS 154

*Investment and Financial Policies for Latin
America* FELIPE HERRERA 162

A Note on Spain's Economic Recovery
IGNACIO HERRERO 172

4. *The Newly Developing Economies* 176
Patterns for Private Participation
PAOLO N. ROGERS 176

Utilizing Internal Investments AMIRALI H. FANCY 188

Problems in Giving Aid MARCEL A. DEMONQUE 195

Management and Growth SIR LESLIE ROWAN 202

5. *Government-Business Relationships for Growth* 211
Government's Responsibilities WALTER L. GORDON 211

The Responsibilities of Business
SIR SIK-NIN CHAU 221

How Much Public Enterprise?
EDGAR F. KASIER 229

A Program for Economic Growth
ABOL HASSAN EBTEHAJ 234

III. STRENGTHENING BUSINESS LEADERSHIP — 245

Plenary Addresses: Some Fundamentals — 247
    Beginning at the Beginning   LOGAN T. JOHNSTON 247
    Ethical Principles   VITTORIO VALLETTA 254
    The Growing Importance of Organization
        JOSEPH A. GRAZIER 259
    Developing High-level Leaders   THOMAS J. BATA 267
    New Responsibilities   CRAWFORD H. GREENEWALT 274

1. Business and Public Policy — 281
    Business: Enemy or Citizen?   M. A. RANGOONWALA 281
    Preserving the Free Enterprise Concept
        HANS HOHN 287
    Providing a Good Climate for Business
        I. C. THYGESEN 293
    Industry-Government Cooperation in Australia
        G. G. FOLETTA 298
    Influencing Public Policy in Britain
        SIR NORMAN KIPPING 304

2. Financing Corporate Growth — 309
    Helping the Smaller Company   HENRI DEROY 309
    Risk Investment without Ownership Control
        SIR NUTCOMBE HUME 315
    Commercial Banking in Japan   KIICHIRO SATOH 322
    Growth Through Auto-financing
        FERNAND J. COLLIN 327

3. Technology and Growth — 332
    Budgeting for Research and Development
        HANS C. BODEN 332
    The Two Technologies   MAURICE J. PONTE 338
    National Policy and Technological Investment
        MALCOLM P. FERGUSON 348

Prerequisites to Technological Progress
GUNNAR RANDERS 356

Stimulating Technological Development
K. Y. KING 359

4. *Long-range Corporate Planning: Case Studies* 363
Worthington Corporation
WALTHER H. FELDMANN 363

N. V. Philips P. F. S. OTTEN 369
The Thyssen Group HANS-GÜNTHER SOHL 380

5. *The Multinational Company* 386
Why Expand Overseas? SVEN T. ABERG 386
Facing Political Realities ENRICO BIGNAMI 396
Local Autonomy and Central Control
PAUL RYKENS 405
The Parent Company and Local Management
WALTER LATTMAN 411

**IV. CHALLENGE FROM FOUR
CONTINENTS** 419

Plain Talk from an African A. ROMEO HORTON 421
Private Enterprise and India's Plans G. L. MEHTA 426
Alliance for Progress in Latin America
EUGENIO MENDOZA 433
Freedom Calls Again HENRY C. ALEXANDER 438

SUMMATION J. E. WALLACE STERLING 447

*Organization of the International
Industrial Conference, 1961* 456

I

A World Perspective

What can we do, as businessmen, to strengthen the free system the world over? How can we work more effectively to strengthen man's faith in freedom by furnishing him the opportunity to develop and maintain his own dignity and to work toward his own personal aspirations? How can we best help to reduce the starvation, disease, and illiteracy that are stifling the majority of the earth's people?

NEIL H. MC ELROY

1

A World Perspective

For centuries mankind's afflictions were endured because they were accepted as a natural state of being. Great sections of the world were isolated from progress. But today men everywhere know that a better way of life not only exists, but is attainable. To millions upon millions, this knowledge is coming to motivate every judgment, every act.

THE TASK FOR BUSINESS LEADERSHIP

By Neil H. McElroy *

It is a great pleasure to join in welcoming you to this Conference. The environment of the city in which we meet, on its record, is conducive to accomplishments of historic importance. San Francisco, as you know, was the meeting place of the international conference which drew up the charter for the United Nations 16 years ago. It was in this city, a decade ago, that 48 nations joined in signing an enlightened peace treaty with Japan. And four years ago, business leaders of the free world closed ranks in this same city in which we are gathered as they met in a dramatic International Industrial Development Conference.

Today the business statesmen from 60 nations are meeting to-

* Chairman, The Procter & Gamble Company; former U. S. Secretary of Defense (1957–59); director, General Electric Company and the Chrysler Corporation. Mr. McElroy is a member of The Business Council, the Council for International Progress in Management, the Policy Board of the Business Council for International Understanding. He is a councillor, trustee, and former chairman of the National Industrial Conference Board.

3

gether to consider the opportunities for private initiative to speed the progress of free peoples everywhere.

There is a common purpose among us that can produce more than the individual gains we shall make through a free exchange of ideas and information. That exchange is a desirable end in itself; but beyond it, this conference holds the seed of a new vitality among free institutions that can decisively affect the course of world affairs.

From our meetings will come no proclamations or ringing manifestoes. We shall not leave here agreeing with each other on every matter we discuss. But I am confident that we shall leave better prepared and more deeply inspired to meet successfully the momentous common problems we face.

AN OPPORTUNITY AND AN OBJECTIVE

The great, overriding opportunity afforded us here is to strengthen the alliance for the progress of the whole free world.

We cannot overstate the importance of this high objective. For we have far more at stake than the improvement of our individual enterprises, or of our individual national economies. At stake is the survival of the kind of society in which our enterprises and our economies are possible. We are at a crucial juncture in time when the abilities of our economies to stand separately depend on our willingness to work mightily together for their defense and their growth.

FACING THE FACT OF TWO WORLDS

We face the fact that we have in the world today two strong political and social philosophies that are moving mankind in two opposing directions. One is the Communist philosophy, which embraces the gospel of state-dictated decisions with respect to the public and private affairs of its citizens. A fundamental political determination of international Communism is that free nations must be subverted to Communism or be destroyed.

The other is the philosophy of the free world, which holds that free choice is the right of all men and that the purpose of the state is to serve individual opportunity and freedom. On the one hand, we see totalitarianism set out as the price that *must* be paid for economic progress. On the other, we have the promise that human freedom is not only compatible but interdependent with the raising of standards of living on a great world scale. It makes no difference what may be the form of the political organization of our free world countries; it matters not whether your country or my country is committed or uncommitted, or is a developed or a developing country. We are united in the resolve that we shall not permit the domination of the world by international Communism or by any other superstate.

In support of that issue, we are locked in a vast struggle over virtually the entire face of the earth. We must accept the likelihood that we shall be engaged in this contest for decades to come. The totalitarian leaders are set in their course. We are dedicated to ours—to the determination that all men are entitled to the blessings and opportunities that only a free society can supply. As we have come to grips with these differences, we have faced many crises. Without question, we shall be tested by many more, not of our making, but as a result of consistent aggressive action by the Communist world.

Today the critical focus is on Berlin. The situation the Soviets have chosen to create there is, of course, cause for grave anxiety. I do not discount it in any way. But I would point out that the contest between the two major social philosophies is not concentrated in a single location or type of endeavor. It is with us, without pause, in many forms and in many places throughout the world. We must give our continuing attention to the over-all demands which this massive competition places upon us.

Of course, the most apparent is the opposing confrontation of military power. The development and maintenance of such awesome weapons of destruction as we know today is not something that moral men would desire if they could choose. But for the free nations there is no choice, if independence is to be preserved. Our very maintenance of great deterrent power is the world's best assurance that this struggle will not be settled by a resort to force. If we nations of the free world continue to combine our defensive strength in a solid front, and if we have the wisdom and steadfastness to keep our weapons in tune with our rapidly advancing scientific capabilities, our opponents are not likely to risk combat as the route to decision.

The outcome, then, will be decided in other ways.

TO MEET THE ECONOMIC CHALLENGE

The fact is that the Communists—most recently in the draft program of the Soviet Communist party, prepared under Mr. Krushchev's direction—have expressed confidence many times that freedom can be defeated by nonmilitary methods, notably subversion and economic competition. There is no lack of evidence of the diligence with which they propose to move in these fields.

Our ability to carry on the struggle of *economic competition* will underlie all the factors that determine the ultimate course of events. Equally, let us agree that this is the field of competition that we should most welcome. There is ample evidence that a free society has the inherent potential to give its people far greater economic benefit than the state-directed economy of a totalitarian society.

A SHOWCASE OF FREEDOM

The contrast between West Germany and East Germany is an example standing vividly before the eyes of the world. Any traveler who goes from prosperous West Germany to dispirited, dull East Germany sees it immediately. Since 1949, more than 2½ million people have left their homes in East Germany to take up new lives across the border. These people represent one out of every seven citizens formerly under Communist East Germany's rule. Until passage between East to West was forcibly halted, they continued to pour across into West Germany at a rate of more than a thousand a day.

What are their reasons for wanting to leave East Germany? It is not only that their spirits revolt against the police state; it is that the free society offers them genuine *economic* opportunity. Across from the stagnant, regimented routine of East Germany is a bustling, productive, rewarding society in which they can earn a good living for themselves and their families while working in dignity and without fear. In the two parts of Germany we have a clear demonstration of the superior drive and productivity of a free as compared with a Communist economy.

Each of our nations, of course, must decide for itself how it intends to build its economic strength. But this fact should not obscure an equally essential one—that the continued freedom of each of our nations to make individual national decisions will depend on our willingness to make them in the interest of our common effort. Unsolved differences between any parts of the free world complex will represent a weakening of our total position. Any rationalization of our problems will serve to strengthen it.

We are meeting here to consider specific problems and opportunities in our international business relationships. The subjects on our agenda are well designed to give us maximum results in these considerations. But along with the subject matter, pervasive questions almost surely will be present in every meeting —every exchange of views—in every expression of conviction— between us.

What can we do, as businessmen, to strengthen the free system the world over? How can we work more effectively to strengthen man's faith in freedom by furnishing him the opportunity to develop and maintain his own dignity and to work toward his own personal aspirations? How can we best help to reduce the starvation, disease, and illiteracy that are stifling the majority of the earth's population?

For centuries these afflictions were endured because they were accepted as a natural state of being. Great sections of the world were isolated from progress. But today men everywhere know that a better way of life not only exists, but is attainable. To millions upon millions, this knowledge is coming to motivate every judgment, every act. Nor is it difficult to understand such motivation when we consider that over half of the world's people live where the average per capita income is less than $100 a year.

The Communist strategy is to take advantage of the discontent that occupies men's minds when they conclude that their existing society cannot meet the problems that keep them in hunger and despair. The Communist tactic is to win not by dissolving this discontent but by agitating it until even the surrender of liberty seems a bearable price to pay for the *promise* of a better lot. The record shows, of course, that a better lot, in terms of standards of living, is far easier for the Communists to promise than to deliver.

Even in relatively promising Communist economies, the direction has been backward. Throughout the satellite empire in Eastern Europe, food shortages are chronic. In China, the Red regime has only intensified the threat of famine that stalks the Chinese people.

THE BURDEN OF PROOF IS ON US

Nevertheless, the burden of proof is on the protagonists of the free society. We cannot succeed simply by pointing to the pitfalls of the police state. If we are to win the minds and loyalties of men, we must lead the way in causes they will support. The greatest cause to the greatest number of the world's people is the elimination of the grinding poverty that envelops their lives.

This is not a task that can be achieved solely by our governments. It is a need that, in the ultimate, calls for large measures of the skill, the daring, and the resourcefulness of private initiative. Working with cooperative government, business enterprise is the most dynamic force on earth for employing the constructive energies of men.

If we apply this force more massively to the erasure of poverty and the raising of living standards, we need have no fear of exhausting our resources in the process. On the contrary, over the long term the goal of lifting standards of living the world over is compatible with the essential business goal of profitable operation—profits to be reinvested in greater opportunities to benefit more people.

What greater incentive for market development could there be than the potential that is represented by that half of the world's population striving now to find the means to become effective consumers in the market place? The problem on which I am touching is perhaps the most complex and difficult with which mankind is concerned. Fraught with imponderables and discouragements, it nevertheless demands urgent progress toward solution.

I would call your attention to two basic responsibilities that are vital to it. The first is for each of us to manage our own respective functions within our own economies with the greatest proficiency of which we are capable. The productivity of our free society depends on the initiative of its individual units, each putting such demands on itself for improved efficiency that the composite result will outstrip the progress of any dictated efforts of an authoritarian system.

MANAGEMENT SPELLS THE DIFFERENCE

It is management that spells the difference between success or failure for any business enterprise or for any free society. And when I say management, I mean those few men who, by the nature of modern management, give direction to the entire operation. Their direction, if it is capable, contributes in a critically important way to the productiveness of the assets—both personal and material—of the enterprise. It helps to assure vigorous national growth and to produce maximum citizen opportunity.

Ineffective management is a devastating drag on an economy. It wastes important resources in capital and labor and lowers the total capacity of the nation to provide sufficient jobs and adequate income for its people. Wise, yet dynamic direction of our individual production and distribution units, then, is at the very foundation of our separate national strengths and our total progress.

BUSINESS LEADERSHIP MUST PARTICIPATE MORE BROADLY

Even as we acknowledge that principle, however, we recognize that far more is required of business leadership. We cannot devote ourselves to our business pursuits to the exclusion of other vital national interests.

The political and social determinations of our respective countries are—or should be—matters of basic concern to us. The problems and needs of our governments call for the broad participation of business executives. It is essential that business should have an articulate voice in the formulating of political programs that have impact on the economy.

Business leadership has reason to be deeply interested also in the nation's educational progress. The course of world history is turning as surely upon the relative levels of education among peoples as upon any other factor. Our influence can be great in the advancement of universal and unfettered education in our respective countries. As we exert our influence in behalf of better education, we fortify our free institutions, because sound education is essential to sound self-government; it is indispensable to the best development of human and natural resources; it is a matchless builder of individual dignity; it enables a people to appreciate other cultures, and to be more able to evaluate its own loyalties in the historic struggle between totalitarianism and freedom.

THE NEED FOR PLANNING AND COOPERATION

Our second responsibility is to plan together, in the most practical terms possible, to assure that our free industrial enterprise will grow in its value as a positive world force.

We businessmen have a long way to go in all of the areas I have noted—in management efficiency, in political and social participation, in advancing better education, and in making a maximum contribution to the alliance of free nations. All of us here represented have much to offer in terms of cooperation for progress. Let us consider our opportunities together with a new magnitude of imagination, boldness, and pioneer spirit. Let us run the gamut of exploration into those areas of cooperative action that can lead to greater free world economic strength.

We have seen such cooperation cast in dramatic form in the development of great regional marketing programs, such as those in Europe and Latin America. We may well expect that other such developments can be—and will be—worked out in the near future.

Finally, let us keep in mind the importance of how our progress as economic entities looks to other nations, especially the newer nations. All that we accomplish in friendly and productive cooperation serves as a showcase of the values of a free society to those undecided peoples who ask: Which kind of social and political organization will produce the better life for us?

The competition most visible to mankind will not be in technology and science in themselves. It will be in the purposes to which these great forces are put. If each of us in his own country, and all of us in concert, will demonstrate the clear purposes of our society—the constant improvement of our living standards in an environment which protects all the satisfactions of living, working, worshiping, and thinking in freedom—we shall forge decisively ahead.

*As businessmen we no longer can continue
to look only at the industrial problems of the
world and think we are doing our full duty
or, as we are prone to call it, "minding our
business." There may very well be no industrial problems to worry about if we do
not look up from our concentration on producing and marketing problems and start
thinking right away as to how we are to
solve the greater issues with which the world
is now faced and will be faced perhaps before our industrial problems can be solved.*

THE CALL FOR LEADERSHIP

By John J. McCloy *

Dealing with something that is so much more political than
industrial probably cannot properly be called keynoting this
meeting, but I suppose it is difficult to list anything more important to industry the world over than the political conditions
under which it operates. At any rate, I have determined to speak
of several things that are related more to the political than to the
industrial conditions we now face in this world.

It seems inconceivable, but it is a fact, that we today find ourselves again face-to-face with threats of another war—a bare sixteen years after the close of the last one. However high our hopes

* Special Adviser to President Kennedy on Disarmament; counsel, Milbank,
Tweed, Hope & Hadley (N. Y. City); director and member, executive com-
mittee, American Telephone & Telegraph Co., The Chase Manhattan Bank,
Westinghouse Electric Corp.; director, Allied Chemical Corp., Metropolitan
Life Insurance Co., Chase International Investment Corp.; chairman, The
Ford Foundation. U. S. Military Governor and High Commissioner for Ger-
many (1949–52); president, International Bank for Reconstruction and De-
velopment (1947–49); Assistant Secretary of War (1941–47).

12

and firm our determination to do all possible to avoid it, we cannot blink the fact that the situation is serious.

What is the malady that so plagues human society that we have so frequently to face the threat of war? In my lifetime I have taken part in two World Wars, in each of which, at least so far as the United States and those who fought with the United States were concerned, the result was a total victory. In each case we felt, as we endured the struggle, that if we could but achieve the victory, the future would be made secure from another war. After each, there was a universal determination to establish the means by which wars could be avoided. Serious efforts were made to erect institutions designed to bring about a condition where resort to force or threats of force in the settlement of international disputes would be outlawed. How dismally we have failed!

What is wrong with the world's thinking and its statesmanship? In all conscience the weapons of the last war were horrible enough in their devastating effects to impel men to abjure their use again, but when compared to those we now know how to employ, they might almost be termed primitive. How can the human race keep on doing this to itself? There are probably a number among you who think they can foresee the consequences of a thermonuclear war, but I doubt whether there is anyone in this audience who truly can give any dependable appraisal of what the total effect of such a war would be upon mankind. Yet we do not have the reliable substitute for such a futile and suicidal means of settling our disputes. The question confronting us is what is to be done about it, and there is a grim urgency pressing for the solution.

CRISIS AFTER CRISIS

We may slide by the ominous Berlin problem and the German problem by a means not yet too clear, but what about the *next* crisis, for these things have a dangerous habit of following one another. It is not reasonable to expect that we can forever move from one crisis to another, always averting disaster only through the deterrence involved in a nice balance of terror.

On the last day of 1960 I retired from the chairmanship of a bank with the thought that the time had come in my life where others could well take up my duties of administration and I could devote myself to the performance of those tasks which I most wanted to do. I was not seeking a pasture by any means, but I did labor under the illusion that I could devote a little more time than before to reading, good companionship, hunting, fishing and a more normal family life and so on. You know that refrain. Then, with no warning, I was asked to become an Adviser to the President on matters of Disarmament in a period when the whole prospect of disarmament, international understanding and confidence in a divided world was at a very low ebb, indeed. A good part of my previous government experience had been with armaments—preparing the country for war or helping maintain the country in war, as had been the experience of those I see before me today. I had a rather clear insight into what wars and modern weapons, including atomic weapons, could achieve, and it required little argument to convince me how profoundly necessary it was for mankind to seek the means of ridding itself of this scourge if we were to hold forth to those who take our places the prospect of their living their lives in decency and peace.

A COMPLEX AND DIFFICULT TASK

For over eight months now I have been struggling with this matter of disarmament and I am prepared to say that I have never faced as complicated, as difficult, or as challenging a problem in or out of business, in or out of war, in or out of the law, as this one. It involves or could involve every aspect of our national life—foreign policy, defense policy, economic policy—indeed, our whole social structure. I use the term "disarmament" in its widest sense to include the reduction or elimination of arms, the control of arms, also the maintenance and improvement of our peace-keeping machinery.

The President asked me to advise him not only in regard to policy in respect of disarmament, but also to make recommendations as to the form of the organization within the government which should be set up in order to deal with this very important issue. This I have attempted to do, and the bills now before the

Congress to set up a statutory agency to deal with this question are the result of the President's acceptance of those recommendations. And if one may ask why the President is requesting the Congress of the United States to set up such an agency at the same time we are building up our strength in the face of threats of war, I believe the answer is that it is now of all times that we should examine seriously this matter of disarmament to see if it can advance us toward the achievement of a peaceful world.

Disarmament and its attendant problems have been with us in one form or another ever since the close of the war—every United Nations meeting deals with them and in the coming sessions of the United Nations the issue will again crowd the docket, and there will probably be a large number of resolutions about it induced by a wide cross-current of motives. We have had negotiations going on, sometimes two or three at a time, dealing with the subject of disarmament, and we have used a variety of means and methods to make progress with it. Some, I am obliged to say, were devised on too short notice and with too little preparation to cope with the seriousness of the problem and its manifold complexities.

THE TEST–BAN FAILURE

The first problem with which the new United States Administration had to deal was the test-ban negotiations at Geneva. It required the most intensive effort to work out a definitive and practicable position, clear it with the many agencies of government which had a deep and lively interest in the subject, and do the same thing then with our allies and associates who with us share responsibilities for the security of the free world. By dint of much scientific analysis, careful consideration of many security problems, we were, in good time, able to put forward a proposed treaty for a test ban which I felt that any nation seriously determined to find a means for banning future nuclear tests could readily accept. It was made possible by a convocation of scientists and experts knowledgeable in this field, and I do believe that no objective individual or group with an awareness of the factors involved can escape the conclusion that the United States made every reasonable effort, including the granting of solid concessions some of which involve real risks, in the hope of achieving agreement. I think our position at Geneva amply demonstrated our willingness and determination to effect an agreement that all could live with. Now it is futile to recount the weary and frustrating course those negotiations took at Geneva. President Kennedy, the Secretary of State, Arthur Dean, and all of us held the highest hopes for a prompt conclusion of an agreement which might well have been the significant forerunner of further agreements leading both to the relief of some of the burdens of the arms race and to the significant lessening of tensions. I repeat, I do not see how the President of the United States could have clung more tenaciously than he did, not only to the hope of concluding an agreement but also of adjusting his position to meet any reasonable demands of the Soviet Union.

It now transpires that from the very beginning of the talks the Soviets had no interest in concluding a test ban. The nature, the speed, and the number of the recent Soviet nuclear explosions make it abundantly clear that all during those negotiations the most elaborate preparations had been going on in the Soviet Union for the resumption of tests. We informally, but none the less sincerely, offered on several occasions to permit Soviet observers to check for themselves, in this country, to confirm the fact that we were not testing, provided they would permit similar observations in the Soviet Union, but to no avail—a circumstance which now can be better understood. This whole sorry affair is bound to cast doubt on the prospects for other agreements. The fact that the Soviet Union now seeks to merge test-ban talks with talks on so-called comprehensive disarmament, after they themselves demanded a separation of these two only three years ago, a demand to which we earlier reluctantly agreed, accents the time we have lost and the discouraging nature of the exercise in international negotiation through which we have just passed. I think that this phenomenon is one of the most unfortunate developments which has occurred in the history of man's recent search for constructive steps in the field of disarmament and the maintenance of peace.

THERE MUST BE CONTROLS

We have assumed risks during this long period of negotiation because we did conform to a moratorium on tests of all character, whether above or below ground, when it was quite clear that we with our open society could not and would not conduct clandestine tests while it was next to impossible for us to know whether the Soviets were testing secretly. Since their heavy control over the dissemination of information within their country continues, we have to insist upon reasonable verification measures within the Soviet Union if we are to know that obligations taken are being fulfilled. In spite of their many protestations of willingness to install strict control measures, our experience has been that when it comes to the actual agreement and implementation of those measures, as in the test ban, they are promptly repudiated as being attempts at espionage.

I mention all this not by way of recrimination. But I do want to add further evidence to the already imposing array of facts to show that the United States, contrary to incessant charges, has more than proven its seriousness and determination to get ahead with the reduction of the arms race as a contribution to the maintenance of peace. We have, as I said, constantly stressed the need for controls, and it is always in this feature that we have met the greatest obstacles in our talks with the Soviet representatives. Constantly the charge of espionage has been cast because as practical people we have sought to find the means by which disarmament can really take place with the assurance that obligations are being fulfilled. I cannot conceive of a better demonstration of the need for controls and verification and of the need for careful analysis of any better general statements of willingness to submit to them than is given by the Soviet conduct in the test-ban negotiations.

AMERICA'S RECORD ON DISARMAMENT

What continually dumbfounds me is the fact that our conduct and actions in the way of actual disarmament, so deeply contrasting with the facts as related to Soviet armament, seems to mean nothing in the face of the mere statements of Soviet desire for disarmament. I know of no more striking example in the history of a determination to lay aside the implements of war than was contained in the Baruch Plan where, after alone achieving the invention of the atom bomb, we sought immediately after the war to subject it and all the materials which could aid in its production to strict and clearly defined, clearly spelled out, international control. How in the face of this and our record of deep reduction of our forces and armament after both World War I and World War II, when others retained theirs, can we justly be accused of threatening the peace of the world by the maintenance of large armaments? I fail to understand it, but the fact is we are so accused. Or, at best, we are equated with those who have never done as much. The most effective and the most drastic examples of disarmament in history made by any great power have been made by the United States. The charge has, as a matter of fact, frequently been leveled at us with some justice that we have prejudiced the cause of peace because we have disarmed so promptly and so rapidly after the passage of the emergency. We demobilized over 11 million men in a little over a year after World War II, while the Red Army was maintained at a level so high that in relation to ours it simply could not be said to have disarmed. The fact that there has been a rather prevalent opinion abroad among those who go under the title of "unaligned" that the Soviet Union, of all nations, has been more sincerely devoted to the cause of disarmament than we, is simply another tribute to the power and persuasive effects of incessant propaganda. And, in some cases, to the extreme hesitancy of many nations who cherish their nonalignment to express any open criticism except in one direction. I really shudder to think what form the resolutions from Belgrade would have taken had the United States been the first nation to resume testing—and in the atmosphere at that. There is a certain wry compliment involved in this, I am told. It is that more is expected of us than from others—that the nonaligned nations have less to fear from us than they have to fear from others. It is not a particularly warming compliment, however, nor is it particularly well designed to induce restraint upon the other party.

WE MUST CONTINUE THE SEARCH

All this is most discouraging, but the obligation to continue to search for the solution is clear. If we are to deal intelligently and practically with this matter of disarmament with the world in the state in which it is now, it seems obvious that we must be certain that we are well equipped to deal with it. It requires study and skill to make our own sensible proposals, and the same requirements are needed if we are to analyze correctly the proposals that are made to us. The subject demands continuity of thought and preparation. We need the highest order of talent we can find in the scientific field, as well as the best strategic thinkers. We need skillful draftsmen and negotiators. We need statesmen aware of the forces and the opinions which play about the world. Our security, if not our survival, demands it. It is far too vital a subject to be buried in a subordinate bureau of an existing government department, and I say this to other governments as well as to my own. And I am not talking of the United States alone when I say "our." I am talking of the free world, the world that wants to live in peace and freedom. It is dangerous to come forward with an ill-thought-out proposal to meet a particular negotiating due date. On the other hand, it is not enough to refuse to take any action at all when the situation clearly demands that we should. Security can be prejudiced either way.

Perhaps I have dwelt too long on this subject, but in my judgment it does carry some deep implications for you as leaders in your respective countries, and as industrialists, but I feel a little sensitive when some of my friends say, "Why is McCloy, who has been so long involved in preparing for the defense of our country, asking Congress now of all times to pass a bill to set up an agency to deal with disarmament problems?" I believe I have already indicated the answer. You may have noted that the reason for it seems to have been recognized by the representatives of our people. The Senate Foreign Relations Committee unanimously reported out such a bill as I have described, and it passed the Senate by a large majority. I think it is interesting to note the type of men who testified in its favor. First, there was the President's own strong message, which was given a warm and unsolicited endorsement by former President Eisenhower. It was endorsed by General Lemnitzer, by Secretary McNamara, by Under Secretary Gilpatrick of the Defense Department, by General Gruenther, by General Clay, by General Hull of Korean fame, by Secretary of State Rusk, by former Secretary of Defense Lovett, by former Secretary of State Herter, by Ambassador Cabot Lodge, by Thomas Gates, former Secretary of Defense, by Fred Eaton, a former negotiator at Geneva, by Ambassador Wadsworth, also a former negotiator, also by Neil McElroy and others of similar standing. These men certainly cannot be considered insensitive to the security needs of the country and of the times. Their character and experience provide another demonstration of the attitude with which serious men, all of whom have been charged at one time or another with the protection of this nation's security, view the problem which not only this nation—but mankind as well—faces in this thermonuclear era.

NOT BY DISARMAMENT ALONE

But disarmament is not alone the answer to the cause of peace. History will show, I believe, that some wars have been induced by disarmament rather than by armament. Disarmament itself is certainly not synonymous with peace or with the millennium. It could, if improperly implemented, produce disaster, but if continuous and prolific arming with thermonuclear and other mass destructive weapons is not stopped, and if we do not find the honorable substitute for war, one day it is almost inevitable we will all share a common disaster. Concurrent with any drastic development in disarmament, there must be erected a better method than we now have for maintaining the peace. We have to have better and more frequently accepted means of settling our international disputes. Unless we do, we shall never have full, or I should say perhaps even significant, disarmament. We may have some forms of arms control, but even here these can readily be swept away if we do not find the means wherein our procedures for settling our international disputes are effective and at hand.

THE SEARCH FOR PEACE IS NOT UTOPIAN

There are some who will say that this is Utopian—that great nations will never submit what they term their vital interests to any form of abjudication they do not control. I recognize that this creates problems, for us as well as for other nations, particularly the Soviet Union, with its governmental philosophy. But with the existence of 100 megaton bombs (5,000 times as great as the Hiroshima bomb, and it is not clear that we could not make one 50,000 times as big) or the use of refinements in bacteriological, chemical, and radiological warfare that likewise defy imagination, the alternative is a very real and a very sinister one. Viewed in this light it may make the search for a better means of settling our differences seem much less Utopian and much more necessitous.

I am not going to speak of Berlin. We all can sense the seriousness of that situation, unless we just refuse to think about it. All should know that we do not intend to surrender our rights and we all should now know something, at least, of the intent of the leaders of the Soviet Union in regard to Berlin and Germany. We all know that we are not dealing only with a single city, Berlin, or only with Germany, for that matter. We know we are dealing with the standing and integrity of the whole free world. The subject is too delicate for us to be proffering solutions from this platform, but as businessmen we no longer can continue to look only at the industrial problems of the world and think we are doing our full duty or, as we are prone to call it, "minding our business." There may very well be no industrial problems to worry about if we do not look up from our concentration on producing and marketing problems and start thinking right away as to how we are to solve the greater issues with which the world is now faced and will be faced perhaps before our industrial problems can be solved.

In the first place we have to recognize that there has developed within the world a deep cleavage—ideological, economic, and social. It is one of the great developments of history. We find vast areas of the world emerging from a protected, underdeveloped state into independence with an intense desire to share the affluence of a life of whose existence they have only recently become aware. It is the era of rising expectations and, in addition, we are faced with a tremendous population explosion with its attendant demands. This explosion is not very far ahead and it is an explosion that may also be measured in megatonage so far as its effects on mankind are concerned. And we are faced with the need for meeting and avoiding the threats of cataclysmic war.

WHERE BUSINESS FITS IN

Where does industry and business fit into all this turbulence? What is our obligation and our imperative? I do not know the full answer but somehow in this connection I am reminded of that story they tell of Carlyle when someone reported to him that a famous lady philosopher of the day had finally decided she would accept the universe. "By Gad, she'd better!" said Carlyle. Business and industry had better pause and look at the universe and its condition, for the very environment in which it lives and moves is taking on some extremely menacing shapes. Its ills are becoming too much for just the statesmen of the world to deal with, much less the statesmen of any one nation, however strong and wealthy that nation may be. Vast challenges lie right ahead. We can see the economic and scientific challenges right on our doorstep. There is a dynamism bred of a movement which is stirring vast numbers of people situated in some of the largest areas of the world, and the industry of the free world must find its proper relation to it.

THE IMPERATIVE NEED FOR UNITY

I feel that the organization of the Common Market and the unification of Europe may point the way—it may give us the direction light for our course. We have seen how dangerous dictatorships may become, how unreliable they are, how frequently they breed excesses and wars. If they can marshal great masses of people, however, which they bid fair to do, does not the free world have to set about the organization of its resources, human and material, in a more serious and better form than we have thus far been able to advance? We are experiencing now the difficulties of coordinating a policy between this continent and the European continent. Time lost now may be very, very painful. At the same time there are tremendous forces doing their utmost to divide us and frustrate our determination and our strength. The European continent is itself painfully far from having and asserting the unity that the times demand. There is still in my judgment an outdated inclination in Europe to dwell on its own weakness. For too many years Europe has been dwelling upon its weakness and its inability to play a major part in the determination of world affairs. With over 200 million people, with resources and capacities which make those of Russia and China seem quite miserable, with the finest accumulation of technical and managerial skills that probably exist anywhere, with cultural and artistic reserves that still lead the world, wherein does the weakness of Europe lie except in lack of cohesion, in lack of proper organization and ability to express its strength.

When this great reserve of strength, properly organized and speaking with the general unanimity which its common position and interest should, with proper effort and will, make possible, is added to that of the American continent, the British Isles and other parts of the free world, all other combinations fall quickly into a very much less imposing perspective. There would be no thought of attacking such strength if it were clear that it was determined to protect its common interest and heritage. Not only would the problems of peace in the world be advanced, but most of the problems of the underdeveloped nations of the world would very promptly be brought into far better control. No other group can approach the capital resources, skills, or the markets on which improvement in these areas will depend. All this sounds like a large order, but what has been accomplished already in Europe is an indication of what the energy of a relatively few men and minds can achieve. The times demand large orders in view of the threats that beset the free world.

I read a book the other day that I am sure many of you have

read. It is Clarence Randall's "Folklore of Management." It may not be a profound book, but it is a very readable one and it does explode a number of the fetishes with which industry and its leaders have been deluding themselves in the face of an interdependent, changing, and menacing world. There should be counterparts of that book, and I can think of their titles right away. I would like to see one written on "Folklore of Politics," and another on "The Folklore of Labor." The point is that the time has come to reappraise all our compartmentalized thinking, and rapidly.

ACCEPTING THE WORLD AND ITS CHALLENGES

Your presence here in such numbers and distinction is a clear indication that you have, like Carlyle's lady, accepted the world. You know very well it is more than the industrial, commercial and economic aspects of the world that now demand your attention. Together we face the emergence of the ultimate weapon, the challenge of space, the great ideological conflict, the rising expectations of billions of people, the increase in the world population, the development of science, the threat of suicidal war, the still unorganized potential of the free world, the need above all to preserve and carry on the mighty revolutionary traditions of the freedom of the individual which once again are being threatened. Are not *these* the keynotes which any such distinguished and experienced group as this gathered in these days should weigh and consider, no matter what else may be on the agenda for discussion?

The industrialized nations, old and new, have experienced economic growth of unprecedented character.... In the underdeveloped countries the postwar interval may well have been a period of preparation for achieving a faster rate of growth in the near future. Thus far, the application of scientific knowledge in these areas has resulted principally in expanding population faster than real output.

ECONOMIC GROWTH: THE RECORD

By Martin R. Gainsbrugh *

Within little more than a decade or so after its introduction, the measure known as gross national product has become the most frequently cited statistic in the entire system of economic intelligence. It is today the most widely employed single indicator of the aggregate economic activity of a nation. In the hands of the skilled business analyst changes in the gross national product and its derivatives provide the keys to determining the current state of business as well as why business has grown better or worse.

With the passage of time, interest developed in the use of these measures not only for purposes of current analysis but also to observe trends over the longer run. However, the further back in time the accounts are started, the greater are the hazards of

* Chief economist, National Industrial Conference Board; president, American Statistical Association. Mr. Gainsbrugh was chairman of the Business Research Advisory Council of the Bureau of Labor Statistics (1955–57), member of the Council of Economic Advisers' Business Advisory Committee (1947–57), chairman, Committee on General Business Expectations, Board of Governors of the Federal Reserve System (1955), and member of the Textile Industry Advisory Committee of the U.S. Department of Commerce (1959).

incomparability. This was particularly so for the contribution made by the family and the home, much of which is not reflected in national accounts. Removal of the influence of price change over time is also not without its statistical hazards. Even so, by World War II the usefulness of these measures had been broadened by shifting the emphasis from a business-cycle orientation to longer-run historic comparisons.

COUNTRY–TO–COUNTRY COMPARISONS

Following World War II, public and professional interest turned to comparing the income and output of one country with another. Under the auspices of the United Nations, an organized approach was made toward standardizing the techniques and conventions of national accounting. The economic fashion of the day is now international comparisons of economic growth.

Here, again, as the new field of use was opened up, the degree of comparability and reliability was further strained. The agrarian and less-developed countries continue to derive much of their product from within-the-family operations that are excluded or given low valuation in modern conventions of social accounting. This serves to understate the income level, but to overstate the rate of growth. A new hazard is introduced by the necessity to express the output of each nation in terms of a common world currency. Of late, the public seeks an equally quick yet definitive comparison of growth trends in the national products of the free and totalitarian societies. Involved here is the comparison of the output of nations in which what is to be produced and its value is government-determined with the output of nations in which resource allocation and value is primarily determined within the free market. Without question this places the greatest strain yet imposed on the reliability and significance of national accounting as a basis for international growth comparison. For this and related reasons no such comparison is attempted here.

MEASURING ECONOMIC GROWTH

Economic growth has been measured in several ways, ranging from the simple contrast of rates of change over time in total output to highly detailed comparisons of output per unit of labor or of capital input. In this review the center of interest is the extent to which the various nations have demonstrated an increased ability to turn out more goods and services per head and such alterations as may have occurred in their relative growth performances since the turn of the century. In Table 1 the rates of

Table 1: Annual growth in total and per capita real output in the 20th century and per capita national income in U.S. dollars in 1957–1959, selected countries (World War I and II years omitted for United Kingdom, Germany, Italy, and Denmark; World War II years from Norway, Japan, Australia)

| Country | Duration in years (1) | Annual percent increase in | | Per capita national income in U.S. dollars, annual average 1957–1959 (4) |
		Total real output (2)	Per capita real output (3)	
United Kingdom ...	30	1.67	1.37	900–999
Germany, Federal Republic of	35.5	3.31	n.a.	800–899
Italy	47.5	3.01	2.21	400–499
Denmark	43.5	3.34	2.23	900–999
Norway	51.5	2.82	2.02	800–899
Sweden	55.5	3.31	2.61	1100–1199
United States	49	3.10	1.60	2100–2199
Canada	49	3.63	1.83	1500–1599
Australia	44	2.81	1.11	1100–1199
Japan	44	4.51	3.31	200–299
Argentina	53	3.31	1.01	400–499
Union of South Africa	34.5	4.70	2.70	300–399

SOURCES: Cols. 1, 2: Simon Kuznets; Cols. 3, 4: United Nations.

change in total physical output are examined for a limited number of nations for which reliable long-terms records are readily available. Later, a brief summary will be given of the course of national output during the past decade for virtually all the free nations. Throughout, output is matched against population growth, to determine the extent to which there was more for all to share.

Included in the table are the major industrialized areas of the Western world (excepting France and the Netherlands) as well as Japan, Australia, and Argentina. The entries range in population from the several millions of each of the Scandinavian nations to Japan's total of nearly 100 million and the United States with almost twice that figure. The aggregate for the dozen nations, however, is only about 500 million, or roughly a sixth of the world's total population.

The rates of growth shown for real output were computed in such a way as to exclude the distortions of the war and immediate postwar years for those nations most directly affected. For this reason, the record spans a minimum of about a third of a century's growth experience for the United Kingdom and Germany as compared with a half-century or more for nearly all others.

Insofar as the national accounts permit comparison in dollar terms, they reveal the span in national income per capita to be broad indeed, despite the heavy concentration of industrialized nations in the sample. The average per head of population ranges currently from several hundred dollars in Japan and the Union of South Africa to well over $2,000 for the United States.

RISING POPULATIONS AND RISING LIVING STANDARDS

One central conclusion leaps from the figures here presented as it has from all similar assessments. Economic growth in every country shown has been far in excess of population growth; in some instances output has increased at a rate double or treble that of population. And population, in turn, has been advancing at an unprecedented rate in this century.

World population is now nearly double what it was at the beginning of the century. The net gain in just the past six decades already approaches the absolute population peak ever previously achieved by mankind. In the face of this "swarming of population," living standards have been improved more sharply than in any period of similar length in this or any earlier civilization.

The illustrious dean of the school of national accounting, Simon Kuznets, from whose historic studies are drawn most of the data here used, underscores this conclusion in typical guarded language:

Modern economic growth of nations has two distinctive features: in *all* cases it involves a sustained and substantial rise in product per capita, and in *almost all cases* it involves a sustained and substantial rise in population.... The distinctive feature of modern economic growth is the frequent combination of high rates of growth of the total population and of per capita product, implying even higher rates of growth of total product.

What of the rest of the world, particularly the agrarian or developing economies? Here the empirical data are virtually non-existent for the long term. The results, even for more recent years, must be used with caution, because of the serious limitations surrounding comparability with the heavily urbanized, industrialized areas of the world. For the dozen nations in Table 1, growth over the past six decades has been at an unprecedented rate, yielding at minimum a doubling in living standards, even after allowance for the unparalleled increase in their underlying populations.

Yet even today we know that per capita income of many members of the society of free nations still yields only stark subsistence at best. For this and other reasons dredged from the scraps of evidence available, the body of professional opinion is that economic growth in the developing areas has lagged well behind that of the rest of the industrialized world.

HIGH GROWTH RATES IN NEW AREAS

High growth rates, however, are not the exclusive possession of the long-industrialized nations, nor is the rank and array of high-growth countries today identical with that at the turn of the century. Japan, Argentina, and the Union of South Africa— all three countries with per capita incomes currently well below that of the Western world—rank high in terms of annual growth in total real output. Indeed, Japan's increase in per capita real output of 3.3% annually is the highest rate shown, implying at least a trebling in the flow of goods and services to its inhabitants within the past two generations.

A recent study of economic growth over an even longer period, namely the past century, amplifies this conclusion about the continuing alteration in the ranking of the various nations in the array of world economic growth. The National Institute of Economic and Social Research, London, in "Economic Growth: The Last Hundred Years," a study recently released, finds:

> There is no convincing evidence of constancy or normality in the international pattern of growth rates; almost any hypothesis of constancy which one tries on the figures gets a negative answer—with the one exception that Japan, in almost any period one selects, comes at the top of the table.... Nearly all countries—again, except Japan —have had fairly long periods of both rapid growth and slow growth.

Countries with low rates of economic growth currently may find considerable comfort in the Institute's conclusion that there is no long-term historical inevitability about growth rates.

Before we turn to the record since World War II and the greater wealth of data provided for that period, several other findings of major moment can be culled from the longer-term data.

POPULATION GROWTH AND ECONOMIC GROWTH

Economic growth, while influenced by population growth, is not dependent upon that factor. Sweden for example, ranks high in terms of its annual increase in total real output (3.3%) although its long-term rate of population increase is the lowest of any nation included in Table 1. Conversely, the Netherlands, boasting the highest rate of population increase of Western Europe, is reported to have the slowest growth of total product per man-year.

The National Institute's findings are that the rapid rise in population may have stimulated economic growth, but that it has "not been a major determining factor in the last hundred years. There is absolutely no indication that it is a necessary condition of economic growth; some of the fastest-growing countries have had relatively stable populations."

NO SIGNS OF DECELERATION

Prior to World War II the impact of the Great Depression led to considerable acceptance, particularly in the United States, of the mature, if not stagnant, economy thesis. With the passage of time that decade now appears to have been more a product of the peculiar economic philosophies then prevailing than a harbinger of secular stagnation. Viewed over the longer run, the 30's emerge as a decade of contraction suspended between decades of earlier and subsequent growth and expansion.

In his earlier work, Kuznets did find some evidence of retardation in the rate of growth of product per capita for several nations, but these instances may have been heavily influenced by the depressing effects of wars—in the instances of Japan and Germany—and the prolonged depression in the United States. The National Institute's later study reaches this guarded conclusion:

> It is not safe to say—on the basis of a single comparison of pre-1953 and post-1953 averages—that growth rates are slowing down secularly. ... It is true that since 1950 it is the richest nations that have shown the slowest growth: this might suggest that, after a certain point, the transfer of working population from the manufacturing sector to the service sector could have a slowing-down effect. But it is far too soon to be certain about this.

MORE LEISURE AND MORE GOODS

The draft program of the Soviet Communist Party to be presented to its 22nd Congress in October repeats the familiar thesis of worker exploitation. Two illustrations will suffice: "The workers in capitalist countries will be fated to engage in backbreaking labor to enrich the capitalists. ... Capitalism extensively exploits female and child labor."

Instead, the 20th century has seen a substantial and continuing reduction in the hours of work in virtually every industrialized country as its growth curve mounted. In 1909, manufacturing production workers in the United States labored 57 hours per week on the average for 19.3¢ an hour, or $9.84 a week. In 1960, hours of work averaged 39.7 per week; hourly earnings (from which many fringe benefit items are excluded) averaged $2.29, and average weekly earnings had risen to an all-time peak of $90.91. This record stands in striking contrast to the Soviet charge that "Capitalist automation is robbing the worker of his daily bread—the living standard is dropping."

Child labor has been virtually abolished in the United States and is rapidly disappearing among the industrialized nations. Paid sick leave, extended vacations with pay, pensions and related benefits have become almost a universal practice throughout the Western working world. The increased employment of women in an ever-widening range of occupations and industries is far more a reflection of emancipation than of exploitation. The worker in such societies is far more the beneficiary than the victim of economic growth, as these critics contend.

DISTRIBUTION OF THE GAINS

Reliable national income figures do not extend back far enough in the 20th century to permit any sweeping generalizations about how the gains in product have been allocated to the various factors of production. From data for the last quarter century, however, it has been demonstrated that nations with higher incomes per capita are also those in which the compensation of employees tends to be a higher proportion of national income. Even more in point, the share flowing to employees has risen substantially postwar as compared with 1938 among the higher-income countries; for the less-developed nations it has held at about the prewar ratio.

The trend in distributive shares of the national income of the United States, available for the past three decades, offers little support for the charge of exploitation of the workers, most recently voiced in the Communist manifesto previously cited. Employee compensation comprised about 58% of the national income in the United States in 1929; today it exceeds 70%. While much of this reflects the enlarged role of government in modern society, even for the private and the corporate sectors the long-term trend is clearly upward, rising from 74% of all income produced by corporations in 1929 to nearly 80% in 1960.

Income of the self-employed is also largely a return for labor. Such income and employee compensation are frequently brought together for analytical purposes. This share is by far the largest component of national income and shows no diminution throughout the 20th century. The possibility of increasing it by encroachment upon the share of income from assets is far more limited than is generally recognized, particularly among the low-income countries. The proportions of total product that are not distributed (retained as corporate savings or government profits) or are distributed to the small group of pure *rentiers* usually amount to only a few percentage points.

CAPITAL FORMATION AND ECONOMIC GROWTH

Last in this limited list of factors related to economic growth is what many regard as its key determinant, capital formation, the contribution of tool-power and technology toward lengthening and strengthening the arm of the worker. Capital formation embraces all new construction (including homes), equipment and inventories (both private and public) before capital consumption (e. g. depreciation). This combined total reflects the set-aside from each year's total output that remains available for the production of future goods. Given a larger stock of capital goods to apply to future production, it should follow that output would be forthcoming at a higher rate.

The longer-term record offers several illustrations in support of this thesis. Output per capita rose at a low rate in Great Britain in the 20th century; Great Britain's proportion of national output set aside for capital purposes throughout the first half of the century was about the lowest on record among the industrialized nations. Japan, particularly in recent years, the United States and Canada exhibit high rates of capital formation, 20% or more of total output, and above-average rates of growth in per capita incomes.

Again Kuznets' findings can be employed to highlight trends in this century. Capital formation, he concludes, is directly and positively related to income per capita. In high-income countries it ranges upward from 20% of national output. In contrast, this set-aside ratio declines to 14% in the low-income countries.

Here, however, his acceptance of the simple link between capital formation and economic growth ends. Different rates of capital formation are not too closely linked with differences in per capita income. Several high-income countries have had low proportions of capital formation and the converse. The conclusion is sobering, and a testimonial to the need for husbandry and prudent management.

... one may say truistically that capital formation does not matter as much as capital utilization, and utilization depends upon a host of economic and social conditions which sometimes permit attainment of high rates of growth with little capital, but at other times impede the growth-inducing effect of even larger amounts of capital.

ECONOMIC GROWTH IN THE 1950'S

Interpretation of economic growth rates in the 50's is complicated by the influence of recovery from the destruction and dislocations caused by World War II. This is particularly true for the early years of the decade, especially for the highly industrialized countries where destruction of life and physical capacity was widespread or the economies were completely mobilized for the war effort, or both.

In Table 2 the growth performance of eleven of the major industrialized countries in the 50's is matched against their long-term growth rate over the past half-century or more. The comparison here is of economic growth in terms of the rate of increase in real national product *per head of the employed labor force,* which in most countries parallels the rate of growth in per capita income. The annual per cent increases in economic growth so measured, for the entire decade, 1950–59, and the last half, 1954–59, are stated as percentages of the long-term rate for each of the eleven countries that were among the first to industrialize.

The record of economic growth of this group of countries, impressive as it was for the long term, is overshadowed by their rate of economic growth in the 50's. In all eleven countries the annual rate of growth exceeded the long-term rate by wide margins. Indeed, in five countries (Japan, Italy, Germany, France, and the Netherlands) the growth rate of the 50's was more than double the long-term rate. In only three countries was the excess as little as 10% to 20%; in the remaining three countries it varied from 33% to 94%.

Table 2: Comparative annual growth rates in national product per man-year as per cent of long-term growth rate

Country	1950–1959 Growth rate	1954–1959 Growth rate
Japan	110	162
Italy	292	217
Germany	200	140
France	140	120
Netherlands	209	164
Norway	94	56
Sweden	33	43
United States	10	10
Canada	18	6
Denmark	12	56
United Kingdom	42	33

SOURCE: "Economic Growth: The Last Hundred Years," *National Institute Economic Review,* July, 1961.

Expansion in the 50's was undoubtedly stimulated by the catch-up phase following World War II. This, however, is far from providing a full explanation of the strong rate of growth. The annual rate of growth for the period 1954–59, well after the catching-up period, is also impressively above the long-term rate, although somewhat lower than for the entire decade (for Japan, Sweden, and Denmark the rate was actually higher).

The high growth rates in the industrialized countries are not necessarily a transitory phenomenon attributable to the aftermath of a devastating war. Instead they support the earlier conclusion of no retardation in the rate of growth despite the long number of years of industrialization of these countries. The high rates of growth in the 50's are thus consistent with historical precedents.

STIMULUS OF INFLATION

Inflation usually occurs after prolonged wars. The post-World War II period was no exception. The growth rates here presented have been corrected for price change. Even after correction, however, rates of the 50's undoubtedly still reflect the expansionary influence of inflation. In the latter part of the decade, however, the inflationary pressures were much reduced. A high growth rate, nonetheless, was achieved during these same years. Moreover, high growth rates are associated with substantial additions to capacity. Thus, they have served to eliminate one source of inflationary pressures.

One other positive accomplishment of the postwar period is worthy of emphasis. Recessions since the last war have been both short and mild; in many countries they have been merely temporary declines in the rate of growth. The industrialized economies of the free world have avoided a deep secondary postwar recession. This is in sharp contrast to their experience in the second decade following World War I.

THE BURDEN OF DEFENSE

Two aspects of the postwar growth record engender little or no pride of accomplishment. It is a convention of national accounting systems to consider governmental expenditures on defense, as is true of all government expenditures, as part of the national product. The share of defense expenditures in total gross national product is shown in Table 3 for fourteen countries for 1950, before the full impact of the Korean War was felt, and for 1958, as the nations of the free world began to adjust to the stark realities of the cold war. (For 1960 the world total for defense expenditures was placed in one unofficial estimate at nearly $125 billion.)

In all except four countries there was a significant rise in the defense share of gross national product. In the United States the share doubled, from 5.5% to 11.1%, and in Canada the share increased by two thirds. Increases were more restrained in the United Kingdom, France, and the Netherlands; even in traditionally neutral Sweden and Switzerland defense costs rose substantially. Thus, not all of the economic growth of the 50's was translated into heightened economic welfare. Whether the rate of economic growth was accelerated by the armaments race remains a moot question, depending, of course, upon whether and how the resources diverted to the defense buildup would have been otherwise employed. The economic effects of disarmament are under serious study in many quarters.

Table 3: Defense expenditure as per cent of total gross national product (at factor cost)

Country	1950	1958
United States	5.5	11.1
United Kingdom	7.0	7.7
France	6.2	7.0
Canada	3.6	6.1
Greece	7.0	6.3
Netherlands	4.4	4.7
Italy	4.6	4.3
Belguim	2.3	3.5
Turkey	6.4	3.0
Norway	2.4	3.9
Denmark	1.8	3.2
Sweden	4.3	5.9
Switzerland	2.7	3.3
Iceland	1.4	1.2

SOURCE: "Defense Expenditure," *National Institute Economic Review*, July, 1960.

THE PER CAPITA GROWTH GAP

This discussion has thus far been concerned with the economic record during the 50's of the highly industrialized countries. The comparable record for the underdeveloped countries gives no more ground for satisfaction than did the longer-term view. Here the reviewer is still compelled to rely on crude approximations of national accounts as measures of economic growth. However, two British analysts, Andic and Peacock, recently released a compilation of per capita national income in U. S. dollars for 1949 and 1957 for 62 countries outside the Communist bloc. Of the 62 countries in the free world (shown in Table 4), 42 had per capita incomes in 1949 below the average per capita income of the free world.

What progress did these underdeveloped countries manage to make during 1949–57 toward closing this per capita gap? More specifically, how many of these countries had higher per capita incomes relative to the free world average in 1957 than they had in 1949?

Of the 42 underdeveloped countries, 24 had improved their per capita income relatively. Eighteen, however, were further below the free world per capita income in 1957 than in 1949. It is particularly significant that these 18 countries accounted for 43% of the free world's population. Thus, nearly half of the free world's people live in areas where the per capita income gap widened in the first postwar decade. The population explosion in these newly developing countries, resulting from rapidly declining death rates and steady but high birth rates is a partial explanation. The inherent difficulties in quickly establishing the prerequisites for sustained economic growth is undoubtedly another restraining factor.

The widening per capita income gap noted earlier for the long sweep is thus even more clearly revealed by the analysis for the more recent years. Both facets of this review thus serve to highlight the critical challenge facing the free world as it enters the closing third of the 20th century. The industrialized nations, old and new, have experienced economic growth of unprecedented character. They have made more progress toward eliminating mass poverty in the past six decades than in any past period known to man.

In the underdeveloped countries the postwar interval may very well have been a period of preparation for achieving a faster rate of growth in the near future. Thus far, the application of scientific knowledge in these areas has resulted principally in expanding population faster than real output. It is to be hoped

Table 4: Per capita income in each of 62 countries as per cent of the per capita world (62-country) income, 1949 and 1957

	1949	1957		1949	1957
South Korea	10.7	27.0	Greece	39.1	58.2
Uganda	11.0	11.4	Colombia	40.4	30.6
Burma	11.0	9.6	Jamaica	40.6	51.4
Thailand	11.0	17.6	Panama	56.0	50.8
Ecuador	12.2	30.2	Chile	57.5	72.0
Kenya	12.8	15.4	Austria	66.1	108.6
Philippines	13.5	38.8	Italy	71.9	80.6
Pakistan	15.6	10.4	Portugal	76.5	39.4
Belgian Congo	15.9	14.8	S. Africa	80.7	67.2
Bolivia	16.8	13.8	Malaya	85.9	71.0
India	17.4	12.4	Cuba	90.5	72.4
Nigeria	20.5	13.8	Puerto Rico	95.4	94.6
Ceylon	20.5	23.2	Germany	97.9	148.2
Dominican Republic	22.9	47.8	Venezuela	98.5	161.2
Guatemala	23.5	32.4	Argentina	105.8	95.0
Honduras	25.4	36.2	Finland	106.4	129.6
Paraguay	25.7	23.0	Israel	119.0	144.4
Iraq	26.0	27.0	Ireland	128.4	90.2
Syria	30.6	30.6	Iceland	145.6	143.6
Peru	30.6	24.6	France	147.4	169.4
Egypt	30.6	22.4	Netherlands	153.5	138.0
Japan	30.6	50.4	Luxembourg	169.1	213.2
S. Rhodesia	30.9	24.4	Belgium	178.0	184.0
Brazil	34.3	50.2	Norway	179.0	182.8
Mexico	37.0	46.8	Australia	207.6	214.8
Spain	37.9	62.0	Denmark	210.7	173.8
Costa Rica	38.2	54.8	United Kingdom	236.4	190.8
Lebanon	38.2	60.8	Sweden	238.5	255.2
Turkey	38.2	73.0	Switzerland	259.6	244.6
Ghana	39.1	32.2	New Zealand	261.8	233.2
			Canada	266.1	291.6
			U.S.A.	444.3	420.2

SOURCE: S. Andic and A. T. Peacock, "The International Distribution of Income 1949 and 1957," *Journal of the Royal Statistical Society,* Vol. 124, Part 2, 1961.

that in the years ahead greater managerial skills coupled with heightened scientific knowledge will tilt the balance in the direction of output. That this should come about is as essential to the continued well-being of the industrialized nations as it is for the satisfaction of the physical needs and rising aspirations of the underdeveloped countries.

*What has been accomplished by the exist-
ing industrial nations ... has not passed unnoticed among the developing peoples. They
see no reason why what has been done in
the West should not be done everywhere:
they want it and they want it quick. The
revolution of rising expectations is indeed
a revolution. No government of a new nation can ignore its compulsive power. These
governments, if they are to survive, must
respond and make questions of economic
growth issues of government policy.*

ECONOMIC GROWTH: THE OUTLOOK

By Sir Oliver Franks *

I keep meeting people who see no real problems in the development of that half of the world which is neither already industrialized nor part of the Communist bloc. Britain, they point
out, was the first to become an industrial nation and to generate
enough capital to make the processes of growth self-perpetuating.
Then came the United States and Germany, other European nations, and Japan. Nowadays there are many more nations than
there used to be. They want the benefits of industrialization.
Excellent! What happened to us will happen to them. They will
industrialize themselves: their economies will grow; they will
progressively generate more capital for investment. This will all
occur by the same methods as it occurred to us—by the development of markets, the power of competition, and the search for

* Chairman, Lloyds Bank Limited; British Ambassador at Washington
(1948–52); member, Radcliffe Committee on The Making of The Monetary
System (1957–59); chairman, Committee on Administrative Tribunals and
Enquiries (1955–57); trustee, Rockefeller Foundation.

profit. The economic growth of the world will come about, in the future as in the past, through the techniques and incentives of free enterprise.

To me this easy view is romantic, sentimental, idealist dreaming. It has no contact with reality. It ignores the general context in which economic growth among the developing peoples can take place in the world today. It presupposes a modicum of political stability, progressive development, a modicum of peace and order. This existed from the end of the Napoleonic wars to the first World War, a hundred years without a world conflagration during which the older nations became industrialized. It was the period in which world affairs were largely run by the Western European powers, which succeeded in containing their rivalries sufficiently to avoid general war. Two great nations remained outside the system, the United States and Russia, each working out its destiny in its continental domain and only in a limited way interested in the affairs of the world at large. These were, as we are so often reminded, the bad old days, swept away forever by two World Wars.

But what have we in place of that imperfect but operative system of order and stability? There is no working concert of the predominant powers. Instead, tension and hostility between the two great powers, the United States and Soviet Russia. It is a rivalry that goes beyond the normal struggle for place and power and affects the whole structure of society, the general philosophy of life. Each, with its friends, faces the other, armed with all the weapons of mass destruction, a confrontation that is basically unstable, precarious, unpredictable. If there is to be enough stability and order in the world to permit regular economic growth, it has to be created—the hard way—by intelligent decision and persevering action in the teeth of natural tendencies. So far the achievement has been sufficient, but it is the continuing task of the highest statesmanship.

TODAY THERE IS AN ALTERNATIVE

But even so it cannot be just assumed that the development of the underdeveloped peoples will take place in the historical way through the methods and techniques of private enterprise. An alternative is on offer, the alternative of the Communist system in which governmental decisions determine all the workings of the economy. Let us abstract our minds for one moment from the Communist philosophy, its denial of freedom as we know it, its social and moral values, and look only at the Communist system as a method for economic growth. We cannot say there is nothing to it. It is not true, and it is not what many millions of men think, who live outside the Communist bloc but regard the Russian achievements in economic growth with wonder and admiration. They have seen Russian machine tools, scientific precision instruments, steel plants for themselves; they have heard of Russian atomic weapons and Russian space travel.

There are two prescriptions for economic growth in the world; which will be the more widely chosen? The world context permits us to take nothing for granted here. It must be a matter of high policy and hard work to lead the developing peoples so that they wish their economies to grow in freedom, in a broad way on lines similar to our own.

No easy historical parallel obtains between the economic development of the older industrial nations and that of the younger nations today. In place of a parallel there is a contrast, and for a compelling reason. What has been accomplished by the existing industrial nations—the strength and productive power of their economies, especially the vast output of goods and services by the American economy which in recent decades has revolutionized the whole standard of living not just for some, but for all, citizens—has not passed unnoticed among the developing peoples. They see no reason why what has been done in the West should not be done everywhere; they want it and they want it quick.

THEY EXPECT MORE AND DEMAND MORE

The revolution of rising expectations is indeed a revolution. That large numbers of people all over the world should believe that they and their children can live better than their forefathers is brand new. That life at subsistence levels need not be the iron rule for most men and women is a new idea of violent, explosive quality, for good or evil, destined to alter the face of the world. No government of a new nation can ignore its compulsive power. These governments, if they are to survive, must respond and make questions of economic growth issues of government policy. It follows that the governments of the developing peoples are involved from the beginning; they are compelled to intervene in the economy and initiate action to stimulate and encourage growth. Industrial development cannot be, as it was with the older industrial nations, something which happens within the economy solely because of the enterprise of private citizens. In strong contrast, in nearly all developing countries governments are right in the business of industrialization. They dare not stay out. This is another element of the world context today.

OUR OWN REVOLUTION IN THOUGHT

But our own governments, the governments of the older industrialized nations, are involved too. For them the economic development of the many younger nations has become a major object of policy. Hence the existing programs of aid to developing peoples. Here, too, we have a revolution in thought. Who would ever have dreamt in the earlier pioneering days of industrialization that the nations which had progressed furthest and fastest had a duty or policy interest in forwarding the same development in others? It would have been considered sloppy nonsense. But not today. What has led the governments of the industrialized nations, here on the North American continent or in Western Europe, or the Japanese, to consider yesterday's nonsense now to be a vital interest of policy?

I suppose that if we leave out of account all those who live in the older industrial nations and all those who live in the countries of the Communist bloc, the rest of the world, the developing nations, contain around 1,250 million inhabitants. They are the citizens of the Central and South American countries, of Africa, the Middle East and South Asia, of Southeast Asia, and the Pacific islands. Almost all these peoples are experiencing the revolution of rising expectations and aim at rapid economic growth. Some have gone a long way on the road to industrialization, some only a little, yet others have barely started.

A VICIOUS CIRCLE AND HOW TO BREAK IT

We can, if we choose, wonder about the wisdom of all this, and whether the revolution can possibly satisfy the expectations that have been aroused. Such speculations are beside the point. Most of the new nations intend to develop at all costs. We industrialized earlier and discovered the secrets of material prosperity and political power. They are not going to miss out now. But in their efforts they face a vicious circle. You all know what it is, how low living standards combined with free, broadly democratic societies cannot produce sufficient savings to sustain the rapid economic development they will not forego. They need more capital to increase output, but low output prevents sufficient saving for capital formation. This circle can be broken in one of two ways. It can be broken by tyranny which, by enforcing hardship and depressing the standard of living, forces the savings for rapid development. Or it can be broken by a flow of capital from outside which, added to home savings, gives a free society the chance to develop and remain free.

TYRANNY—OR WISE AID?

Does it matter to us which way the circle is broken for half the world? Suppose the way out of tyranny and dictatorship were taken. The North American continent and Western Europe would look like an island and a peninsula in a world divided from them by basic beliefs about the place of freedom and enterprise in human society. It is therefore a matter of enlightened self-interest for the West, indeed generally for the older industrial societies, that the alternative solution to the vicious circle be adopted. But this involves programs of aid; it involves direct intervention by our governments; it inevitably implies a limitation on the sphere of free enterprise. Yet this course has been adopted as a matter of high political decision by the governments of the very peoples who believe most strongly in freedom and the working of the ordinary processes of industry and commerce.

For the issue in the end is about the kind of world we want our
children to live in; whether most of the world will attach value
to individual human freedom; whether trade and enterprise
should find a large world in which to be active and prosper.

THE CONTEXT

This, then, is the context in which the economic growth of
the developing peoples is set. It is the framework within which
the relation of private industry and commerce in our countries
to the developing nations must be considered. It is a world
polarized in tension and hostility between the great powers,
without any system of order or stability; a world in which Communist methods of economic development have demonstrated
considerable achievement and acquired in many quarters considerable prestige. It is a world caught in the revolution of rising
expectations so that the governments of the developing peoples
are irresistibly carried into the business of growth and development. It is a world in which our governments, the governments
of the industrial nations, feel compelled for reasons of high policy
to get into the same business through programs of aid. It is a
world which does not automatically present all the opportunities
to private industry and commerce in their relations with the
developing peoples, but rather one in which opportunities have
to be sought out and made for enterprise in the light of a
thoroughly realistic appreciation of existing trends.

PRIVATE ENTERPRISE IS RIGHT FOR ECONOMIC GROWTH

Why do we attach so much importance to the principles and
methods of private industry and commerce making a major contribution in these matters of economic growth and development?
First, because we believe in their efficacy; we think they have
the power to command success. But more than that the concentration of responsibility and decision in too few hands is prevented, as it is something which tends to rigidity and to stifle
enterprise. To attempt to run a whole economy by centralized
decision collects all freedom and responsibility into a narrow
compass outside which men become the instruments of policy,

giving effect to decisions they did not make, responsibility for which they do not share. Where there are many centers of decision there is freedom and independence, and the whole economy acquires flexibility. There are many places where risks are assessed and taken, new ideas given their chance. We think this is the best way to material progress, but at the same time it is a safeguard of that political freedom we have inherited. It is reasonable that private enterprise should have a lot to do with economic growth among the peoples of the world.

WHAT THE STATE SHOULD AND SHOULD NOT DO

I propose therefore to put before you some considerations which seem to me relevant to the making and taking of opportunities in this context. First, a negative point. It will not forward the cause of private enterprise to indulge in endless and unremitting guerilla warfare against all manifestations of government activity. After all, even at home most of us agree that defense, some public utilities, the postal services, the road system are matters for public authority. There is a proper function for the State and for private industry and commerce. And the same is true in the external economic relationships we have with the developing peoples. There are things the State should do and things that are the province of private enterprise. It is not possible to draw a boundary between the function of the State and the function of free enterprise valid for all times and places. We are talking of practical affairs, not metaphysical dogmas. But two propositions seem to me clearly evident. First, when a new nation is beginning to develop its economy from scratch, then much of the initial capital investment from outside is bound to be governmental, and take the form of aid. The things that as a rule have to be done first belong to the infrastructure of the economy—communications and essential services, harbors, roads, epidemic prevention, and the like. They will not be done if the condition of external capital investment is commercial terms. They have to be done if the productivity of less-developed countries is to increase enough to provide trading markets offering opportunities to manufacturers and merchants. This is plain common sense and the principle is, I believe, fully recognized and accepted by business organizations like the International Chamber of Commerce.

AID IS NEEDED TO START GROWTH

At the start, then, aid is needed to do what trade cannot do. This is the appropriate sphere of government action. On the other hand, in proportion as the economy of a developing country progresses and the ability to save and invest domestic capital increases, so the opportunities of trade and industrial investment on commercial terms are multiplied. The relation between aid and trade should be such that the first makes the second possible and the second progressively takes over from the first.

There are certain attitudes of mind that are relevant to industry and commerce in industrialized nations in their relations with the growing economies of new nations. One affects their posture towards their opposite numbers, private industry and commerce in the developing country. That the private sector should flourish and grow with the growing economy is very important. When all allowance has been made for external capital assistance from international institutions such as the World Bank, from governments or from private sources, the blunt fact remains that the main source of saving in an underdeveloped country must be that country itself. As Maxwell Stamp says, "The business firm which ploughs back a large proportion of its profits is one of the most efficient means known for saving and increasing the resources available for expansion." And to quote the same author again, "Business is the great nursery and forcing ground in which a middle class can be developed, a middle class with a stake in the community, a reservoir of managerial and professional skills and experience in leadership. The benefit to a developing country of having large numbers of men who have had the responsibility of 'meeting a payroll,' of managing a factory, of building up and organizing a business, can only be fully appreciated by those with experience of a country without these advantages."

BUT WHAT OF "CONDITIONS"?

All this is obviously true of one of the more advanced and sophisticated developing nations which I had the pleasure of visiting with Mr. Sproul and Dr. Abs not long ago—India. Certainly our people in industry and commerce wish the private sector in India well, hope to see it expand, and look for opportunities of doing business with it. Sometimes there is a temptation to go further and ask, even insist, that the Indian Government take positive measures to foster and expand private industry and commerce. Why not make this a condition of the aid which flows to India from the Western nations and Japan? Well, what about freedom, independence, sovereignty? Are peoples newly come to nationhood more or less sensitive to infractions, real or supposed, of their sovereign powers of decision? What right have aid-giving nations to prescribe the internal policies of a developing country? Clearly none, none at all. But aid is for the benefit of the developing country; if it wants the benefit, it must accept the conditions that go with it. So it is argued, and it is true that the intention in giving aid is to help the economy to grow and benefit the people of the aided country. But this is not why we give the aid. Great nations do not embark on major programs of aid from sheer generosity, from an other-regarding altruism. They give aid for much the same reasons as they embark on other foreign policies, out of enlightened self-interest, out of the best judgment they can make of the kind of world they want and what they can do to promote it. In this, the real context of aid, it does not pay, it is self-frustrating and self-defeating, to attach political conditions. The only people it could help would be the Communists.

PROTOTYPE OF WISE AID

I have always thought the United States got this absolutely right at the time of Marshall Plan aid in relation to Britain. At that time we in Britain had a Socialist government, and there were people over here who were concerned lest through Marshall Plan aid American resources should strengthen Socialism in Britain. In fact, no conditions were attached and, a minor point, the record shows that the attitude of the United States did not make Britain Socialist for all time. But the real issue was that the United States had a policy about the kind of world across the Atlantic it was in the long-term interest of the United States to promote. It wished to defeat hunger, misery, and chaos and all their train of social and political consequences. You know how great was the success achieved. In the last few years there has been no more flourishing part of the world than Western Europe.

Therefore, let the leaders of industry and commerce in the developed nations not hesitate to express their convictions on the role of their activities in the economy, nor fail to emphasize the importance they attach to private enterprise playing its part, flourishing and growing, with the growing economy of the developing nation. But let them not defeat their own objectives by seeking to attach conditions to aid.

There is another subject on which I should like to touch: the attitude with which private enterprise in the developed nations should enter a developing country when it invests capital and puts up a plant. As an economy grows, there should be increasing opportunities for risk capital to be employed in this way. On the whole, the governments of developing countries have become increasingly conscious of the need to foster this kind of relationship and of the advantages it brings. It is not just that the infusion of capital of this kind only involves payment across the exchanges when the business succeeds and dividends are earned. It is far more important that with the capital come ideas, know-how, skilled personnel, and experience in management that multiply the utility of the capital. Mr. Sproul, Dr. Abs, and I saw numerous examples of this fruitful cooperation in India and Pakistan—American, German, and British.

A FOREIGN COUNTRY IS A FOREIGN COUNTRY

But if this process is to be really successful long-term, it must be acceptable and this concerns attitude. A foreign enterprise, setting up in an underdeveloped country, must act on the belief that it has entered a new community and has obligations to it. That developing new nations should worry about foreign domination is not surprising; there are advanced countries with similar preoccupations. In this regard certain procedures have been widely adopted by the industrial and commercial corporations that have achieved most success in these overseas operations. One is to employ, train, and promote local personnel to technical and managerial positions. This is costly in time and effort but very important. It is partly a matter of satisfying natural patriotism, but it is much more than that. Foreign enterprise has to demonstrate that it is a partner with the developing country in making the economy grow. The training and placing of local men is a demonstration of faith in the future of the economy and it counts high in prestige.

Then there is another point—whether or not to allow some participation to local capital. I favor this myself, though I am aware that there can be drawbacks. Undesirable influence may be exercised on dividend policy; still more, it might affect the flexibility of work programs in the particular plant overseas in relation to the other plants of the corporation. But a foreign country is a foreign country. If a corporation wishes to stay long-term, and to grow with the economy of the developing country and so make increasing profits, it seems to me a matter of long-range self-interest to let the citizens of the country have an equity interest. Then the corporation can say "we" in approaching the government and other institutions in the country on the basis of a factual mutuality of interest. It is a helpful attitude to be able to say "we" to one's hosts.

A TWO-WAY FLOW OF TRADE

In a recent article Mr. Axel Iveroth of Sweden has drawn attention to a further issue where the attitude of private enterprise has importance. The article deals primarily with Europe but the sentences I am going to quote apply equally to all the established industrial nations.

In the long run it is greatly in the interest of the whole of Europe that the economies of the underdeveloped countries should be expanded, so that these countries' growing industries can become larger customers also for our more highly technical export products. This means at the same time that we must accustom ourselves to the idea of accepting these countries' finished goods on a rapidly increasing scale in our market, and not merely buy raw materials from them.

This is true. In the old days one could think of the exchange of goods between a developed and an undeveloped country as the exchange of manufactured for primary products, raw materials, and foodstuffs. But this cannot be the prevailing pattern now when the exchange is not between developed and undeveloped but between developed and developing economies. This inevitably involves an increasing exchange of technologically advanced for simpler manufactured goods.

Here are real difficulties. Think again for one moment of the case of India. Historically, Indian exports have been primary products the world market for which is not elastic. Further, as the Indian economy has moved forward and standards of living have begun to rise, more and more of these primary products have been consumed at home; for example, the export of hides goes down as fewer people go barefoot. The chance in the next ten or twenty years of India earning a reasonable amount of foreign exchange and therefore being able to pay for the goods we wish to export, being able to keep up with the due instalments of capital and interest on borrowed money—all this turns on a large expansion of exports in manufactured and intermediate products like textiles, sewing machines, or pig iron. I consider that India ought already to be making a great effort to find markets for such products and expand them, but it is obvious that these new markets will have largely to be found in the rich, developed nations. And this in turn involves structural changes in our economies that have economic, social, and political implications.

WILL WE TAKE THE MEDICINE OURSELVES?

What is the attitude of industry and commerce going to be? Are its leaders going to recommend for themselves a stiff dose of the medicine they recommend to others—open markets, free competition, and search for profit? Or will there be appeals to governments for help, applications for tariffs or quotas, for administrative, governmental decisions to prevent the natural working of the free enterprise system? The Western world has not really faced this issue yet, and it is an awkward one which is likely to become acute. Protestations of a desire to help underdeveloped countries have a hollow ring unless we are prepared to admit their products to our markets. Paradoxically, we could find some of our countries feeling it politically easier to go on giving aid rather than open their markets, though everyone knows that in reality to allow export earnings in the developing countries to increase is of far more lasting value to them, and indeed to the sort of world we want to come into being, than aid can possibly be.

A KEY PROBLEM—THE BALANCE OF PAYMENTS

I come briefly to my last topic. One of the most important parts of the industrial and commercial system built up by private enterprise in the Western world is the market mechanism for the international balance of payments. Overseas trade and overseas investment depend on the effective functioning of the foreign exchange markets.

Today it is not quite clear that we can unquestioningly assume this effective functioning. What bothers people is the fact that no nation, however large its reserves of gold and internationally acceptable currencies may be, can indefinitely sustain a large unfavorable balance on its external payments. But aid and trade alike as means of overseas investment can make or magnify such an unfavorable balance. They can accentuate the transfer problem. Nor is this an abstract point. It concerns reality. Last year the United States, with one of the currencies most widely used for the settlement of international transactions, was deeply concerned about a large continuing deficit on its balance of payments and the extent to which overseas capital investment might increase the transfer problem. This year the United Kingdom, with another widely used international currency, has also been in difficulties because of a continuing large deficit on the balance of payments and troubled about the additional transfer problems created by international investment, trade or aid, overseas. There have been, and there still are, risks that this transfer problem might force a reduction in aid or capital investment overseas by private enterprise.

I want to express a platitude, something elementary but also true, and not always remembered. The financial relations between the developing countries and the developed industrial countries cannot as such create or intensify a transfer problem. These relations, all taken together, neither initiate nor moderate an international disequilibrium—for obvious reasons. The developing countries are very unlikely to use the foreign currency they receive to build up their reserves. The terms of the agreement make this impossible with capital investment by private enterprise. And it will not happen with aid from governments. The developing countries are too poor, the political pressures too great for luxuries like building up reserves. To take the case of India again, she has in fact used up practically all the very large sterling balances with which she had entered the first Five-Year Plan. Capital exported by developed countries to underdeveloped countries leads to the export of goods by the developed countries to the same amount.

THE MARKET SYSTEM CHALLENGED

On the other hand, individual developed nations can find their balance of payments affected by the amount of capital they export by trade or aid. There is at present in my judgment a real problem of imbalance between the leading industrial countries. But this transfer problem, as I have said, is not created by the general movement of capital from the developed to the developing nations. It comes about through the failure of us, the industrialized members of the Western world, to find a satisfactory basis for the working of the mechanism of international payments between us.

This situation intimately concerns the upholders of private enterprise. It is a challenge to industry and commerce on their own ground, the market system. It is watched by both interested and unfriendly eyes. It is very important that we do not let things drift, with only an occasional corrective jerk by one nation or another. If we, the developed countries, are unable to secure in good time the conditions for a satisfactory adjustment of our balance of payments and transfer problems, if we are unable to invest overseas by trade and aid as we judge it wise policy to do, I do not think history will forgive us.

WE CANNOT AFFORD FAILURE

I have said the mechanisms of the international balance of payments between the developed, industrial nations are part of that whole commercial and industrial system which we operate and believe to be superior. We cannot afford the judgment that our system could not take the strains imposed upon it. Such a judgment would alter the balance of the world. It is a Communist doctrine that the capitalist system of free enterprise will break down through its own internal contradictions, though it is the part of a good Communist to hasten the day. Internal contradiction means inability to operate the system to accomplish our purposes, to let it get out of control, to permit a facilitating mechanism to be the cause of difficulty and failure. It is the part of free enterprise, of industry and commerce, to go to work to prevent this happening. It can be done perfectly well if only we are not dilatory or complacent but resolute and clear-headed and prepared to think through and apply the principles we accept.

II

Interdependence of the Free World

We have far more at stake than the improvement of our individual enterprises, or of our individual national economies. At stake is the survival of the kind of society in which our enterprises and our economies are possible. We are at a crucial juncture in time when the abilities of our economies to stand separately depend on our willingness to work mightily together for their defense and their growth.

NEIL H. MC ELROY

1. *Population Pressures and the Consumption Explosion*

> *One of the potent factors that is causing people to have less than they want to have, and hence is creating unrest and resentment, is the uncontrolled and meaningless expansion of human numbers.... Unless the unremitting population pressure is released in the near future by reducing the birth rate, it seems likely that it will be tragically released by a rise in the death rate from the use of modern armament.*

THE DEMOGRAPHIC OUTLOOK

By Kingsley Davis *

Four years ago, at the predecessor to this conference, I ventured the opinion that the world's accelerating population growth, particularly extreme in the underdeveloped countries, cannot continue indefinitely. Either the traditionally high birth rates would have to be brought down or the miraculously low modern death rates would go up. Either science would have to be applied to the control of fertility or the scientific control of mortality would be lost. This opinion rested not only on the widely acknowledged proposition that rapid population growth and a high ratio of people to resources are obstacles to economic development, but also on the view that they are conducive to political instability and social unrest, which can potentially wipe

* Chairman, Department of Sociology, University of California; director, International Population and Urban Research, University of California; United States representative to the Population Commission of the United Nations (1955–61); president-elect, Population Association of America; American editor of UNESCO's *Current Sociology*.

out hundreds of millions of people through warfare with nuclear and biological weapons.

Looking over events during the four years since the previous conference, I see no reason to modify this outlook. The world's population has continued its rapid expansion, but the tenuousness of the structure on which this increase rests has become still more apparent.

AN ESSENTIAL CAUSE OF UNREST

My intent is not to suggest that population pressure is the sole or even the most important cause of tension in the world today, but rather to say that it is an essential cause in the sense that it must be eliminated if tension is to be reduced. In other words, neither poverty nor international conflict would be necessarily avoided by stabilizing populations; yet, unless the latter is accomplished, no other solution will work either. Both the problem of economic development and the problem of peace depend for their solution upon certain conditions, of which demographic restraint is one. Although it may be possible over a short period to substitute one of these conditions for another, as time goes on the substitution becomes increasingly difficult until it becomes impossible. With the world's 3 billion people multiplying currently at a rate that will double their number every 36 years, it looks as though the attempt to substitute purely economic and political measures for demographic measures cannot succeed for more than a few years.

By definition, a demographic problem is one that is caused by demographic processes—that is, by some kind of deleterious consequences flowing from the interrelation between births, deaths, migrations, changes in the age-sex structure, etc. It follows that, to solve any demographic problem, a demographic solution is required—an alteration of one or more of the demographic processes so as to produce a more desirable consequence. Nothing else will solve the demographic problem. For this reason, the frequently heard idea of using purely economic or political measures to alleviate conditions that are partly caused by rapid population growth is false. Unless the proposed economic or political measure can be shown to exercise an influence on the demographic processes—in the case of too-rapid population growth, by lowering the birth rate, raising the death rate, or causing drastic migration—it cannot be regarded as a demographic solution.

Thus, sending food free or at less than the cost of production to a country whose shortage is at least a partial consequence of its population growth, does not solve that country's population problem. It may solve the immediate problem of hunger or of political unrest, and for that reason is desirable; but, if anything, it tends to make the population problem worse, because it helps reduce mortality without doing anything to lower fertility. Similarly, a public health program that lessens the role of infectious diseases does a great deal for the welfare and productivity of the current generation, but if it leaves the birth rate untouched or increases it the demographic effect may be so deleterious as ultimately to nullify the gains.

When a problem has several causes, it is erroneous to reason that the remedies must be mutually exclusive. If a man is suffering from chronic indigestion due to emotional disturbance and a poor diet, it would seem foolish to argue that *either* the emotional or the dietary factor must be cleared up, but not both. Similarly, it seems illogical to argue that population restraint and economic measures are somehow so mutually opposed that if one is adopted the other cannot be. Proponents of policies designed to lower the rate of reproduction in currently underdeveloped countries do not generally claim that such measures alone would guarantee economic development; but proponents of economic measures often claim that these alone will solve the problem of poverty. They do this either by denying that population growth contributes to poverty (which is the current Soviet line) or by ignoring the question. The truth seems to be, however, that the demographic problem cannot be reasoned away by spurious logic or swept under the rug by official silence. Population growth has become so rapid that it is visible, often painfully visible, to the ordinary man. And demographic research and statistical analysis have advanced to the point where the economic and social consequences, at least in direction and broad degree, are becoming indisputable. It is doubtless for this reason that world opinion, both official and unofficial, is changing rapidly with respect to population, and that population policies are being more frequently adopted as integral parts of developmental programs.

RECENT TRENDS AND PROJECTIONS

Four years ago, most of our data ended with 1955. Now we can carry them forward to 1959, and in some cases to 1960. Furthermore, in 1958 the United Nations published its projections of future population growth for the countries of the world. Between 1955 and 1959 the world's population grew at the fastest pace ever known, as the following figures show:

	World population (millions)	Average annual per cent rise in prior period	Years to double at this rate
1900	1,608	0.64 *	110
1930	2,013	0.75	93
1950	2,476	1.04	67
1955	2,690	1.66	42
1959	2,907	1.94	36

* From 1850: A. M. Carr-Saunders, *World Population.*

The absolute gain during the four years from 1955 to 1959 was 217 million, or about the current population of the entire USSR.

It is the underdeveloped areas that are contributing most to the earth's population explosion. The following table, taken from United Nations data, shows that these regions have outdistanced the more advanced regions in every period since 1930. Their ratio to the industrial countries fell considerably during the 1950–55 period when the latter were experiencing their postwar baby boom, but it rebounded to almost two-to-one during the 1955–59 years. Thus there is no observable reversal of the paradoxical condition in which the poorer countries experience the fastest population growth. This means that the negative economic and political effects of the population explosion are worse than they would be if the growth were distributed differently. Even with gains in the *proportion* of people who are literate, well-fed, and well-housed, the absolute number who are illiterate, underfed, and poorly housed tends to rise. In other words, despite all the efforts made to attain higher levels of living, there are probably more impoverished people in the world today than there ever were before.

Population growth in more industrial and less industrial countries, 1920 to 1980

Year	More-industrial countries [1]		Less-industrial countries [2]		Ratio of increase of second type to that in first type
	Population (millions)	Per cent increase per decade	Population (millions)	Per cent increase per decade	
1920	565	..	1,245		
1930	625	10.6	1,388	11.5	1.1
1940	671	7.4	1,575	13.5	1.8
1950	703	4.8	1,790	13.7	2.9
1955	752	13.5	1,938	16.6	1.2
1959	790	12.3	2,117	22.1	1.8
Projected					
1980	1,013	11.8	3,208	17.8	1.5

[1] Includes Northern America (United States and Canada and their possessions outside the Caribbean), Australia-New Zealand, Japan, USSR, Northwest Europe, and Central Europe.

[2] Includes Africa, Central America and Caribbean, South America, Asia (excluding Japan and USSR), Oceania (excluding Australia and New Zealand), and Southern Europe.

DECLINING DEATH RATES

The main impetus to population growth in the less economically developed countries remains the rapidly declining death rate. The crude death rates for seventeen of these countries in 1955–59 were, on the average, 15.9% lower than they had been in 1950–54. This represented a slight let-up in the pace of death control, as could be expected with the low levels already achieved, but still enough of a drop to enhance the rate of population growth very substantially in these countries. The decline in the death rates for the seventeen nonindustrial countries I have kept under review was as follows:

Years	Average percentage decline in crude death rate from previous half-decade
1925–29	6.0
1930–34	4.6
1935–39	6.3
1940–44	8.5
1945–49	19.2
1950–54	20.1
1955–59	15.9

It is a moot question as to how much of the reduced death rate is due to public health measures and how much is due to other factors, such as a general improvement in living conditions. I believe that by far the most important factor has been public health work utilizing modern techniques of sanitation, immunization, diagnosis, and treatment. If the decline in the death rate were almost wholly the consequence of economic advance, the rapid population growth to which it gives rise would be less worrisome, for it would occur only where economic gains are being made. The truth seems to be, however, that the chief causes of reduced death rates are those associated with the control of infectious diseases. In many cases these diseases can be eliminated or reduced by mass measures at low cost, independently of whether or not the country in question is prospering economically. The death rate in Mauritius in 1955–59 was 58.4% less than it was in 1940–44; in Ceylon it was 50.7% less; in El Salvador, 46.8% less; and in Taiwan, 55.6% less. There has been no corresponding rate of economic growth in these countries; on the contrary, one gets the impression that they are perilously near to economic stagnation. In Mauritius, for instance, the real national income per head declined from 1,078 rupees in 1953 to 956 rupees in 1958 (at constant prices), while the population grew by 17%. Ceylon's agricultural production index rose by only 3% in the period 1954/55 to 1958, although the population grew by 12% in those years. Furthermore, neither the death rate nor population growth can be turned on and off with the ups and downs of business.

We thus see that in many of the currently underdeveloped countries the growth of population is occurring independently of the economic situation. It can therefore become an obstacle to such development, either negating it altogether or lessening its rate. Coale and Hoover, in their recently published research on India, find that if the birth rate in that country were reduced by 50%, the effect would be to raise the output per consumer, given identical assumptions on other matters, to something like one-and-a-half or one-and-three-fourths what it would be with sustained fertility. They feel that their findings apply generally.

POPULATION CONTROL OR ELSE

The picture people often have in mind when they think of the contemporary population problem is that of crowds of ragged peasants slowly starving on the land. The picture has probably never been accurate, and is least so today. Human beings desire so many other things than food, and are subject to so many other vicissitudes than starvation, that other causes of death, such as disease, warfare, violence, and recklessness, have generally been more important in the death rate.

Today, in an era of rising expectations, there is little likelihood of mass starvation but a distinct likelihood of warfare. The maintenance of peace among nations can hardly be achieved by such superficial means as pronouncements deploring warfare, agreements limiting armaments, or votes in the United Nations Security Council. These are measures that deal with the symptoms rather than the causes. One of the potent factors that is causing people to have less than they want to have, and hence is creating unrest and resentment, is the uncontrolled and meaningless expansion of human numbers. This factor is operating in industrial societies, where such amenities as space, clean air, recreational facilities, and water are becoming scarce in relation to the multiplying hordes who seek them; just as it is operating in nonindustrial societies where even elementary education, clothes, and shelter are hard to get. Unless the unremitting population pressure is released in the near future by reducing the birth rate, it seems likely that it will be tragically released by a rise in the death rate from the use of modern armaments.

It takes much longer to train a first-class engineer or chemist than to build an atomic energy reactor or a large steel mill, yet in many countries where rapid development and industrialization are being planned, education and training are seldom considered as a necessary part of the total investment and total plan, but are introduced as an after-thought. Economic development results from human will for improvement, depends on human vision as to what is possible, human labor for construction, human skill in execution, and human desire for consumption.

DEVELOPING HUMAN RESOURCES

By Alexander King *

The dominant trend of our age is towards an ever-greater rate of change in the scientific, economic, social, and political sense, against a background of specialization and interdependence. This interdependence is of many kinds: the interdependence of individuals in society, of different specialists at the work place, of industrialized and underdeveloped countries, and more generally of the nations that are no longer able to march alone.

It is becoming self-evident that the nature and rate of change is determined by a complex interaction of economic, social, tech-

* Director for Scientific Affairs, Organization for Economic Cooperation and Development; deputy director of the European Productivity Agency, Organization for European Economic Cooperation. Dr. King has held a number of posts with the government of Great Britain, including Deputy Scientific Adviser, Ministry of Production (1939–42); head of the United Kingdom Scientific Mission in Washington and Scientific Attaché to the British Embassy (1943–47); head of the Scientific Secretariat and Lord President of the Council, London (1947–50); and chief scientist in charge of Intelligence and Overseas Divisions, Department of Scientific and Industrial Research London (1950–57).

nological, educational, and political factors, and that the examination of any of these in isolation can at best be but limited, while it is often misleading. Economic development rates, for example, are clearly influenced by technical and social factors, both in the case of highly developed countries and of those just emerging from an agricultural subsistence economy. They cannot be explained on simple economic grounds alone. The very fact of the economic "take-off" of many new countries is obviously related to political influences, and to the initial impact of education leading to a psychological readiness that was hitherto lacking.

It is somewhat surprising, therefore, to realize that until recently the main lines of economic thought showed very little interest in the nature of the noneconomic determinants of growth. There is as yet, for example, little precise knowledge of the contributions of education or of technical progress. The rise of great industries, originating from fundamental scientific discovery, developing on the basis of research and creating a demand for advanced and special education, have usually been accepted as a fact rather than as a factor, in spite of their influence on capital demand and capital accumulation. Certainly much technological innovation results from economic pressures of various kinds, yet many of the discoveries of fundamental science give rise to technological developments that create new demands for materials, equipment, or services, which until then were utterly unknown and hence were not merely satisfying an existing or foreseeable demand of the market.

This has been especially true with regard to human resources, which have been regarded as an input factor demanded by the economy rather than as a creative factor which may determine its nature and direction. Economic development certainly creates demands for skills and competence of all kinds and permits also the general cultural advantages of education. But its rate is influenced by the quantity and quality of human skill available and it can be seriously hindered by inadequacies of education and training. At a time when there is need to increase growth rates, investment in education and in the management of human energies and skills becomes an exceptionally important item. To regard education in this light does not in any way imply a belittling of its importance for cultural purposes; the two are inextricably tied together.

CONDITIONS FAVORING ECONOMIC GROWTH

It is generally recognized that there is need to increase the economic growth rates of countries at all stages in development if social and economic goals are to be attained. This is necessary for nations at the beginning of their development, where the economic basis does not yet exist to provide better possibilities of living. It is equally important for the highly industrialized countries in their own social and economic evolution, and for the provision of greater resources to help the less developed.

We badly need to know more, therefore, about the nature of economic growth and of the complex and interrelated conditions that determine its rate. This is a field that requires the combined efforts of the economist, the social scientist, and the technologist. Among these are several factors that especially require study. Let me list them:

1. The adequacy of the general educational system

2. The availability of opportunities for higher and specialized education

3. Technician and vocational education

4. The necessary level of scientific research activities that will provide new technical possibilities, or in the case of less-developed countries, sufficient awareness of relevant technological possibilities elsewhere

5. Those economic and fiscal conditions that encourage investment and innovation

6. How to establish a social climate conducive to the acceptance of change and to equity in the distribution of the products of economic growth

7. How to provide a sufficient number of good managers for the public service, local administrations, industry, and commerce

8. How to maintain an informed labor force convinced of the need for economic development and free from exploitation

9. How to foster the will to change

It is striking how many of these facets of growth involve human resource creation and use. All nations are concerned in a general way with most of them, but usually as separate problems or services. Their interrelation is seldom fully realized, and it is only now dimly appreciated that they could, if sufficiently understood and if incorporated within a national strategy, provide a dynamic impetus to social and economic development.

THE PRODUCTIVITY MOVEMENT

One of the few deliberate attempts that have been made to improve the use made of human capital has been the productivity movement that arose in Europe after World War II. It was greatly aided by the Marshall Plan, and has proved a powerful means for recovery and advancement. The problem here was initially much narrower than that of economic growth and was conceived in static terms rather than in the dynamic context of growth. Initially launched under conditions of industrial weakness resulting from the war and under a grave shortage of capital, the productivity drive aimed at increasing the product of existing inputs rather than creating new resources or better ones. It strove to increase the output per man-hour of industrial labor, the effectiveness of management, and the agricultural yield per acre. Emphasis was on the introduction of improved techniques, on the management of industrial processes, and distribution. Large numbers of European industrialists and labor union representatives visited the United States to learn of methods and attitudes that had evolved without the disruption of war. In practice, the techniques proved less interesting and more easy to acquire than the attitudes, and the European productivity movement quickly concentrated on problems of management education, management-labor relations, improved vocational training, market research, and the like in an attempt to shape a new approach in Europe.

Institutionally, this movement forms an interesting case history. In nearly all the European countries a national productivity council with an executive center was created, generally with full participation of management and labor. Governments played different roles, ranging from zero to complete dominance, from country to country. A European Productivity Agency (EPA) was created within OEEC as a sort of federal center, to provide stimulus, experience, and services, before most of the national bodies had been set up.

The success of this activity has been manifest. Management education institutes were created all over Europe, the free trade unions were supported, and new joint attitudes of management and labor were evolved towards increasing productivity and solving industrial-labor problems.

The productivity approach, with its stress on effective management, has been essentially an organized utilization of human resources. It is now spreading to other parts of the world. In Asia, for example, there are now national productivity centers in many countries, and an Asian productivity center with federal functions similar to those of EPA. A similar pattern seems to be emerging in Latin America with the help of the Organization of American States.

That there were limitations on the narrow productivity approach was quickly realized by the directors of EPA. Turkey, for example, had considerable underemployment and balance of payments difficulties, so that productivity per man-hour had little meaning and no popular appeal. Yet the *techniques* of the productivity drive were directly applicable. This led to a gradual reorientation of action for such countries in the direction of economic development and resource (including human resource) planning. Furthermore, as the European economies improved and capital became available, it became obvious that the actions that had proved successful in the reconstruction decade should be reconsidered in view of the longer-term problems of economic growth. For this reason it was proposed that within the new Organization for Economic Cooperation and Development, the European Productivity Agency should be abandoned as such, and its activities replaced by a deeper approach to factors favoring economic growth and resource development.

DEVELOPING SCIENTIFIC AND TECHNICAL PERSONNEL

The evolution of policy with the EPA made clear the importance of education, training, and effective utilization of manpower. But action had concentrated on the improvement of vocational training methods and on management education. Recognition of scientific and technological developments, and the shortage in OEEC countries of scientists and engineers, made it necessary to take special measures with regard to their education and use. The OEEC programs in this field initially included studies of the supply and demand for scientists and engineers in Europe, examination of the problems of scientific and technical education in member countries, modernization of school science policies, reform of the curricula in the teaching of mathematics, chemistry, and physics, and an attack on the specific educational problems of the Mediterranean countries. These programs have, however, quickly matured in a direction somewhat similar to those of EPA, namely in the consideration of how to improve the quantity and quality of skilled manpower in terms of resource building, national investment, and the long-term growth of the economy. These activities, which will be deepened and strengthened in the new OECD, represent a coherent human resource approach in relation to economic development and are being studied in other regions of the world.

NEEDED: A HUMAN RESOURCE STRATEGY

If the highly industrialized countries are to continue a healthy development and if the less-developed countries are to advance quickly, the creation and utilization of the necessary human resources must be planned well in advance and in the closest relationship to general schemes of economic development. They must not be left, as is still usually the case, until the needs have already been demonstrated. It takes much longer to train a first-class engineer or chemist than to build an atomic energy reactor or a large steel mill, yet in many countries where schemes for rapid development and industrialization are being planned, education and training are seldom considered as a necessary part of the total investment and total plan but are introduced as an afterthought. Economic development results from human will for improvement, depends on human vision as to what is possible, human labor for construction, human skill in execution, and human desire for consumption. If such schemes are to be successful, in a practical as in a social sense, there is need for a much deeper consideration of human resource and consumption aspects. Specifically, two things are necessary: first, national and regional strategies must be devised for the development of human resources of the highest quality appropriate to future economic expansion needs, considered as part of the national investment policy and planned sufficiently for in advance; and secondly, there must be a much deeper knowledge of the influence of education, science, and human skills on economic growth, this to be achieved by well-planned studies and by exchanging experience already gained in this area.

In the industrialized countries, such an approach is necessitated by the rapid rates of technological and social change, as well as the increasing demands of competition in the world markets. This will certainly require considerable changes in educational policy at all levels and in the development of educational technology, where it is likely to be rapid. The present rates of technological change are already rendering obsolete the knowledge of scientists and engineers educated a decade ago; the need for providing better and more regular facilities for retraining must, therefore, be an important part of educational policy, as indeed the concept of education as a process which continues throughout life, rather than as a once-and-for-all process at the beginning of a career. The need for much larger numbers of technically trained people both for domestic employment and to help overseas will necessitate reform in teaching methods, in curricula, in selection of talent, and in the provision of opportunities. Finally, there is need for a more systematic approach to the assessment of future needs for higher skills in relation to economic and demographic projections, in order to enable educational investments to be planned systematically and in advance. This conception of a human resource strategy will require the closest cooperation between economists, educational policy workers, and those responsible for national investment.

For the less-developed countries, the need for such a strategy is more obvious and more urgent. The use of scarce funds has to be accurately aimed at the development goals of the country, and hence education has to be regarded as part of the general development plan; if not, frustration and chaos will result. Yet the role of education is subject also to a variety of political and social pressures that may at times be in opposition to economic objectives and make decisions difficult. For example, the social and political necessity for a quick achievement of universal literacy may make it impossible to provide sufficient funds for the higher education of an elite that must manage the country's affairs, including its new industrial developments, and in addition create the teachers without which universal literacy can never be attained. The need here is for careful planning of educational investment in relation to general national policy and, within this, to decide on the best means of distributing the investment, taking account of political and social as well as of economic objectives.

A CHECK LIST FOR THE DEVELOPING COUNTRIES

Many problems have to be clearly formulated before such a process can be sensibly undertaken:

1. What precisely are the national objectives, in terms of tangible and intangible goals, economic, social, political and even prestige?

2. What is the time scale of the operation?

3. What human as well as financial resources will be required at the various stages?

4. What expert help as well as financial aid can be obtained from external sources, bilateral and unilateral?

5. How can institutions (including educational) be built up with outside help, which will continue effectively when the foreign experts have gone?

6. How many people can be educated and to what level? Who will select them and how?

7. What curricula will be used in education? What methods adopted to accelerate the importing of knowledge and of experience at different levels?

8. Can plans be projected sufficiently ahead for the yields (financial and human) of earlier schemes to be used as the input of later programs?

9. In how far are economic, social, and political aims compatible, and how can education and information help to make them so?

In a number of countries a start is being made on the introduction of educational and manpower aspects into general development planning. For example through the Mediterranean Regional Project of OEEC, small groups of economists are working in six countries to assess educational investment needs in terms of economic and demographic projections and social policy up to 1975. These groups are working in consultation with one another and with international experts. The promise of the approach is sufficient for the addition to these teams of the apprentices who may later undertake similar work in other areas.

There are areas in which the industrialized countries are in a position to give considerable assistance without suspicion of political aims or of indirect gain. It is becoming ever more obvious that technical assistance is likely to be successful only if it is given with complete altruism and in a spirit of participation. Paradoxically, it appears that only if assistance is honestly free from political objectives will friendship, mutual trust, and long-term political advantage be gained.

*How can we raise the standard of living and
cut down the still relatively high death rate
when it is so difficult to support the existing
population even at a low standard of living,
if the population of Asia alone continues to
increase by about 30 million every year?*

MEDICAL AND BIOCHEMICAL
IMPLICATIONS

By S. Chandrasekhar *

Of all the problems faced by man in mid-century, none is more
grave than that posed by man's uncontrolled fertility. The population problem affects every aspect of man's social life—individual, national, and international. It affects the health, happiness,
and security of individual families. It affects the economic development and social progress of nations. And it affects international
security and peace, for problems of population pressure are connected, albeit latently, with issues of peace and war.

WORLD POPULATION GROWTH

It took man many thousands of years to multiply to a billion
and a half by 1900, but it has taken only a little more than half

* Director, Indian Institute for Population Studies; director of demographic
research for UNESCO in Paris (1947–49); Indian UNESCO delegate to numerous international conferences on population and related matters. Dr.
Chandrasekhar has lectured at universities in the United States, Norway,
Hong Kong, Canada, and Middle Eastern and African countries.

a century to double that number—an incredible and unprecedented rate of increase. And now the United Nations estimates that at the current rate of increase, the world might have 6.2 billion people by 2000 A. D.!

In other words, the population of the world is increasing by about 45 to 55 million a year. For thousands of years during man's early history the rate of increase of the world's population was infinitesimally slow, between .01% and .02% per annum. And a few centuries ago, when man was slowly becoming the master of his environment, the rate of increase ranged between a quarter and a half of 1%. And the annual rate of growth, which was about 1% before World War II, increased to 1.6% a few years ago, and today is about 2%. As Kingsley Davis aptly puts it, "Viewed in the long-run perspective, the growth of the earth's population has been like a long, thin powder fuse that burns slowly and haltingly until it finally reaches the charge and then explodes."

Of these 3 billion people in the world today, Asia claims over half. Asians are increasing faster than Europeans, and at the current rate of increase Asia might have to take care of 60% of the total world population by 2000 A. D., an increase she can hardly afford at the present rate of her economic development and social progress.

DECLINING DEATH RATES

This tremendous increase in the world's population, particularly in Asia, in recent years is due to man's increasing control over disease and death. The effectiveness of death control is not uniform all over the world, for while the death rate in the more advanced and civilized countries of the West is about 10 per thousand, the rates in Asia are relatively high—about 30 to 35 per thousand in Burma and Nepal, and about 15 per thousand in India and Indonesia. However, since the end of World War II, the death rate in many Asian countries has begun to decline, thanks to the work of the World Health Organization, American technical aid, and the efforts of various national governments in providing a modicum of modern sanitation, environmental hygiene, health education, the wonder drugs, and basic health services.

Once the improvements effected in preventive and curative medicine in the United States of America and Northwestern Europe are made available to the rest of the world—to Asia, Africa, and Latin America—the population explosion of the future will be all the more alarming.

The sciences of medicine and biochemistry are bound to continue to make enormous progress. The implications of biochemistry affect two vital aspects of our life—that of obtaining an adequate supply of food and that of maintaining and improving health. Medicine and agriculture have always looked upon biology and chemistry as active allies in man's struggle with Nature. Every new discovery in these sciences directly affects our current demographic explosion. They can, in a word, immeasurably alleviate human suffering, reduce the incidence of morbidity to an incredible minimum, control and eventually conquer disease, prolong the active and useful part of life, and postpone death as far as possible, and at the same time find the necessary resources for the sustenance and habitat of man. That is to say, these achievements are within the limits of human possibilities, theoretically and technically.

THE UNDERDEVELOPED WORLD'S LEVEL OF LIVING

But the countless applications of the marvels of modern science have not begun to affect the daily lives of a great majority of the world's population. Even the most casual look at the conditions of human life in the underdeveloped parts of the world shows how backward and distressing life is for the average man. The level of consumption of the basic requisites of civilized human existence in terms of food, clothing, housing, educational and health facilities, leisure and certain cultural amenities is shockingly low. Accurate statistics on all these matters are not available but they are not really necessary, for anyone who has traveled in Asia or Africa knows the wretched poverty in which a majority of the people live.

Food is Asia's biggest problem. According to a recent United

Nations' Survey, four out of five people, or 80% of the three billion people of the world have never had and will not have in the foreseeable future what an American or European family takes for granted as a good square meal. And an overwhelming majority of the underfed and unfed live in Asia. Most Asian countries are faced with food shortages and in a few countries the shortage is chronic, bordering sometimes on famine conditions. There is not enough food even of the coarsest and least nutritious variety to go around. But if the levels of consumption, both in quality and quantity, recommended by nutrition experts are taken into consideration, a hundred million Asians, not to speak of Africans, suffer either from malnutrition or undernourishment. And the hunger in Asia appears to be increasing every day for, while food production is increasing, the number of mouths to consume it is increasing at a faster rate.

It is the same story with clothing, housing, health, and education. As for education, there are some 550 million children from five to fourteen in the world today, of whom only about 300 million are enrolled in schools. A majority of the remaining 250 million children are in Asia and Africa—children who have no chance of obtaining even a few years of schooling in this generation and who will grow up to swell the existing army of adult illiterates. And yet some of these developing countries are trying to be democracies, and this despite the utter incompatibility of predominant illiteracy with effective democratic institutions.

In brief, the level of living of the vast majority of Asians and Africans is well below the poverty line. The entire vicious circle starts with incredibly low incomes. The per capita annual income of the Asian ranges between $50 and $120, depending on the particular country he lives in. This low income is in striking contrast to the per capita income of some $2,000 in the United States and Canada and about $1,000 in Europe. Millions of Asians and Africans earn in a day little more than what a package of cigarettes costs in America. This low income is both the cause and the consequence of the misery of life in the underdeveloped countries.

THE PROBLEM

In its simplest form the problem is: How can we raise the standard of living and cut down the still relatively high death rate when it is so difficult to support the existing population even at a low standard of living, if the population of Asia alone continues to increase by about 30 million every year?

The peoples of the underdeveloped world cannot lower their standard of living any further, even if it were possible. Nor can anyone suggest raising the death rate! What then is the way out?

NO EASY SOLUTION

First of all, there is no easy solution to the world's population problem. Certainly part of the solution is to put the underdeveloped countries on their feet, and *massive* economic and technical aid is needed to make the underdeveloped countries going concerns. Are the advanced and affluent countries prepared to do this? The United States of America has been more than generous. But the poverty is so deep that we need such aid multiplied many times. If this were done—and this is a very big "if"— the population explosion could, theoretically, mean expanding markets, a boundless demand for goods and services, more houses and plants, a higher wage bill, higher consumption—in fact, a beneficent chain reaction. But the available resources are limited and before mankind can eat new "foods" from the sea or the air or any synthetic "pap" that biochemistry can give us, the population numbers will have increased fantastically. What is more, all the rich countries may not be willing to underwrite the development of the underdeveloped countries. And who can blame them if they question why the fruits of their hard work and efficiency and planned fertility should be shared at the altar of the boundless fertility of the backward.

Only massive economic and technical aid to the underdeveloped countries of the world accompanied by universal birth control can provide a real solution to this problem. In the present context the population explosion does not mean a consumer explosion; it only means the multiplication of poverty.

Today the conventional birth control methods have by and large failed among the masses in Asia. What is needed is a really cheap, effective, acceptable, and harmless birth control "pill." Here again, the aid of American science and technology is needed to perfect just such a pill.

All this—massive economic aid and the perfection of an ideal contraceptive, and quickly—will mean a tremendous outlay, and patience with the problems of the underdeveloped world. But once the underdeveloped peoples have been enabled to become solvent, their prosperity is bound to bring vast benefits to the advanced Western countries. Prosperity, like social justice, is indivisible. The world has become so small and interdependent that we can no longer afford a world half prosperous and half starved.

First, a survey of the consumer market in the affluent U.S. Then, from Sears' remarkably successful experience in Latin America, Mr. Kellstadt observes that modern merchandising—accompanied by local manufacture and recruitment—provides a sound stimulus to economic growth in underdeveloped countries.

THE CONSUMPTION EXPLOSION

By Charles H. Kellstadt *

I shall begin by describing some of the most significant characteristics of the United States market. First is the fact that the level of consumer income here per capita is considerably higher than anywhere else in the world. Second, the income of the population is relatively well distributed. Differentials in average incomes between the lower and higher income areas within the United States, between the lower and the higher-paid occupations, and between racial groups are narrower than prewar. Wages and salaries, moreover, have been rising over the long term, even after allowance is made for the inroads of inflation. As a result

* Chairman, Sears, Roebuck and Co.; director, Chemical Bank New York Trust Co., Continental Illinois Bank and Trust Co., First National Bank of Miami, Allstate Insurance Co., Eastern Airlines, Ford Motor Co., Simpsons-Sears, and Whirlpool Corp. Mr. Kellstadt is a trustee of the National Industrial Conference Board, the Committee for Economic Development, Eisenhower Exchange Fellowships, and the American Heritage Foundation. He was unable to attend, and his address was read by Mr. Arthur Rosenblum, Director of Business Research, Sears, Roebuck and Co.

there is a large and growing proportion of middle-income families. In addition, consumer markets have been stimulated by the spurt in population growth following World War II. The current rate of increase, 1.7% per annum, is about the same as the world average but is well above that of most other industrialized countries.

Other factors have intensified the postwar demand for homes, automobiles, and other durable goods. Among these were the backlog of demand built up during the war; the high savings and low debt position of consumers at the end of the war; and the more marked propensity of young adults to get married, raise children, and buy homes in the burgeoning suburban developments ringing our major cities. Backed by this combination of unusually favorable conditions, demand blossomed to mass-market dimensions for an unusually large number of products and services, sometimes in surprisingly short periods.

By the beginning of the current decade, almost two-thirds of American families had attained the status of home owner. An even larger proportion, more than three out of four families, owned automobiles. All but a relatively few homes enjoyed such conveniences as mechanical refrigeration, electric washers, and modern cooking facilities. Television became as common as radio sets are in European households. Millions of homes have been equipped with power lawn mowers, freezers, electric blankets, clothes dryers, air conditioners, and so on through a long list. These are some of the material evidences of the highest standard of living ever reached in the history of the United States. Not only have we been able to produce and distribute more goods per capita than ever before, but we have given our workers increased leisure from their daily toil. We were able to do this and simultaneously maintain a great military establishment, which drained 10% of the total national output in the decade of the 50's.

There have been increasing indications in recent years, however, that consumers' appetites for durable goods have become pretty well satisfied except for replacement needs. This slowdown in durable goods markets has occurred while incomes were still rising. Demand for food, clothing, and other nondurable goods has continued to expand quite steadily and outlays for services have been gaining even more rapidly. I believe that the growth rates of these three major categories of spending will continue to follow a divergent pattern well into the 60's.

The existence of a large and prosperous middle class already well equipped with time and energy-saving mechanical servants is certainly one of the major factors to be considered in appraising future trends in consumer demand. There are others, such as the changing needs for products and services resulting from different rates of growth among the various age groups, and the changing tastes and desires affected by the rise in sophistication and educational level of the population, and by the gradual transformation in where and how people live.

A CHANGING CONSUMER MIX

We know, for example, that the adult age group which most frequently provides customers for new homes, autos, and household durables, namely those between the ages of 25 and 45, will show relatively little increase during this decade. On the other hand, we shall see the big crop of the baby boom years, now swelling the ranks of the teenagers, reach the age of marriage in increasing numbers as the decade progresses. The stage is being set for the biggest marriage boom in our history in the late 60's. But with typically low average incomes at this stage of the life cycle, these young couples start their family life in rental units and can satisfy only their minimum needs for cars, furniture, appliances, and other household items. Spurting demand for a wider and more expensive range of items will come several years later with the rise in earnings of the family breadwinner, the addition of children, and the move to larger, more permanent living quarters.

A rising tide of young people will be entering the labor force all during the decade. This will have important implications for prospects of further growth in per capita incomes and therefore consumer demand. Labor force projections by the Bureau of Labor Statistics indicate that a disproportionately large part of an estimated increase of 15 million people in the labor force from now to 1970 will consist of young men and women under 25 and women over 45. These workers earn less than the average received by all workers. It is possible, therefore, that the relatively more plentiful supply of workers and the change in their composition by age and sex may have a dampening effect upon the growth in consumer wage and salary income which is the predominant source of buying power.

The more rapid growth in spending for services at a time when consumers are already well supplied with goods illustrates the truth of the statement that consumer wants are insatiable. One of the important reasons why services have been taking an increasing share of the consumer income is that in general prices of services have been rising faster than the prices of goods. It is not so easy to restrain increases in unit costs of producing services in the face of rising wage rates through greater mechanization, as is the case with manufactured commodities. Even apart from the price factor, consumers tend to spend a larger part of their incomes for services as they move up the income ladder. With an assist from jet air transportation, trips to Europe or the Caribbean are becoming increasingly popular as the way to spend the lengthened vacation periods. Travel and recreation are favored outlets for spending.

Rising college tuition fees and related expenses will, in combination with an expected sharp increase in the college student population, especially in the latter half of the decade, account for a bigger slice of consumer income than ever before. Because more people can afford to do so, they are spending a larger part of their incomes to get well and stay well. Our population includes a growing proportion of older persons who need more than average medical care. Rising costs of repair and maintenance of the vast stock of homes, automobiles, and appliances owned by consumers, and to service outstanding debt incurred in their purchase, also help to swell the share of the consumer dollar spent for services. With a large and prospering middle class, growing more sophisticated and better educated with the passage of time—there were 40% more people with college educations in the population in 1960 than in 1950—markets for luxury items, for goods of better quality and value, for the aesthetic and cultural, are on the upswing. "Hi-fi" and pleasure boats are becoming mass rather than class markets.

Producers and distributors have been moving rapidly to cater to this changing market. Product and market research effort has been stepped up as never before to develop new products or improve the old. Any group in the population of sufficient size and buying power, by age, sex, race, or any other significant characteristic, is virtually sure to receive special attention. In the meantime, advancing technology, rising wage rates, and the intensification of domestic and foreign competition are acting as a three-pronged spur toward increasing the productive efficiency of manufacturers. The keener competition from lower-cost producers abroad and an abundance of productive capacity in most industries at home are helping to dampen the upward creep in prices of manufactured goods.

The distribution sector of the economy, which is more aggressively attuned to the changing needs of the consumer market than its counterparts anywhere else in the world, has been undergoing a series of transformations. Retail outlets have been following the migration of the population into the suburbs. Certain changes in distribution which have been going on, and which will continue, are aimed to attract customers by making it easier, more pleasant, and more economical to shop. Thus the trend toward the clustering of new retail outlets in attractive shopping centers with ample parking areas, the extension of store hours to facilitate family shopping, and the broadening of credit buying to cover an increasing range of goods and services.

LATIN AMERICA AS A MARKET

Now let us look south of the border and see if we can draw implications from my company's experiences there that offer clues to future progress in some of the so-called underdeveloped nations of the world. Latin America has about as large a population in total as the United States and Canada combined, and has much higher birth rates. There are broad differences in the sizes and populations of these countries, in their stages of industrial development, their current rates of economic growth, their average per capita incomes, their dependence on foreign trade, and their degree of financial and political stability. Living standards are considerably lower in even the most advanced of these nations than in Western Europe, to say nothing of Canada or the United States. Large numbers of people in Latin America live in poverty.

However, a broad drive toward economic development has been gaining impetus during the postwar period in most of Latin America. It was estimated recently that with one-sixth of the population of all underdeveloped countries Latin America had a third of the income and about 37% of the total investment. Especially encouraging progress is being made in the larger countries—Argentina, Brazil, Colombia, and Mexico. Already in 1957, there were more television sets per capita in Mexico and Brazil than in Sweden and Switzerland, more refrigerators per capita in each of these two Latin American countries than in the Netherlands, and as many washing machines per capita in Mexico as in Italy.

THE SEARS ROEBUCK EXPERIENCE

Sears entered the Latin American market with its first store in Mexico in 1947. By the end of 1960 it had expanded to 16 stores in Mexico, 9 each in Venezuela and Brazil, 6 in Colombia, 2 in Peru, and 4 in Central America, as well as sales offices in various countries. Total net sales passed the 100 million mark in United States dollars last year.

Sears' original plan was to stock these stores for the most part with goods made in the United States, since local manufacturing sources for many of the merchandise items we planned to sell either did not yet exist or were too small, antiquated, or otherwise unsatisfactory. This idea had to be abandoned as embargoes were imposed on a wide range of consumer goods imports because of exchange difficulties and national policies aimed at rapid industrialization in various countries.

Sears, therefore, had to concern itself in a major way with the development of local manufacturing facilities. This included a considerable amount of technical and financial assistance to existing and new manufacturers. We had to help organize and reorganize manufacturing and office procedures. We had to take the initiative in improving the design and quality of product, and in introducing new products. We had to sell the advantages of modernized plant and equipment, and inculcate producers with the attitude that it is good for manufacturers as well as for consumers to provide the best possible product to sell to the consumer at the lowest reasonable price. This, I might say, did not come easily. In solving these formidable problems of merchandise procurement, Sears was fortunate in being able to draw upon the large reservoir of practical knowledge and skills possessed by its personnel in the United States.

There has been a steady growth of local manufacturing facilities for consumer goods in these countries. In 1960 we purchased practically all our merchandise requirements in Brazil, Mexico, and Colombia from local sources; about three quarters in Peru, and nearly half in Venezuela. We bought merchandise from nearly 7,800 different sources in Latin America last year, an increase of nearly 10% from 1959, and in countries like Colombia, Venezuela, and Peru, the number of local producers is increasing even more rapidly. Local industries manufacturing ready-to-wear clothing are usually among the first to be established successfully. Blue jeans, sport shirts, and women's dresses in American styles have won considerable popularity among Sears' Mexican customers.

However, a growing list of nontextile items such as pressure cookers, food mixers, and other kitchen utensils, which were introduced in Mexico by Sears, have met with brisk and growing demand. All major appliances are now being produced in Brazil and Mexico. Refrigerators and stoves are being manufactured in Colombia. The first refrigerator ever made in Peru was placed on sale by Sears in July, 1961; stoves and washers are in the production planning stage. Venezuela may have locally produced refrigerators next year.

It was originally thought that the customers of Sears stores in Latin American cities would come from the top 25% of the income classes. Experience has proved this estimate too narrow. One reason is the steady growth of a middle-class income group, and a second is the popularization of instalment-credit buying. Nearly half of our Latin American sales are on credit, almost as high a percentage as in the United States. Credit losses, incidentally, are comparable to our experience in this country. Instalment credit is only one of the modern retail distribution aids and techniques pioneered by Sears and now widely practiced by competing retailers.

DISTRIBUTION—A KEY TO GROWTH

In 1953, the National Planning Association published a case study on Sears Roebuck in Mexico. This was the first of a planned series of studies of selected examples of operations by United States corporations abroad. While these operations have been undertaken for profit, they have also made positive contributions "toward raising living standards and helping to integrate, into countries less developed than in the United States, the foundations of a more mature economy."

The report cited the Sears record in Mexico as a practical demonstration of the importance of the modernization of distribution to the expansion and sound industrial growth of economies emerging from agrarianism, achieving its effects through the broadening of consumer demand and the passing on of benefits from mass production.

One important conclusion drawn from this study was that too little attention has been given to the influence of the distribution process in promoting growth in comparison with the traditional emphasis on development of mining, agriculture, manufacturing, power, and transportation.

The Latin American people themselves deserve considerable credit, of course, for what Sears has been able to accomplish in their countries. First, there was a large core of manufacturers who proved to be willing, even eager, to adopt our methods. Secondly, the personnel recruited by Sears within these countries were of high quality and ambitious, which made the job of training them easier and facilitated the success of our policy of promotion from within. Our Latin American corporations now employ more than 9,000 persons, and fewer than one per cent of them are North Americans.

Latin American consumer markets, in short, present the prospect of unusually rapid growth and change in the years ahead, compared with other undeveloped sectors, or even with some more industrially advanced countries.

THE COMMON MARKET AS A MARKET

The Common Market countries are highly industrialized and densely populated. Their populations are growing relatively more slowly than in the United States. Average income per capita is about half as high as in this country but is rising faster. Investment in new plant and equipment has been stimulated by growing markets, increased competition, labor shortages, and government policies friendly to industrial expansion. The shortage of skilled labor and more rapid rise in manufacturing productivity have caused European wage rates to climb even faster than in the United States.

Here is a market that is relatively unsaturated with consumer durable goods. Strongly rising consumer purchasing power, reinforced by growing use of instalment credit and coupled with a strong desire for better living, is laying the basis for a probable boom in home construction and durable goods buying of prolonged duration. Mass markets that have been opened by the removal of restrictions on trade are an important factor in this stimulation of European economic development. The broadening of the membership of the Common Market to include Great Britain and other European countries, which appears more and more probable, should impart additional strength to these prospects.

MORE THAN ONE BILLION "HAVE NOTS"

Of the present 3 billion inhabitants of this globe, slightly over a billion live in the Communist bloc countries, the majority in Red China and the Soviet Union. Less than 600 million live in what economists would classify as the "developed" countries of the free world. The rest of the world's population is concentrated in the underdeveloped nations of the free world, nearly 1½ billion persons.

If we exclude from this group the countries that are showing visible signs of progress, namely the largest countries in Latin America, there remain well over a billion people who are living at or close to subsistence levels. The problem of helping these multitudes to take significant steps toward better living conditions is formidable, but it is of primary importance to the free world.

Sociologists talk about the "revolution of rising aspirations" as a growing force in world politics. In plain language, the masses living in the poor countries are becoming increasingly aware of the difference between their way of life and ours through radio, movies, tourists, and other forms of contact with our world. They have become increasingly impatient with governments that will not take action to ameliorate their poverty. Unfortunately, they will learn, as some already have, that standards of living can be raised only slowly. More education and training is needed for the working force and that takes time, measurable in decades. The population will have to produce more and save more of its earnings to invest in capital goods. This is hard to do when the increase in output must largely be used to provide for the growing number of dependents which the population explosion is causing in many of these countries.

Particular attention is being focused on India, one of the largest as well as one of the poorest nations of the free world. It has a population of over 400 million, twice as large as all of Latin America. Handicapped by a primitive and inefficient agriculture which does not yield enough food for its population; by social, language, and religious divisions among its people; by a shortage of domestic capital in comparison to its astronomical needs for investment; and by a high rate of population growth which further reduces its ability to save capital, India, nevertheless, has certain valuable assets and potentialities for growth.

Its national government policies and programs are framed with the objective of removing or reducing the major obstacles to economic progress. I certainly do not pose as an expert on the complex problems of India but it would appear that here, as in

Latin America, investment in modernization of retail distribution facilities and methods would have fruitful results. Despite the small proportion of middle-income families, there should be enough of them in its larger cities to provide markets of adequate size for the gradual development of new consumer manufacturing and distributing industries. The problem of personnel recruitment should be no greater than in Latin America since India has a relatively large core of educated people. Moreover, attacking the problem of raising consumption standards through the approach used by Sears in Latin America requires relatively small amounts of capital as compared to development of basic industries. It is at least as effective and rapid in developing modern business "know-how," initiative, and other attitudes essential to the growth of free enterprise. It contributes to a better balance in economic growth, and effects a speedier and more orderly transition to modern ways of living.

A PREDICTION

I would summarize my views about the outlook for consumption in various sectors of the free world as follows: Total consumption of goods will rise somewhat more rapidly than population, the growth of which has been described as "explosive." Even though per capita consumption may not increase appreciably in many densely populated countries, other areas will continue to show improvement, raising the over-all average. I expect to see an increasing flow of investment capital and technical help from the more advanced industrial nations to the less-developed countries as the latter begin to establish appropriate conditions to use and, in turn, derive adequate benefits from such assistance. Demand for manufactured goods, particularly durables, will climb more rapidly, especially in areas like Western Europe, Japan, and Latin America, supported by rising per capita incomes. The consumer market in the United States will be one of an even richer product mix including a steady stream of new and redesigned products, and a greater emphasis on quality items. And an increasing share of the American consumer budget will be devoted to various kinds of services.

2. The Changing Structure of World Trade

> *Latin America has no alternative but to be self-dependent. To the extent that it succeeds, its industry will eventually absorb a substantial part of its raw materials. Its populations, with a much higher level of income, will also consume an equally substantial share of its foodstuffs. In an integrated market there need be no anxiety concerning the vagaries of world demand.*

PRIMARY COMMODITY PROBLEMS

By José Garrido Torres *

Instability of income resulting from price fluctuations of primary products in world trade constitutes a challenging problem. It is particularly serious for underdeveloped countries that ordinarily depend on one, two, or three of them for the major part of their foreign income. As they must import heavily because of the lack of diversification in their production, a sharp deterioration in the terms of trade adversely affects the operation of their economies.

Besides reducing their purchasing capacity for current imports, this upsets the execution of development programs, planned

* Member, National Economic Council of Brazil; editor of *Conjuntura Economica;* member, Technical Council of the National Confederation of Commerce, and consultant to the Inter-American Development Bank. From 1947 to 1952, Dr. Torres was director of the Brazilian Government Trade Bureau in New York, and in recent years he has served as alternate governor of the International Monetary Fund, executive director of the Superintendency of Currency and Credit, and president of the Brazilian National Economic Council.

or under way, for capital goods, raw materials, and services that must be imported.

This is not just a question of stabilizing the level of foreign income. It is also one of trying to raise it through special efforts to expand the volume of exports to pay for added imports, and these special efforts are frustrated when prices of exports drop. It is true that underdeveloped countries may be able to count on foreign private investment and capital loans from developed nations and international financial institutions. They may even derive revenue from the tourist trade. Ultimately, they must cover profit, interest and royalty remittances, and the servicing of their debts by whatever earnings they can generate with exports.

These countries depend vitally at present, therefore, on foreign trade. In the final analysis, their aspiration for economic development depends on their import capacity. This explains their preoccupation with preserving their purchasing power in foreign currency. In this respect their anxiety can be compared to that over unemployment in industrialized nations. Thus, they have adopted valorization schemes of doubtful long-term results. But they have resorted to them as an alternative to international agreements that are not accepted by competitors or by consuming countries.

Industrialization has seemed to them all the more imperative, owing to other factors that accentuate their vulnerability. I refer to the restrictive policies of some governments in their traditional markets of protecting agricultural products, to replacement of natural products by synthetic ones, to preferential treatment given to the output of colonial or associated territories, and to competition with surpluses of subsidized crops in world markets.

Eugenio Gudin, of Brazil, has said that the underdeveloped countries have "reflex economies." They do not generate booms nor cause depressions. They just benefit from the former and suffer the impact of the latter. GATT has called attention to the fact that while international trade has experienced significant expansion, this is mainly among industrialized areas. Participation in it by the underdeveloped has been diminishing in relative terms. The tendency is for industrialized areas to depend less and less on those that produce raw materials, while the opposite is true of the latter. Some time ago that agency sounded a warning. If synthetic production were to continue, the improvement registered in terms of trade by nonindustrialized areas would rapidly disappear, while the revenue they derive from exports would diminish in absolute values. It follows that the gap existing in terms of per capita income between industrialized and nonindustrialized countries, instead of narrowing, is widening.

There is a widespread belief that terms of trade tend, in the long run, to favor countries that export manufactured goods over those that specialize in supplying primary ones. There are those who even argue—some with clearly ulterior political intentions—that this is the design of developed "imperialist" nations whose selfish policies are bent on keeping the unjust status quo.

The problem has become increasingly political. This makes it all the more significant because, as the cold war gains momentum, finding solutions is today a pressing matter to be pursued through effective international cooperation.

TOWARD SOLUTIONS

I should like to touch on two classes of solutions. The first is a product-oriented one. The second is market-oriented. According to the latter, primary products would tend to have their problem solved through regional economic integration.

International price agreements seem to be rather unpopular nowadays owing mainly to the difficulty of coordinating domestic supply with world demand, and to the danger that rigid patterns of production would reduce productivity. It is usually said that the harmful results of world price instability should be resolved by the adoption of national policies in the producing countries that would favor the mobility of factors of production in response to the variations in world demand. It is argued that these policies should be supported by a strengthened International Monetary Fund. Examination of the social and economic conditions in the underdeveloped countries leads, however, to the conclusion that this is obviously a long-term solution. As a report of the Committee for Economic Development stated recently: "The dependence of the export earnings of most Latin American countries upon sales of one or two primary commodities creates the danger of more serious, wider and longer, swings in earnings than could well be handled by such means."

In the search for solutions, the Act of Bogota favored a product-by-product approach, as the most realistic and the most conducive to fruitful results. It implies that, as conditions vary from commodity to commodity, they may not enhance a general conclusion applicable to all Latin American problem-products.

A report on this problem was prepared under the sponsorship of GATT in 1958 by a panel of outstanding economists. They recognized that the most important contribution of the industrialized countries would be their avoidance of wide swings in the business cycle and the maintenance of a steady rate of domestic growth. For the underdeveloped countries, these economists recommended national measures aimed at stabilizing agricultural markets on the "buffer-stock" principle, or upon that of the "variable levy—deficiency payment." On the other hand, a "buffer fund" would have the advantage of carrying the product physically from the time when its value is low to the time when it is high. But they saw no technical objection to the operation of a combined "buffer-stock—buffer-fund" device.

The GATT economists endorsed the principle of equal representation of importing and exporting countries. They held that a "buffer-stock" agreement has advantages over others based upon long-term contracts or export quotas, and that it would be more likely to succeed if its operations were not based on a rigid price formula.

The international "buffer-stock" idea seems quite appropriate for minerals. Copper, lead, and zinc are generally used as good examples. To the argument that it costs money, the reply is being given that this money would most likely be spent in any case in aid to their supplying countries. However, there are those who do not think it advisable to apply that mechanism to foods and agricultural raw materials because of the nature of these commodities.

Buffer-stock or buffer-fund schemes would serve many purposes. If carried out according to plan, they would make world prices effective domestically. They would curb increased output of commodities already in oversupply, extend the benefits of low-cost production to consumers of the industrialized countries, and discourage the latter from dumping the surpluses of their subsidized output. They would also bring about the necessary adjustment of some high-cost domestic activities in the developing countries.

However, this type of action runs counter to the national policies of developed countries, whose price-support programs and import quotas favor their domestic producers. Such policies are just as restrictive of free competition as the schemes described. They are at variance with their avowed objectives of cooperation and with their professed commercial doctrines. They represent serious friction points between developed and underdeveloped countries.

RIGID ECONOMIC DOCTRINES INADEQUATE

If the search for solutions were to continue exclusively in economic terms, finding them might be a hopeless task, especially if performed within a laissez faire ideal model. The experts who produced the report for GATT admit, in rather guarded language, that "there is some substance in the feeling of disquiet among primary producing countries that the present rules and conventions about commercial policies are relatively unfavorable to them."

Fortunately, rigidity of doctrine is giving way to the stark realities of today's world, and political considerations must have primacy in shaping out thoughts in an era of cold war.

A distinguished Brazilian economist, Octavio Bulhões, recently suggested a new approach that seems worth considering. He suggested that the United States examine the idea of applying a tax on the consumption of imported raw materials and foodstuffs from Latin America when their prices suffered serious drops. The revenue thus collected could be earmarked and turned over to an international institution for investment in our area. It would compensate Latin America for at least some of the substance it loses when its terms of trade become adverse. Reports from

Washington last July seemed to indicate that Ambassador Robert F. Woodward, Assistant Secretary of State for Latin American Affairs, could have picked up the idea or had it himself, as he is supposed to have suggested to a U.S. Senate committee that the price of coffee to American consumers be increased by 10 cents a pound by way of a contribution for aiding Latin American development.

A COMPROMISE PROPOSAL

Speaking for my country at the International Monetary Fund meeting in New Delhi in 1958, I proposed a more positive role by that agency, partly in these words: "... when the imbalance is due to a temporary slack in demand for a country's products or to an oversupply situation, it could perhaps be corrected by making use of commodity surpluses."

The following scheme was suggested for consideration: first, countries applying for drawings against the IMF would be allowed to offer commodity stocks in lieu of national currency; and second, the IMF would have the option of accepting the commodity collateral or of abiding by its present rules, depending on whether or not a satisfactory agreement is reached with the applicant country on production, price, and disposal policies for surplus commodities.

Arguments against such a procedure are twofold: first, the countries might feel tempted to unload their burdensome surpluses on the Fund without taking steps to promote consumption or curb overproduction; and second, the evaluation of the stocks might present difficulties, since the country holding the stocks might wish to have them priced at levels that exceed the long-run equilibrium price.

While these problems exist, adequate precautions could be taken to make the system operational. It would be a compromise between the national "buffer-stock" idea, which requires heavy unproductive investment by primary producers, and international "buffer-stocks," which spread the burden of stockpiling but present numerous operational difficulties.

At the 1961 conference of the Inter-American Economic and

Social Council at Punta del Este, the primary commodity problem received careful attention. The resolutions passed lead to the expectation that a serious effort will be made to find adequate solutions. Besides setting down the principles and norms that should guide domestic related policies, there was agreement on the need to offset wide fluctuations in volume and prices of exports of primary products. Experts appointed by the Secretary General of the Organization of American States are to prepare a report that should contain recommendations for action before March 31, 1962. Also a draft plan for a compensatory credit program is to be circulated among the member governments and their views obtained before the next meeting of the Commission on International Commodity Trade.

Latin American economies have been among those most affected by the instability of the price behavior of primary products. After the last war a vigorous effort was made at industrialization which, in several respects, did not produce the desired results. This was due, among other things, to the limited dimensions of national markets. Latin American countries remain today vitally dependent on what happens to the prices of their staple commodities in the world market. Their prospects are not rosy. To the difficulties experienced so far, it is feared that a new and serious one will be added. That is the sharp competition that Africa, in particular, could offer them as a result of a combination of cheap labor, rich natural resources, abundant capital, modern technology, and a sure market that is firmly reserved for it by an expanded preferential system covering a vast European area. Latin Americans are concerned not only about holding their traditional European markets; they also fear for the extended effects of such a competition in the rest of the world.

ECONOMIC INTEGRATION—A WAY OUT

The countries to the south are taking cognizance of new trends in the world economy and are now looking for a way out through closer association. There is a growing conviction that isolated national development has been frustrating because there seems to be little possibility for large-scale economies. As its natural resources are largely complementary, Latin America needs to unite economically, although divided politically.

With a large volume of demand provided, there can be high productivity, competition can arise, and specialization will occur, both in national exports and in business operation. The process is far from easy and may take a long time. But a start is now under way, no matter how timidly, through the newly established Free Trade Zone. Latin America has no alternative but to be self-dependent. To the extent that it succeeds, its industry will eventually absorb a substantial part of its raw materials. Its populations, with a much higher level of income, will also consume an equally substantial share of its foodstuffs. In an integrated market there need be no anxiety concerning the vagaries of world demand.

Economic integration would spell firmer, sounder, and faster progress because it should activate and expand trade within the area. But it would also mean greater, though modified, participation in a more remunerative trade with the rest of the world, as it would mean a larger and more attractive field for investment from outside sources. It would mean economic prosperity, social peace, and political stability, providing a most desirable and solid pillar to the free world. To achieve this will require decisive cooperation from the United States and from Western Europe.

These changes may not do away with product-oriented agreements entirely or for many years to come. But if it is a worthwhile objective, every effort should be made to bring it about, for as Latin America progresses towards it—towards diversification and self-dependence—the primary commodity problem will correspondingly diminish in importance.

In the long run, interdependent countries should try to meet each other's needs by producing what it is economical to produce, and by importing some goods that are not economical to produce. I firmly believe that a rational division of labor on an international scale contributes to the world economy as a whole. I would propose that when two countries are concerned, they should agree upon some flexible formula in accord with the spirit of orderly marketing.

COMPETITION AMONG INDUSTRIAL NATIONS

By Hatsujiro Yoshida *

I shall present my views under four points. First, I should like to discuss the progress now being made in the liberalization of world trade. I need not remind you that foreign trade during the postwar period was under continued restriction because of the adverse international payment situation. This restricted trade was naturally aimed at protecting the domestic industry of each nation but, as a result, the function of free competition among developed nations was not given full play in the world market. Later, with the reconstruction and development of the economies of Western European nations, it was no longer necessary for them to maintain a restrictive trade policy. I would like to say, however, that Japan is also striving positively toward a liberalization of

* Chairman, Daito Woolen Spinning & Weaving Co., Ltd.; executive director, Federation of Japan Economic Organizations; governing director, Japan Federation of Employers' Associations; member, board of trustees, Japan National Committee, International Chamber of Commerce. Mr. Toshida died February 26, 1962.

trade, and it will not be long before we will have completed the process. Nowadays the liberalization of trade is regarded as matter-of-fact the world over, serving as the media of unrestricted fair competition among industrial nations. Where competition is given a full part to play, whether on a national or international scale, it will be the basic principle upon which a nation's progress and economic prosperity are predicated.

Secondly, I should like to touch briefly on structural changes in world trade and competition of industrial nations. In summary, after World War II an industrial nation's trade recovered much faster than that of a nonindustrial nation. The total export volume of industrial nations showed a growth of as much as 2.4 times during the 12-year period between 1948 and 1960, as compared with only a 70% increase in exports by nonindustrial nations. In a period of five years from 1953 to 1958, the export volume between industrial countries grew by 58%, while that among nonindustrial nations increased by only 25%.

These statistics indicate that trade between industrial nations has expanded in direct proportion to the recovery of world trade and to the progress of trade liberalization. In other words, the greater the framework of freedom in which competition is allowed, the more the volume of foreign trade among industrial nations expands. On one hand, the increased trade of industrialized countries was a result of international division of labor, nurtured through international competition where each industrial nation is contributing its unique products and skills; on the other hand, this increased trade is making competition among industrial nations more intense than ever before.

EFFECTS OF REGIONAL INTEGRATION

Thirdly, I would like to speak about regional economic integration and its impact on competition among industrial countries. This is a new factor that has added to the intensified competition among industrial countries. The European Common Market, for example, gave an impetus to the creation of the European Free Trade Association, which is expected to join the Common Market in the near future, and to the Free Trade Association in Latin

America. The Common Market is the most fully integrated economic bloc of all. We understand that it is not aimed at creating a bloc economy or an autarchy, but rather at integrating an economy based on the principles of free competition and free trade. Nevertheless, so long as the thinking which underlies the Common Market is to draw some kind of line between member and nonmember countries there always exists a danger of neglecting its trade relationship with countries outside.

What role is this new factor going to play in the development of international free competition and free trade? Or what effect is this new factor going to exert on the future of industry and trade of less-advanced industrial countries and particularly the developing countries that have won their independence in recent years? These are the problems of great importance that deserve our serious consideration.

NEWCOMERS TO INDUSTRIAL COMPETITION

My fourth point concerns the progress of industrialization and competition. Here again, new factors have recently appeared. They are the drive toward industrialization on the part of non-industrial nations and also the desire for greater industrialization on the part of less-industrial nations. Those countries that were liberated from colonial rule and gained independence after World War II have been exerting great efforts toward industrialization. Some have not succeeded yet in reaching even the first stage of industrialization, while some others are gradually changing from importers of industrial goods into exporters of light industrial goods. Participation by the newly developing nations in world markets will have the effect of intensifying competition among industrialized nations themselves.

The so-called "market disturbance," recently taken up by the GATT, stems from this phase of competition between the developing and the industrial nations. It arises from the fact that in a newly industrializing nation where labor productivity in some cases is high, the cost of product is bound to be comparatively competitive. As an attempt to solve the problem, we hear that GATT experts studied both the multiple and bilateral formulas in an attempt to find a solution. The multiple formula, however, involves many difficulties, since it touches on the principle of non-discrimination endorsed by GATT. It is considered that voluntary coordination between two nations affected is the most practical solution, but the voluntary restrictive measures should be made on a flexible basis even under the bilateral formula. In essence, the principle is that a certain industry of the newly developing nation is definitely favored with various advantages as compared to the same industry of the already industrialized nation. It follows that as long as the principle of free competition is to prevail, the industry of the developing nation is destined to continue its steady expansion. Under these circumstances, trade coordination between the two countries should be aimed at finding ways of making its impact gradual. If competition is to function fairly among industrialized nations, their task should be to develop their advanced technology and create new industries utilizing the higher-formed technology. In the long run, interdependent countries should try to meet each other's needs by producing what it is economical to produce, and by importing some goods that are not economical to produce. I firmly believe that a rational division of labor on an international scale contributes to the world economy as a whole. As a solution to the problem of competition related to market disturbance, I would propose that when two countries are concerned, they should agree upon some flexible formula in accord with the spirit of orderly marketing.

This same problem was taken up in the recent International Textile Conference in regard to cotton goods. It is truly to be regretted that the proceedings of the conference were led in a direction where the restriction of imports by each advanced nation was even more facilitated. This direction is not toward progress based on free competition and free trade. It offers no prospect for a basic solution of the problem.

ONLY BY FAIR COMPETITION

In my view, intensified competition among industrial nations is a prerequisite to the progress of their economies. With the addition of new factors to competition, however, the relationship between them is becoming ever more complex. Under such circumstances it is very difficult to find an easy solution, such as an attempt to dispose of the problem by import restriction. Even a minor miscalculation may involve a serious deviation from our fundamental philosophy that the progress and prosperity of world economy can be built only by fair competition. Can we be sure that a regional economic integration created by advanced industrial countries will always move in a direction conducive to the advances of a rational internationl division of labor?

Competition between industrialized countries is thus faced with difficulties. It is interesting to note that the Reciprocal Trade Agreement Act of the United States is to expire next year, and the question of what the Kennedy Administration will do is drawing world-wide attention. In the past the United States has performed a leading role in the prosperity of the world economy by supporting free competition and free trade. Its role in the future of the world economy will be decisively important.

I am firmly convinced that the goal of a prosperous world economy through expansion of free trade can be achieved only through powerful leadership exercised by the United States. Only in that way can the fair competition of industrialized nations be guaranteed and the unremitting advance of the free world be assured.

A Belgian industrialist canvassed the possible consequences of European economic integration, within and between members of a regional group and on the other parts of the free world. He believed that it is much too early to forecast with any assurance.

THE IMPACT OF REGIONAL GROUPS

By Léon A. Bekaert *

Economic and commercial integration in vast areas of the world will inevitably lead to some reorientation and displacement of existing trade. It would be premature, however, to make precise projections of these effects, which will largely be determined by an unusually large number of imponderables. Some are inherent in the evolving and still incomplete character of the different integration formulas now being worked out. Others depend on the reactions of nonmember countries. I feel, therefore, that any hypothetical forecast would have to be surrounded by so many provisos that right from the start it would lose any practical value.

* President, Federation of Belgian Industries. Mr. Bekaert was seriously ill and unable to attend. He died December 19. His talk was read by A. G. Closon, managing director, Brufina, and a member of the Managing Committee of the Federation of Belgian Industries. Mr. Bekaert was president, managing director, or manager of a number of important Belgian and French enterprises. He was a regent of the National Bank of Belgium from 1937, and was a member of the Conseil Central de l'Économie and the Conseil Supérieur de la Recherche Scientifique.

How could one plan, for example, the effects of European integration? The level of the EEC (Common Market) tariff toward outside countries is still under negotiation in GATT. That is where outside countries are endeavoring to obtain concessions on the products they consider most exposed to the restrictive incidence of this tariff. Furthermore, neither the common commercial policy nor the common agricultural policy has yet been decided, and the present association status of overseas territories is only provisional. Would the hypothesis of a merger between the Six and one or more of the Outer Seven, with or without the association of the Commonwealth countries, be adopted? And what would be the terms of the merger?

These are only a few of the factors that can profoundly affect the consequences of regional integration.

TRADE GROWTH WITHIN THE COMMUNITY

The first consequence normally expected of a regional grouping is a quicker development of trade within the community than with outside countries. It would be wrong, however, to attribute this movement solely to tariff or quota discrimination in favor of products produced by member countries.

Even the prospect of an integrated market may create new flows of trade or intensify existing ones. Indeed, it was just such a vast anticipatory movement of businesses and trade that has made it necessary to accelerate the EEC and EFTA treaties, in order to catch up with economic reality.

What other explanation is there for the disproportionate increase in trade within the European Economic Community in 1959, with the very small tariff preference of 10% which set them in motion? Other factors in the transitional period are bringing about specific flows of trade both within the integrated group and with outside countries. For example, there are the structural adaptations of firms and national economies to the new dimensions of the market. The prospective opening of a great integrated market incites industrialists to a general effort at rationalization. Firms give up certain products in order to specialize more in the categories in which they are the most competitive. And each member country will import from other countries of the zone the goods of which it has abandoned production, and will export goods in which it has specialized and developed production; hence, there is likely to be a big development in trade within the community.

It follows that the process of adaptation necessitates considerable investment, and this means orders for equipment, either from within the zone or outside it. The effect of this investment on trade with outside countries will obviously be more immediate if the member countries of the zone do not themselves produce the necessary equipment, and are forced to go outside for them. Seen from this angle, the repercussions of European integration may be different from those of Latin American integration.

If the transitional period is likely to entail a big increase in trade within the community then, a fortiori, the definitive period should further assist this movement. Yet this quicker growth of internal trade is not an absolute law. One may well wonder whether, after a few years, internal and external trade will not tend to develop along parallel lines once again, thus attaining a new point of balance.

COUNTERBALANCES TO GROUP INCENTIVES

It must be added that the "incentive" of preference—which varies according to the level of the common outside tariff in a customs union, or national tariffs in a free trade area—may be cancelled by extra transport costs. Such might be the case, for example, of Austria and Switzerland in the European Free Trade Association, for these countries are nearer to the EEC than to their partners in the EFTA. That might also be the case of countries in the Latin American Free Trade Area. It is important, therefore, that countries which enter a regional group should have easy, direct lines of transport between them. To a certain extent, therefore, a difference in transport costs may counterbalance tariff preference.

Again, such factors as the existence of traditional trading relationships with outside countries, differences in production costs, and other comparative advantages, will continue to exercise a preponderant influence on the evolution of trade within the integrated group.

Another factor that may have strong influence is the absence of any international standardization of products. Perhaps this factor is not so important in new countries. But when highly industrialized countries set up an integrated zone among themselves, this absence of standardization—in most cases the result of national tastes and habits—may slow down the effects that would normally be expected of zonal preference.

TRADE WITH OUTSIDE COUNTRIES

The tendency toward rapid development of internal trade inevitably involves certain displacement of previous trade channels and, in one way or another, breaks up the existing balance. Nevertheless, although the effects of commercial or economic integration on various products and various countries must necessarily be different, integration may give rise to new trade which, for the outside world as a whole, makes up for the negative effects of these movements.

Real, total damage could be done only if the regional integration of countries largely dependent on international trade were to have consequences contrary to what was expected, that is, a contraction of economic activity and not an expansion. In this case, we may reasonably anticipate that integration, in the manner in which it is conceived, must lead to quicker economic growth.

Under the pressure of competition, we are witnessing a migration of production factors—of less productive units toward more productive ones. This migration, which normally takes place within each country, now extends to the member countries of the integrated group. We also find that integration makes possible a better technical and economic concept of enterprises and is at the origin of the creation of new production units, among which are subsidiaries of foreign firms anxious to become "insiders." It is an open question whether this increase in production and general well-being will be merely a leap forward or an accelerated, continuous growth.

In my opinion, the answer will be a combination of the two.

There will first of all be rapid economic development while firms adapt themselves to the new aspects of an integrated market. The early years of the European Economic Community confirm this tendency. And it is through the over-all expansion of national economies that regional integration can contribute to an increase in imports from outside countries, and thereby to their prosperity in general. It is in this way that EEC imports from outside countries have developed in the course of the last few years. This evolution is certainly fundamental, and is confirmed by the facts, but it is nevertheless governed by a series of economic factors. It is not inherent in *any* integration formula, *anywhere* in the world. The condition for such a movement to take place is that the economies engaged in the integration process must be largely dependent on international trade, and diversified in terms of both commodities and geographical areas.

As regards Western Europe, the import trade/production ratio is very high. According to calculations made by GATT, this ratio is at least three times higher than that of North America. The number of different products imported as well as the number of countries supplying Western Europe is also definitely higher.

On the whole, variations in the volume of imports to Europe are roughly proportional to fluctuations in industrial production. It follows that any given fluctuation in industrial activity in either direction would have more widespread and much larger effect upon the export proceeds of the primary producing countries than a similar fluctuation in North America.

The GATT survey concludes that the maintenance of prosperity and the continuity of economic development in Western Europe are matters of key importance to the world economy at large and, in particular, to the nonindustrial areas that depend so heavily on the proceeds of their exports.

THREE CONCLUSIONS

This leads to three conclusions. First, the situation of basic product producers will normally be different from that of producers of manufactured products. Secondly, an integrated zone that is largely dependent on import trade may no longer be so when a larger number of outside countries is associated with it. Finally, the wider the extent of the zone, the more liberal the tariffs and trading policy will have to be to correct the restrictive effects that might be experienced by outside-country trade.

At first sight, the situation of outside primary producing countries is more favorable than that of producers of manufactured goods, for the over-all economic expansion of the integrated zones must have direct repercussions on imports of basic products. It must be added that tariff discrimination is practically nil for these products, since neither the EEC common outside tariff nor the national tariffs of the EFTA countries generally applies duties to these products. Increased demand within the zones, following upon the economic growth, will consequently have a predominant influence on primary product imports.

A recent study by *The Economist* Intelligence Unit on the effects of European integration in the trade of Commonwealth countries confirms this point of view. According to this survey, the incidence of the EFTA will be very small and will certainly not cause any deterioration of Commonwealth trade as a whole with the United Kingdom. It is hardly necessary to add that for certain products the situation may be less favorable.

As regards the EEC, the same survey remarks that two-thirds of imports from the Commonwealth consist of raw materials, which come in duty free. In that context, an expansion in trade is to be expected. For other products, the consequences of integration may be very different. EEC imports of certain temperate zone foodstuffs (15% of total imports from the Commonwealth) might suffer under the EEC agricultural policy. Some tropical products might be exposed to keener competition as a result of free trade between the EEC and overseas territories. The future for goods manufactured by the Commonwealth and by other outside countries will depend largely on the policy of the Six.

IF THE SIX AND SEVEN MERGE

Those are a few of the perspectives. As I emphasized in the introduction, it is impossible to project the situation that would arise in the event of the Six and the Seven merging. One thing is certain, however. It is that Great Britain would take part in the policy-making of the whole group, and her influence would no doubt be cast toward a reduction in duties on manufactured products from the Commonwealth and an increase in imports of agricultural products.

Certainly, national economies in Europe are competitive, and tariff preference might create or intensify intra-European trade, to the detriment of outside countries. This danger is all the more real in that it is on these manufactured products that customs duties are highest. Here again, the more the area is geographically extended the more it is liable to evolve toward a self-sufficient economy in which the import trade/production ratio becomes lower and lower.

I cannot examine this problem in detail, but it seems possible that a merger between the Six and the Seven, with which would be linked a status of association in respect of EEC overseas territories and possibly of the Commonwealth countries, might raise problems for certain outside countries that would not enjoy zonal preference. However, this element does not seem such as to cancel out the long-term advantages that a more extensive zone would offer: greater possibilities of developing economic activity and increasing real income, and hence increased import requirements, not only in basic products but also in manufactured goods.

Finally, it is quite clear that discrimination will have very different effects according to whether it is installed when the general business conditions are expanding or contracting.

The purpose of these remarks is to show how extremely difficult it is to form any accurate idea regarding the possible consequence of regional integration on international trade. As is always the case in economics, a large number of closely interdependent factors will determine this evolution. I have endeavored to indicate certain tendencies: the rapid development of trade within the community, the increase in production, and the corresponding increase in raw material imports. I have also drawn attention to the effects in the opposite sense of an integrated zone grouping a large number of countries. On the one hand, there is the danger of self-sufficiency of the group, but with a greater fraction of the world benefiting by a real freedom of trade. On the other hand, more rapid economic growth is likely to stimulate trade with outside countries. When the countries making up an integrated zone do not belong to a geographically united area, the effects of the integration may be slower.

Difficulties may arise, especially for manufactured products, but even for these products the increased prosperity within the integrated zone, and the liberal nature of the trading and tariff policy of the zone, may compensate for the negative effects of discrimination.

In the present political circumstances, co-ordination of policies is required from countries at various levels of development. The reconciliation of national interests can best be achieved in a world-wide forum where governments meet on a footing of equality and on a basis of definite rights and obligations in the field of trade.

INSTITUTIONAL ARRANGEMENTS TO ADVANCE WORLD TRADE

By J. Royer *

Before the end of World War II, the principal trading nations decided to negotiate a set of international obligations in order to restore some order in the chaotic situation that had prevailed in international trade since the depression in the 30's. They sought to limit the scope of governmental interference with the exchange of goods—to ban certain regulations and procedures that had been found particularly detrimental to the flow of goods. In this way they hoped that the natural economic forces would bring about an orderly expansion of world trade and enable all trading nations to enjoy the benefits of a reasonable international division of labor. These restraints and obligations were embodied in the Havana Charter, and are now accepted and applied by govern-

* Deputy executive secretary, GATT (General Agreement on Tariffs and Trade).

ments that account for more than 80% of world trade through the General Agreement on Tariffs and Trade. They have proved extremely valuable, as the spectacular increase in international trade since the end of the Second World War has shown.

Although the analysis of the situation by the drafters of the Havana Charter and the GATT has proved correct and the solutions suggested by them effective, it is only fair to note that the expectation that this type of international cooperation would suffice has not been entirely fulfilled. Reliance on economic forces alone will not achieve what appears to be one of the most essential requirements of the age. That is the maintenance of a sufficiently rapid and orderly rate of economic growth in all parts of the world, and the gradual disappearance of the tragic discrepancy between living standards in the industrialized and the less-developed countries.

In present circumstances it does not appear practical to reconstruct the patterns that obtained during the 19th century and the beginning of the 20th century in the field of monetary and trade policies. In those days by far the major part of world trade took the form of exports of manufactured goods by a small group of industrialized countries to primary producing countries, and of exports by the latter to the former of raw materials and foodstuffs. The pattern, of course, was not always so simple but, by and large, the trade between the industrialized countries and the primary producers followed the simple pattern which has been indicated.

COMPLEX PATTERNS OF TRADE

Now the pattern of trade is far more complex. On the one hand, the primary producing countries have tried to diversify their economies, and practically all of them are committed to a policy of industrialization and of import substitution. On the other hand, the industrialized countries, while usually prepared to refrain from developing or even maintaining the production of industrial raw materials, are reluctant to discourage domestic production of agricultural products. Most of them are committed to agricultural policies aimed at ensuring the farming community an income that could not be obtained if trade in agricultural products were subject to market forces. In order to isolate the domestic market from those forces, the importing countries see to it that domestic prices are divorced from world prices and that no competition is allowed from imported products.

To sum up, foreign trade which formerly was largely of a *complementary* nature and did not require governmental action to protect domestic producers against competition from foreign sources has now been replaced by trade of a *competitive* nature. As a result of this change, domestic producers, both in the industrialized and the developing countries, insist more and more on protection from the government, and consumers need more and more a moderation of such protection to maintain their purchasing power and to ward off inflationary pressures.

This sweeping change in the pattern of trade accompanied by the political urge for rapid development in the primary producing countries has brought about a growing unbalance in the trade between the two groups. In spite of the remarkable achievements of the multilateral system of trading set up after World War II, it would be overoptimistic to expect that the growing trade deficit of the developing countries could be offset during the next 10 or 15 years by the natural evolution of economic forces. Governments will have to collaborate and use more fully the existing international institutions in the trade field to adjust their commercial and economic policies if this important and disquieting problem is to be solved. The optimum pattern of trade and division of labor between these two groups of countries will require joint action by governments.

REGIONAL GROUPS

Another striking change in the pattern of trade is the growing importance of regional trading groups. The international structure which was accepted by the trading nations in 1947 was based on the principle of equal chances for all. It was, of course, a standard practice in bilateral trade agreements to provide an exception in favor of customs unions, but the practical effects of such a clause had remained negligible until recently. Nowadays, the situation has changed completely, and regional groups are springing to life in Europe and in other continents. Insofar as these regional groups are conducive to an expansion of trade between each member of the group and the other countries either inside or outside the group, their establishment is consistent with the philosophy of expanding world trade, and in everybody's interest. At Havana the trading nations had tried to limit the exception to the most-favored-nation clause to the so-called "outward-looking" customs unions and free-trade areas, while maintaining the ban on preferential arrangements and forms of customs unions and free-trade areas that would be "inward-looking" and restrict the total volume of trade.

Our experience during the last few years has shown that it is not easy to draw the line between an "outward" and an "inward" form of regional integration. So much depends on the policy followed by the regional group after its formation that the outsiders insist on a dynamic system of checking to ensure that the measures taken do not adversely affect their export interests.

The changing structure of world trade thus requires the building up of existing institutional arrangements, and these can be effective only if they are based on clear international obligations and on the willingness of the countries concerned to accept freely a common discipline enforced by majority decisions.

Another development has made it even more essential to rely on institutional arrangements. It is the desire on the part of countries having an active trade with members of a regional group to be associated with the group in one way or another, so as to ward off possible adverse effects on their trade. This situation could involve varying deviations from the most-favored-nation clause and lead to arrangements hardly distinguishable from a purely preferential agreement. All countries in the world cannot join regional groups. Those that remain outside would have to be protected against a deterioration of their status. It is more and more necessary to rely on a constant scrutiny of the policies followed by the various countries so as to define the type of setup that would conform to the common interest at any given moment.

POSSIBLE SOLUTIONS

During the next 10 to 15 years, the chances are that the exports of the developing countries will fall short of the minimum import requirements of these countries by an amount which may well exceed $10 billion. This deficit will have to be met by one of the following methods, or by a combination of methods. The developing countries might slow down the rate at which they are trying to develop their economies. This solution does not appear to be acceptable, because these countries are not prepared to accept the continuance of their present stagnation and poverty. And the industrialized countries cannot afford the political consequences that such a negative solution would imply.

A second solution would be to finance the imports not covered by export earnings by a generous aid program. But this would involve such an increase in the present level of grants that it would probably not be politically acceptable to the industrialized countries. Even if those countries were to contribute 1% of their national income for that purpose they would be able to raise only about $8 billion, which would leave a very substantial balance to be covered by other means.

A third solution would be for the Western countries to realize that they cannot increase substantially their purchases from the developing countries, and for the latter to direct their exports more and more toward Communist countries. The Communist countries would sell capital goods and buy agricultural products and consumer goods that are required by their population and hardly compete with their domestic agriculture and light industry. This is, of course, a possibility which cannot be ignored, but which may have political implications that neither the Western countries nor the developing countries might find to their liking.

There is another possible solution. It is for the Western industrialized countries to absorb increasing quantities of exports from developing countries. This solution is, of course, politically and socially difficult to accept, but appears unavoidable. The opening up of the markets of industrialized countries to exports of developing countries would perforce compete with and displace to some extent the production of domestic farmers or manu-facturers. It would require energy from the governments and forbearance on the part of sectional interests; it could be limited to token or temporary gestures. It should, however, be sufficient to supplement the financial aid which the industrialized countries are prepared to give at any time. The policy should be one of "trade and aid," and would have to be devised on a multilateral basis so that the burden would be shared equally by all.

Appropriate institutional arrangements would be required to implement such a policy. There does not appear to be any need for new organizations. Existing ones, such as the GATT, the OECD, the World Bank and its subsidiaries, are well equipped to deal with such problems, once the governments have made up their minds about the policy to be followed and are prepared to educate their public opinion in a frank, open way.

DEVELOPING COUNTRIES MUST COOPERATE

In view of the unprecedented effort which such a program would impose on the populations of the industrialized countries, they would be entitled to ask the developing countries to enter into a close collaboration with them. The developing countries should frame their policies in such a way as to obtain the maxi-mum results from the financial and commercial aid which the industrialized countries would be prepared to give them. In a number of cases, the expansion of exports of manufactured goods from developing countries to industrial states might require tran-sitional arrangements to avoid the disruptive effect which un-bridled competition would necessarily involve. The developing countries would probably have to agree to exercise some restraint in the development of such exports and, in a number of lines such as textiles, some intergovernmental understanding might be necessary to ensure an orderly expansion of trade.

The role of commercial policy and of international collabora-tion in trade matters should not be limited to such arrangements. The developing countries would have to rely more than has been the case so far on an active commercial policy to get the best results from their economic development program. Foreign competition is one of the most valuable safeguards against inflation. It affords effective protection against the artificial fostering of uneconomic industries which, by imposing excessive prices on the consumer, deprive him of the very benefits which the economic development programs were intended to give him. In many developing countries economic development has been based exclusively on import substitution without much attention being paid to the price at which the domestic production could be sold.

AN END TO SELF-DEFEATING POLICIES

A recent study has shown that, in the developing countries of Latin America, new industries are protected by excessive duties or similar charges or by severe restrictions, while their profitability is seriously hampered by abnormally high tariffs or drastic restrictions on the raw materials, intermediate products, or capital goods which they need to import. In the cases of raw materials, the average incidence of duties and similar charges ranges from 36% to 68%; for capital goods the average levy varies from 23% to 50%. This state of affairs could easily lead to a wastage of domestic and foreign reserves.

Even when the government is prepared to grant exemptions on a selective basis for the import of such products by industrialists, the general effect of such exemptions is to give to the privileged importer a *de facto* monopoly and encourage him to jack up the prices of his product. When the exemption is granted in the case of consumer goods, the exemption is usually limited to what is necessary to supplement domestic production and does not allow any real competition between the domestic and foreign products.

The need for overhauling such obsolete tariff and commercial policies is becoming apparent, and governments seem to be aware of the risk of developing a hothouse economy. But such reforms always meet with internal resistance, and international cooperation may assist the government concerned in carrying out the necessary changes.

If they are to maintain a balance between exports and imports, the developing countries will probably need, during the next 10 to 15 years, to increase very substantially their exports to the highly industrialized countries. It would be unwise to expect that the whole increase can be accounted for by a development of traditional exports of primary products or that the successful conclusion of international agreements on the stabilization of commodity prices would make it unnecessary to look for new or more resilient markets.

A determined effort will be required on the part of the developing countries to produce new products for export. The development will have to be in the direction of processing materials that so far have been exported in their natural state and of producing a range of manufactured goods. They will have to avoid the temptation of moving toward national or regional self-sufficiency; they will also have to face the cold wind of competition on world markets.

Experience has shown that developing countries tend to select more or less the same lines of development and to overestimate the absorptive capacity of world markets. There is a real need for a scrutiny of development policies insofar as they affect export markets. Otherwise, there would be a serious risk of a complete disruption of the markets of various commodities. The lack of coordination would make it still more difficult for the industrialized countries to reconcile themselves to the gradual opening of their markets to the competition of manufactured goods from developing countries.

STATE CONTROL AND STATE-TRADING

Another important change in the structure of world trade has impaired to a certain extent the efficacy of the institutional arrangements adopted after World War II. It is the part played by governments in the actual conduct of trade.

The urge for an exceptionally high rate of growth has induced most developing countries to adopt planning methods that were practically unknown before World War I. The government has stepped in not only to facilitate industrialization, but also to determine priorities and even to act as an entrepreneur. The experience of planning in Eastern European countries and in continental China has certainly contributed to this development. But even in countries that believe in free enterprise the comparative lack of entrepreneurial skill and the reluctance of private capital to invest in essential but less remunerative ventures have very often led the government to fill the gap. Even when the government is not directly responsible for management, it plays a decisive role in the selection of the industries to be encouraged, the firms responsible for the production, and even in the location of plants.

This comes about from the fact that, in developing countries, no industry can stand without the blessing of the government. It can approve or disapprove foreign investments, facilitate or hamper the granting of credit facilities and, last but not least, grant or refuse to grant indispensable commercial advantages such as the exemption of tariff duties, surcharges, or of administrative restrictions for the importation of needed capital goods or raw materials.

These governments have adopted a new attitude toward commercial policy. They often give a particular firm or particular firms specific advantages; investors may even be required to grant a *de facto* monopoly to a particular firm. The next step, of course, is for the government to enter the field of trade itself, through state-trading enterprises or joint-trading ventures where the government retains controlling interests.

The system adopted by Burma is a case in point. A large part of the import trade has been taken away from private importers and the right to import is given either to government agencies or to joint-venture companies where part of the capital is paid by selected tradesmen and part by the government, which is thus able to control the operations of the importing agencies. The joint-venture companies have to accept certain definite commitments regarding their selling prices and the organization of a distribution system inside the country. The object of this arrangement was not entirely economic; it also served the purpose of encouraging Burmese nationals to replace the foreigners in the import trade of Burma. India has also set up a state-trading corporation whose object is mainly to conduct trade with bilateral partners, especially countries with a planned economy, but also to carry on export transactions in cases where the producers or traders are not efficiently organized.

The expansion of state-trading operations has not been confined to the developing countries. Highly industrialized countries have also maintained or developed certain forms of state-trading. In the industrial sector, state-trading enterprises are not numerous, but they have become an important feature of trade in agricultural products in many industrial countries. With the widespread resort to support prices for a number of agricultural products, some governments have found it convenient and profitable to conduct importing or exporting activities through a state monopoly, even though the actual trade may be conducted by private firms. The state-trading arrangement acts as a screen that has the effect of preventing world prices from affecting domestic prices.

COMMUNIST TRADE MOVES AHEAD

In Eastern Europe and continental China, foreign trade rests, of course, on import and export monopolies. With the exception of Yugoslavia, where domestic producers or cooperatives may import or export goods without using state agencies, practically all the trade in other Eastern European countries has to be conducted through state corporations. Before World War II and during the first ten years after the war, trade with the planned economies represented only a small fraction of world trade. The international arrangements of 1947 could afford to leave it out of account. It is less easy to ignore this sector of trade now that the share of planned economies in world trade, especially with developing countries, has grown substantially. In absolute figures, that trade is still small, but it is steadily growing. From 1955 to 1959, USSR exports increased by 260% to Asia, by 550% to Japan, and by 800% to selected African countries.

Whether state trading exists in a planned economy or in a free-enterprise country, the enforcement of the rules of nondiscriminatory, multilateral trade meets with the same kind of difficulties. The state trading agency is the ideal instrument for restricting imports and discriminating between sources of supply.

There is no need to announce quotas, no need to explain what is behind the purchasing or selling program. As the import or export agency is not subjected to competition from other domestic firms, and often is not obliged to show a profit at the end of the year, there is no guarantee that it will be operated in accordance with commercial considerations. In order to protect themselves against the restrictive influence of such agencies, the exporting countries seek to conclude quantitative agreements with the monopoly or with the importing government. But it is not easy to see how the institutions and commitments which serve as a basis for conducting trade in the free world can be made to work. The problem looks formidable indeed from a technical point of view, even if it is assumed that the political difficulties involved are overcome.

In a free-enterprise country, which accepts the rules of the game, the foreign exporter can compete with success with the producers of the importing country and of foreign countries. Of course, if a country follows a policy of complementarity, *i.e.,* when it accepts foreign goods only when required to supplement domestic supply, the position of exporters may not be much brighter than if they were to export to planned economies. In the agricultural sector where this policy is widespread, the efficacy of the institutional management has been doubtful; but in the industrial sector, by and large, the system works well.

In a planned economy the volume or value of each category of imports is determined by the planning authorities and there is practically no room for real competition between foreign products and domestic goods. Foreign goods are allowed to enter the country only insofar as they cannot or shall not be produced internally. It is only if the plans are not fulfilled that some additional opportunities may be opened for other countries. The upshot of all this is that the free-enterprise countries cannot expect much reward for an active commercial policy with respect to the planned economies; they will get only what remains after the domestic suppliers have sold their entire production and when the other planned economies have sold what has been earmarked for them in the joint plans.

The consensus of opinion so far has been that the extension of the principles which govern trade among free-enterprise countries to the planned economies would give the latter far greater advantages than those which the free-enterprise economies could expect in return. Principles that are so valuable in the other sectors of international trade appear to have very little relevance in connection with trade with planned economies. Would it be reasonable to conclude that nothing should be done to integrate trade with planned economies in an international arrangement? Probably not; a possible solution might be the drafting of a particular code of rights and obligations that would apply to the trade between free-enterprise and planned economies, whereas the existing code would continue to be applicable to trade among free-enterprise countries. From a technical point of view, the difficulties are not insurmountable, but from a political point of view, such a solution appears to be out of reach, at least for the time being. Another promising approach is the system of association which the GATT has experimented with lately in the case of Yugoslavia and Poland. By starting with an arrangement based mainly on consultation procedures, it might be possible to elaborate, step by step, a more binding set of rules that would be custom-made and would take account of the particular circumstances of each associated country.

TENTATIVE CONCLUSIONS

It is too early to forecast how trade will develop in the near future. One thing, however, is clear: institutional arrangements have to be devised or strengthened to enable world trade to expand as rapidly and in as orderly a way as possible. May I submit to you as a starting point four tentative conclusions which appear to me to reflect the experience gained during the last few years:

1. In spite of the criticisms launched against liberal economic policies in many quarters, the experience of the postwar period has shown that the world has been better off because the main trading nations have applied liberal commercial policies since the war and have undertaken international commitments to

guarantee the continuance of such policies. World trade has expanded in an unprecedented manner and a more rational division of labor has led to an improvement of the standard of living in all trading nations.

2. The observance of this code of conduct will continue to play an important role in the future, especially if the governments resort more frequently to the procedures of consultation and conciliation provided for in the code. This should be supplemented and underpinned, however, by closer cooperation between governments within the framework of existing organizations to solve problems, usually of a transitional nature, which economic forces are unable to dispose of.

3. Trade problems can no longer be treated as technical issues; they often involve or reflect major political issues that can be solved only at the ministerial level, after adequate preparation by high-level officials.

4. Trade problems generally affect a large number of trading nations, directly or indirectly. Solutions to such problems cannot be negotiated in regional organizations. In the present political circumstances, coordination of policies is required from countries at various levels of development. The reconciliation of national interests can best be achieved in a world-wide forum where governments meet on a footing of equality and on a basis of definite rights and obligations in the field of trade.

The essential thing is to have regularly available a place to talk, with the right to talk, in an atmosphere of common purpose and understanding.

THE OECD AND FUTURE WORLD TRADE

By W. Randolph Burgess *

The Organization for Economic Cooperation and Development, the charter of which will be shortly put into effect by 20 governments of the Atlantic Community, has crept on the scene so quietly that few people understand its purposes and significance. There have been no dramatic headlines, no great clashes between statesmen. This is mostly because the new organization is a logical and normal outcome of the experience of the Atlantic Community in learning to work together for the past 14 years. It is an evolution, not a revolution; but that does not make it any less important.

* Former United States Ambassador to NATO. Mr. Burgess was Under Secretary of the Treasury (1954–57), and deputy governor (1930–36) and president (1936–38) of the Federal Reserve Bank of New York. He is a former chairman, executive committee, National City Bank of New York, director of various business corporations, and a past president of the American Bankers Association, American Statistical Association, Reserve City Bankers Association, and New York State Bankers Association.

THE FINE RECORD OF OEEC

This new organization really had its beginning in 1947 with the Marshall Plan. It was an essential part of the Plan that the participating countries should organize themselves to see that the funds were spent most effectively for the revival of Europe, and with the fullest participation of the people of Europe, in both planning and execution.

Thus was born the OEEC, the Organization for European Economic Cooperation. Starting with the Marshall Plan, it proved so useful that its scope was gradually enlarged to include a wide range of consultation and action furthering economic progress. It played an important role in the brilliant postwar recovery and mounting prosperity of Europe. The productive output of Western Europe has doubled, and the standard of life has risen to new heights. There were many causes for this astonishing feat, of course, and many agencies were involved. But the OEEC was one of the most influential.

Perhaps its greatest achievement was in breaking down barriers to trade, so that goods might flow more freely. Specifically, it brought about the gradual reduction and near elimination of quotas on the movement of industrial products among European countries. This was the result of persistent consultation, persuasion, and pressure to make people and governments understand that freeing trade from arbitrary restrictions would have benefits far outweighing the temporary hardships to certain groups. The facts have fully supported the argument; European trade has increased by leaps and bounds.

A second achievement of the OEEC was making European currencies sound—making foreign exchange rates stable and reliable. The "Monetary Revival of Europe" is one of the most remarkable economic events of our generation. The facilities provided by the OEEC and the International Monetary Fund helped make possible general currency convertibility in Western Europe and the freer movement of money, goods, and people.

Besides these two outstanding activities, literally 100 committees of the OEEC explored one phase after another of the European economy, seeking to make it work better. There have been notable accomplishments in a wide range of human endeavor, including problems of labor, science, and agriculture, as well as industry.

To sum it up: The OEEC proved the value of a regional organization in which countries with common traditions, ideals, and problems could consult together intimately and frankly, educate each other, bring pressure to bear on each other to remove barriers, and actively stimulate economic and human progress.

CONSULTATION AND PERSUASION—THEN ACTION

This experience has demonstrated the usefulness of carefully organized consultation and persuasion, implemented in many cases by joint action. This, despite the fact that no member country surrenders its sovereignty. No country has power to give orders to any other. The method is to bring to the council table all the available information, to analyze it, to seek conclusions by continuing consultation, and to set up standards and principles for operation. Finally, those standards are made effective by the process of "confrontation," that is, a face-to-face review of what each country is doing to meet the standards.

These methods of operation have their limitations; any country can hold out and so reduce the effectiveness of joint action. But over a period, the methods have proved much more effective than the word "consultation" would seem to suggest. They do work and as of today they are the only methods available to our democracies to bring about the cooperation that is so essential as we face the current challenge from the East.

MEETING THE NEW CHALLENGE

It has been the success of the OEEC that has led to the next forward step, the creation of the OECD, to carry forward the best that the OEEC has done and apply its successful methods to newly emerging problems. For the problem facing the Atlantic Community has changed since the days of the Marshall Plan. Partly owing to the OEEC, there is no longer a problem of European recovery; Europe has recovered.

There is also a change in the relation of the European countries and the United States and Canada. All countries of the North Atlantic Community now share very much the same problems. In a real sense, the United States now needs the help of Europe as much as Europe needs its help in the common problems of economic growth and stability. The recent discussions of the balance of payments are illustrative of this fact. There is need for an organization in which the United States and Canada participate actively as full members rather than as associates, as in the OEEC.

In addition, there has now emerged more clearly the responsibility of the industrialized countries for the well-being of the less-developed countries, which are going through a revolution of ideas and ambitions.

When Presidents de Gaulle and Eisenhower, Prime Minister MacMillan, and Chancellor Adenauer met in December, 1959, and set in train the negotiations for a new economic organization, one of their major purposes was stated in a joint communique as follows:

... In view of the great economic progress of Western Europe, they have agreed that virtually all of the industrialized part of the free world is now in a position to devote its energies in increased measure to new and important tasks of cooperative endeavor.

With general agreement on the need for a remodeled organization, the negotiations to set it up went forward rapidly. A "Group of Four," from France, the United Kingdom, Greece, and the United States, after hearing representatives of all countries and agencies concerned, submitted a preliminary report together with a draft charter in the middle of April, 1960.

A "Preparatory Committee," composed of representatives of 20 countries and the European communities, reported to a meeting of ministers in July, 1960. It agreed in principle on the structure and name of the new economic organization and selected as Secretary General a distinguished statesman and economist, Dr. Thorkill Kristensen of Denmark. He set to work at once with experts of the 20 countries and the economic communities on the final drafting of a Convention. This was signed at a meeting of ministers on December 14, 1960, subject to ratification by parliaments.

OECD OBJECTIVES

The Convention of the new OECD states its objectives as follows:

... to achieve the highest sustainable economic growth and employment and a rising standard of living in the member countries while maintaining financial stability, and thus to contribute to the development of the world economy;

... to contribute to sound economic expansion in member as well as nonmember countries in the process of economic development; and

... to contribute to the expansion of world trade on a multilateral, nondiscriminatory basis in accordance with international obligations.

It will be seen from this statement that the economic philosophy of those setting up the new organization was that the needs of the future can be met only by vigorous economic growth, rather than by any sort of reallocation of existing resources. What is needed is a larger pie to divide rather than a different formula for slicing.

As to methods of operation, the new organization will continue to use the consultation and persuasion that have been so successful in the OEEC and in NATO.

OECD'S TRADE FUNCTION

The OECD, by the convention establishing it, has an important trade responsibility, and it is no secret that defining this function was the most difficult task faced by the negotiators in their full year of work. OEEC's work on trade problems offered only limited precedent because of changed conditions. Tariffs are being dealt with in GATT, and it was generally agreed that it was essential to leave that function with GATT to avoid overlapping. It was also difficult to determine in advance just how the new organization would fit in with the somewhat stormy relationship between the Common Market and the Free Trade Area.

Trade is always a sensitive subject, highly charged with the interests of special groups having political influence. The United States, in particular, has trade problems of this sort and faces next year the question of the renewal of the Reciprocal Trade Agreements Act. Other countries have corresponding difficulties.

Under all these circumstances, there was some sentiment during the course of the negotiations to eliminate all trade responsibilities for the new organization. Fortunately, this sentiment did not prevail. For trade is a major factor in economic growth and well-being. It is not possible to omit trade considerations from any economic analysis. Trade is especially crucial to the countries in process of development, for they are in most cases dependent on a sustained and increasing market at suitable prices for their products.

It was finally agreed, therefore, that the OECD should have an active Trade Committee and that this committee should conduct "confrontations" on general trade policies and practices at regular intervals and when requested by members. It would also examine specific trade problems primarily of interest to members and problems that may arise in connection with the relations of the "Six" and "Seven" and the interests of countries outside these two groups.

These functions may sound rather general and nonspecific, but that is necessarily the case. For no one can safely predict exactly what will emerge in the trade area; results will flow from developing circumstances, as was the case with the OEEC. The very existence of this new and strengthened forum will assure its use. The essential thing is to have regularly available a place to talk, with the right to talk, in an atmosphere of common purpose and understanding. As in the OEEC, talk will be aided by the collection and analysis of all the pertinent facts and statistics.

The recent announcement that the United Kingdom and a number of other members of the Free Trade Area group (EFTA) will seek membership in the Common Market paves the way for a whole series of complicated and difficult negotiations. It seems entirely probable that the consultative machinery of the

OECD will prove useful at one point or another in achieving the goal. The fact that efforts made in the OEEC in 1957 and 1958 to join Western Europe in one Free Trade Area broke down is no bar to the use now of similar machinery. There is now available actual and successful experience in the working of both the Six and the Seven. Many fears have been set at rest. The United Kingdom and its partners are now taking a new approach to the problem. There are new faces at the council table. Above all, nobody is really happy over the division of Europe into groups.

It will be helpful to have a United States representative at the council table with a somewhat more detached point of view, reminding the negotiators of the interests of parties outside the group.

Another trade question, already mentioned, is the great need for steady and growing markets for the products of the less-developed countries. Even a modest dip in the value of their exports will often do more damage to these countries than the benefits from all the aid they receive. The countries of the OECD are the principal importers of the products of the less-developed countries; so this is a problem that cannot easily be shunted to one side but must be dealt with. But it is much too soon to wrap these questions up in neat packages. All that can be done today is to indicate the types of problems and the machinery that will be available to deal with them.

RELATION TO OTHER ORGANIZATIONS

There now exist in the world many international organizations concerned with economic problems. Just to name the list would suggest that there are too many. But they fall into different groups with less overlapping than might be expected.

In one group are those having the Soviets or their satellites as members, such as the United Nations and its agencies. These provide sounding boards for public presentations of policy and have been useful for certain types of action, as in Korea and the Congo. But the presence of the Communists in the councils, exercising their veto power constantly, and the vast membership of small new countries, each with a vote, are serious limitations on effective action.

A second group, symbolized by the World Bank and Monetary Fund, has proved invaluable for specific operations. By good fortune, the Communists elected to stay out of these activities, and they therefore represent the power of the free world. The breadth of their membership gives them not only strength but also acceptability among the so-called "uncommitted" nations. They act through boards of directors with weighted votes, assuring responsible action.

The third group, to which the OECD belongs, is that of the regional organizations. Their more limited membership, including only those countries that have common problems, traditions, and ideals, makes it possible for them to agree on common action much more easily than is true of larger groups. In the case of the Atlantic Community this factor is especially potent. For here we have a group of countries with centuries of similar background and, to a considerable extent, with a common blood stream. In terms of productive capacity and avenues of achievement in science and culture and religion the Atlantic Community is unique.

Within the Atlantic Community itself there are several different organizations whose functions must be kept distinct to avoid confusion and wasted energy. This is especially true with respect to NATO.

RELATION OF OECD AND NATO

Some misunderstandings have arisen as to the economic role of NATO because Article II of the NATO Treaty reads as follows:

The Parties will contribute toward the further development of peaceful and friendly international relations by strengthening their free institutions, by bringing about a better understanding of the principles upon which these institutions are founded, and by promoting conditions of stability and well-being. They will seek to eliminate conflict in their international economic policies and will encourage economic collaboration between any or all of them.

Back of these provisions in the Treaty is the clear lesson of history—that military strength must be supported by economic strength. But the Treaty does not say that NATO itself should deal with economic problems, but that the "parties," that is the countries which sign the Treaty, shall take the suggested action themselves and "encourage economic collaboration between any and all of them."

There has been a tremendous amount of discussion in and outside the NATO Council of the role that NATO itself should play in the economic field, and of the extent to which it should leave economic action to other agencies. The planning for the OECD has stimulated this discussion. A consensus has been reached that it would be more effective and wiser to carry forward most economic functions in an agency other than NATO itself.

One reason is historical. The OEEC was born even before NATO and developed a remarkably effective program and tradition of work. The OEEC also has included five European countries not members of NATO, but which are a logical part of the Atlantic *economic* community and add substantial strength to the effort.

A third very important reason is that a major task now facing the West is assistance to less-developed countries. These countries are extremely sensitive about becoming involved in the "cold war." Aid by NATO would inevitably have a military flavor. But an economic agency, one including neutrals in its membership, can elicit the cooperation essential to success.

Furthermore, NATO has plenty to do in its main task of the defense of the West in military, political, and other aspects. In this specific connection, certain economic questions will naturally fall within the responsibility of NATO rather than that of the OECD. Among these are trade with the Communist countries, assessment of the relation of economic to military strength, appraisal of the economic sinews of war, and the economic capacity of the members of the Alliance for maintaining their military contribution. The NATO Council quite rightly feels free to discuss any economic problems in their relationship to the main function of the Alliance. There will be close liaison between NATO and OECD through overlapping membership and, in certain countries, through common representation.

In fact, the work of the OECD may be thought of as helpful and complementary to NATO in building the strength by which the West may defend itself. Its work thus constitutes in part a fulfillment of the objectives of Article II of the NATO Treaty. Both organizations forge ever-stronger links between Western Europe and North America.

NATO and the OECD have this in common: they draw together the massive intellectual, scientific, productive, and moral resources of the Atlantic Community to defend it from alien aggression, and to promote healthy, vigorous economic growth both in the Atlantic Community and throughout the free world.

*International, national, and private struc-
tures exist to provide financial assistance to
the developing countries. New ones are being created. These institutions are here evaluated, but Dr. Wallenberg stresses the need
for more cooperation between them.*

EVALUATION OF STRUCTURES IN INTERNATIONAL FINANCE

By Marcus Wallenberg *

To meet the challenge of an ever-increasing demand, a sharp
increase in the international flow of capital among the developed
countries as well as between these and the less-developed ones is
highly desirable. Are the existing financial institutions in our
world equipped to fulfil this function effectively? What institutions are active in international finance?

Let us divide them into international and national groups.
I should like to start with the international governmental organizations. The main part of the capital provided by these institutions has emanated from the World Bank, on an average $500
million in annual disbursements during the late 50's. Of this

* Vice-chairman, Stockholms Enskilda Bank; chairman, Allmanna Svenska
Elektriska Aktiebolaget, and deputy chairman, Federation of Swedish Industries. Dr. Wallenberg is also chairman of the Council of European Industrial
Federations, and of the Swedish National Committee, International Chamber
of Commerce.

amount, about 60% has gone to the underdeveloped countries. Most of the World Bank's development loans have been for basic facilities, such as power, transportation, irrigation, and so on, needed to raise productivity in general in the recipient countries. Since it started, the Bank has made loans totalling $5.7 billion, of which more than 30% has gone to develop electric power and some 30% to transportation. Apart from its own funds, the World Bank works with long-term money raised in the international capital markets by sale of its bonds in different currencies. Such bonds, placed in the U. S., Canada, Switzerland, Germany, Holland, Belgium, the United Kingdom, and France, have totaled more than $2.2 billion. The Bank also cooperates with commercial banks in different countries by placing with them part of its holdings of bonds or notes without guarantee. It has played an outstanding role in creating wealth and generating development in a great many countries. Its help has been pivotal in the reconstruction of national economies since the war and in igniting the spark of life for many promising potentialities in all corners of the world. The great prestige of the World Bank's leadership, based on its meritorious performance, has permitted it also to play a useful role in reaching workable solutions to many knotty international problems. The world has a tremendous asset in the expert knowledge and wide experience the staff and associates of the World Bank have acquired through its activity.

HELPING SMALL COMPANIES

To help investments in small companies of varying types and size, the International Finance Corporation (IFC) has been created. In cooperation with local and international entrepreneurs and capital, its goal is primarily to help private investment spread to the world's less-developed countries. Having so far a capital of only $100 million, the IFC has been advancing rather cautiously, but it can, in due time and given greater resources, be of value. Requiring no government guarantees, it is definitely a liberalizing step toward developing private enterprise in less-advanced countries.

The International Development Association (IDA), which began its operations in November, 1960, is one of the younger intergovernmental organizations. IDA has scheduled resources of $1 billion; it allows for the repayment of loans in local currencies, and its management has authority to grant loans free of interest or at a privileged rate. As time goes on, this institution should be a valuable complement to the World Bank and the IFC in special situations outside their scope.

Other international governmental institutions created to help the development of trade on a regional basis are the European Investment Bank and the Inter-American Development Bank, each with an authorized capital of $1 billion. The aim of the former institution is to assist in solving special regional problems in cooperation with existing banks within and outside the European Common Market, as well as with other international government credit institutions. The Inter-American Development Bank, founded last year, has a limited authority to grant loans, with repayment in local currencies, and is cooperating with commercial banks. It appears that this bank will be given certain tasks in connection with the program laid down by the Alliance for Progress at Punta del Este.

NATIONAL INSTITUTIONS

Let us now deal with national official institutions. In most countries, institutions specializing in financing capital exports have been established to grant medium or long-term credits to exporters in order to carry through important contracts to export capital goods or consummate whole projects in the form of so-called package deals. Such institutions work either by giving loans to foreign buyers directly or by assisting the national exporters to arrange a medium or long-term financing not otherwise readily available through customary banking facilities.

The U. S. Export-Import Bank, with a capital of $1 billion, also is one of the most important organizations in this field. Its loan limit is $7 billion and its outstanding volume of loans is now $5.8 billion. Its activities over many years show an impressive support of developing natural resources, industries, and public services of foreign countries, promoting U. S. products and know-how in those foreign countries, since generally "E.I." loans are tied to U. S. deliveries of equipment or services. The Export-Import Bank has shown great versatility and flexibility as to terms in creating undertakings of truly national importance to the recipient countries.

Another interesting U. S. venture is the Development Loan Fund (DLF), having the objective of granting long-term loans with low interest and with repayment in local currencies. These loans are often called soft loans and come close to outright grants. Obviously, the DLF can play an important role in helping countries that are in a transitory stage as to their economic development and where situations exist in which national interests would best be served by loans instead of grants.

In Germany, the Kreditanstalt für Wiederaufbau (Reconstruction Loan Corporation) was established in 1948. Its purpose was to further German capital development projects, grant long-term foreign loans or export credits, and to assist, with guarantees, special domestic activities in industry, farming, and fishing. In 1960, the RLC engaged in business totaling about $500 million, often in cooperation with industry and other credit institutions both domestic and foreign. Of this, 45% went to underdeveloped countries. The institution procures its funds outside its own resources from public money and by placing its own bonds in the market or with credit institutions.

Complementing these activities are a number of export credit institutions engaged either in granting loans or in giving guarantees against various risks. Such risks do exist with international transfer of funds, with possible default in obligations entered into by foreign parties, with the solvency of creditors or risks connected with *force majeure* of various kinds, political or otherwise.

Institutions granting loans include the Commonwealth Development Finance Company of the United Kingdom, with investments of about $40 million, the AOFC of the U. S., with total assets of $30 million and with 85% of its business in Latin America, the Banque Française du Commerce Extérieur, and the Export-Import Bank of Japan.

Among institutions giving guarantees may be mentioned first

of all the British ECGD (Export Credits Guarantee Department), with commitments of about $2.2 billion, the French Coface (Compagnie Française d'Assurance pour le Commerce Extérieur), with commitments of about $1.1 billion, and the German Hermes, with commitments amounting to $2.3 billion. The Italian, Dutch, Belgian, Norwegian, Danish, and Swedish institutions are comparatively smaller, with commitments of less than half a billion dollars each.

PRIVATE FINANCING

An important role is also being played by the commercial banks and by the big industrial corporations engaged in international activity. Commercial banks can contribute to capital exports not only by giving export credits of varying lengths but also by assisting their clients to arrange long-term financing to facilitate their investments at home and abroad. They have acquired over the years an extensive knowledge of international business and have developed valuable contacts all over the world that can be usefully employed to further the flow of international investment.

Exports from industrialized countries toward the less-developed ones tend more and more to consist of sales of complete factories or installations. Exports of such projects obviously require long-term credit facilities. This is a difficult problem. I think it can be solved only through close cooperation between the special institutions referred to and the commercial banks.

Where is the capital to be found that is ready to run the risk of an entrepreneur, in other words the equity money? It is here that the big industrial corporations often play a decisive role. Developing natural resources, founding new industries, or creating or extending public services in power or transportation in more or less developed nations very often require corporations ready to give leadership, management, or know-how on a temporary or permanent basis. Backing these projects with their own money, as these corporations often do as carrier of the ultimate risk, is often the very prerequisite to finding the necessary long-term money to bring the projects to fruition and fulfilment. Combining enterprise and long-term lending, whether institutional or not, opens to my mind great opportunities for sound cooperation between industrialized and less-developed countries in developing the latter's often dormant resources.

POLITICAL RISKS

What can be done to encourage this much-desired flow of private capital into less-developed countries? What inhibitions do prospective investors feel toward investments in this area? Political risks often act as a brake on the potential investor, bringing him to the conclusion that he would rather keep his money closer home. By "political risks" he means the possibility that government measures will impair the rights of foreign investors through nationalization or expropriation, or through discriminatory taxes, currency transfer restrictions on interest, dividends, etc. If risks of this kind could be reduced, there is every likelihood of a substantial increase in the flow of private capital toward the less-developed countries. What remedies are there to encourage confidence in the security of foreign investments?

According to international law a state that exerts its right to expropriate foreign property has to provide fair and prompt compensation in a transferable currency. But if the capital-importing state does not live up to this obligation, the investor may face protracted negotiations with the competent authorities, or long legal proceedings, or turn for support to his own government. This outlook does not stimulate the prospective investor. A remedy might be arbitration. Indeed, arbitration has increasingly become a favored method for the resolution of disputes arising in business relations, and the more such machinery is being used with acceptable arbitration awards the better. The agreement by capital-importing and exporting countries to refer their investment disputes to arbitration or to an international court for settlement is surely one means of stimulating private capital to move to the capital-importing countries.

This need for more effective protection of private investment has already been recognized in several of the developing countries. By legislation or otherwise, they have introduced rules aimed at the protection of foreign property. In other instances, provisions of this kind are laid down in bilateral conventions between governments. Still more frequent are the cases where an individual concession agreement between the private investor and the government of the capital-importing country contains provisions guaranteeing the investor against expropriation for a specified period of time and providing for full compensation in case of taking over. These are steps in the right direction.

PREPARING A BASIC CODE

Another active suggestion for building up confidence in international investments is a multilateral convention open to all states and containing a set of guiding principles regarding the conduct and treatment of foreign investments. The plans for a multilateral arrangement are not new. The Havana Charter called for the preparation of such an agreement. The International Chamber of Commerce has tried to gain universal acceptance of some such basic rules. Its Code of Fair Treatment for Foreign Investments provides a useful pattern for the multilateral instrument that is now needed.

The most promising initiative in this direction, however, is certainly the one taken a few years ago in the Organization for European Economic Cooperation (OEEC). It is still being actively processed by experts and is to be carried on in the Organization for Economic Cooperation and Development (OECD). The OECD is to replace and extend the OEEC, and is charged particularly with the task of promoting the economic development of the less-developed countries. Thanks especially to the diligent work and support of Dr. Abs, Lord Shawcross, and others, there is hope for a new instrument to be born, to add to those already at the disposal of those countries that desire to create a favorable investment climate.

AN INTERNATIONAL GUARANTEE FUND

Another idea is the creation of an international guarantee fund through which the investor could obtain a guarantee, or insurance, against political risks involved. If a common ground could be found for establishing such an institution, it would be an effective addition to the structure of international finance of the greatest importance. When indemnifying the investor, the fund should be subrogated in the investor's rights, so as to enable it to recover from the government or other responsible entity the indemnity paid out to the investor. But in order to determine responsibility, whether through arbitration or in some other way, a set of basic rules accepted by the governments participating in the insurance scheme on the treatment of foreign investments is required.

Plans for an international investment guarantee fund have sprung from the belief that the acceptance of rules of fair treatment of foreign investment, coupled with an effective arbitration machinery, does not always suffice as a stimulus to making investments. Nor do the export credit facilities available in many countries provide the investor with adequate safeguards. He may still have to face the risk of losses because of political events. I want to make it perfectly clear that the risks to be taken care of by the suggested insurance scheme should be exclusively those that are genuinely political. The idea is not to relieve the private investor of the commercial risks.

Investment guarantee schemes, aimed at taking care of political risks, are, as you know, already operating on the national level in the United States, Germany, and Japan. The idea of approaching this matter on a multilateral basis, however, came up for discussion last year at the International Chamber of Commerce Conference in Karachi. It has gained momentum in various quarters ever since. The question is under active consideration within the ICC. It may be mentioned also that a group of businessmen, bankers, and lawyers who have come together in a private international organization called "The International Association for the Promotion and Protection of Private Foreign Investments" have given a lot of thought to this matter.

The latest development in this field, and in my view an important one, is that at its meeting in Tokyo this past summer, the Development Assistance Group (DAG) asked the World Bank to study the matter further. The World Bank agreed to do so, and I believe that it is the ideal body for a study of this kind.

IMPORTANCE OF FINANCIAL STRUCTURES

These rather brief comments have emphasized the desirability of arranging insurance against political risks for private capital. There is, to my mind, a clear reason for this. Looking down the list of international and national institutions or organizations with the object of assisting in the flow of capital between the countries of the free world one must be impressed by the number and power behind them, as well as by the skill with which these institutions deal with their tremendous tasks. In addition, there is the great assistance given by the various national governments, because of special ties or situations, to a number of large areas in the less-developed world.

Furthermore, we should not forget what is done in the monetary field by such institutions as the International Monetary Fund and the Bank for International Settlements in Basle. Their promotional and stabilizing work influences developments far outside their particular sectors. It is of no less importance than the stability in economic, financial, and political matters exercised by our advanced industrial nations in building a basis for extended world development.

Many people can say that the amounts involved are small in relation to demand. That may be so, but what is important is to make sure that the structure is there and that the instruments exist that can be given more ammunition as our goal becomes clearer and our resources grow.

The conclusion I draw is the desirability of developing cooperation between international and national institutions, on the one hand, and the private sector, on the other. The latter is represented by industrial corporations, banks and private investors, which tap and extend financial markets for foreign investments in both loans and risk capital.

India's leaders expect their country to reach the stage of self-sustained growth by the end of the Third Five-Year Plan, which was launched in April, 1961.

INDIA'S MONETARY AND FISCAL DISCIPLINES

By H. V. R. Iengar *

The rate of investment in the Indian economy has been doubled since 1950, and is currently estimated to be about 11% of national income. The rise in the savings ratio has been less, and domestic savings have been supplemented by a substantial inflow of external resources. The crucial determinant of long-term growth prospects is the extent to which savings rise. In this context, the steady increase in life insurance business and in small savings is an encouraging pointer to the outlook for

* Governor, Reserve Bank of India; secretary, Department of Planning and Development; secretary, Constituent Assembly (which drafted the Indian Constitution); principal private secretary to the Prime Minister; secretary to the Ministry of Home Affairs; secretary to the Ministry of Commerce and Industry. Mr. Iengar represented the Government of India in financial and economic discussions with various European countries, and in 1956 was named chairman of the State Bank of India. Currently, he is chairman of the Refinance Corporation for Private Industry, and president of the Indian Institute of Bankers.

146

savings. It also reflects the confidence of the community in the longer-term prospects in regard to economic growth and financial stability.

India's national income in real terms has been rising by almost 3½% a year in the last decade. A somewhat higher growth rate, of about 5% per annum, is postulated under the Third Five-Year Plan which commenced in April this year. This higher rate is based on the fructifying of previous investments and the larger investment rate that is projected. Investment is to rise from about 11% of national income in 1960–61 to a little over 14% by 1965–66. The domestic savings rate is to rise from about 8% to 11%, which requires a higher marginal savings-income ratio than hitherto.

These various estimates do not include the nonmonetary savings and investment that take place in the Indian economy through direct capitalization in agriculture and other ways, probably on the order of about 1% of the national income. For this and other reasons, estimates of savings and investment in the Indian economy are really in the nature of broad orders of magnitude. In the conditions of the Indian economy, the basic approach of having a mixed economy is considered likely to yield the most satisfactory results, with the public sector taking greater initiative in new investment, particularly in the development of social capital, with a view to promoting total investment and directing it into certain priority fields.

Private investment itself is helped forward in a variety of ways. While the share of the public sector in new investment is larger than that of the private sector in Indian Plans, public authorities account for only a minor part of total economic activity in the country. The government's share (including government enterprises and administration) in the generation of net domestic product is today only 10% or 11%. This proportion was only 7% or 8% ten years ago. Again, within the limited sector of organized industry, government enterprises account for hardly one-sixth of the output; even by the end of the Third Plan this will not be more than a quarter.

India offers a most appropriate case study of development with stability. There is an ever-present expansionist bias and, therefore, a certain pressure on prices, arising mainly from an investment program that presses on the resource position. The general price level would, therefore, be a good indicator of stability in the economy. In the First Plan period (April, 1951 to March, 1956) there was no rise in prices; in fact, prices fell by nearly 20%. This was partly due to the fact that at the commencement of the First Plan the price level was rather high, reflecting the Korean boom conditions, and a corrective fall was to be expected. More importantly, during the First Plan period, while real national income increased by about 18%, the rise in money supply was about 10%. Thus, the investment program during this period could well have been larger than was planned for and attained, without untoward effects on prices. On the other hand, prices were rising in the Second Plan period (April, 1956 to March, 1961), and especially since 1958. Money supply increased by 33% while national income in real terms rose by less than 20%. The price rise has averaged 5% to 6% a year. While the extent of this price rise is not alarming, and has also been somewhat moderated in the last year or so, this has been of some concern, and a major decision has been taken in regard to the financing of the Third Five-year Plan—that deficit financing of governmental outlays should be limited to what may be broadly termed the noninflationary level.

FISCAL AND CREDIT POLICIES

The maintenance of reasonable price stability without inhibiting growth is a major policy goal in Indian thinking. This does not imply that there should be absolute rigidity in the price level, or that prices of particular commodities cannot rise. Individual prices may rise or fall, but the general price level should not undergo any abrupt change. The distinction here is between a "functional" rise in prices and an inflationary one. Two related guideposts of fiscal and credit policies in India are: (1) promoting savings in the community; and (2) regulating bank credit with a view to assisting productive activity while preventing speculative, cornering, and unproductive activity. In view of the inadequacy of savings and the shortage of capital, it is necessary that even the relatively unessential activities and demands for funds arising from them are curbed. However, the existence of a large unorganized sector through which nearly 50% of industrial and trading activity is financed limits the effectiveness of policy measures to this end. In such a context the role of fiscal and monetary policies has to be essentially promotional while keeping guard against the emergence of any really inflationary situation.

While small savings are nurtured assiduously, and market loans also are expected to provide somewhat larger sums, it is in the field of taxation that fiscal policy can really fulfill this role. Basically, the objective of taxation, and of fiscal policy generally, is not merely to divert savings into the public sector, but to enlarge the total savings. Thus, tax policy has also to keep in view the investment needs of the private sector and the incentives for productive enterprise. Total tax collections in India amounted to 9.2% of national income in 1960–61, as against 7.7% in 1955–56. This proportion is to rise to 11% by 1965–66. There is also to be a substantial surplus from public undertakings owned by the government.

In recent years, mainly under the impact of the development program, there has been a gradual, almost imperceptible, extension of the monetary sector. This should improve tax yields. Tax administration itself is being streamlined to facilitate collections. Accordingly, the tax system may be expected gradually to show a better response to the rise in incomes. However, in view of the low incomes of the vast majority of the people in the country, the tax effort involved is indeed considerable. This is rendered even more difficult by the existence of a sizable nonmonetary sector that cannot be reached by any conventional tax measures. Apart from marginal adjustments, there is little scope on the whole for enhancing rates of direct taxation; the main approach in this sector is toward a more effective enforcement of the taxes on the statute book. The main reliance for obtaining the additional tax revenues has to be placed on commodity taxation. Numbers of small farmers have to be called upon to bear additional burdens, and taxes have to be levied even on the essentials of life such as sugar, cloth, and foodgrains. Even the poorest are thus called upon to contribute to India's development. This calls for great political courage.

Credit policies have to be in harmony with the accent on steady growth. It is only to be expected, therefore, that in the functions and working of the Reserve Bank of India the developmental aspect is no less important than the regulatory one. Policy decisions have to be taken on an assessment of factors that are not always easy of mutual adjustment. Among these are: (1) the need to contain inflationary pressures, (2) the provision of credit facilities for an expanding level of production, and (3) the rigorous restriction of credit for nonproductive and less essential purposes. The main concern of the Central Bank has, of course, to be with the maintenance of reasonably stable conditions in the economy, as reflected in prices and costs. This is important from the viewpoint of the success of the longer-term development endeavor itself.

THE PUBLIC SECTOR

Even in the industrialized, free-enterprise countries, there has been an enlargement of public sector activity in the postwar years, so that to a varying degree they are all today mixed economies. Thus, in the United Kingdom, France, and other countries of Europe, public investment, including especially that by public corporations, forms a fair-sized proportion of total investment. When government expenditure on goods and services ranges from a third to a fifth of total domestic expenditure, and tax revenues form a similar proportion of national income, the course of the economy can be influenced in no small measure by the conscious use of the fiscal instrument. In these circumstances, the efficacy of the interest-rate mechanism, or of monetary policy in general, gets rather blunted, especially as the public corporations cover transport and public utilities, which are precisely the fields, together with housing, that are generally more sensitive to decisive changes in the interest rate. Again, real growth prospects influence business decisions to a much greater extent than the cost of having to borrow at 1% or 2% more or less, particularly during the process of "creeping inflation" that has been going on in practically all countries.

These are some of the reasons why monetary techniques that were revived in the postwar years as a main instrument of economic policy have not been as effective as was expected. In a developing economy like India's, where public finance increasingly reflects the financing of the development program, this is perhaps even more true. As investment activity is planned and promoted with the longer-term perspectives in view, according to certain broad priorities, direct controls have to operate alongside the more general instruments of monetary discipline and fiscal policy. Nevertheless, monetary techniques, such as the variation of reserve ratios and more recently a slab system of interest rates on accommodation from the Reserve Bank, have been increasingly in use. The yield on government securities is also being gradually increased. In India, as in other developing countries, domestic fiscal and monetary policies should be in tune with the major requirement of promoting exports.

FOREIGN ASSISTANCE

Total foreign assistance required for India's Third Plan is placed at Rs. 32 billion, including U.S. assistance of Rs. 6 billion that has already been arranged for; the gap also includes about Rs. 5 billion (net) repayment of external debt falling due. This forms about 30% of the total investment envisaged for the five-year period. Import saving has an important place in dealing with India's foreign exchange problem. However, the experience of other countries over longer periods and that of India herself in the last few years demonstrates that import requirements on the whole increase as industrialization gains momentum. With the growing needs of the economy, imports of fibers, chemicals, fertilizers, oil, and other items will be larger in 1965 than at present, despite higher domestic output levels of these goods. The import bill in respect of "maintenance imports," as well as the direct import component of the investment outlays, may actually turn out to be somewhat higher than allowed for in the Plan projections. Therefore, the foreign assistance requirements of India's Third Plan have really been placed at the minimum.

The success of our monetary and fiscal policies will depend to a major extent on the availability of the needed external assistance. The greater part of the assistance has necessarily to be provided by friendly governments and through international financial institutions. The inflow of private investment capital can also play an increasingly useful, though supplementary, role. The facilities available for private foreign investment in India are liberal from any realistic viewpoint. Against the background of a large and expanding market and a climate of political and economic stability, there are various tax incentives for new investment, including a development rebate and a tax holiday, equally applicable to domestic and foreign enterprise. Despite the country's foreign exchange difficulties, free remittance of profits and repatriation of capital continue to be allowed.

The growing volume of external debt, however, poses the problem of servicing and repayment; nor can such large-scale assistance be expected to continue indefinitely. The debt looks burdensome as of now, and for some years to come, but with the growth of the economy India's ability to service the debt will also rise and, over a period, the problem should not prove intractable. Meanwhile, the terms of the external loan assistance become a most relevant consideration from India's viewpoint; long-term loans at a low interest rate are needed.

IMPORTANCE OF EXPORTS

Also on the longer-term view, a steady rise in export earnings is essential to enable the economy to reach an approximate condition of external viability. Such viability is an ingredient of self-sustained growth. This does not imply that at the end of a stated period, say, 10 or 15 years, all foreign assistance could or should abruptly cease. Net inflows of external resources over a longer period are quite consistent with viability on external account. No spectacular or abrupt improvement could be expected in India's export picture. To some extent, exports depend on world market conditions and the commercial policies of industrialized countries. Here is another field where the advanced countries can assist India through liberal trade policies, so that increased trade supplements external assistance.

The structure of India's exports renders the task of promotion difficult, as experience during the Second Plan years has amply demonstrated. Only a gradual rise in exports can be expected in the next few years. In taking a view of the export problem and prospects, the Indian planners look beyond the Third Plan. They are aware that, if exports are to rise, the structure of Indian export trade has to undergo a change and competitive ability has to be maintained in world markets on the basis of the quality of goods and their prices. As a latecomer in the export field for diversified manufactured goods, however, India will find her task difficult without a liberalization of trade policies by the industrially advanced countries.

Is there anything more important, more indispensable, or more urgent for an internationally satisfactory monetary order than that each nation concerned should confirm and secure its own financial stability?

CURRENCIES, CAPITAL, BALANCE OF PAYMENTS

By Hermann J. Abs *

Mutual international and intercontinental interests have become so obvious that it can almost be taken for granted that specifically national viewpoints would be disregarded in a survey such as mine. What an encouraging sign this is of the progress we have already made in international cooperation! At the moment, we are witnessing a variety of projects for reforming the international currency system. The object is to increase and more evenly distribute international liquidity; the national foreign exchange balances are to be adjusted and appropriate currency policies are to be adopted by the surplus and deficit countries.

* Managing director, Deutsche Bank; chairman of Badische Anilin- & Soda-Fabrik, Daimler-Benz, Dortmund-Horder Hüttenunion, Deutsche Lufthansa, Kreditanstalt fur Wiederaufbau and Rheinsch-Westfälisches Elektrizitätswerk; vice-chairman of Handel-Maatschappij H. Albert de Bary, Siemens & Halske, Deutsche Shell, and Zeiss-Ikon. Dr. Abs was a member of the World Bank Mission to India and Pakistan on Western Aid Programs in 1960. He is president of the German-American Chamber of Commerce.

Some quarters are even prepared to sacrifice the stability of exchange rates to these ends.

I should like to ask: Is there anything more important, more indispensable, or more urgent for an internationally satisfactory monetary order than that each nation concerned should confirm and secure its own financial stability? Can institutions or even automatisms, funds, drawing rights, or exchange-rate adjustments guarantee a lasting equilibrium if, as a result of differing degrees of discipline in economic and financial policies, there is a marked discrepancy in the development of internal price levels and international competitiveness of the nations concerned? On the other hand, conditions being what they are, who can bear greater responsibility for internal financial stability than national agencies? This ultimate supremacy of national responsibility applies even in regard to the members of the European Economic Community, who have agreed to delegate a comparatively wide range of economic competencies to a supranational institution.

Before contemplating any reforms of monetary institutions and practices, it is necessary to condemn a policy that would, because of its injustice and inefficiency, result in a creeping inflation. That holds especially true considering the fact that it would be impossible to coordinate national policies. One country inevitably would inflate more extensively than another; this would inevitably result in balance of payments crises, as well as other disturbances of the monetary system and the international exchange of capital.

All countries concerned should practice national self-aid. This is not irreconcilable with the acceptance of the fact that today more than ever only internationally coordinated self-aid can succeed. But coordination will have to comprise the entire realm of economic and financial policy, including business cycle and foreign trade policy. Otherwise the results can be only very short-lived.

Let me quote a few sentences from a statement made by Douglas C. Dillon, the U.S. Secretary of the Treasury, before the subcommittee on international exchange and payments of the Joint Economic Committee of Congress on June 19, 1961:

In the final analysis, there is no substitute for balance of payments discipline in this, or any, economy—a discipline that reaches through our productivity performance, our price and wage performance, our governmental budgetary position, and our monetary and credit policies. Neither the force nor the form of this discipline is materially different for a reserve-currency country than for any other.

Now that Great Britain and a number of other EFTA countries have declared their willingness to join the European Economic Community, the tendency toward a closer international harmonization of economic policy may soon be expected to spread over the whole of Western Europe. Without such harmonization, how can the nations involved succeed in achieving a permanent removal of duties and quotas?

At a time when the idea of combining the EEC and the EFTA is passing from the stage of Utopia to the realm of feasibility, more intensive cooperation on the Atlantic level is also assuming actuality. Let us hope that the successor of OEEC, namely the OECD, of which the U.S. has also become a full member, will have the foresight and courage to aspire to a common market for all the Atlantic peoples. This would simultaneously increase the productivity of Western industrial states to the benefit of the developing countries.

A SUPRANATIONAL CENTRAL BANK IMPRACTICAL

The idea of a supranational central bank is contrary to the principles that I have outlined. The realization of such a project demands a measure of preparedness to give up national sovereignty in the sphere of economic and financial policy in favor of supranational agencies that would hardly be possible to attain in the foreseeable future. It seems questionable whether it would be sound to envisage a solution of this kind even in the more distant future. I am afraid it would never do to establish a uniform currency system if other important competencies were to remain decentralized.

The thought of a supranational accounting unit, which has been advocated at least on the European continent, should also be rejected. The peoples partaking in world trade have ample reason to welcome the existence of the dollar and the pound sterling, two currencies that are of outstanding importance for international trade. It is desirable that this situation be further consolidated, and to this end the two currencies ought to be made less susceptible to short-term capital fluctuations. This susceptibility is revealed as soon as the key currencies are changed into gold or other currencies either because of a lack of confidence in their stability, or as a result of interest arbitrage, or for other reasons. If caused by a prolonged deficit in the trade balance and the balance of long-term capital movements, such suscepti-bilities become dangerous. This is to be expected if a country's economic and financial policy becomes unbalanced generally.

Jacques Rueff, whom I hold in high esteem, recently considered it a "fundamental collective error" which could develop into "a surprising and scandalous episode" that the present gold-exchange standard allows the credit basis to be doubled. Indeed, the foreign exchange that flows out of a deficit country might be bought and paid for by surplus countries in currency which has been created for this purpose by the central bank and subsequently placed back on the debtor country's market. Yet this need not auto-matically result in inflationary tendencies, because there are vari-ous compensating factors. Unfortunately, the admirable mecha-nism of the gold standard cannot at present be established for many different reasons, but the current system seems to have proved quite sound, at least as far as the fundamentals are con-cerned. Therefore, its inherent weaknesses will be the less aggra-vating the sounder the economic policy of the governments con-cerned. This conclusion, as you will have noticed, is the substance of my statements today.

No agency would seem better suited than the International Monetary Fund to counteract liquidity crises by negotiating as-sistance credits. These should never be granted automatically, however—that is, without investigating the particular circum-stances of each case and possibly without asking the receiving country to assume certain obligations.

Such assistance will be effective only if it facilitates the debtor country's efforts to make fundamental adjustments. Yet we must beware of interpreting a disequilibrium of the trade or payments balance or the national economy altogether as being of a structural nature. During the last fifteen years, we have witnessed a great deal of change not only in the terms of payment, but also in the flow of commodities and capital. Many of these phenomena, which at first seemed permanent, turned out to be temporary.

Moreover, the present foreign trade and exchange position of a number of European countries has been vastly overrated. The Federal Republic of Germany, for instance, during the last five years achieved an average annual foreign trade surplus of about $1 billion, while during the identical period the United States annual commodity exports succeeded her imports by $4 billion. To my mind, the real problem consists in establishing a suitable structure and adequate volume of capital exports, rather than in the superior or inferior competitiveness of the national export business.

DANGERS IN TINKERING WITH EXCHANGE RATES

It is amazing to see what great hopes are occasionally attached to changes in exchange rates. Again and again we hear that surplus countries ought to revalue or at least permit a temporary revaluation of their currencies by introducing flexible exchange rates with ample allowance for oscillation. The following objections must be raised against interfering with exchange rates:

1. The stability of exchange rates is one of the basic prerequisites of intensive and steadily expanding international capital, money, and even commodity movements. Alterations of the exchange rates often fundamentally upset the basis of business calculations and carry an element of uncertainty into international economic relations that is impossible to neutralize. Therefore, they are disturbing even if they occur only rarely.

2. Manipulation of the exchange rates as a means of influencing the business cycle must also be ruled out because its effects do not show as promptly as required for business-cycle adjustments.

3. Warnings are also in order against manipulation of the exchange rates for reasons of structural policy. As already mentioned, one must beware of readily attributing economic dis-

turbances of all kinds to structural causes, by which long-lasting phenomena are usually meant.

4. Revaluations of flexible exchange rates have a serious disadvantage in that they are apt to cure symptoms, thus diverting attention from the real problem.

5. Currency revaluation in countries enjoying a temporary foreign exchange surplus cannot even curb speculative money and capital movements. The Deutsche Mark revalution in March, 1961, is a classical example of how, on the contrary, a revaluation increases the tendency toward pronounced speculative capital movements by undermining confidence in the stability of the existing rates of exchange.

6. Those in favor of revaluating one or another currency should bear in mind that what seems right in one case soon might be considered fair in another.

Accordingly, alterations of exchange rates can be contemplated only as a last resort in removing difficulties of a long-lasting nature.

PROMOTING THE EXPORT OF CAPITAL

Is the suggestion, especially on the part of the United States, justified that the present surplus countries must do more to promote capital exports, both in the interest of developing countries and in order to contribute toward a more suitable distribution of international liquidity? I should like to answer with a conditional yes. But a clear distinction must be made between short-term funds supplied by surplus countries and long-term capital exports in the form of loans or participations. I have already discussed the first category, which includes temporary liquidity assistance.

What of long-term capital exports? I may say that the Federal Republic of Germany can be counted among the countries in which the willingness to expand capital exports is steadily increasing, partly for economic and partly for political reasons. Last year, my country raised about $1.5 billion in various kinds of contributions, including debt service and restitution payments. During the current year, the government alone has agreed to extend long-term financial aid to developing countries in the amount of $1.1 billion. Altogether, German capital exports in 1961 are expected to be considerably higher than in 1960.

Commercial capital exports, that is, capital transfers by private business, still encounter difficulties that could be resolved.

Thus it appears exceedingly difficult in practice but extremely urgent to adjust tax legislation affecting capital movements, one example being the tax on securities. As a result of differences in national laws and procedures, progress in listing foreign securities on the various national stock exchanges is rather sluggish, although the internationalization of capital investment via investment certificates has been comparatively successful.

The volume of direct private investment in developing countries is still far from sufficient. Why is this so? One of the main reasons is that the investment climate in some of these areas is still very unfavorable, in some places even worse than it was some years ago. As a result, private investors, in particular small and medium-sized companies of the Western countries not having at their disposal sufficient risk capital and manpower, are still reluctant to invest their capital abroad. In this respect, I do not hesitate to say that the Cuban Government by its illegal measures against foreign investment has rendered a very bad service not only to its own economy but also to other developing countries.

On the other hand, a country like Argentina which, under the leadership of President Frondizi, for some years now has pursued a policy of creditworthiness and fair treatment of foreign investment, is now being rewarded by an increasing volume of private capital from abroad. Pakistan and Malaya are other examples.

NEED FOR AN INVESTMENT CHARTER

To repeat, under given circumstances a considerable improvement in the over-all investment climate will not be achieved until like-minded countries both in the industrialized and the developing world get together on a mutual and reciprocal charter, as to the basic rules regarding fair treatment of foreign private investment, once such investment has been accepted by the countries concerned. Such fair treatment would have to comprise: (1) no discrimination vis-à-vis nationals and between foreigners of different nationalities; (2) strict adherence to undertakings given; (3) no direct or indirect deprivation of foreign investment without prompt, just, and effective compensation; and (4) submission of disputes to international arbitration.

Since 1957 a belief has been growing both in developing and in capital-exporting countries that such a convention is one of the most important preconditions for the solution of the economic as well as the political problem of the less-developed countries. Many more countries and organizations are now working positively on this very subject than was the case a few years ago. Among them are the international chambers of commerce, the OECD, and quite a number of other private groups. Recently the Development Assistance Group has also discussed this matter, together with other related subjects, in a very constructive way.

Before such an understanding is reached among a limited number of countries, a fair amount of legal, political, and psychological difficulties will still have to be overcome. But if the parties recognize objectively that it is in the best interest of all concerned, especially of the developing countries, that proposals of this kind have been put forward, these problems eventually can and will be solved.

The Latin American countries must mobilize their own resources to a greater extent, prevent the flight of domestic capital, raise tax rates, improve tax collections, increase savings, and discourage luxury consumption. But an important amount of the additional capital required should come from abroad, and a large part of it can very properly come from official agencies.

INVESTMENT AND FINANCIAL POLICIES FOR LATIN AMERICA

By Felipe Herrera *

Latin America is in a period of transition. Its growing pains are manifested in economic, social and political tensions, and instability. At Punta del Este we reached significant policy agreements that I am sure will contribute greatly to the growth and stability of the area during the next decade. The countries of the hemisphere established an economic goal that will require great efforts to achieve, namely, a minimum per capita growth rate of 2.5% per annum in each country.

This means that there must be far greater effort to mobilize domestic resources in order to produce the investment capital necessary to assure or surpass this rate of growth. During the past decade Latin America derived from domestic resources 90%

* President, Inter-American Development Bank; former executive director, International Monetary Fund, representing Argentina, Bolivia, Chile, Ecuador, Panama and Uruguay; former Minister of Finance of Chile, and Under Secretary of Economy and Commerce.

of its investment capital, but even a greatly intensified domestic effort will not be enough. It is for this reason that the United States Government promised at Punta del Este its financial cooperation by agreeing to assure the major part of the foreign capital flow of $20 billion considered to be needed in Latin America during the next ten years.

The action at Punta del Este was significant not alone because of this guarantee of financial assistance. There is now a hemisphere agreement to deal with excessive variations in the prices of primary products and to accelerate the process of economic integration as an essential for the economic and social development of the continent.

A NEW DEVELOPMENT BANK

The Inter-American Development Bank was established after lengthy negotiations in Washington among the members of the Organization of American States. Formed by agreement of 20 of these states, it began operations on October 1, 1960. I think it has already had a significant impact on Latin America. As you may know, the Bank is capitalized at $1 billion. Of this amount, $850 million comprises its ordinary resources for lending on regular banking terms, for projects in countries that have the capacity to repay in the currency lent. Of these ordinary resources, $400 million is to be paid in by the member countries, while $450 million represents callable capital available to assure the payment of Bank borrowings.

Thus the Bank, after use of its paid-in capital, must rely on the capital markets for its ordinary resources. Its operations in this field, therefore, are basically no different than those of other well-known international development banking institutions. During the past year we have approved loans of $92 million. We also have a Fund for Special Operations of $150 million, which is available for lending on soft terms primarily in countries that have been stagnating and have a very limited foreign exchange repayment capacity. Loans of this type amounting to $37 million have been approved.

Another function of the IDB is the provision of technical assistance, primarily in formulating development projects. This aid can be furnished at various stages, including the planning of economic development, the creation or reorganization of domestic development institutions, and the preparation of specific projects on which loans will be sought either from the Bank or from other lending institutions.

In Latin American experience, the need for financing preinvestment expenses has become more and more obvious. Until now, we have relied upon technical assistance provided by national or international agencies in specific fields. These studies have contributed to a greater awareness of our problems but, though indispensable, this type of technical contribution needs to be complemented by the formulation of programs and projects.

In the Inter-American Bank we make loans to meet this kind of expense. For example, we recently approved a loan to Argentina of $640,000 to finance engineering studies of a possible electric and irrigation development program in the El Chocon area. In addition, we believe that the Latin American countries should be able to look forward to sufficient funds on a nonreimbursable basis to cover essential needs in this area.

Action of this kind would have untold ramifications in procuring additional external financing resources—resources that are assured by virtue of the new inter-American economic policy. The discovery and evaluation of the physical resources of a country are now relatively easy; there is an ever-increasing number of usable techniques to investigate the true potentialities of our soils, our seas, our forests, and energy sources.

SOCIAL INVESTMENT

In Bogota, all of our countries recognized for the first time the need for external financing of social investment in such fields as improved land use, housing, water supply and sanitation, and education. This led to the establishment of the Social Progress Trust Fund, whose administration was recently entrusted to our institution. The number of applications for assistance that we have received in these areas justifies the creation of this Fund for the financing of projects which under traditional international lending criteria are not considered "bankable." In fact, we have already approved loans of over $25 million.

I should like to point out that while these social investment programs cannot be viewed as alternatives to economic growth, they do facilitate and strengthen a comprehensive economic policy. They should make a significant contribution to stability, without which economic progress is meaningless.

The activities I have outlined show that the resources of the Bank, other international lending institutions, and even the extensive public capital which comes from the United States, must be supplemented by the flow of private investment. I believe the Bank can play a significant role in channeling these funds into promising areas. We have made a modest beginning by securing significant participation in our loans by both United States and European banks. My recent five-week trip to Europe provided evidence that Europe is anxious to contribute to the acceleration of economic growth in Latin America.

A "COMPLEMENTARY" FUNCTION

There is now general agreement that foreign aid can be used more efficiently if based on national or even regional development plans or programs. With such programs, we can better carry out one of the basic principles of our statutes. We are not a "substitute" financial source, but rather a "complementary" one. I would say that we should take an "active and promoting" complementary position in the formulation of these programs. The Bank should act on the request of interested countries as an organizer and agent for financial "partnerships" similar to those recently formed by other sources to finance the five-year plans of India and Pakistan. We have made a beginning, in cooperation with others, with the so-called "Operation Triangle" to rehabilitate the Bolivian mines, supplementing our own support with contributions from West Germany, the United States, and Argentina.

Like other underdeveloped countries throughout the world, the Latin American republics face an unprecedented need for additional investment in capital resources. The very rapid growth of population requires ever-increasing amounts of investment both in the social and economic fields. By 1970 there will be 250 million Latin Americans and by the year 2000 there will be 600 million, if present rates of growth continue. These countries must mobilize their own resources to a greater extent, prevent the flight of domestic capital, raise tax rates, improve tax collections, increase savings, and discourage luxury consumption. But an important amount of the additional capital required should come from abroad, and a large part of it can very properly come from official agencies.

In the decade of the 50's, World Bank disbursements for Latin America were $675 million and those of the Export-Import Bank, $2 billion. These loans have been supplemented by recent activity on the part of the Development Loan Fund and the International Development Association. In the same period private sources of international investment played a vital part by adding medium- and long-term investment of $8 billion, of which more than $5 billion was direct. Private firms from outside our borders also make a significant contribution by bringing in advanced technical methods, accounting systems, market analysis and distribution techniques, general management procedures, and other special assistance.

Overhead investment today must be provided in a planned and integrated manner in all areas of a country, including areas remote from the centers of population. This task is so enormous that it must be done by governments, who must seek aid from international sources in order to move forward.

Public investment in economic and social overhead is of great benefit to private business. It increases labor efficiency and productivity, permits a broadening of the market, results in lower production costs and facilitates competition. After the public facilities are provided, it is possible for small and medium-sized industries to enter.

We in the Inter-American Bank have been making an effort to develop techniques for assisting the development of private enterprises, especially medium-sized and small industries. It is obvious that the Bank cannot successfully lend to a very large number of small enterprises. We have found it desirable to lend a reasonable portion of our funds to local development banks for relending to small private enterprises. Loans of this type have been approved for institutions in Mexico, Guatemala, El Salvador, Haiti, Nicaragua, Venezuela, Colombia, Brazil, Argentina, Chile, Paraguay, and Ecuador.

PROSPECTS FOR PRIVATE INVESTMENT

Historically, foreign investment in Latin America has been directed toward the extractive industries, especially petroleum and such public utilities as railroads, electric power companies, and telephone companies. There is a growing feeling in Latin America that the direction in foreign investments should change rather basically. While private investment generally is still welcome in the extractive industries, it is felt in a number of countries that this should be done only in partnership with the public sector or where the majority interest is owned by nationals of the country.

The obvious area for future foreign private investment in Latin America is the manufacturing sector. We are particularly concerned in its entry into medium-sized and small industries. It is quite possible for the domestic businessman in Latin America who has a good background, training, and the necessary initiative to enter fields where limited capital is required.

STEPS TOWARD ECONOMIC INTEGRATION

One of the significant obstacles to the growth of a healthy manufacturing sector that can compete with imports is the limited size of the market in most of our countries. It seems clear that the size of the market has been a significant factor in the more rapid industrialization of Brazil, Mexico, and Argentina.

So well aware of this are the Latin Americans that they have made strenuous efforts to widen the market by the creation of the Central American Common Market and the Latin American Free Trade Zone. While the Central American Common Market will still be small, its population of 10 million people will permit the establishment of a number of medium-sized industries. The potential of the Latin American Free Trade Zone, with a population of 145 million people and a combined gross national product of $43 billion, representing in these terms approximately 70% of Latin America, is very great, although at this moment it is hard to predict the rhythm of its development and the general direction of its policies.

It is certain that there will be greatly increased opportunities for investment of new capital as the Latin American Free Trade Zone develops. In this connection I should like to indicate that there is apprehension among many Latin American economists and statesmen regarding the weak position of the domestic manufacturing sector in these countries and its inability to compete satisfactorily with foreign enterprises. There is great concern for the strengthening of the domestic entrepreneur to assure reasonable control by domestic enterprise.

Foreign private institutions may make loans to the Latin American enterprises, with advice and consultation going along with the loans. There may be joint ownership of stock companies. Private development banks or institutions similar to small business investment corporations may be established with mixed capital for the purpose of lending to medium-sized and small enterprises in Latin America. Frequently, licensing arrangements are worked out to share the advantages of know-how and patent techniques. In some cases, a joint operation may benefit by having production in the hands of the domestic entrepreneur and export sales and distribution carried on by the international firm. Another possibility, which of course does not exhaust the list, is that a high-grade Latin American company, in association with a reputable United States or European firm, may be able to float securities in the capital markets of the developed countries.

COOPERATION BETWEEN PUBLIC AND PRIVATE CAPITAL

In many ways government and private enterprise can work together directly. For example, the corporation that has mixed government and private ownership is sometimes useful. Chile, Brazil, and Mexico have done very well in this respect with CORFO, the National Development Bank, and the Nacional

Financiera often owning a minority or a majority of the common stock as well as providing loan capital. Government policy can then be implemented without any substantial loss of the efficiencies of private management. Also in those countries the public lending institutions sometimes make loans to private firms, helping them to finance their activities at a time when the private commercial banks may not feel it is possible to do so. In some cases governments have constructed and leased public facilities to private companies. Governments may construct hotels and then place their operation in the hands of a private firm, with an appropriate division of the profits. Mixed enterprises are also being formed to exploit natural resources. The State may grant a concession for exploration or development and provide capital in the form of timberlands or other natural resources, with profits to be shared according to the capital contributed.

FROM PRIMARY PRODUCTS TO INDUSTRIALIZATION

In most of our countries the bulk of exports consists of only two or three items—products like coffee, cotton, copper, bananas, cacao, wool, tin, and petroleum, with volatile prices. Experience as far back as we can remember makes us worry about depending too much on primary industry of this type. The instability of foreign exchange earnings is notorious and the adjustment of output is very difficult and even impossible except over a long period. In addition, we have found that the long-run demand for primary materials simply is not growing fast enough to produce the foreign exchange that is needed.

We must industrialize if we are to have full employment and rising levels of living for our rapidly expanding population. There is no general formula to answer the question whether emphasis should be placed on primary or secondary industry. It is a function of the size of the market, the raw materials available, and the particular stage of development of the country. In other words, small countries with limited natural resources that are emerging in their economic development must limit themselves to light industries processing available materials. But as a country's economy grows and incomes rise, there is a growing need to import from abroad not only to meet the requirements for capital goods, but also because people wish a wider variety of consumption goods.

It is logical in this process of development that the countries of Latin America should not limit themselves to the production of primary products, nor should they limit themselves to the production of consumer goods that act as substitutes for imports. They must think in terms of developing basic industry and of producing industrial goods for export. They need to diversify their economies, provide employment, and enjoy the higher incomes associated with industrialization, especially in view of the highly protectionist agricultural policies pursued by many industrialized areas. In this connection, I should like to emphasize that it will become increasingly essential for industrialized countries to reconsider those restrictions and also those on manufactured goods.

Although very short in terms of time, our experience as international bankers already has brought us into contact with a number of practical problems, some of them arising from conflicts of interest that extend beyond national frontiers. For example, we all place great emphasis on the transfer of technical know-how from industrialized countries in order to accelerate Latin America's industrial development. This is being done on an increasing scale, to a large extent through licensing of patents and provision for technical consultation. Payment is made through royalties.

In some cases, however, the holders of patents for industrial processes have imposed restrictions prohibiting the sale of the resulting products to countries other than the one in which the licensee is located. This conspires against the objective of integration in Latin America. We cannot be content or complacent in observing how in this instance an instrument of development, such as technological progress, is being converted into an instrument to reinforce restrictive monopolistic practices.

In the case of coffee, a commodity which is the very lifeblood of some of our members, we find that the high tariffs maintained by some industrial countries impede consumption at serious cost to our area, even though no real economic justification now exists for the policy.

I have mentioned some of these problems to emphasize the need for serious reconsideration and reorientation of trade policies throughout the world if we are to reap the full benefits of integration and of accelerated economic growth.

Spain's experience illustrates how a country under the most difficult circumstances could, in a comparatively short time and with a rather small amount of external aid, progress to a point where it can even attract free foreign investment.

A NOTE ON SPAIN'S ECONOMIC RECOVERY

By Ignacio Herrero *

The Spanish economic situation at the end of the civil war called for immediate and urgent steps, that were from the start tremendously hampered by the outbreak of World War II only a few months after hostilities had ceased in Spain.

From that precarious moment, the process of our recovery can be divided into three periods. The first comprised the years between 1940 and 1952. Its characteristics were a lack of capital for investment, the impossibility of obtaining capital goods and foreign aid, and a very low rate of production owing to the obsolescence and destruction of capital equipment. Faced with this situation the measures adopted by the government varied only in detail from those that other countries have had to adopt under similar circumstances.

All new industrial plants had to be authorized by the Ministry

* Chairman, Unión Española de Explosivos S. A.; director, Banco Hispano Americàno, Banco Urquijo, Banco Herrero.

of Industry, in order to canalize our limited capital resources toward those fields of production whose output was more urgently needed. Within this selective criterion approved industries that were additionally declared of high national interest received preferential fiscal and financial treatment. Finally, state capital entered the industrial field through the gate of the Instituto Nacional de Industria, an organization officially entrusted with the launching of industrial initiatives for which private enterprise could not or would not provide sufficient capital.

During this period progress was inevitably very slow. Inflation could not be sufficiently checked by rigorous price fixing, quotas, import licensing, differential rates, and all those measures that are less successful in checking inflation than they are in hampering trade.

The second period began in 1952, when the Spanish economy was making some leeway, thanks to 12 years of unremitting effort and the beginning of external aid. The ICA began to contribute from 1951, and in 1955 and 1956 the Development Loan Fund and the Export-Import Bank came to the rescue. Total American aid rose from $63 million in 1951 to $140 million in 1959.

During this period industrial output rose steeply; the index numbers show 91.8 for 1952 and 157.9 for 1959. However, this expanding production kept up a strong inflationary pressure that could not be entirely bridled, and comparatively few controls were removed. Although rationing of consumer goods disappeared, there remained price fixing, control on new industrial investment, import licensing, and differential exchange rates.

At last in 1959 there was an important change in the government. Navarro Rubio and Ullastres entered the cabinet as Finance Ministers with a firm program for the stabilization of our currency and the breaking down of trade barriers.

Here I must recall Dr. Abs' opinion that if you expect outside help you should start by helping yourself out of your own difficulties. With the welcome help of international institutions, the stabilization of our currency was carried out in an astonishingly short time and with the minimum impact on our industrial progress.

Too short a time has elapsed since the stabilization of the peseta for us to be able to draw a very detailed balance on results, but you all know that Spain is now considered by the Western World as a good lending risk. We have joined the World Bank and the International Monetary Fund. The Eximbank and the Development Loan Fund are normally procuring capital for our public investment schemes and for some private ventures.

Most important of all, as a symptom and as a promise of long-awaited normality, is a renewed flow of foreign private capital. In this short period of time important private firms from abroad have joined forces with Spanish groups in building the modern industrial plants that Spain so badly needs. This is only a beginning. The interest of American and Western European industrialists in Spain is growing every day.

Even more encouraging is the interest shown by private investors in Spanish issues on the stock markets of the Western World. Our leading equities are beginning to be quoted outside Spain and important orders are placed every day by foreign brokers on the Madrid stock exchange. One step more and I believe that our leading private groups will even be able to place bond issues abroad.

The external demand for our equities must be met by capital investment from within, if a proper balance between foreign and Spanish holdings is to be established. Savings in Spain are bound to grow with industrial development, and measures are being taken to canalize these savings toward productive investment. Investment trusts are being encouraged by fiscal and other concessions, and the Comite de Inversiones a Medio y Largo Plazo is authorized to issue bonds with state backing to finance private enterprise with loan capital. The capital needs of state-owned industries will be met by the savings banks and similar institutions.

Spain's experience illustrates how a country under the most difficult circumstances could, in a comparatively short time and with a rather small amount of external aid, progress to a point where it can even attract free foreign investment.

COMMON PRINCIPLES FOR PROGRESS

As the last speaker on this panel, I might presume to restate some of the common principles we have noted as to aim, means, and method. Our aim in the developing countries should clearly be to promote economic expansion, free from inflation, while assuring full production and full employment in the industrial nations.

Modern economic analysis and what we can already call field experience assure us that this should be quite possible with the means at our disposal. We all know that in order to prevent inflation in expanding economies the gap between savings and the rate of investment must be bridged by the influx of foreign capital. We also know that the opening of new areas to economic development provides the only positive outlet for the surplus manufacturing capacity of the advanced countries.

The problem is mainly one of choosing the method by which transfers of capital goods can be achieved with best results for both parties. As to this choice of methods, I think we can discover quite a lot of common ground. We all agree, I think, that it is essential to establish the difference between what Dr. Abs terms "liquidity aid" and medium- and long-term financing of productive enterprise in the developing countries. The first function —the "liquidity aid"—should be carried out by international banking institutions, more or less on the same principle on which commercial banks grant short-term credits to their clients. The second function should be carried out by international institutions, by national governments, and by the free transfer of private investment capital.

This transfer of private savings constitutes a most convenient method for financing industry in developing countries. Very rightly, the necessity for a code protecting these transfers has been stressed. In an ideal picture of the world to come, intergovernment lending should be relegated to the role of filling up the gaps that are left over after the natural flow of private capital toward the undeveloped resources of the world.

4. The Newly Developing Economies

> The private sector cannot undertake to re-
> place the public sector in the fields and in
> the circumstances in which typically the
> public sector must operate. It must resist
> and oppose any unwarranted intrusion and
> invasion by the public sector. Privileges and
> unfair advantages in favor of the public sec-
> tor and to the detriment of the private sector
> must be singled out and defeated. This
> would be much more effective than the futile
> theoretical lamentations that too often are
> heard in international business circles.

PATTERNS FOR
PRIVATE PARTICIPATION

By Paolo N. Rogers *

The private sector has contributed to the economies of developing countries in a measure and to an extent much larger than is
generally known. A recent report prepared by the Organization
for European Economic Cooperation shows that total private
contributions to developing countries, classified under various
categories and including export credits, amounted to $3 billion
in 1956; $3.7 billion in 1957; $2.9 billion in 1958; and $2.4 billion
in 1959. The total contribution in the period of four years
amounted to approximately $12 billion. Data for 1960 are not yet

* Director of foreign relations, The Olivetti Company; Italian delegate in
various international economic organizations; deputy chief of the Italian
Technical Delegation at the Italian Embassy in Washington from 1946–55;
senior Italian executive officer, Allied Commission in Rome from 1944 to
1946, in charge of liaison with the Italian Government, and in the same
capacity with the UNRRA Italian Mission in 1946. Dr. Rogers is a member
of the editorial committee of *The American Review,* and a member of various
commissions in the Italian section of the International Chamber of Commerce.

available, but it would appear that contributions were slightly higher than in 1959 but below the level of 1957.

AN ANALYSIS OF CONTRIBUTIONS

How do these contributions to economic development by the private sector of the Western countries compare with those of the public sector, and how does the over-all contribution of the West compare with that of the Soviet Bloc?

Public contributions, according to OEEC classification, including grants, reparations, loans, bilateral contributions, and contributions to multilateral agencies were: $3.2 billion in 1956; $3.7 billion in 1957; $4.3 billion in 1958; and $4.5 billion in 1959. Public contributions thus totaled $15.9 billion. It would appear that the upward trend was also maintained in 1960, with a slight increase over 1959.

Lumped together, the contributions of the public and private sectors of the Western countries yield the following annual totals: $6.2 billion in 1956; $7.4 billion in 1957; $7.3 billion in 1958; and $6.9 billion in 1959. Total Western contributions for the four years therefore amount to almost $28 billion.

According to United States statistical sources, the contribution of the Soviet Bloc to developing economies, including grants and loans, has been as follows: $608 million in 1956; $227 million in 1957; $556 million in 1958; and $894 million in 1959. Bloc contribution in the four-year period is therefore $2.3 billion. This upward trend is confirmed by results in 1960, when total Soviet Bloc contributions amounted to almost $1.2 billion.

In percentage terms the contributions of the private sector in relation to the over-all Western contributions were: 1956, 48%; 1957, 50%; 1958, 40%; 1959, 35%. For 1960 the percentage should be nearly the same as for 1959. The important role played by the private sector is even more evident when the over-all contributions of the West and of the Soviet Bloc are lumped. Over the period of four years, the percentages were: private sector, 40%; Western public sector, 52%; Soviet Bloc, 8%. For 1960, the following "guesstimate" can be formulated: private sector, 30%; Western public sector, 56%; Soviet Bloc, 14%.

These data lend themselves to important conclusions. The first is that the West has been and still is making by far the largest contribution to developing countries. Secondly, the Soviet Bloc contribution is still comparatively small but increasing at an accelerated rate. Thirdly, the private contribution is of great significance both in absolute and relative terms. This percentage participation should not only be maintained but also increased if the private sector is to assert itself as a fundamental factor in development.

FORMS OF PARTICIPATION

In the past, industrial investments aimed traditionally at assuring full ownership by the foreign investor, or at least a majority share-holding. More recently, the concept of partnership has gained increasing popularity, and joint investments by foreign private capital with local private or public investors have become less rare. Since these joint enterprises provide the ground for better mutual understanding and closer cooperation, the private sector should make a definite effort to adopt this system whenever practicable.

A second field in which the private sector participates massively in development is trade with developing countries. There are three aspects which should be emphasized: one concerns the balance of payments; the second, credit facilities; and the third, risks.

BALANCE OF PAYMENTS RESPONSIBILITY

The balance of payments of developing countries suffers endemically from deficits. This situation requires free enterprise to adopt special rules of conduct and great caution. The potential demand of developing countries is theoretically unlimited, but the limited availability of financial resources shrinks this potential demand to a severely reduced real demand. Development does not necessarily produce a gradual across-the-board increase in real demand. Economic planning and budgetary and balance-of-payments deficits not only limit real demand, but to a certain degree tend to distort it. Therefore, exports to developing countries must be selective. Exporters must offer, against scarce for eign exchange resources, goods that are useful in the context of development plans and not merely useful, or even necessary, in general terms. Failure to exercise self-discipline in this respect only serves to unbalance developing economies and cause more rigid and drastic controls than would otherwise be adopted.

USE OF CREDIT FACILITIES

Credit facilities are closely linked to the problem of the balance of payments. In order to overcome specific payment difficulties it has become common practice for exporters to finance their customers through medium-term delayed payments. According to OEEC sources, guaranteed private export credits were offered in the amount of $1.5 billion in the period 1956–59. Again, this represents a form of helpful contribution by the private sector. Delayed-payment facilities are a valid instrument for expanding commercial penetration in developing economies, but they pose a dilemma: they should be used extensively in order to satisfy urgent needs and thus provide a multiplying factor in development. On the other hand, an intensive and indiscriminate use of this system may lead to burdening the developing economies excessively and cause bottlenecks at a later stage.

ATTITUDE TOWARD RISKS

Free enterprise is and must be motivated in its actions by the expectation of profit. This expectation provides the measure of the economic validity and soundness of its operations. Risks therefore must be evaluated in the proper perspective and be considered as an economic component of any individual operation. Businessmen must approach this factor coldly in technical terms, with the proviso that the profitability of an investment in an area in the process of development must necessarily be assessed for a longer than normal period and for a higher than normal risk.

Insurance covers certain risks to a greater or lesser degree and provides a practical instrument to permit and encourage this approach. In the majority of cases, the insurance covers commercial risks, political risks, and the risk of currency inconvertibility. It has been estimated that as much as 25% of exports from

Western countries to developing countries has been covered by insurance. This system should be greatly increased, particularly if present provisions are improved and costs reduced in the light of experience.

TECHNICAL COOPERATION

There are three separate areas in which technical cooperation can be offered by the private sector, as distinguished from technical cooperation offered by the public sector. The first is overall assistance given in an advisory capacity by consulting economists, engineers, and other specialized professional consultants. Private companies have often established *ad hoc* consortia. These consortia provide general consulting services and help in formulating development programs, which include industrial, agricultural, health and welfare, and infrastructural plans. When general development programs have been adopted and bids are solicited to implement them, these consulting consortia provide the best and most practical channels to secure the participation of the various member companies and thus become the natural liaison between foreign suppliers and local customers.

Private industrial cooperation is also carried out through license and patent agreements and through the furnishing of know-how. They constitute powerful catalysts which bring together private companies in industrialized countries with their counterparts in developing countries and provide a basis for the conclusion of partnership arrangements.

COMMERCIAL AND FINANCIAL COOPERATION

Private commercial cooperation plays an important role in development. Trading activities should, whenever possible, precede industrial investments. Foreign investors should test the potentials of a market through trade, in order to be in a position to evaluate the prospects of embarking on industrial activities.

The private sector also participates in development through investments of a purely financial character. These investments are channeled through the traditional banking system, supplemented by the international public banking system. The private sector has responded abundantly, for instance, to the World Bank's repeated calls upon it.

BOLDER PARTICIPATION NEEDED

While available data show that the participation of the private sector in the over-all growth of the developing economies is very significant, this is not widely recognized. While there are many reasons for this, the principal one is that it is the very essence of private enterprise to operate individually, so there is very little inclination toward showing collective results and achievements.

It is inconceivable and unrealistic that the private sector should aim at being the only protagonist of development and that it should play its role merely in accordance with classical and traditional patterns. The real risk, however, is that because of a certain amount of skepticism or complacency or other paralyzing factors, the other extreme should prevail, namely, that the private sector be deprived of its share by default.

Progress appears to be slow with regard to the mobilization of the private sector as a whole. The long-term self-interest is dimmed by short-term risks, most of them real, some of them imaginary, involved in investments and operations to be effected in distant countries and in insufficiently known circumstances and surroundings. Opportunities too often escape the attention of those who could take advantage of them. Development in its various stages and ramifications takes place day by day, without adequate dissemination of information. One can almost detect a curtain between the developing countries and business circles in industrialized countries. This curtain must be raised through mutual efforts on both sides.

Granted that many and serious difficulties must be removed to reduce risks, provide incentives, maximize guarantees, and generally to improve the climate, there is serious doubt that the private sector has adopted a bold and aggressive approach and fully exploited existing opportunities in the present technical and psychological climate.

It should be emphasized that developing economies need in most cases to test the validity of the private system on their own ground. Suspicions and ill feelings, arising from past experiences based on atypical private business practices, both domestic and foreign, can only be removed by proving through new experiences and sound practices the viability and the usefulness of the private system in the context of economic development in the present age.

The question is whether private enterprise will be enlightened and aggressive enough to undertake what clearly appears to be an uphill effort, where risks and unknowns are great, where the short-term outlook is dim, where the very aim and purpose of private enterprise—the expectation of profits—is conditioned by abnormal factors. The feasibility and advisability of any such bold and aggressive action must be measured not in ideological terms but strictly in economic terms. The short-term view may lead to negative conclusions, but it would appear that the broad picture is clear enough to allow for a sober, positive conclusion at a glance.

PSYCHOLOGICAL ASPECTS

The very terminology commonly used in connection with economic development is cluttered with such expressions as "aid," "assistance," "donor countries," "recipient countries," and the like. Such terms have conveyed the false, yet widely shared, impression that participation in economic development is entirely and exclusively the business of governments and of the public sector. The statistics given earlier show this impression to be far from the truth. Nevertheless, it is difficult to correct it. Aid plays an important role in development, but it is misleading and technically wrong to overemphasize its impact and importance. If, instead of crystallizing our thoughts on "aid" and "assistance," we were to become accustomed to think in terms of "participation," we would be proceeding on correct technical grounds and on a sounder psychological approach.

It is not easy to offer suggestions as to how the private sector could be placed in the right focus. So far, there is a rather discouraging record of the private sector's achievements in the psychological field. For some reason or other the collective manifestations of the private sector show an appalling weakness. The private sector places itself on the defensive or, at the other extreme, adopts an unduly aggressive and antagonistic attitude toward the role of government and of the public sector. It shows an unwarranted suspicion and distrust of planning, failing to recognize that planning is a fundamental prerequisite to development and to an orderly and secure participation by the private sector itself.

Private enterprise individually shows a much greater degree of flexibility and adaptability. Individual businessmen and companies have carried out successful undertakings everywhere in developing countries and have shown in abundance their ability to adjust to new situations, to conform to local requirements, and to contribute in evolving and innovating structures, systems, and methods. Nevertheless, very few of these rich and vast achievements have resulted in a more generalized experience or provided a pattern available to the private sector collectively.

This serious deficiency is not a matter of propaganda and publicity. It is a question of attitude, deeply affecting the psychology of the whole sector. It is a weakness of which inimical principles and systems are taking undue advantage, and it may lead them to an undeserved degree of success through our default rather than their virtue.

RELATIONS WITH THE PUBLIC SECTOR

For historical and functional reasons, it is for the state, the government, and governmental organizations—the public sector at large—to establish the focal instrument, to provide the motivating mainspring, to set up pilot units, and finally to induce development. In most underdeveloped countries strict planning and rigid allocation of resources, human and material, quantitatively and timewise, are required. This does not imply per se a statist socio-economic system. It simply poses certain problems for private enterprise.

All this is recognized and accepted by enlightened businessmen individually when they undertake operations of their own in developing countries. It is not equally recognized by businessmen collectively, who tend to oppose the interferences and invasions of the public sector and resist them in theory. But it is not a matter for theory; it is plainly a practical matter. The private sector cannot undertake to replace the public sector in the fields and in the circumstances in which typically the public sector must operate. It must resist and oppose any unwarranted intrusion and invasion by the public sector. Privileges and unfair advantages in favor of the public sector and to the detriment of the private sector must be singled out and defeated. This would be much more effective than the futile theoretical lamentations that too often are heard in international business circles.

OBSERVATIONS ON IMPROVING PRIVATE PARTICIPATION

It should be emphasized that a precondition to successful operations in developing countries is to be thoroughly informed as to the peculiar social, political, cultural, and economic characteristics of these countries. It is equally essential that developing countries be thoroughly informed of the prospects of economic cooperation by the private sector through appropriate contacts in their governmental, political, commercial, industrial, and cultural circles. This informational activity must be specific and cannot be adequately carried out at the official level alone, as a part of the bilateral or multilateral political and economic relations maintained between governments. It is, instead, the typical task of private diplomacy.

PRIVATE DIPLOMACY

Private diplomacy, although not a new corporate instrument, is bound to be more widely used in our times as the result of the intensification and expansion of international economic relations. It is its function to precede, to second, and to protect business operations undertaken by private enterprise in foreign countries. It must be regarded chiefly as a complement to, and not as a substitute for, public diplomacy.

The sphere of operations of private diplomacy is limited and conditioned by precise and concrete interests that a given company may have in particular countries. It is not a miniature Foreign Office handling international problems on a large and all-comprehensive scale, but rather a flexible instrument to be used as needs occur in specific areas and with regard to specific issues. Within these limitations, however, private diplomacy must follow closely major political and economic developments and try to make sure that the corporate interests are adequately protected when they are likely to be affected by such major events. Any negotiations between governments affecting bilateral trade, tariffs, currency regulations, migration, or similar matters, are also of direct interest to individual companies and therefore the subject of private diplomacy.

Private diplomacy must operate in close cooperation with public diplomacy. Public diplomacy in turn should use private diplomacy as a valuable source of information and inspiration in determining the broad lines of international relations.

TRADE RELATIONS

While it is typically the task of governments to negotiate and regulate trade relations, the private sector also has an important and effective role to play in this vital area. Investment and trade in developing countries should not in fact be conceived as a one-way traffic, lest sooner or later the movement becomes frozen because of the inability of the developing economies to meet their financial obligations. Private enterprise must therefore multiply its efforts and sharpen its understanding of the special and urgent need to help developing countries increase their earnings from exports, even to the extent of becoming, so to speak, promotion agents to assure the continuity, expansion, and profitability of this export trade. This can be done and is being done on an *ad hoc* basis. Sales of manufactured goods linked to the importation of primary products, direct or through intermediate consortia, private barter agreements, and switch operations on a triangular or multilateral basis, have in many instances achieved useful results.

By showing an active understanding of the problems of the developing countries, by lending helpful cooperation, the private sector can prove to be a valuable and friendly instrument, can stress the meaning of its unreserved participation and can be regarded as a friendly partner in the whole venture.

FINANCIAL RELATIONS

Another area for improvement is in the relations between the private sector and the intergovernmental financial agencies. The problem should be considered from the point of view of the supply of capital and of the allocation of capital. Ever since the World Bank decided to go into the open market to procure supplementary money, it has met with encouraging success in drawing upon private sources, which have readily and confidently subscribed successive bond issues. This new money, however, has been allocated mainly to the public sector. Omitting other considerations, it would seem that the primary cause of this apparent contradiction is the statutory requirement of a government guarantee for any loan extended by the World Bank.

This is an obstacle that has stood in the way of a closer relationship between the World Bank and the private sector as a potential beneficiary of loans. The subsequent establishment of the International Finance Corporation and more recently of the International Development Association have modified this situation somewhat but not substantially. In any case, there seems to be a gap, both technical and psychological in character, between intergovernmental financial agencies, operating on a world-wide basis, and the private sector as recipient of their financial assistance.

A more encouraging prospect for a better relationship is offered by the recent establishment of regional intergovernmental financial agencies, such as the Inter-American Development Bank and the European Investment Bank. These agencies are, so to speak, on the scene, and therefore prove to be more accessible to local private enterprise; their procedures and statutory requirements are more flexible and better suited to accommodate the ways, the methods, and the operational programs of private business. It is up to the private sector to take adequate initiative, to provide frequent contacts, to submit concrete cases, so that the instrument itself can be progressively adjusted and made available to meet a wide variety of demands and needs.

ATTITUDE TOWARD SOCIAL PROBLEMS

A final point that deserves attention is the attitude of the private sector toward social problems. It should be emphasized that development is an aspiration of countries and people on two counts which run parallel: economic improvement and social improvement. The insufficient educational, cultural, sanitary, and technical infrastructures of developing countries are a reflection of insufficient income. The private sector cannot ignore these fundamental shortcomings and must participate in their gradual elimination just as much as it participates in economic progress.

CONCLUSIONS

Individually and even more collectively, private enterprise must exercise a continuous and constructive self-criticism in order to meet the test and the challenge posed by developing economies. It is in the interest of countries in the process of development to ensure the largest possible participation by the private sector, just as it is in the interest of the private sector to ensure for itself the largest possible share in the economic development of those countries.

Whether private enterprise participates in a large or small measure, whether it participates at all, economic development will take place anyway, because it is an irreversible trend. But the pace, the achievements, and the harmonious coordination of developing economies with more advanced economies will depend upon the behavior and the participation of the private sector in the very near future.

The only security of investment anywhere in the world of today is the strength of the free world itself. Without that, investment even in the highly developed nations is as insecure as it is anywhere in the developing economies.

UTILIZING INTERNAL INVESTMENTS

By Amirali H. Fancy *

While internal investment can play a vital role in the economic growth of the developing economies, it can hardly become operative without the cooperation of the developed world. The problem of development in these regions is not so much lack of money or manpower. It is lack of machines, managerial skill, and technical know-how. None of these requirements can be met unless foreign exchange is available.

Economic growth in these countries is dependent on investment that is either purely external, or external and internal. But

* Chairman, Fancies Investments Limited, Pakistan; member of the Standing Advisory Council, Ministry of Industries, and advisory committees of the Ministries of Commerce, Finance, and Investment Promotion Bureau; chairman of Pakistan Refinery, Steel Corporation of Pakistan, New Jubilee Insurance, Platinum Jubilee Finance & Investment, and Pakistan Chrome Mines; managing director, Industrial Managements; director of Pakistan Industrial Credit & Investment, Development Construction, National Bank of Pakistan and Landhi Industrial Trading Estate.

in no case is it purely internal. This is because the utility of internal investment is solely dependent on the availability of external investment.

Developing economies are the countries that have for one reason or another lagged behind. They are still in the same state of poverty, disease, and ignorance that the regions now called "developed" experienced before attaining their present state of plenty and prosperity. They have not only the desire but also the zeal to attain better conditions of living, and they do not lack courage in the struggle to change their present conditions. The big question mark staring them in the face is Time. Left alone they may eventually achieve what has been achieved by others. But have they the time at their disposal in the present-day world? They are making every conceivable effort and their efforts do produce results, but the population problem hardly permits any impact of those efforts on their standard of living; on the contrary, exploding population simply continues to multiply their problems every day. If this is what developing economies are, what is it that we intend to do about them?

Why should we as private businessmen consider measures to remedy the situation? If it is advice that is needed, we are prepared to give it and have been doing so for the past few years. But we have seen that mere advice does not produce results.

It is only by accelerating the pace of development in these regions that the situation can be remedied, and mere advice will not bring that about. We must put in our hard-earned money if we want the developing economies to achieve the take-off period, so that thereafter they may stand on their own legs.

INVESTMENT REALITIES

We are motivated, quite legitimately, by self-interest, and we do not consider any investment proposal on the basis of philanthropy. Before putting in our money, we have to examine the economics of a proposal. This is exactly what we do even for investment in our own country. For investments abroad, similar considerations can hardly be questioned. Some of them are: demand and supply, price levels, return on investment, structure of taxation and tax laws, remittance of profits, attitude of the government and the people toward foreign investments, experiences of others, political stability and, most important of all, security of investment. Such considerations, symbolized by the words "investment climate," are made every day on a countless number of investment proposals from different regions.

Many developing countries have enacted laws, laid down priorities, and established institutions to provide the desired investment climate for attracting foreign investment. Investments have undoubtedly been made in these countries by foreign investors, but is it anywhere near the requirements of those countries? We are constantly told that capital is shy and that it has to be attracted. No one says just how!

What are the reasons for this shyness? We know that investment in foreign countries is not at all a new problem. Almost all the developed free nations of today owe much of their progress to private foreign investments. This kind of risk is an inherent characteristic of free private enterprise and it is this aspect alone that has made private enterprise an accepted doctrine of the free world. If, therefore, private foreign investment could go to developing economies of the past, which presented no better prospects than the developing economies of today, why this talk of shyness of capital now?

A DIFFERENCE IN "CLIMATE"

I am convinced, however, that there *is* a difference between the developing economies of the past and those of the present, in so far as the investment climate is concerned. Let us be frank and admit that despite the presence of many factors conducive to investment, the flow of private foreign investments in the developing economies is slow. And it is slow because of apprehensions about the security of investments in view of the complex political situation of the world today. Just a few years ago there was no such threat to political stability in any country such as is posed today by the emergence of a rival ideology in powerful opposition to the very concept in which we believe. Before our eyes nations in distress have fallen prey to the machinations of the other camp. I will agree with anyone who holds that investment in the developing nations is far less secure today than it was a few years ago. I also agree that even the slightest apprehension of ultimate risks can be a positive deterrent to foreign investments. But it is also my firm conviction that the only security of investment anywhere in the world of today is the strength of the free world itself. Without that, investment even in the highly developed nations is as insecure as it is anywhere in the developing economies.

We talk a great deal about the free world, but we never seem to consider it to be an indivisible whole. This is evident from the indifference with which we view the passing over to the other camp of those who till yesterday were a part of the free world. We never take it as our loss. We have gone on losing from time to time, yet think and often boast that we are gaining in strength. In other words, we submit to the amputation of our limbs and see them grafted onto a body that needs them to give us a fight.

Is the free world really gaining in strength everyday? If the answer to this question is obviously "No," what do we propose to do? Do we intend once again to wait till the free world gains enough strength to put an end to world tension, to eradicate the threat to free nations, and to restore peace and tranquillity and thus create ideal conditions for investments anywhere? It is not my intention to rub it in, but in essence all the talk of shyness of capital and insecurity of investments in the developing countries means just this and no more.

We must realize that there is no security without strength, and no body can be called healthy and strong if some of its parts and limbs are weak and diseased. The free world is just one body, but one with some limbs that need strengthening. Only if that is done will the free world have health and strength to resist disease and to survive.

ONLY ONE SOLUTION

It is through large-scale private investment in the developing economies that progress can be accelerated and poverty, disease, and ignorance eradicated. Thus health can be restored to the free world and strength acquired. There is no other means to achieve this end. We are left with no choice. Of course, there is one alternative. It would be to write off the underdeveloped world as a total loss and to withdraw from these regions and conserve the resources of the developed nations in the hope of freeing the world or of saving ourselves by relying on their strength alone. That alternative appears absurd on the face of it.

Is the threat posed to the free world or, to be precise, to its private investors, by the rival ideology an entirely new challenge? Is private enterprise competent to meet it? My answer to these questions is a straight "Yes." Private enterprise has survived just because it has met many a challenge of varying nature and degree. This is not opinion but fact. Although making profit is its motivating factor, taking risks is its very foundation. Uncountable billions have been sunk in water, put beneath the earth, and flown into the air, all in the hope of returns but not without the risk of total loss as well. Is there any single investment possible without involving any risk whatever?

It can be said that the present situation involves greater risk than normal. The answer could be that it is absolutely unlikely that all investments in every developing country could be a total risk. If that were so, how horrible the prospect would become for freedom to survive. I would like to repeat, therefore, that we are left with no choice. Let us, therefore, resolve to make every conceivable effort to assist the developing economies and strengthen the free world as fast as we possibly can. Let us prevent the inroads of the rival ideology into our camp. It is high time that we call a halt to this process and reverse it with all the means at our disposal.

WHAT RECIPIENTS MUST DO

If the objective is clear and the line of action well defined, I have no doubt that the benefits will be mutual and positive. I must stress that this should be realized on both sides, by both investors and recipients. The recipients must create conditions conducive to investment. They must shed all prejudice against foreign investments and must resist any tendency to discriminate between themselves and the foreigners in economic planning and activity. Both the goverments and the people in the developing countries must, by their behavior and their over-all attitude, create an impression of genuine desire for mutual collaboration based on good will and mutuality of interest. Association with foreigners in the past may have been none too pleasant for some of the developing nations, but it must be remembered that collaboration on the basis of equality and good will has a different connotation altogether. The past is dead and must be forgotten, otherwise the future is likely to be far more unpleasant than the past has ever been. It is heartening to note a visible change in the minds of some of the people who till recently appeared to be in two minds about their future course of action. A very sincere desire is evident in most of the developing economies for collaboration with like-minded people, irrespective of their nationality.

WHAT INVESTORS MUST REALIZE

With such a climate it is the responsibility of the people belonging to the developed world to respond to the offer of cooperation effectively and without the loss of time. But I must warn against the tendency shown by some of the foreign investors in the developing countries to exploit the situation. By this I mean the desire to remit the profits home as soon as possible, profits that are often as large as the original investments or even larger. Besides draining the meager resources of the developing countries, such a policy naturally gives rise to suspicion and discord.

The objective of development must assume equal importance with profits. Profits may certainly be remitted, but some of them must also be reinvested to accelerate development. Joint ventures must be preferred rather than avoided, as is being done presently. Utilization of internal investments for the purposes of economic growth has specific significance. It means a substantial reduction in the demand for foreign exchange on any single undertaking and thereby makes it available for other projects. And it makes the nationals of the recipient country partners in the progress of their homeland. Association of indigenous capital and training the locals in the art of management and techniques at the enterprise create a sense of oneness, despite all the differences of color, caste, and creed. This feeling is vital, not only for the growth and progress of any enterprise, but also for identifying the nations of the free world as an indivisible whole despite great diversities of language, climate, and culture.

If the West is to get together for the purpose of setting up and carrying out a common policy of aid to developing countries, it does not mean that the world should be divided into zones of Western influence. Quite the contrary, Western countries ought to define, in common and with the aided countries themselves, the means for carrying out this aid.

PROBLEMS IN GIVING AID

By Marcel A. Demonque *

The aid Western nations are giving to the developing countries is tending more and more to be placed on the highest moral plane. This means that the West is giving up the trappings of colonialism and the protectorate. This is why the West is trying to give financial aid the appearance of a gift or a low-interest loan that the country assisted may use as it sees fit. This is also why the West is furthermore realizing that aid to developing countries can no longer be just financial; it must also be technical. For this same reason, the very form of this technical assistance is changing. Assistance is no longer limited to lending technicians capable of implementing the financial projects or using the machinery supplied. It also involves the training of local "elites" capable of

* President, Ciments Lafarge, France; board member, Counseil National du Patronat Français; president, Commission on Economic Cooperation; vice-president, Commission on International Economic Relations; counsellor and director of the Centre d'Études Prospectives and Bureau d'Informations et de Prévisions Économiques. M. Demonque is president of Société Nord-Africaine des Ciments Lafarge, Algiers, and Lafarge Aluminous Cement Co., London, and director of several companies.

governing, of administering the economy, and of applying modern technical methods to the efficient organization of agricultural and industrial production.

This facet of technical aid can be expected to continue to develop and to be gradually substituted for the other forms. It must furthermore be expected that trained local administrative, economic, and technical cadres will be formed on the spot rather than in the Western countries themselves. That is to say, Western aid will have to supply the training in each developing country by sending more instructors. These forms of financial and technical assistance tend to lose all direct political character. But does this mean that there are thus no indirect political consequences?

COMPETITION IN AID

We would not be objective if we overlooked the fact that assistance to the developing countries has become an instrument of competition between the Western countries on the one hand, and the countries of the East on the other. In those nations where the assistance of the West is insufficient, or is badly handled and finally fails, the aid of the Eastern countries has a much greater chance of being substituted. In that event—and it has already come about in several cases—there lies a secondary but not negligible reason for the West to attach the highest value to insuring that its aid to developing countries does not fail.

Two of the factors frequently accompanying this failure are, first, the desire to assert a political tutelage along with the aid, and second, the fact that the aid appears—or might appear—as originating from the desire to obtain new business and trade. In other words, every time that Western aid is reduced, or seems to be reduced, its essential purpose—which is ethical—appears to be of secondary importance, and the effort to aid is threatened with failure. By that very fact it opens the door to aid from the Eastern countries.

One undesirable aspect of Western mercantile methods often appears in the rough competition between the public and private organizations—of the various Western countries or of even a single Western country—that enters into the different forms of aid.

One might imagine that this rough competititon might be favorable to the developing countries by enabling them to obtain the best conditions for loans, merchandise, and equipment. Experience shows that in the majority of cases things have not happened that way. Enticed by those offering the most, the developing countries frequently point the development of their economies in a wrong direction.

NECESSARY CONDITIONS FOR WESTERN AID

It should be admitted that aid to developing countries has become one of the most serious tasks with which the West is confronted. The first condition for an aid policy is that it should not be set up or oriented to serve only the interests of the one giving it. Instead, it should be worked out in advance with all interested parties; that is to say, with the countries being aided, so that one may adapt the aid to each given case through preparation, in advance, of rational development studies. The second condition is that competition among Western countries, or among their nationals or customers in the countries to be aided, is, in a manner of speaking, absurd. It scatters and often destroys forces that are already tragically insufficient when compared with the huge fields in which they must act. The third condition follows logically from the second; the West should work out a common policy of aid to developing countries.

NEED FOR A COMMON POLICY

If the West is to get together for the purpose of setting up and carrying out a common policy of aid to developing countries, it does not mean that the world should be divided into zones of Western influence. Quite to the contrary, Western countries ought to define, in common and with the aided countries themselves, the means for carrying out this aid. Together they should determine: first, the type and conditions of financial aid (loans for export, medium-and long-term credits, guarantees to private investments); and second, the type and conditions of technical aid (analysis of resources and needs, development studies, missions of experts, formation of trained cadres). Once these definitions have been made, they should be uniformly respected when carrying out the aid program.

The West should develop the multilateral form of aid, since it is more consistent than bilateralism with the desire of the aided country not to appear protected by any single Western nation. Multilateral aid also permits the establishment, in complete objectivity, of development plans, case by case; it also makes it possible to look for the best adaptation of the various kinds of financial aid.

Along with the development of the multilateral form of aid, the West should apply itself to making as complete a listing as possible of the public and private organizations specializing in development and engineering studies. If need be, it should encourage the creation of additional organizations of this type. Finally, it should keep the developing countries closely informed on all the possible lines of investigation that it can put at their disposal.

The West should encourage the creation of schools, or aid those already existing, for the purpose of training persons for specialized assistance in administration, economics, science, techniques, and technology. Under the same conditions, all Western countries ought to promote the training of teachers capable of dedicating themselves to the task of education in developing countries. The allotment of these teachers ought to be done by common agreement, taking into account the linguistic peculiarities of the countries to which they are to be sent. The tasks of all the international organizations that can aid developing countries should be smoothly coordinated.

LOANS AND GIFTS

The practice of tied loans, even when there is some justification in existing circumstances, is not desirable. This does not mean, however, that all privileged relationships must be avoided between the aiding country and the country aided. Frequently there are natural relationships between the two, owing to complementary economies or geographic proximity, or the same language, that have a normal influence on trade between them. But the practice of the tied loan, when it becomes systematized, removes from Western aid both a part of its moral value and a part of the efficiency it could have if applied apart from any direct or immediate self-interest. The use of the financial gift is not in itself to be ruled out, but it can appear humiliating; long-term, low-interest loans are surely the most efficient formula for financial aid. I would like here to reemphasize the importance of establishing common methods for carrying out loans by the West. In spite of the real difficulties in application, the West should look for all solutions leading to a distribution of its food surpluses and to a stabilization of the market prices of raw materials coming from the developing countries.

PRIVATE INVESTMENT AND GUARANTEES

Private investments in developing countries present a special problem owing to the risks arising from world political instability. Along with the legitimate development of financial and technical assistance by governments, private investment remains an important method of providing assistance. Thus, it is of great importance that private investments should be guaranteed against political risks.

Several Western countries already provide guarantees to those of their nationals who invest in developing countries, but the conditions and rules of application have not been made uniform. Frequently, they are only tentative, timid, or isolated steps which are often used as a means of competition by those who have them against those who do not have them. For this reason they can aggravate the division of assistance policies by preventing the West from pulling together its most efficient means of achieving policy goals.

An international mutual guarantee organization has already been proposed with regard to the guarantee for private investment. On this point, I should like to call to your attention the fact that any guarantee given by an international organization is difficult to negotiate, that the problems raised by the guarantee can be properly analyzed and dealt with only at the lowest rung of the ladder, that the feeling of security a government can offer (personalized as it is by the backing of common and statutory law) is stronger than the feeling of security offered by an international organization based on a specific statute.

The surest and simplest guarantee that can be given to private investment in developing countries is that given by the government of the investor country. But, if the governments of the Western nations are to guarantee risks that can with time turn out to be burdensome, it is probable that their timidity and, indeed, their worrying uncertainty about any guarantee system, will remain great. Thus, it is desirable that a reinsurance organization should be constituted among the Western nations, the purpose of which would be to reinsure all or part of the risks guaranteed individually by each government. Such an international organization should also have the role of establishing a code of guarantee regulations; this code should strictly bind the various associated Western governments. Among other things, this would make it possible to keep international competition for private investments in the developing countries from being based on guarantee systems differing greatly from one country to the next.

CONCLUSIONS

Western aid to the developing countries should no longer pursue direct political ends, since it would be resented as an indirect form of colonization or political protection. But its failure brings along with it almost necessarily an indirect political consequence: the substitution of aid from the countries of the East.

In these conditions, the task of aiding developing countries—which purely moral considerations impose with ever-increasing force and urgency—demands that the West follow some strict obligations: the obligation of collective discipline and organization, as well as the obligation to amend the classical free enterprise philosophy which, in itself, is no longer an efficient tool in the solution of this problem.

More precisely and concretely, the West should carry out disinterested financial and technical assistance (of which multilateralism and general agreements are the best guarantors); the training of local cadres; the training in all Western countries of teachers capable of teaching in developing countries; the listing of national organizations specialized in technical assistance; the creation when necessary of international organizations purely for technical aid; a systemization, respected by all but not necessarily entirely uniform, of the rules for making loans to the developing countries; a guarantee against political risks given by each Western country to private investments made by its nationals in the developing countries; a complement to this latter guarantee in the form of reinsurance of the governments by an international organization for the purpose; and the unification by that organization of the methods for carrying out the guarantees given by the various countries that are associated with it.

In other words, Western aid to the developing countries will have its full effect only if it is not developed within an anarchy of purposes and methods. All Western countries carrying out aid in one form or another should closely coordinate their programs. In this, every effort should be made to associate the aided countries themselves; and some sacrifices should also be made of the absolute freedom to lend, sell, and invest.

One is bound to ask whether there has not been too great a tendency to allocate too much effort to building up machines and factories, and too little to the human beings who will run them. We have seen financial and physical aid programs organized on a scale that no one would have thought possible—but not human aid programs.

MANAGEMENT AND GROWTH

By Sir Leslie Rowan *

A massive movement of countries to political independence has occurred during the postwar years. This imposes the need, common to them and to us, to ensure that this political independence is based on a foundation that will have lasting strength, namely, economic self-reliance and freedom from extraordinary external assistance in a competitive trading system.

This objective is the harder to reach because of the conjunction of three features common to most developing countries. First, they have expanding populations, in many cases already dense, with widespread inertia among the masses to social and economic change. Second, there is a grave shortage of skilled manpower at

* Director of finance, Vickers Limited; private secretary to Sir Winston Churchill, 1941–45, and to Lord Attlee, 1945–47. Sir Leslie has served as permanent secretary, Office of Minister for Economic Affairs; as economic minister, Embassy in Washington; and as second secretary, H. M. Treasury. Currently he is a director of Vickers-Armstrongs, Barclays Bank, and Canadian Vickers, and is chairman of Robert Boby, and Overseas Development Institute.

all levels and in all spheres. Third, it is vitally necessary for them to develop their wealth and resources at great speed.

The solution of these three issues imposes one of the major challenges of our time. The response to this challenge must be a composite one, from outside and from within. Upon the success of the response will depend not only whether the resources, human and material, provided to and available within developing countries are in fact well used or wasted. Upon it will also depend whether we, in the developed countries, maintain and strengthen our links with such countries and improve our mutual trade.

It is a challenge that will be at its sharpest in the 1960's, though it will not end with the 1960's. I say this not just because I think that we, and the developing countries, will during this decade be most subject to the challenges of Communism. My view is based on two purely practical considerations. First, the years of transition immediately following independence raise peculiar difficulties of their own. They are years in which it is a vital interest to us in the developed countries to seek to maintain the links between the developing countries and ourselves—links built up over so many years and so difficult to re-establish once they are snapped. Second, political independence and economic development, marching forward hand-in-hand at a great pace are most demanding of skilled manpower at all levels and in all spheres—political, social, educational, industrial, and financial.

These years of transition are therefore extremely important. They are the period when the greatest help is needed and from which, if the response is right, the greatest advantages to all can flow. But the converse is also true. Penalties of failure will be greater than in normal times, even if we do not have to consider how the Communists would seek to exploit such failures. Thus, all our efforts are needed, from all sources.

In this context it is perhaps worth while to emphasize that the essential quality of private enterprise is, as the name implies, to be enterprising, or to take sensible risks. It is exactly this spirit of enterprise for which the developing countries call. The real issue is to find a fruitful partnership between private enterprise, whether within or without the developing countries, and the authorities in

such developing countries. The first essential element in this re-
volves round the questions of attitude and approach.

CONCEPTS OF PARTNERSHIP

We face here basically questions of mutual understanding and
of the concept of partnership, which involve duties and obligations
on management both in the investing and in the developing countries. Equally, of course, they involve encouragement from the
public bodies and governments of the investing countries and
receptivity on the part of the developing countries.

If we consider management originating from the investing
countries, we can reasonably assume that it has the necessary
technical qualifications. One might also assume, though this is
not by any means always the case, that management will acquire
a knowledge of local conditions, the habits and history of the
people, and not least by any means, some knowledge of their
language.

All this, however, can be wasted unless there is an attitude of
understanding on certain wider issues that color all our activities.
Many examples could be given, but perhaps three of the most important will suffice.

First, it is equally wrong to assume that the adoption by developing countries of our techniques and industrial practices
implies that they will adopt our political system. It is wrong
to conclude that, if they do not adopt our political systems, we
cannot as private enterprise work with them. This is not an
argument for Communism or dictatorship. It is an argument in
favor of realizing that in all our own history we have at times
needed strong hands at the center. This is perhaps necessary
more than ever when a country is trying to meet concurrently
the three needs mentioned at the outset.

Second, it is wrong to assume that in developing countries economic planning and central control are political devices of an
objectionable kind, necessarily inimical to private enterprise. On
the contrary they may be not only necessary but also, in some
cases, the basic condition under which private enterprise can have
any real hope of success. This is not an argument in favor of na-

tionalization, and more particularly not an argument in favor of a policy under which industry and private enterprise are expected to invest in a country with the threat of nationalization held above its head. It is basically an argument in favor of recognizing that developing countries, with their central planning organizations, can often offer great benefits to private enterprise, and that without such organizations there may be real danger of chaos. A country can perhaps afford the full working of the market economy when its people's bellies are full; it is a different matter when most of them are hungry.

Third, it is wrong to assume that our time scales or priorities are necessarily those that will appeal to all developing countries, or be relevant to their problems. For example, our system of training or the period we devote to training may suit us. It is not by any means clear that it will suit them. Equally, priorities that we attach to mechanization may be very different in one of the developing countries where the great problem is not shortage but surplus of manpower.

If these and other similar basic issues are clearly worked out in the minds of management from an investing country before they seek to go into the developing country, then they can provide a fruitful basis for what must be the continuing relationship, namely, partnership. Equally, these attitudes on the part of management in developed countries must be matched by an attitude of receptivity in the developing countries.

Here, again, many issues are involved. It is vital that recipient countries should recognize that our political and economic systems are built up principally on choice rather than direction. There will be no fruitful basis for partnership if they seek to decry the private enterprise system in its proper sphere, for it has built up the surplus savings and resources from which the investment in their country can be made.

It is wrong to assume that the profit motive cannot contribute to the public good. Without the expectation of profit, investments will not be made; without the realization of profit, they must fail. Profits are therefore essential and should be regarded by developing countries as such, provided private enterprise on its part recognizes its moral as well as its commercial and creative obligations and is ready to render service while it seeks profit. For developing countries, private enterprise has one great advantage: normally it provides both finance and management, initially by sending out its own employees, and then by training local management either on the spot or in its own works and factories at home. In fact, to do its job, private enterprise must seek to provide a package deal—finance and management both from home and locally; and this comes with few if any other methods of external investment.

Above all, such countries, with their very low national wealth per head on the one hand, and necessary dependence on external investment on the other, must show in both their attitude to such investment and their general policies that they recognize that while labor on the whole is static, capital is volatile and can be fugitive.

Unless these things are understood in developing countries, scarce resources of money and men will stay at home within developed countries and there is no method under our system for directing them to do otherwise.

One other major fact that must affect our attitudes and then our actions is the comparative state of education in its widest sense. In most fields of activity manpower in developing countries represents a rather distorted hour glass. At the top, there is a small but high-level administration, in some cases as good as can be found anywhere. I choose India because I know it best; those at the top in any sphere in India are as good as you can find anywhere in the world. At the bottom there is a vast reservoir of manpower, from which the mass needs of industry, agriculture, and so on, can be found and trained. But these two are joined by a narrow neck and here in this middle and junior management structure lies the great weakness and the great need. It is, in military terms, the noncommissioned officers; in industrial terms, the foremen, skilled tradesmen, and artisans; in government, the executive and clerical grades. Without these middle grades, a modern state just cannot work, any more than an army can work without its NCO's.

Here then is a great difference. We in private enterprise, when seeking to go into developing countries must not only understand it but seek to do something about it if we are to make sense of our partnership.

COMPONENTS OF POLICY

The scale of the problems and their urgency call for a policy in all three spheres—through international bodies, and through both national governments and private enterprise in developed and developing countries alike. But through all these spheres there run three major issues. Upon their outcome will depend in the future to a great extent the pace and stability of economic development in the new countries, and the role that private enterprise plays in it.

The first is education. The second is whether we in the developed countries show the right balance between the material and the human components in our help. The third is whether we rely on these things just happening, or whether in all spheres there is a conscious effort of organization.

Education. Our own experience must show us the vital importance of both general and technical education to development and industry. A literate and inquiring people is the real and only basis on which to build. What is much more necessary to argue is the degree to which it is given priority in our thinking and action, and the extent to which we seek to put forth an organized effort.

We in private enterprise should be playing a much more active role in ensuring that international bodies and national governments give the issue of education in developing countries the priority it deserves in their schemes of assistance. The need is indeed recognized; it is the practical follow-up that is now required.

In this, as indeed in the whole field of development, the main effort must be made locally. But it cannot all be done locally. Here we need to ask ourselves two questions. Are our efforts, whether at the level of government or at that of private enterprise, adequately organized? And are they adequately known and the knowledge made available to developing countries?

The British Commonwealth Conference, held in July, 1959,

represented a major new effort on the government level, but no such organization exists on the private enterprise level. We may hope that with the new Department of Government set up in the United Kingdom to coordinate all overseas technical assistance, our national effort will be much better organized at all levels. From organization it is an easy step to put available knowledge to proper use.

Perhaps each of us should ask ourselves, in relation to our own government and our own private enterprise: (1) is our effort in this wide field of educational policy towards developing countries adequately organized, and (2) if I were a Minister in a developing country responsible for such matters, would I find ready-to-hand information about what is available?

If we could all answer "Yes" to these questions, then we should have taken a major step forward.

The Human Component. The next major issue—the priority given to the material as opposed to human component—naturally overlaps largely with the issue of education. But it raises some wider issues that are perhaps worth some thought.

One of the major differences in the economic field in the post-war years, as compared with, for example, the 1930's, is the degree of international cooperation. Countries now seek to discuss matters together so that solutions can be found that do the least harm or the most good all round, rather than to go their own ways. Not only this, but as everyone knows, powerful and well-endowed bodies have been built up. Some are world-wide, such as the United Nations and its special agencies, the International Monetary Fund (IMF), and the International Bank for Reconstruction and Development (IBRD). Some are regional: the Organization for Economic Cooperation and Development (OECD), the Economic Commission for Europe (ECE), the Organization of American States (OAS), the Inter-American Development Bank, the Economic Commission for Asia and the Far East (ECAFE), the Colombo Plan Organization in the Far East, and the Economic Commission for Africa (ECA).

There are others, but these will suffice to show that the institutions are not lacking. In their various ways they have provided resources to developing countries to build up some of their basic needs—communications, power, agriculture, and so on, thus helping to provide the foundation on which private enterprise can build. We, as private enterprise, have a direct interest in the future operations and success of these bodies.

Despite their great success in these matters, one is bound to ask whether there has not been too great a tendency to allocate too much effort to building up machines and factories, and too little to the human beings who will run them. We have seen financial and physical aid programs organized on a scale that no one would have thought possible, but not human aid programs. This latter can be tackled in many ways, and at all levels. But it needs great organization. I suggested one possible way some time ago in lectures at Cambridge, England:

I have referred to the consequences of the withdrawal of empire, the rise of nationalism, and the surge of development in so many countries. From these have flowed the cutting of old ties, gross shortages of skilled administrators and technicians just when conditions demand them in great numbers and, in many cases, a suspicion of anyone who wears a national hat. It is precisely here that the international bodies have played a major role and one which it is vital to expand.

The United Nations is doing much to train experts, so is the International Bank for Reconstruction and Development; and all have sent their own experts to countries which have asked for them. But perhaps because of my past experiences I feel that the West could make no better investment than in an International Administrative and Technical Civil Service which I should put under the International Bank for Reconstruction and Development. Nothing in my view would help more to ensure the best use of the material resources, in any event inadequate, to meet the needs of developing countries, or to ensure the training of local administrators and technicians on whom the future of any country must depend. Such people would, of course, have all the executive responsibility attaching to any post they might occupy and not be merely advisory. This is the crucial point.

Under such a scheme any country should on proper application be able to acquire the services of a first-class expert in any particular field. Under the present system this cannot happen for two reasons: first, they cannot afford it in many cases; secondly, the first-class expert, whether a public servant or private person, hesitates to go because he is uncertain what the future may hold if he strays away from home and from the sources where his future lies. Both difficulties are removed if the international institution pays and employs the expert as a permanent servant. It should be reimbursed by the recipient country (and this in my view is most important) the salary which it would pay a local holder of the post; this provides both a safeguard and an assurance of local continuity. Such a system has indeed a further advantage; it adds to the independence of the advice which the expert gives, for his future will depend on giving honest and fearless advice, rather than in seeking to placate local interests.

There are no doubt many other ways. For example, there is the suggestion made recently by Gustav Papanik, of the Harvard University Center for International Affairs, for an Institute for Development Planning. What we need is for this aspect to be given the priority it deserves and for the effort to be organized on the scale and with the imagination that have applied to the programs of material assistance.

Organization. The need for an organized effort runs through all this paper. These things will not just happen. And if, as I believe, progress in them is of crucial importance to private enterprise, then we have a major task ahead of us. I have sought to argue the need on all levels—international, governmental, and private enterprise—of greater emphasis on management in the development of the emergent countries. It is not an issue that presents the same excitement or propaganda value as the more spectacular industrial or other schemes. But it is an issue on whose successful outcome depends in large measure the success of such schemes, and the success that will attend the efforts of private enterprise.

5. Government-Business Relationships for Growth

The extent of direct government interven-
tion in the management of the nation's econ-
omy in order to accomplish the desired rate
of growth will differ from one country to
another. It will depend upon the stage
of industrial development that has been
reached, the degree of urgency for improv-
ing the standard of living of the people, the
historical background, and the social and
political conditions that prevail.

GOVERNMENT'S RESPONSIBILITIES

By Walter L. Gordon *

All of us today would probably agree that government should play a positive role in promoting economic growth. There will be marked differences, however, in what would be regarded as its proper role from one country to another. In the United States, for example, with its highly complex and fully developed industrial economy, with its established banking and credit facilities and its more-than-adequate accumulations or pools of private capital, there are excellent arguments for keeping day-to-day business and economic decisions as free and decentralized as possible.

* Partner, Clarkson, Gordon & Company, Canada; partner, Woods, Gordon & Company; president, Canadian Corporate Management Company. Mr. Gordon assisted in the organization of the Foreign Exchange Control Board in 1939, and was special assistant to the Deputy Minister of Finance from 1940–42; chairman of the Royal Commission on Administrative Classifications in Public Service (1945), and of the Royal Commission on Canada's Economic Prospects (1955). His paper was read by Herbert H. Lank, president, Du Pont of Canada Limited.

It is this decentralization of responsibility for economic decision making that is meant when people speak of the advantages of "free enterprise." But the so-called free enterprise system will not work effectively even in the United States unless the government does its part in promoting the kind of policies that will encourage a high rate of annual economic growth and high levels of employment at stable prices.

In less-developed countries, and also in countries whose economic, social, and political development has not followed the same paths as in the United States, the role that government should play in promoting economic growth may necessarily be more direct. This may be true in India, for example, with her population problem, her poverty, her low rate of capital formation, her quite different social and historical background, and with her different experience in the ways of doing business. So it may be desirable in India, or the Indian people may think it is desirable, for the government to direct and control a larger proportion of the total capital expenditures each year than would be appropriate in the United States or Canada.

The extent of direct government intervention in the management of the nation's economy in order to accomplish the desired rate of growth will differ greatly from one country to another. It will depend upon the stage of industrial development that has been reached, the degree of urgency for improving the standard of living of the people, the historical background, and the social and political conditions that prevail. In France, to cite another example, the largest manufacturer of automobiles is a state-owned enterprise. Not long ago, the coal and steel industries in the United Kingdom were nationalized. When the Conservatives came back to power, steel was denationalized, but the government still runs the coal mines. In Canada, the Federal Government operates among other things the largest railway, the principal airline, the national broadcasting system, a large uranium mining enterprise, the only synthetic rubber plant, and controls the marketing of wheat.

Although conditions and the points of view of the people vary, all national governments have this in common—their primary aim and responsibility in the domestic field must be to ensure a satisfactory rate of annual economic growth, high levels of employment, and stable prices. If they refuse or fail to do this, their prospects of re-election, at least in those countries that have free elections, may be disappointing.

One approach to this subject is to concentrate on the nature of the government's responsibilities for promoting economic growth in one country, while pointing out that this may not be appropriate in the case of others. I should like to do this using my own country as the example. It has been suggested that I should touch on the government's responsibility for monetary policy, debt management and fiscal or tax policy, the role of private foreign capital, the more positive kinds of action the government should take from time to time, and the government's regulatory functions.

CANADA'S SITUATION

Canada is one of the largest countries in the world. Her population of only 18 million is concentrated in a narrow band along her southern border running some 4,500 miles from the Atlantic to the Pacific oceans. Canada is a federal state with two cultures and two official languages. Wide differences exist in points of view, in the nature of economic activity, and in the ways of doing business from one province to another. In view of this and the great distances involved, it is important in our case that responsibility for day-to-day decision making should be decentralized as much as possible. Such decisions should be left in the main to the thousands of individuals who together comprise the Canadian market place. But when, as sometimes happens, these individual decisions do not keep the economy sufficiently active to maintain employment at high levels, the Federal Government should not hesitate to step in with positive programs for getting things into high gear again. Similarly, in boom times it is the government's responsibility to apply the brakes when this is called for.

I do not claim that Canadian governments have always lived up to the responsibilities I have suggested for them. In the last few years, our rate of economic growth has not been nearly high enough and unemployment has been heavy. Moreover, about as many people will be added to the nonagricultural labor force in the five years 1960–65 as were added in the whole decade of the 50's. This means we shall have to encourage a very high annual rate of economic growth in Canada if jobs are to be provided for all those who will need them. Apart from questions of defense and foreign policy, this must be the primary preoccupation and responsibility of the Canadian Federal Government.

Not very long ago, the Radcliffe Commission in the United Kingdom recommended that the government through its Treasury officials should assume a greater degree of responsibility for monetary policy controlled through the operations of the Bank of England. Some of the Commission's specific proposals were criticized at the time. Nevertheless, since its report was issued the responsibilities of the Chancellor of the Exchequer relative to the Bank of England have been emphasized. There are two points here. One is the general principle that responsibility for monetary policy, like any other policy, should always rest with elected members of the government. The other is that, when the government's responsibility for the whole range of economic policies is acknowledged, the prospects for pursuing coordinated policies are increased.

Somewhat similarly, the Commission on Money and Credit in the U.S. submitted a number of proposals for improving the relationships of the Federal Reserve System and other parts of the government. This is desirable in order that monetary policy may be coordinated and integrated with fiscal policy, debt management, and all the other economic policies of government.

The same thing is true in Canada. With us, a restrictive monetary policy, high interest rates, and difficulties in obtaining credit weigh especially heavily on small businessmen and farmers and less heavily on the larger corporations. There are more small businesses, relatively speaking, in the areas of the country where economic activity and income levels are lowest. It follows that a restrictive monetary policy in Canada weighs most heavily on the very areas that already lag behind.

Many Canadians are bothered by the increasing degree of

absentee ownership of our industries and resources. For example, 57% of all manufacturing in Canada was controlled by nonresidents in 1958 (the last year for which statistics are available), up from 43% in 1948. To a considerable extent, it is the larger companies in Canada that are controlled by nonresidents, and in many cases these companies are much less dependent on bank credit than are the smaller, locally owned concerns. The effects of a restrictive monetary policy in Canada, therefore, may impinge much less directly on many foreign-owned concerns than upon business enterprises that are owned and controlled by local residents.

MONETARY POLICY AS A TOOL

Until quite recently, we have pursued a tight-money policy in Canada and this has influenced the inflow of foreign capital and the exchange rate. High interest rates in recent years have widened the spread that normally obtains between interest rates in Canada and the U.S. This attracted an inflow of capital from U.S. institutions and other sources. In turn, there was a strong demand for Canadian funds, so that the exchange rate for our dollar was at a substantial premium until very recently. The Canadian economy is a relatively open one. This means that Canadian manufacturers producing goods for the domestic market are up against stiffer competition from imports than would be the case if the Canadian dollar is at par or at a discount. It means also that Canadian exports command lower prices when converted into Canadian currency. Both influences tend, of course, to increase unemployment.

These facts are mentioned, not to denigrate the importance of monetary policy as a tool in influencing the rate of economic activity, but to point out the danger of using it indiscriminately in Canada and perhaps in other countries also. To be used effectively, monetary policy should be integrated and coordinated with fiscal policy, debt management, and other economic policies. And this can be done successfully only if the national government accepts full responsibility in all these fields.

It is important to appreciate also that monetary policy may

be a more effective instrument in restricting the rate of economic growth than it is in stimulating it. An easy credit policy and lower interest rates are obviously called for when the rate of economic growth is unsatisfactory and unemployment is too high. While important, such policies may not be sufficient by themselves to get the economy out of the doldrums. The times may call for new approaches in the management of the national debt, for lower taxes, for tax incentives, and sometimes for positive action by the government in order to stimulate economic activity in certain areas. On the other hand, if it becomes necessary to restrict the rate of economic activity under boom conditions, higher taxes or the withdrawal of tax incentives may be less damaging in the long run than an overly restrictive monetary policy, some of the effects of which in Canada have been referred to.

Generally speaking, governments should aim at balancing their budgets on the basis of reasonably full employment. In poor times, this method of government budgeting will produce deficits and an increase in the public debt. In good times, it should produce surpluses that should be applied to reduce the debt. But it is important that those responsible for the management of the debt should do their work in close cooperation with the officials who are responsible for other aspects of the government's economic policies. For example, in boom periods when inflationary pressures may be severe, the government may find it necessary to restrict credit and to increase taxes. In such circumstances, if surplus revenues were used to retire debt, the amount of cash in the hands of the public would be increased. The effect of this would be to counteract or offset the other policies referred to. At such a time, therefore, it may be desirable to hold surplus government revenues in specially earmarked bank accounts for a time, rather than apply them immediately in debt retirement. This example may be sufficient to demonstrate the importance of integrating debt management with other government policies.

Governments should make considerable use of tax policy in order to stimulate or restrict the rate of economic activity. In times of recession, a reduction in taxes can be used to stimulate consumer spending and thus breathe new life into the economy. In times of high economic activity and serious inflationary pressures, an increase in taxes is one way to restrict and check a boom. The Commission on Money and Credit went so far as to suggest that such changes in the rates of personal income tax be made more or less automatic in their incidence.

It may be some time before democratic governments in most countries and the citizens they represent will be ready for a proposal of this kind to be applied in any automatic way. But the principle is clear enough. Fiscal policy should be used by governments forthrightly and without hesitation as one of the most important tools at their disposal for stimulating or restricting the rate of economic activity.

Tax policy can be used in other ways as well. For example, it is desirable in all nations to encourage industry to keep its plants and equipment as up-to-date as possible. This can be facilitated by very generous depreciation allowances in poor times when governments wish to stimulate private capital investment and by less generous allowances in boom periods if industry is tempted to create more capacity than is likely to be needed. To cite another example, the mining industry in Canada has been greatly assisted and encouraged by the fact that new mines are not subject to income tax for a period of three years. It should be possible through similar incentives to persuade business enterprises of various kinds to establish new facilities or to enlarge existing ones in depressed areas of the country where unemployment may be relatively high.

THE FOREIGN INVESTMENT PROBLEM

Another way for developing countries to influence the rate of economic growth is to encourage the investment of foreign private capital. Canada, for example, has gained tremendously from the foreign capital that has been invested in her natural resources and manufacturing industries since the war. This was accompanied by managerial, scientific, and technical personnel, and "know-how" that we were short of. It brought access to research facilities and technological developments in other countries, and often in the case of the resource industries the assurance of markets without which the new ventures could not have been justified and financed. This foreign private capital was attracted to Canada because the investment climate was inviting, because there was no discrimination against foreigners or foreign-owned business establishments, and of course because the opportunities for profit were very great.

I said earlier that many Canadians are now worried that too large a proportion of our industry is controlled by people who do not reside within our borders. This is true. Too much absentee ownership is probably unwise for any country. But this does not mean that underdeveloped countries should go to the other extreme, and adopt a hands-off policy against all foreign private capital. My only reservation, based on Canadian experience, is that a policy of encouraging foreign private capital should not be allowed to go too far without adequate safeguards and controls. This is very different, however, from a policy that would discourage altogether any appreciable investment of foreign private capital.

CONTROLLING CAPITAL EXPENDITURES

In addition to the methods I have mentioned for influencing the rate of economic growth, governments should not hesitate to take more positive action to increase economic activity and to relieve unemployment when this is necessary. In Canada, for example, our government is being urged to take measures that would stimulate capital expenditures at the municipal level until such time as private capital spending picks up again. In underdeveloped countries, the problem is to supply the seemingly unlimited demand for capital and consumer goods of all kinds. In the more developed countries, on the other hand, the problem is not so much one of production and supply as it is one of providing or stimulating new and sufficient demand. In Canada, our stock of social capital—and by this I mean such things as hospitals, schools, universities, low-rental housing projects, urban and rural redevelopment schemes, appropriate dwelling quarters for our older citizens, parks, recreational and cultural centers, expressways, rapid transit systems, and so on—is relatively low. There is an opportunity for us, therefore, when the rate of annual economic growth is not sufficiently high, to increase capital expenditures on such public services and projects until such time as private capital expenditures reach more satisfactory levels. This is the kind of action government can take to encourage a high rate of economic growth.

NEW THINKING NEEDED

Governments have other responsibilities of a regulatory kind that cannot be neglected if the economy is to work well and smoothly. I should like to mention an area where, perhaps, some new thinking needs to be done, in Canada, at least. Our antitrust laws are based on the principle that free competition is a vital and fundamental factor in maximum economic development and growth. In the absence of competition, inefficiencies and higher costs may stultify the operations of monopolies and oligopolies. Quite apart from the question of increased profits, this may result in higher prices. Under Canadian law, combinations in restraint of trade are a criminal offense and offenders can be severely penalized. But we know that in some Canadian industries there are too many manufacturers for any of them to be able to take advantage of the economies of large-scale production. This also means higher costs and higher selling prices than otherwise would need to be the case. Theoretically, the weaker enterprises should be driven out of business. But this may not happen in practice if the concerns in question are each subsidiaries of some large foreign company that is prepared to subsidize their operations rather than admit failure by letting them go under.

Even if the process of natural rationalization could proceed unhindered, it might lead to a condition where one or a relatively few companies dominated the situation in their particular fields. Having overcome their competition in one way or another, what is to happen then? In the kind of cases I have mentioned, it might be desirable or even necessary for the government to step in. But having done so, what should it do about the situation? I am not prepared to say. I raise the matter only to illustrate the need for a continuous re-examination of some of our basic economic theories and beliefs as our industrialized societies evolve and change.

Some new thinking is needed also, especially in North America, about spreading the benefits of increased productivity in particular industries among the population as a whole through price reductions. In some European countries, questions of appropriate wage and price increases or reductions are discussed by senior representatives of management and labor in the context of what is most desirable for the country as a whole. A proposal that this should be done in Canada would probably be received with some astonishment, or perhaps with the suggestion that whoever made it should have his head examined. Nevertheless, this is a question that governments, even in North America, may be faced with in the not too distant future if they are to be successful in achieving a more satisfactory rate of economic growth and reducing present levels of unemployment. It is not a question that can be ducked indefinitely.

In the short space of a generation, we have come to expect governments to accept responsibility for seeing that there is a satisfactory rate of annual economic growth, that employment is maintained at high levels, and that prices remain stable. This will call for considerably more forward planning and for the exercise of great skill and judgment on the part of the authorities. In some countries, including Canada, some new organizational machinery will be needed for these purposes. And more talented young people will have to be encouraged to make government service their career, either as elected representatives or as appointed officials and civil servants.

Businessmen, among others, can help this process of evolution if in their literature and public speeches they will explain the new responsibilities that governments are now expected to assume and the difficulties involved in doing so. It would be helpful if some of them would understand the fallacy of expecting government to accept increased responsibilities while criticizing it for increasing the expenditures necessary to carry out such responsibilities.

What have been the attributes of Hong Kong's success? I cannot venture a formula, but perhaps it would not be far wrong to say that the cornerstones on which Hong Kong's present prosperity rests are free enterprise, free trade, and a people determined to live in freedom and independence.

THE RESPONSIBILITIES OF BUSINESS

By Sir Sik-Nin Chau *

In discussing business responsibilities in a developing community, certain broad assumptions must be stated. We assume, first, that the government of the country is stable, enlightened, and responsible; secondly, that an atmosphere to encourage private investment prevails; and thirdly, that the government has a considered development policy. Let me add that it is essential that government consult with private enterprise when formulating development policies. It should never be expected that civil servants alone can formulate such policies to optimum effect, although it is for the authorities to ensure that good policies are

* Chairman, The Hong Kong Chinese Bank, Ltd.; chairman, Federation of Hong Kong Industries and Hong Kong Management Association; chief Hong Kong delegate to ECAFE conferences in India (1948) and Australia (1949), and chairman of the ECAFE subcommittee on trade held in Hong Kong in 1955; chairman of Dairy Farm, Ice & Cold Storage Co. (Hong Kong), China Underwriters Life & General Insurance Co., Repulse Bay Enterprises, Far East Insurance Company, Oriental Express, Nin Fung Hong, and Sik Yuen Company; director in several other companies. Sir Sik-Nin was a member of the Hong Kong Legislative Council from 1946 to 1959.

221

implemented to serve the best national interests. The government must also see that the necessary encouragement and assurances are available to responsible private enterprise and, equally important, that the assurances are honored.

Given these conditions, private enterprise, before embarking on a venture, will be able to satisfy itself whether the project is one that falls within the framework of national objectives. If so, the venture may be undertaken with confidence. In all this it is understood that the necessary raw materials and manpower should be available.

USE OF MANPOWER IN A DEVELOPING ECONOMY

In any area, manpower will have its own national characteristics, traditions, and skills. These traits may be so strong as to make manpower the most vital single influence on development policy. A farmer who has spent all his life hoeing the land is hardly likely to have the manual dexterity needed for the transistor radio assembly line, and the man who has led a completely free and roving life will not settle easily in repetitive, stationary work. Thus, the selection of the type of enterprise to accord with the quality and type of the human material available is an important responsibility of business in a developing community. Employment of the kind that the people can understand and master is employment that will give them a sense of fulfillment and lead to happiness. The habits and customs of people can be changed, but this needs time and should be given time.

Included in manpower considerations will be the question of technicians and managerial staff. Specialist skills may not be available among the local population, and in cases where it is necessary to recruit from abroad the long-term view should be taken. The technicians concerned should have skill in their specialty, but this should be combined with the ability, readiness, and patience to teach and to train. Indeed, it is the responsibility of every businessman to have at heart the education of the nationals of the country. This is an essential part of development. He should cooperate with government and other bodies in establishing balanced education programs, in contributing financially and otherwise to educational institutions, and he should take particular interest in ensuring the provision of adequate technical and higher education. This serves his own as well as the national interest and will help to ensure that industry can progress on sound and solid domestic foundations.

TRAINING FOR INDUSTRY

If industry in a developing country is to proceed on healthy lines, the proper training of domestic managers must be one of the major priorities. In the initial stages, there will be the inevitable shortage of managerial talent and this shortage must be corrected, otherwise it will continue to be a serious limiting factor in development.

In the training of both managers and technicians, local training should be augmented by training overseas under advanced conditions and environment. This not only trains in skill, but also broadens outlook and the understanding of responsibilities. The private enterprise that makes this investment sows seeds of progress for itself and for the developing country. Again, looking ahead, sound business should assist in every way in the establishment of a national center for developing managers and management skills.

A PRICING PRINCIPLE

It will be recognized that price will determine the marketability of the industrial products of a developing country. First, in the home market, prices must match the purchasing power of the community and, in the export market, the initial lower quality standards must be offset by lower prices. Yet business must face the responsibility of improving standards of living in the developing country. The two, however, are not necessarily incompatible, for it is possible to upgrade living standards and keep costs low through skilled management.

A CONCERN FOR PEOPLE

Business should take its responsibility to assist in improving the standards of living very seriously, but also realistically. It is wiser to have a steady upward movement on a broad front than to have violent change on a narrow front. Thus, the community of businessmen and the government should exchange views in order to keep reasonably in step with each other and with progress. Sometimes, however, ill-considered comparisons of living standards in developing countries with those in technically advanced countries will take the platform, followed by the argument that violent leveling remedies are necessary. The argument is unsound economically and does not allow for the normal processes of evolution. It may overlook the fact that the man accustomed to lower standards is sometimes happier than one with higher standards.

It is most important, of course, that the working man and his environment should be closely studied. Particular consideration should be given to establishing standards of food and nutrition for the man and his family, to ensuring the adequacy of his shelter, the sufficiency of his raiment, the suitability of the conditions in which he works, the facility with which he can obtain medical services when required, the availability of schooling for his children, and his ability to acquire a reasonable quantity of private possessions. These are criteria by which this emancipation can be measured. In setting these standards, local conditions, customs, and creeds must be studied and respected. It is unwise to believe that patterns of living found satisfactory in one country will ensure equal happiness when imposed in another. The greatest responsibility of business is to provide the means whereby people can achieve greater happiness and, in my view, this transcends all other considerations. Increased material wealth there certainly must be, but not at the expense of a violent upheaval of ancient customs and moral standards.

TRADE UNIONS AND TRADE ASSOCIATIONS

Another responsibility that business in a developing country cannot ignore is the encouragement of the growth of healthy trade unionism. The promotion of trade unionism will often be a government undertaking, but industry also has a stake in the development of trade unions. The danger that trade unionism will become the tool of political forces is too apparent to need emphasis. All too often the unions become little more than segments of political parties, neither serving the interests of the workers nor fulfilling the legitimate functions of a trade union. Once established, their existence cannot be ignored. Trade unions are an inevitable part of the process of industrialization. In a developing country, the employer usually has the opportunity to influence their development, and he can do much to ensure that the proper duties of a union are kept before the workers. In his own interests, the employer should exercise this influence.

The establishment of trade associations should also be encouraged. Through the collective voices of chambers of commerce and industry, government can be advised of the needs and problems of business. Business and government can thus achieve closer cooperation for the benefit of the community as a whole.

THE FOREIGN INVESTOR

The foreign investor in a developing country has special problems and responsibilities. His first responsibility is so elementary that its importance is sometimes overlooked. I refer to a study of the laws of the country. A foreign investor is interested in the development of a country, first and foremost, because it offers him a good return in relation to the risks involved. He should not, however, consider himself a privileged person. Only after he is satisfied that he is prepared to abide by the laws of the country should he contemplate investment.

There may be a wide range of opportunities for investment of varying types and risks. One form beneficial to the developing country is that in which foreign capital combines with local interests, thereby closely identifying itself with the community. A joint venture should provide balance in interests and in security for both parties. A joint venture has catalytic effects not present in other forms of investment. By its very nature it contributes to the advancement of local skills and the growth of industry in the country.

The enterprise that enjoys participation of foreign capital will often be looked upon to set the standards for wages, social services, and other amenities. But these standards should be related to local conditions and should not be disruptive in their effects. They should not be too high for local enterprise to emulate, nor higher than government itself is willing to establish. Close liaison and coordination between the foreign investor, the government, and other local bodies is therefore of prime importance.

In a developing country, a fair proportion of the profits of an enterprise should be retained in the undertaking for further development. Where foreign investment is concerned, this plowing back of profits is an essential article of faith that the community will expect. This faith of the investor in the enterprise will help to build confidence in the economy and the financial stability of the area.

This responsibility on the part of foreign capital to help the newer countries to elevate the lot of their peoples is not without benefits to the more mature nations. In improving the material aspirations and purchasing power of the countless millions in the emergent nations, the highly industrialized countries are opening up for themselves exciting new markets for their products.

HONG KONG'S SUCCESS

I know that many of you here today will be wondering to what extent the views I have expressed can be related to the success of Hong Kong in its development. I'm afraid my answer is likely to be disappointing, for Hong Kong has a reputation for being the exception to the general rule and, indeed, there is such a miscellany of contradictions that they defy analysis.

Hong Kong is a developing yet a mature economy; it is the epitome of free enterprise; yet it has, at least on paper, an autocratic government. It possesses practically no raw materials, no land for industrial development, and suffers from a chronic shortage of water. Yet it has built a vigorous industrial power whose activities have evoked the admiration and in some instances, I must admit, the animosity of other industrial powers.

Until the 1950's Hong Kong was essentially a mercantile community. It relied on its entrepôt trade with China for its livelihood, and around its fine natural harbor it had developed stevedoring, warehousing, shipping, insurance, banking, and commercial services comparable to the best in the world.

In the latter part of the 1940's and the early 1950's the great social upheavals on the mainland of China brought a flood of refugees to the Colony, and an increase in population from 1½ million in 1946 to more than 3 million. Hong Kong's traditional entrepôt trade decreased to relatively negligible proportions under the influence of changing patterns of China mainland trade, and this should have been the Colony's death knell. But in keeping with its contrary character, it wasn't. The refugees brought with them entrepreneurs and labor, skilled and experienced in industry. The fusion of these with Hong Kong's particular advantages attracted capital.

In the postwar era Hong Kong has, from its own resources and without recourse to the substantial outside financial and technical assistance we see poured into other countries, provided lowcost housing for 750,000 people, built new schools that in 1960 were opened at the rate of one a week (we have a school population of a million between the ages of 5 and 15 years), doubled its hospital bed accommodation, more than doubled its water storage capacity, leveled hills and pushed back the sea to provide land for housing and industry, and given employment to a population swollen to twice its normal size. All this has been possible because industry has been able to develop unfettered. Unlike many other developing areas, the Government of Hong Kong has followed a policy of noninterference with legitimate free enterprise, which has been left to its own direction and financing. It is to be emphasized, however, that Hong Kong has been blessed by a long line of able Governors who have chosen local men of wide business experience and foresight as their advisers. Thus, Hong Kong has had political and economic stability—two ingredients essential to the growth of free enterprise—and another incentive to private investment, low taxation.

Hong Kong is proud of its record of achievement and of the tremendous strides it has made in so short a time. But the time is rapidly approaching when the period of unrestricted development, resulting in saturation in certain industries and presenting a potential threat to the economy of the Colony, must give way to planned development. Knowing the resilience of the people of Hong Kong, however, I am sure that even this they will take in their stride.

What have been the attributes of Hong Kong's success? I cannot venture a formula, but perhaps it would not be far wrong to say that the cornerstones on which Hong Kong's present prosperity rests are free enterprise, free trade, and a people determined to live in freedom and independence.

Only by working together—people with people, business with business, government with government, and any number of combinations of these—can we meet the needs of the peoples of the world.

HOW MUCH PUBLIC ENTERPRISE?

By Edgar F. Kaiser *

Mankind is undergoing a fantastic speed-up. Great movements in the past turned on a battle, a king's whim—sometimes on a group decision like the Magna Carta. However dramatic the historical turning points may have been, each event was obscured at the time by a history which meandered leisurely through the ages. The world had a century to catch its breath. Today electronic communications, space exploration, jet plumes in the sky, and television, make all of the peoples of the world as one. So, when the news of the moment is encouraging, the world sighs almost instantaneously with relief. When the drum beat of increasing tension is the reality of the day, this mood too, is communicated to all corners of the globe.

Acceleration of the times tends to obliterate the subtle but important differences between nations—between their aspirations, their requirements, their way of doing things. Living in this his-

* President and director, Kaiser Industries Corp.; chairman, president and director of various affiliated Kaiser enterprises in engineering and construction, automotives, aluminum, building materials, shipbuilding, and steel.

torical whirlwind, it is convenient to attach glib labels to the most complex political and economic developments. Shades of meaning too often are lost in our desire to make categorical short-cuts. Thus, we consider the world as either free or enslaved, democratic or totalitarian, free enterprise or communistic.

If those of us who are leaders in the private enterprise system shrink from this pell-mell rush of historical forces, we will leave a mockery for future historians to study with despair. We who have strong beliefs in the integrity of mankind and man's indi-vidual and collective ability to do great things must help to channel the events of our times. We must take the opportunity to lead and to inspire constructive change. It is proper that we constantly debate how to do what must be done. But in seeking the best way—in finding new ways—we cannot afford to be in-hibited by a superficial debate which merely concerns the labels of our philosophies or our prejudices.

THE DELUSION OF LABELS

Americans have endured a "history by label." In the early days of the 19th century, when we spanned our great continent with steel rails, Americans liked to call themselves "rugged indi-vidualists." As a land of new opportunity, we naturally attracted opportunists, men who were often armed with the skills and spirit to take advantage of our land of great bounty.

The importance of labels—of the quick name-tag—was em-phasized again in the depression of the 30's when many cried "Socialism" as our government took vigorous action to save us from economic chaos. The end of the free enterprise system in the United States was hard upon us, if you believed many spokes-men of that day. Actually, though, it was a realization on the part of a democratic majority that government has a responsi-bility not only to the people but to their economy—to assist business, to regulate it when necessary, and generally to work in close consort with it.

It is popular in some circles today to view the postwar period in America as the "Welfare State." Simultaneously we should note the emergence of another phenomenon sometimes called "corporate socialism"—not private enterprise directed by government, but rather combinations of business that have grown into bureaucratic structures like government, with hired managers instead of elected managers. In many cases they have health insurance and pension programs far in advance of government. This new pyramid form has decided drawbacks, but its strengths are sufficient to make it inevitable in most of our major fields of business, finance, and industry.

More and more, emergency arouses government action. It often is charged, and the accusers often are right, that government is too eager to take over responsibilities that should be left to free enterprise. If the arguments of those who follow this line of reasoning were followed to their logical extreme, however, private enterprise should have won World War II all on its own. Instead, World War II was a magnificent example of energetic partnership between public and private enterprise. So, in times of emergency, I think all of us hope our governments are strong and flexible and able to unite us.

Hundreds of millions of people have learned in a decade or two that starvation, serfdom, illiteracy isn't necessarily a permanent state of affairs. The underdeveloped nations have learned that so many of them know so little and they are therefore hungry to develop the greatest single resources of their nations and continents—themselves.

Think how many generations it took for man to develop the free enterprise system. But now in the developing countries these generations can and must be compressed into a few years. The people of these countries demand it. Common decency and fairness insist upon it. Historically it is inevitable—one way or another.

But in many nations now finding themselves struggling to tap their physical and human resources, there is not enough *private* capital to build great highway systems, to irrigate arid lands, to develop inexpensive power to make the machinery of economic progress run at the demanded speed. So these peoples have combined what they hope are the best elements of public enterprise and private enterprise, and we must join them in the struggle to make their futures worthwhile, both as individuals and collectively.

If the economic power of our private enterprise system does not support these peoples, in whatever way is best for them, we simply will have permitted a vacuum by default, which the leaders of other systems will delight in filling.

We of the Kaiser enterprises have had the privilege of working in partnership with both public and private enterprise—usually a combination of both—in India, in Ghana, in South America. We often have been asked: "How can you do business with India? Doesn't the government of India run the economy there? Do you want to do business with 'Socialists'?" This type of question, no matter how sincere, usually comes from people who have let themselves be blinded by labels. Certainly it is true that the Government of India is formulating many ambitious, long-range, economic plans for that country. But, as all of us know, there is debate in India itself about the proper roles of the public and private sectors. There is no debate, however, about the importance of the job to be done—only about the best way of getting it done.

ONLY BY WORKING TOGETHER

Only by working together—people with people, business with business, government with government, and any number of combinations of these—can we meet the needs of the peoples of the world.

If private enterprise backs away from this job through fear of a label, it would be a tragedy. Private enterprise must provide the leadership which will shape the groundswell of change into a high tide in the affairs of man. By ignoring the deepest kind of involvement, by backing away, by blindfolding itself, private enterprise will be swept from the main stream and left to perish on an isolated shore. It will fail only if the leaders of private enterprise suddenly lack the very things which have distinguished the history of private enterprise—courage, foresight, flexibility, and the ability to capitalize on opportunities.

During this speed-up of history, this blurring of today's headlines into tomorrow's, the characteristics that have made private enterprise an enduring and productive economic force have not changed. What has changed is the recognition that private enterprise alone cannot do the job. All of us must recognize that the designation of an economic system is increasingly less important than the dignity and development of the individual. At the same time, no system, or combination of systems, will improve the lot of an individual who does not make a contribution to his own development by hard work, increased learning, and responsibility of decision.

Private enterprisers, with their deep belief in the responsibility of the individual, have been far too dynamic and adventurous to forfeit the game now by quibbling over doctrinaire ground rules. Two-thirds of the peoples of the world beckon them to become partners with government in meeting a most satisfying challenge. It is an opportunity that history will not permit to linger.

When aid is channeled through an international agency, conditions can be laid down ensuring that the economic development is soundly planned, efficiently executed, and honestly administered. There is little scope left for men whose acts and policies are dictated by personal motives. Military and political considerations do not interfere. Recipient governments have no choice but to accept the international rules of honest and efficient administration, or to refuse aid and risk the wrath of their own people.

A PROGRAM FOR
ECONOMIC GROWTH

By Abol Hassan Ebtehaj *

I start from the proposition that a high rate of investment is fundamental to rapid development. The need is well understood. But the means for achieving high investment targets is still the subject of considerable controversy. Three factors, in my experience, are essential tools in achieving a rate of investment adequate to assure economic growth. They are: first, a framework

* President and chairman, Iranians' Bank. He was Iranian Ambassador to France (1950–52); director, Middle East Department, International Monetary Fund (1953); and managing director, Plan Oranization (Development Board) in Teheran (1954–59). He was governor and chairman of Bank Melli Iran (1942–50); and in 1944 was chairman of Persian delegations to the Middle East Financial and Monetary Conference in Cairo, and to the Bretton Woods Conference.

234

of sound national planning; second, an adequate response from private investors; third, international agencies competent to supply whatever capital and manpower the underdeveloped countries require from abroad.

A framework of sound national planning is considered necessary by most students of the problems of underdeveloped countries; but private businessmen, especially those of more developed economies, are not yet convinced that planning encourages a high rate of investment.

A LONG–TERM PLAN ESSENTIAL

It is my view that a carefully conceived, comprehensive, long-term plan not only encourages investment but is absolutely essential if an underdeveloped country is to attain a rate of investment consistent with rapid growth. I distinguish five basic reasons for a development plan:

1. Investment requires discipline, and the first important function of a development plan is to express a country's solemn undertaking to invest a certain portion of its income in development projects.

2. Planning minimizes bottlenecks. Often the underdeveloped nation is in the position of a factory manager who has raw materials in a warehouse but no means of carrying them to the machinery for processing.

3. The Plan is a major means of communication between underdeveloped countries and their international creditors.

4. The Plan is also an important means of communication within the developing country between planners and the public at large. Its targets are of great importance in unleashing the latent energies of an underdeveloped people.

5. Finally, the Plan is a tool for comparing the relative merits of competing projects.

Discipline ... the clearing of bottlenecks ... an international audit ... social targets ... and a comparative analysis of projects: these seem to be the basic elements in a sound development plan for an underdeveloped country.

PLANNING AND PRIVATE BUSINESS

How does planning affect the private business community? Development planning contains no element intrinsically hostile to private business initiative. Quite the contrary, a sound plan establishes a predictable framework within which private business decisions can be made. The plan, somewhat like the rule of law, defines limits within which private business can work more freely, more predictably, and with less uncertainty than would be possible without a plan. The only restrictions implied by a development plan are those restrictions required of all persons, companies, and nations who would be thrifty and who would, as Mr. Beise so wisely phrased it four years ago, balance the "needs of this generation with those of generations yet to come."

Planning assures the businessman that essential basic utilities and services will be available to serve his needs. Businessmen are the first and loudest to call for government investment in essential community services. Development planning foresees these needs and finds the most economical means of making them available promptly enough to encourage rather than thwart the process of growth.

A published plan with stated procedures for selecting development projects and for awarding development contracts subjects a government to public scrutiny at home and abroad, and thus helps protect honest businessmen from graft and corruption. Stated targets and procedures are particularly important in those many instances when a developing country seeks capital and other assistance from abroad.

The essence of my talk is that there should be continual collaboration between these two prime-movers in the development process. The first responsibility of private businessmen in a developing economy is to understand the Plan, to criticize it, to help perfect it, and to implement its projects whenever possible. By keeping the cost and quality of local products fully competitive with imports, private industry helps determine whether development goals can be achieved without prolonged balance of payments difficulties.

By keeping up with worldwide developments, private enterprise determines how promptly modern techniques are brought to bear on the problems of underdeveloped nations and employed to accelerate their rate of growth. Where industrialists fail to expand and modernize, the government is frequently obliged to interfere or even to compete with them.

The private sector must share with government the spirit of hope, a willingness to work, the determination to succeed, and a constant experimentation with new ideas and techniques. The extent to which private investors share their country's aspirations is a crucial index of the potential for development.

My thesis is that some degree of national planning is essential to the high rate of investment that is required if underdeveloped countries are to break the vicious cycle of poverty and stagnation. The government must be the planner. But the government will also be an originator of new activities, the chief engine of growth, a major source of innovation, and a large-scale enterpriser to the extent that private investors and businessmen fail to recognize or to exploit their myriad opportunities for expansion.

HELP FROM OUTSIDE

Development is not solely a national effort on the part of either or both the public and private sectors. External capital and talent are needed. I have come to believe that appropriate international institutions are of singular importance and, in fact, indispensable to the achievement of rapid economic progress. Outside assistance to underdeveloped countries, if they are to achieve high and rapidly rising economic goals, must be: first, adequate in amount; second, nominal in cost; third, assured of continuity; fourth, reasonably long term; and finally, most important of all, under international supervision.

First, aid must be provided in whatever amounts developing nations can absorb, not just what lenders believe they can afford or are willing to give. No development program will succeed if it is not tailored to the needs of the nation for which it is designed.

Second, loans should be extended to developing nations at very low rates of interest. I have in mind a "service charge" of only

1%. If this idea shocks you, coming from a banker, let me suggest that grants of land to railroad companies, that were the development corporations of another century, did not destroy the free enterprise system. Colleges have been built with land grants, which are the equivalent of low-interest loans. Many other ventures in the development of new frontiers have been encouraged and financed by low-interest loans in one guise or another.

Although I recommend long-term loans at very low rates of interest, I do not favor grants. Every country can and should be expected to repay capital borrowed for development purposes. Grants are often not appreciated by recipients, and are seldom used wisely. Grants are offensive morally, and should be replaced in international affairs.

It is a great encouragement for one who has advocated this type of approach for many years to see the creation of an institution such as the International Development Association. Although the capital of $1 billion is by no means adequate, the terms under which IDA extends development credits closely approximate the principles I have been advancing for many years.

My third and fourth proposals are continuity and long-term assistance. It is hard to design and build a house in one year; it is impossible to build a dam in that period, let alone an integrated series of developmental projects. Continuity is essential for less-developed nations.

SHORTCOMINGS OF BILATERAL AID

Finally, I would insist that development aid be channeled through an international institution. The bilateral government-to-government approach of recent years, despite increasingly generous allocations of cash, suffers from inherent weaknesses that cannot be cured. A donor or creditor is biased, often unconsciously, by his own background. He assumes a certain legal framework, administrative traditions, a pattern of landownership, and tax administration with which he is familiar. But many factors that are assumed in the context of one economy are inappropriate to another.

Representatives of a creditor nation are under pressures from private business concerns and other interested parties that cannot be wholly resisted. Under the present bilateral approach creditor governments are diverted from development projects by military and political considerations.

Even if a recipient government became convinced in all good faith of the fairness of certain bilateral programs offered by another country, it would soon be condemned in the public mind. Opposition leaders will charge the government with selling out to the imperialists, and the public will believe those charges.

No matter how false the accusation that other nations will use "development schemes" to exploit poverty and restrict freedom, it is a popular belief that must be recognized. Bilateral aid poisons the relationship between nations, frustrates the donor, and causes revulsion in the recipient.

Donor nations are obliged to channel aid through the receiving country's officials whether they be qualified, honest, efficient, or otherwise. Where the recipient government is corrupt, the donor government very understandably appears, in the judgment of the public, to support corruption. Where the recipient government resists reforms that are essential to rapid growth, the donor is powerless to insist on change. No foreign government representative can raise a question about corruption without insulting the very officials who are suspected. Corrupt officials indignantly dismiss such questions as an unwarranted interference in their internal affairs.

The bilateral approach cannot bring about reform. Furthermore, government-to-government aid delays internal pressures toward reform by providing considerable material resources to corrupt regimes and by unwittingly fostering the fear that development aid will be stopped if the old regime is overthrown. Under bilateral programs the lending government cannot impose a creditor's normal discipline for fear of jeopardizing the entire fabric of international relations.

I can think of no better summary of all the disadvantages and weaknesses of the bilateral system than the modern history of my own country. Not so very many years ago in Iran, the United States was loved and respected as no other country, and without having given a penny of aid. Now, after more than $1 billion of loans and grants, America is neither loved nor respected; she is distrusted by most people, and hated by many.

ADVANTAGES OF AN INTERNATIONAL PROGRAM

The alternative to bilateral approach is an international program with rules of development spending that apply to all countries equally and are openly administered under a board of directors that includes debtor as well as creditor nations. An international agency frees development aid from the lingering suspicion of imperialistic interference. Potential contractors and private business interests cannot easily influence the decisions of an international agency. Military and political considerations do not interfere.

When aid is channeled through an international agency, conditions can be laid down ensuring that economic development is soundly planned, efficiently executed, and honestly administered. There is little scope left for men whose acts and policies are dictated by personal motives. Recipient governments have no choice but to accept the international rules of honest and efficient administration, or to refuse aid and risk the wrath of their own people. Capable and dedicated local officials can, in the interest of development, accept administrative rules and financial disciplines from an international agency that would be strongly resented if imposed by a foreign power.

The availability and effectiveness of foreign technicians in economic development programs will, in years to come, be determined largely by the auspices under which development is encouraged. Growth is not merely a matter of money and machines but equally fundamentally a question of management and organization. An international agency can draw upon men from all nations. From this broader field a higher average level of competence can be assured than from a single country. A team of technicians drawn from many nations suffers less from the limiting biases of men whose experience is mainly in one country.

Bilateral programs are often staffed with men who will not risk the future of a foreign service career by playing the unpopular role that is required for a tough financial administration of development projects. But an international agency can be staffed with specialists whose attention and abilities are focused squarely on the soundness of the development plan and the integrity with which it is administered, and whose future careers depend solely on their success in guiding economic development policy.

A keen observer of economic development problems, Barbara Ward Jackson, has recently recommended an "expanded international administrative service" whose "professional and objective character would be underlined by its international status." In her view, "It is administration that will often be the weakest link in development," because, although the developing world is piling up diagnoses and prescriptions, "the crucial issue remains that of persuading the patient to take the medicine."

In my own experience the possibility of utilizing foreign planning and administrative personnel is best illustrated by the work of Lilienthal and Clapp in the development of Khuzestan (in Iran). To be sure theirs is primarily an American firm, but no one in 1956 would have accused President Eisenhower of using these two great advocates of the Tennessee Valley Authority as front men for American aid! Their reputation for integrity and imagination, not their nationality, attracted us to them. And the team they sent to Khuzestan was an international one led by men of international reputation. The project that resulted required them to use all their planning and administrative skill not merely to build dams and other facilities but also to train a local organization to take full operating responsibility within as short a time as possible. No mere advisers could have accomplished what they have; and no team of bilateral-aid supervisors could have been given the hiring and firing responsibility that this foreign firm was asked to accept.

I do not claim that the problems of underdeveloped countries can be solved simply by shifting the development effort to international agencies, but I do believe that some of the major psychological, institutional, and administrative difficulties that stand in the way of success for bilateral programs can be eliminated by an international approach.

DEVELOPMENT MUST BEGIN AT HOME

The main effort in development must still come from the developing countries themselves. Here are the most difficult tasks. Their rate of saving must be increased despite poverty that allows little margin for saving. Their social institutions must be transformed suddenly and with painful effects. The underdeveloped countries themselves must find their own political mechanism for effecting rapid changes without too great damage to individuals or to the basic traditions of their society.

I would insist that developing countries accept certain obligations in order to qualify for international aid. I have spoken at length in support of a very generous program—greater resources, over a longer period of time and at lower rates of interest. I should also make clear the conditions to be imposed strictly on all recipients. There seem to me seven major requirements:

1. Applicants for aid should prepare a national development plan and obtain approval of this plan from the international agency.

2. The plan must call for investment of a magnitude that is within the country's absorptive capacity.

3. The plan must require a maximum contribution to development from the recipient's own resources.

4. Recipients would have to accept international rules regarding the selection of projects and the awarding of contracts. These rules would be designed to preclude special or unfair advantages to any one class or group as a result of the implementation of the development program.

5. Recipients would agree to accept budgetary and administrative supervision from the international agency throughout the development period.

6. Recipients would be pledged to fiscal, financial, and monetary policies consistent with a sound development program.

7. In consultation with the international agency a National Development Organization would be established by the recipient if no such organization was already in existence. The Development Organization would be responsible for seeing that all proj-

ects in the Plan were implemented and that projects initiated by the Plan were properly maintained.

Countries that show a determination to make the administrative and social changes that are necessary to achieve a high rate of economic growth will not hesitate to accept the international rules I have outlined.

There is, no doubt, a group of countries that show no firm intention to make the changes and to undertake the sacrifices necessary for rapid economic development. Such countries cannot be helped by any program of foreign assistance in the absence of a willingness to work toward development goals. This group of countries will consider more seriously the possibilities of economic development if a number of nations move forward to demonstrate success under proper international auspices.

By handling development aid through a competent international agency, we can remove one of the major causes of world tension. The Soviet Union would be invited to participate as a principal contributor of both capital and technical assistance. It could either join the agency and work within its rules, or remain outside, clearly labeled as the only industrialized power in the world that is unwilling to give aid without political strings. Here is a disarmament scheme which depends solely upon us, and which, in its very nature, prevents sabotage by duplicity.

Social and political unrest is a manifestation of the despair and the lack of faith of the people, of their distrust of incompetent and sometimes corrupt governments, and of the whole pattern of bilateral agreements that seem to support the bankrupt system. This is no longer a matter of economic development designed to expand world production and trade. It is the most vital question that threatens the very existence of the free world.

III

Strengthening Business Leadership

Businessmen and the industries over which they preside have come to provide the foundation for national progress and national prosperity. It is in these circumstances that business leadership finds a new obligation and a new opportunity.

CRAWFORD H. GREENEWALT

The overriding responsibility of business leadership is not the preservation of our business system alone, but the preservation of the individual freedom on which that system is built. As business managers, we take the first step toward meeting this responsibility by formulating and dedicating ourselves to forthright corporate constitutions: bodies of beliefs that explain, promote, and guarantee the rights of the individual.

BEGINNING AT THE BEGINNING

By Logan T. Johnston *

In a free industrial society, the decisions of business have a more profound effect on the economic well-being of people than the decisions of any other institution, including government. As business enterprises grow, and more people come to depend on them, the businessman's job of effective management is influenced by a great number of new considerations that require new methods.

Unlike the pattern of earlier days of capitalistic enterprise, businesses can no longer be the extensions of the personality and "know-how" of one or a few outstanding individuals. The size and diversity of the modern corporation pose problems whose nature and scope prove too difficult for individuals—problems that yield primarily to group effort.

Businesses of today must develop systematic, formalized methods of managing their affairs. They must employ precise planning

* President, Armco Steel Corp.; director, American Iron & Steel Institute, and various industrial enterprises.

247

methods, efficient organizational structures, a standardized vocabulary for better communications, and well-defined procedures for business conduct. They must develop management as a profession, with practices and techniques that apply to each segment of the business community—tools with which to build a firmer foundation for decision making.

In the understanding, acceptance, and application of such tools and techniques, management shares major common denominators with medicine, law, and the other professions. But the concept of management as a profession certainly doesn't end here. It goes far deeper than the attempt to evolve standardized techniques for operating a plant or a business unit.

It also contributes to a clearer picture of the position of the manager with respect to his company, the people with whom he deals, and the depth of his duties. Acceptance of professional management can prevent managers from taking their duties too lightly by elevating them to the level of their highest responsibilities.

The concept of management as a profession leads the manager to recognize the philosophical importance of his responsibilities and the degree to which reflection must precede action in today's business world.

NEW RESPONSIBILITIES FOR THE MANAGER

In the past the businessman has not been known as much of a philosopher. Whether in consequence of his defined duties or simply because of personal interest, he as been almost solely a "doer"—an executor of acts, whose abilities were directed toward the "hows" of business, rather than toward the "whys."

Today, however, the breadth and implications of world-wide business require the businessman to be more reflective than in any other age. In recent years industry all over the free world has discovered that it is responsible not only for the *economic* well-being of people, but that it is also involved in their social, civic, and cultural well-being.

As a result of this fact alone, the mix—the proportion—of action as opposed to reflection in the businessman's life has undergone a distinct change. He is learning that constant examination and re-examination of his managerial doctrine is necessary to the health of his enterprise.

The social sciences, too, have affirmed the need for such examination. They have presented us with evidence proving beyond any doubt that the businessman has what I call "value responsibility," and that it permeates free society.

In the exercise of all the businessman's managerial duties lies the power to create or to destroy the purpose of enterprise, to strengthen or to weaken its values, to raise or to lower its standards of conduct.

If we, as business leaders, accept this fact, then the practice of professional management is significant not only in terms of business, but in terms of total human endeavor. This fact also indicates that the development of techniques for strengthening business leadership will be meaningless if we teach only their use, and not their meaning.

Leadership development must therefore begin with an honest exploration of managerial beliefs and first principles. It must provide a sense of purpose and perspective. It must discuss and weigh values, because the requirements of future leadership in business demand men whose moral vision is at least as great as their "business vision."

The first and fundamental responsibility of professional management is *to formulate . . . set forth . . . communicate . . . and adhere to a philosophy of doing business that reflects the bedrock beliefs of a free business system.*

FIRST PRINCIPLES

Do not misunderstand me. I do not mean a philosophy in the formal and structured sense, but rather a philosophy that springs from faith, with first principles that arise from belief.

As such, a philosophy of first principles lies at the heart of all professions. In fact, Webster's first definition of profession is "an open declaration, as of . . . faith and purpose." Actually, the first principles and philosophy I speak of are common to all free societies. They emanate from basic democratic beliefs in the rights and responsibilities of the individual.

In business and industry, then, first principles are guideposts to conduct that are understood and accepted by all those who are a part of the enterprise, and all whom they touch. They are not, by any means, an endless series of "shalts and shalt nots," but a tangible and basic body of corporate beliefs that answers such questions as these: Why are we in business? What obligations do we have and to whom? What standards have been set from which we can determine if we are discharging them?

I have worked under such written guideposts or policies for thirty-five years and have come to know the stabilizing effect they have. Such statements of principle comprise a kind of *corporate constitution* and give a sense of direction to the corporate body. They define and clarify the relationships among management, employees, stockholders, customers, communities, and governmental units. They also act as a constant reminder to managers to lead by example rather than by edict.

But the most important effect they have is on the individual within the corporation. Whether a manager or an hourly worker, he looks on them as his own guarantee that, as an individual, he has the same rights and opportunities as any other individual. It is this guarantee that assures him of his chance to grow and prompts him to develop his talents to the highest possible degree. There is tremendous value in such an assurance, for it not only gives a meaningful position to the individual, but encourages the best effort toward achieving corporate goals.

THE NEED FOR SETTING DOWN THE PRINCIPLES

There are, to my knowledge, only a few corporations that have attempted to formulate and set down such a body of beliefs and to breathe life into them by practicing them. It can be argued, of course, that in the past such tangible statements of purpose have been unnecessary. But even if this were once true, that day is past.

No businessman in the free world can any longer make the assumption that his subordinates have reflected upon, understood, and accepted the principles on which our systems of business and government are built. To do so would be to play host to his own destroyers.

We are all aware, I am sure, that among the numerous critics of business these days are those who accuse us of ignoring first principles. They charge that "big business" demands conformity, suppresses the individual, teaches expediency at the expense of conviction, profits at the expense of the public health, encourages materialism. Such charges have become so popular in this country in recent years that some of our best-selling books have had titles like "The Organization Man," "The Waste Makers," "The Affluent Society," "The Hidden Persuaders"—all of which have attacked the business community.

While a number of these anti-business outcries are simply anachronisms—empty echoes of days past—not all of them can be ignored or passed over just because we have heard them many times for many years. Certain of them deserve our attention because they may be valid and we—like the Pharaohs who brought misfortune down upon their own houses—may have brought them upon ourselves.

Take, for example, the things that we in America tend to stress about what we believe to be the best economic system ever devised. We have publicized and republicized the physical benefits enjoyed under this system. We have sung eulogies to our standard of living. We have repeatedly advertised—and not unjustifiably —that free business systems are the most productive. We have all encouraged the emergent nations to adopt a free competitive system. In all, we have emphasized that under democracy and capitalism nations can enjoy that most obvious freedom: freedom from want.

But the truth is that some nations within the Communist world enjoy freedom from want also, and are quite capable of rapid growth and of having economies almost as productive as most of those of the free world. Furthermore, if I may paraphrase a question asked by our friend and colleague, Clarence Randall —if free enterprise is, as we think, God's gift to mankind, what has happened to the celestial communications system? Why is so much of mankind turning to Statism?

WHERE FAILURE MAY LIE

One possible answer is that we have failed to communicate first principles convincingly enough, and consequently even our own people do not understand our way of life. In ringing bells and singing praises to the benefits of our system, we may have come to the superficial conclusion that our system is best because we have the best *things*. If this is the impression that we are creating, then we may be confusing and clouding the true value of democratic free business, namely, *that it has created freedom from want without denying the rights and the dignity of the individual*.

We have proved the worth of a system under which the individual can develop his talents freely. Neither his hopes nor his future are regimented. Instead, his abilities are unleashed. His choices are his own, and the responsibility for success or failure lies *in his own hands*.

Therein is the crucial distinction. Therein is the strength of the free business system and the foundation on which democracy will stand or fall. And therein also is the message which businessmen—through the establishment of and adherence to tangible guideposts for corporate endeavor—must bring to their people, forcefully and with dedication.

OUR RESPONSIBILITY AND OUR GOALS

With the cloud of Communism hanging over so much of the world and threatening all of us, the overriding responsibility of business leadership is not the preservation of our business system alone, but the preservation of the individual freedom on which that system is built. As business managers, we take the first step toward meeting this responsibility by formulating and dedicating ourselves to forthright corporate constitutions: bodies of beliefs that explain, promote, and guarantee the rights of the individual.

Once such constitutions have been set down, communicated and accepted, then we can use the tools and techniques of professional management with a more complete understanding of their importance and effect. And beginning at the beginning:

We can set policies that affirm our first principles and then apply these policies all the way down the line.

We can underline the contributions that the realization of our objectives will provide to each individual whom the company touches.

We can organize enterprise to provide maximum opportunity to individuals so that they may exercise their fullest abilities in achieving both their personal goals and those of the company.

We can lead, with consistent attitudes and a thoughtful concern for the meaning and effect of each decision on all people concerned.

These are not easy goals. To reach them, we must use the techniques of professional management so that they reflect our philosophy and our first principles.

Then their use—not only by top management, but by *all* management from president to foreman—will forcefully demonstrate that the preservation of individual dignity and integrity in business transcends all other things.

*Let us make no mistake about it: either be-
cause of us, or in spite of us, social evolution
will be achieved.... It is for our imagination, understanding, and responsibility to
boldly take the initiative in this evolution.
If we do that, we will provide ourselves, and
those who watch and judge us, with the only
valid demonstration of the enduring efficiency of our free enterprise system.*

ETHICAL PRINCIPLES

By Vittorio Valletta *

It is now evident to everyone that business leadership and
management depend on principles of general importance. To
clarify these principles, to systematize them, and to strengthen
them is the purpose of this international conference.

Ethical principles of the leadership of private enterprise, as I
use that term, embrace the summation of the essential human
values of all of man's work and economic activity. In our time,
when swift and prodigious technological developments make
production the preeminent phenomenon of modern life, the economic problem of providing capital and consumer goods is first
of all a problem of moral and social responsibility. The question,
then, is how to obtain the maximum result in terms of the public
good in order to promote social welfare. For free men, such as we

* President and general manager, FIAT S.p.A.; director of many Italian companies in finance, manufacturing and construction; member, Economic Problems Committee, Italian Manufacturers' Association; president, CEPS (European Committee for Economic and Social Progress). Mr. Valletta's paper was
read by Vincent Garibaldi, U.S. representative of FIAT.

are and want to be, this question relating to the means and ends of productive enterprise clearly calls for an ethical assessment of our business leadership.

The American businessman must be credited with a particular sensitivity to these problems. A very explicit statement I recently read in the *Harvard Business Review* put it this way: "Position, bigness, success—these are not our only values." And it added that production should be directed to provide "human satisfaction."

THE ESSENTIAL ETHICAL PURPOSE

It seems to me that these words properly point up the essential purpose of our corporate decisions and actions. Certainly, the prospects of riches and power can influence individuals. But, in the final analysis, productive efforts and managerial endeavors should legitimately have no other objective than to provide human satisfaction to both workers and consumers—that is, to all citizens. In other words, the true justification for our economic leadership is a proper sense of social responsibility in the performance of our activities.

But how is this social responsibility to be understood? First of all we must endeavor to meet the demands of consumers with a productive response adequate to their purchasing power. The first step toward an economically sound approach to consumers by producers is just this: To organize our production so as to increasingly close the gap between the level of prices and the level of purchasing power until they finally coincide.

I am glad to have this opportunity to recall what has been accomplished in this connection by the true pioneering spirit of the great North American industry, particularly the automotive industry. These developments rested upon the basic concepts of Henry Ford and other great productive groups—concepts that were very bold in their day.

Today these concepts are universally accepted and followed in the automobile sector and many others. Outside the field of durable consumer goods of a mechanical nature, much remains to be done by all productive enterprise to satisfy the ethical imperative that their economic position and power must be directed towards attaining ever higher living standards for increasingly more people.

It is needless to point out that this social imperative is also in the self-evident interest of businessmen themselves. Continual expansion of product outlets is a necessity, but it cannot be taken for granted as a result of the increase in the number of potential consumers that is provided by the population growth everywhere in the world. It is necessary that potential consumers become actual consumers through providing them with gradually higher levels of real income.

A BUSINESSMAN'S SOCIAL ACCOUNTABILITY

What is our answer to this problem, which is essentially of a social and ethical nature? It seems to me that a businessman aware of his accountability to the various social bodies he belongs to—his enterprise, his city, his state, his country, the free nations —must search for a reply at two levels.

Let us consider the enterprise level. Obviously we speak of sound enterprises, those that are equipped to properly coordinate man's work so as to attain increasing human satisfaction shared by more and more people. This is the precise duty and fundamental function of the leader. He cannot regard his economic power as a means for special privilege or profit in excess of a fair return for his work. The business leader is so placed and is vested with command functions solely to promote progressive improvement and expansion of productive enterprise and job opportunities. In this way he contributes to the material, intellectual, and moral well-being of all those who are affected by his conduct and activities.

Americans in particular know that from their ideological inheritance stems this imperative; all men must work, rich and poor alike. We Europeans have recorded in our constitutions this inalienable right and duty of the citizen to work. And all of us from every country know that no form of well-being can exist and develop without work. I believe, therefore, that the conclusion should be acceptable to each and all of us, that to provide work is our mission and the justification of our leadership, for we could not justify it otherwise.

Let us now consider the community level, extending beyond the boundaries of the enterprise. We realize at once that the evolution of the conditions in which we operate gives us an ever greater power for influencing society. The dimensions of enterprises have grown. Directly and indirectly, we exert impact on the economic and social conditions of ever-larger layers of the population. Frequently, a particular company is the main source of income in a city. In the complex network of our trading and investment activities, we often see our industries furnishing the propulsion for economic growth in entire regions.

Therefore, I believe that today's leader must be conscious of these major opportunities for action, provided to him from the development of such economic activity. And he must be conscious of his greater moral responsibility toward the social entities in which he operates. If he—and we—do not recognize this higher responsibility, I do not see how we can hope to strengthen the leadership of private enterprise.

MORE PEOPLE, MORE RESPONSIBILITY

Between 1960 and 1961 mankind surpassed the three billion mark, and the next generation will probably be four billion or more people everywhere blazing their own trails towards greater human satisfactions. Our technical-industrial structures already seem capable of giving an adequate reply to the demand of larger masses of consumers for mass goods and services. But other fundamentals of our society appear still inadequate to the needs of our times. There are needs that can be satisfied not by industry, but only by education and training for a superior way of life.

In the light of these needs we must revitalize our attitude as leaders. For the ability to give an effective answer—such as must be a leader's answer—to the world of today and tomorrow, depends largely on the wisdom of our decisions. Mankind rests all its needs and aspirations on our work. And it is our responsibility to provide work, to expand and organize it for a more worthwhile life for everyone in the world.

In this is the moral value of our function. If he that holds a leading position in the management of men at work does not feel the ethical imperative to perform above personal privilege and interest in creating new sources of work leading to higher living standards, then he forfeits every justification for his position and his action.

Let us make no mistake about it: either because of us, or in spite of us, social evolution will be achieved. It is now in progress. The Pope's Encyclical "Mater et Magistra" documented it with universal eloquence. Therefore, it is for our imagination, understanding, and responsibility to boldly take the initiative in this evolution. If we do that, we will provide ourselves, and those who watch and judge us, with the only valid demonstration of the enduring efficiency of our free enterprise system.

If properly organized, a business enterprise can give top-level attention to its civic, social, and moral responsiblities in the communities and countries in which it operates. In so doing, it can help us as international managers to influence the attitudes and philosophies of people all over the world and thus help win the battle for men's minds.

THE GROWING IMPORTANCE OF ORGANIZATION

By Joseph A. Grazier *

Ever since a business enterprise required the services of more than one person, we have had organization of some kind. Every successful enterprise has been the result of a conscious or subconscious understanding and application of the principles of good organization. What is relatively new is the fact that it is only since World War II that great emphasis has been placed on the forms and techniques of business organization. Why has this emphasis come so late?

The answer lies in the nature of the task of the chief executive today and the extensive and rapid changes in our business environment.

* President, American Radiator & Standard Sanitary Corporation; director of First National City Bank of New York, Johns-Manville Corporation, and the National Cash Register Company; trustee of the National Industrial Conference Board.

What is the responsibility of the chief executive? Is it not to manage, to lead, his company in such a way that he shapes its future while at the same time he produces a profit so that there can be a future? And is it not the common problem of today's chief executive that he himself no longer can do all of the things for which he is accountable? Is there, in fact, any one person anywhere who, alone, is physically and mentally capable of making all of the management decisions which must be made in any business organization?

In today's business world an enterprise grows—or it dies. There is no middle ground. In considerable measure, this increase in size is forced by the marketing revolution. As the world grows smaller, traditional trade barriers are falling, bringing a greater range of customer desires to be satisfied and an increased number of competitors.

CHANGE—CHANGE—CHANGE

We manufacturers used to make what we wanted, where we wanted, and when we wanted. Now we must design and sell what a great variety of customers want, and we must get the product to them when and where *they* want it. If we do not, our competition certainly will. We used to price quite arbitrarily (often cost plus desired margin); but now we must price each product line in each area in terms of necessary return on investment and risk, and under the constant pressure of competitive prices. We used to enjoy simple product lines and relatively long product life. Now we must face a great increase in the number and variety of products and rapid product obsolescence. Most of us once operated with a few manufacturing points serving homogeneous markets. Now we must produce locally at many points and serve many different markets, or give way to someone who will. Other changes of equal impact result from the explosive growth in science and technology.

The change is also being forced by the impact of larger and more powerful labor unions, with high wage rates, intricate contracts, complex work rules, and myriad benefit plans to negotiate and administer.

Tremendous problems in administration naturally result. There are more people to manage, larger markets to serve, greater competition to combat, more divisions to supervise, more complex relationships to maintain, faster moving technology to keep up with. In marketing, in production, in finance, in research, in development. In every phase of business a greater number of more complex decisions have to be made in less time, in more places, than ever before. There are more and more governmental agencies and departments to deal with—and more and more phases of business which feel the impact of government.

HOW CAN THE CHIEF EXECUTIVE DO HIS JOB?

How will the chief executive do his job in the face of all this? Somehow he must decentralize operations, delegate specific authority, and make skilled counsel available at many points if his enterprise is not to fall of its own weight and inertia. How can he do this without a detailed analysis and structuring of his organization?

For most of us, the highly personalized and centralized form of management will no longer work. It won't work because it concerns itself with a few limited areas to the exclusion of others, and thus restricts the very growth, flexibility, and simultaneous action on many fronts which survival demands. But there is more to it than this. We all know that, given strong leadership and vision, the success or failure of an enterprise is determined mainly by the collective performance of its people.

Any major enterprise represents a vast array of individual skills, knowledge, experience, and *potentially* useful hopes and ambitions. Here are great opportunities or great dangers, depending on how we marshal and use these talents through the concepts and techniques of organization and delegation.

Let us look at these concepts and techniques. There is much more involved than charts and job descriptions. Organization, according to one authority, is "a method of breaking down broad and overwhelming tasks into manageable and pinpointed responsibilities and, at the same time, ensuring coordination of the work."

But it is still more than that. It is a method for recognizing and utilizing human abilities for the accomplishment of specified objectives. Getting the best possible person in each position means better results for the company. Knowing that ability is recognized and utilized is a valuable incentive to employees. Indeed, today the managerial talent and prospects you possess or seek to employ demand the opportunity to grow rapidly. To this end, they insist on clear objectives and a structure that tells them where they stand and what is expected of them. They demand clear-cut vistas of growth, and an assurance of fairness in performance evaluation, in compensation, and in other rewards.

SOUND ORGANIZATION PLUS LEADERSHIP

We can all see one thing clearly—sound organization structure is not a substitute for sound, enduring leadership. The two are inseparable. Leadership has slight chance of success in large enterprises without careful organization, but organization without leadership can become mechanistic and fruitless.

Let us be very careful not to confuse the two. Leadership has to do with personal behavior, with the dynamics of the total managing problem, while organization provides the necessary anatomy of the body social, the mechanics of the total managing problem. We can analyze and treat the total problem only if we understand that we really have two problems: the structure of necessary work on the one hand, and the behavior of the individuals who fill these various positions on the other. We find that we must diagnose and treat these problems separately before we are really able to diagnose and solve the managing problem itself. What then, do we find that the organizing process includes?

It includes a clear definition of objectives.

It includes a careful analysis of the activities and component results that are required to meet these objectives.

It includes full communication of these arrangements to all concerned.

It includes continual and timely follow-up to determine whether the structure is working, and to make adjustments in the structure as needs and objectives change and as failures are indicated.

Again, I stress that organization is subordinate to purpose and that it is separate initially from behavior. Thus, it is a tool for leadership, never a substitute.

Some fear the possibility that after a chief executive gets everything nicely organized, he'll find himself without anything to do but cloud-level planning. This absurd image is a possibility in theory only. But it does point up a fact to be noted. When a chief executive delegates, he does not abdicate. He *does not* organize himself out of control, and he *cannot* organize himself out of accountability.

There is an impression among some that "organization" is just another way of saying "overhead." I contend that in today's business world just the opposite is true. Organization properly planned and used will reduce unproductive cost rather than increase it. When people are assigned in terms of objectives, it is easy to locate those who are contributing to the enterprise. It is not so easy without planned organization.

DANGERS AND PITFALLS

To those to whom this emphasis on effective organization is new, let me point out a few dangers and pitfalls. There are those who believe that a set of textbook principles on organization can be set up and applied to every business in existence. Nothing could be further from the fact! Objectives will vary, and organizations must vary accordingly.

We know that it is possible to build a substantial enterprise, productive of adequate return on investment, with a structure as simple as that of the amoeba. There are successful enterprises with a man who acts as chief executive, chief financial officer, chief marketing strategist, labor relations man, public relations expert, head of manufacturing, and chief of research. If this can be done with adequate profit today and adequate provision for longer-range growth and survival, then that is unquestionably the right kind of organization structure for that business. But I believe that there are distinct limitations to this concept and that the odds will be heavily against growth and survival in today's rapidly changing conditions.

In our company we have had to fight against too much precision in organization work. It is easy to become fascinated with the idea of providing for every contingency. This not only cannot be done, but the attempt can be harmful. If you confine an executive too precisely, you will rob him of his vigor and his initiative—and his value to you. Organizational concepts and practices must allow flexibility for constant revision and adaptation to meet changing needs and conditions and the differences in the natures of the men—even the occasional nonconformist— who fill the structural positions. In a few instances we committed the crime of overorganization, creating more positions and providing more people than the work required or could support. When this occurs, prompt diagnosis and prompt and radical surgery are the only cures.

GETTING MAXIMUM VALUE FROM ORGANIZATION

Getting maximum value from organization work requires more than just a few senior managers who understand it and know what they are doing. It requires many managers all the way through the company who understand and accept the managing and organizing concepts chosen as appropriate to the enterprise. We found that a manager might accept for himself the benefits of good organization, but fail to understand how those benefits reach him. He could not, therefore, pass on a proper concept and understanding to his subordinates, an important part of executive development.

Certainly, adequate controls and follow-up are essential to keep every element of the company oriented to established objectives and operating in accordance with corporate policy. It is fortunate that, for the most part, we made provision for adequate controls, supervision, and follow-up; but, unfortunately, the managers were not always trained to use them fully, and they did not always take the indicated corrective action. This is a constant struggle.

Having achieved sound organization, have we merely offset

the administrative problems imposed by size, by the marketing revolution, by the growth of science and technology, and by the changing nature of our work force? Or have we found other values as well? Our experience and our observations suggest that there are, indeed, substantial values beyond these to be gained.

We find that this concept of organization has improved mental discipline throughout our company. Sharp attention to every function was required in order for us to clarify our goals. Attention of this kind leads to a tough-minded, objective appraisal of every operation—and it is training our executives to approach other problems with the same intellectual vigor. It guards against the neglect of situations which may develop into crises if left to themselves, but it also prevents the overmanagement of obvious crises. And it tends to expose and reduce the jealousies and common frictions resulting from ordinary human frailties.

We find we are receiving more productive effort from our key people. Their effort has been sharply focused on their defined responsibilities. Wasteful duplication of effort and unproductive conflict between functions have been cut down. Communications have been simplified and made more effective. A common understanding of the goals of the enterprise is helping executives to take intelligent action for the common good more quickly and more surely.

We are finding that improvement in management techniques is being speeded. Organization work exposes and puts the spotlight on existing problems in planning and in measuring operations. Isolating problems almost automatically speeds the discovery of solutions.

We are finding that the development of managerial resources for the future is being aided. Sound organization provides the framework and the knowledge for a realistic approach to manpower planning at all levels and leads smoothly into sound development activity.

APPLICATION IS UNIVERSAL

Does this situation and experience, perhaps, apply only to my company, American-Standard? I doubt it. Are circumstances greatly different in other companies—or even in other countries? I doubt it. Are the values to be gained from sound organization available only to industry of the United States? I doubt it. Does the degree of industrialization of a country determine reaction to organization? I doubt that, too.

Can any executive in Europe, for example, any longer think only in terms of his own market? What about the actions of his competitors in other countries? Can an enterprise in any industrialized area of the world survive for long by simply attempting to maintain the status quo? Are industrialists in the Western world basically different from those elsewhere? Is not the drive for personal growth and well-being and self-determination just as forceful in newly industrialized countries?

Are we, perhaps, seeing that no area of the world is immune to the influences and the developments affecting the way we must manage if we are truly to lead? Might it not be that the differences from one country to another in these matters may be more a question of *when* than whether?

I believe that there is a common world-wide pattern to the developments that have given rise to the usefulness of this management tool—organization. If this is so, I submit that even the most capable among us cannot lead much longer without careful and planned attention to professional management and, particularly, to the organization aspect of it without which all the rest is futile. I suggest even further that skill in professional management is the next major frontier of business competition, and that that management which leads in this work will enjoy a tremendous advantage.

If properly organized, a business enterprise can give top-level attention to its civic, social, and moral responsibilities in the communities and countries in which it operates. In so doing, it can help us as international managers to influence the attitudes and philosophies of people all over the world and thus help win the battle for men's minds.

The easy, quick, and soft way of developing executives too often results in failure. It is the difficult and challenging tasks that develop the fine inherent qualities in the men who are genuine executive material with the right kind of character, ability, and vitality. These are the tasks that reveal those who are incapable and weak, but who may possess an ingratiating manner.

DEVELOPING HIGH-LEVEL LEADERS

By Thomas J. Bata *

It gives me a great deal of personal pleasure to see young men, often from humble circumstances, rising on merit alone from obscure positions to places of high responsibility and then making a brilliant success of their work.

Our organization has an almost unique opportunity for experimenting, and as a result has its share of success and also its full share of failures in its efforts to develop high-level personnel. The success we have had is partly due to the way in which we are organized, and I must tell you something of that.

The structure of the Bata organization is decentralized. Each individual operating company, with its own board of directors and management, is dedicated to work in the interests of its own country and community. Research, exchange of ideas, and other

* President, Bata Limited, Canada, management center for the Bata Shoe organization. He is also chairman, president or director of a number of companies associated with Bata Shoe. Mr. Bata is a director of the American Management Association.

267

common services are provided by service companies, frequent conferences, and a relatively small staff.

We have 64 factories, and with distributing organizations we are active in 73 countries of the free world. We make over 130 million pairs of shoes a year, operate almost 4,000 of our own retail stores, and now have close to 60,000 people of many nationalities, races, and religions associated with us.

A CHIEF EXECUTIVE'S RESPONSIBILITY

Within the framework of the general concept of the business, I consider that the "development of high-level personnel and the appointment of the right people to the right top places is my principal preoccupation." For the immediate future there are only expenses and difficulties involved in the development of high-level personnel for the longer-term future, and benefits or calamities show up only much later. It is my opinion, therefore, that it is the chief executive of any large organization who must personally take a keen interest in this program and keep up the interest of his executives all the way down the line.

I wish I could report that we have solved the problem of developing high-level personnel. I cannot, and I imagine that this is one of the subjects on which the words "Project Completed" will never be written. It is a subject that is constantly evolving, and one that requires us to keep on learning new concepts and skills. This is probably the reason why it is also so fascinating.

The Conference Board has recently published a most interesting study on this very subject. It includes a comprehensive list of the many methods used to appraise people and give them further management training. In one or another of our companies, we use every one of the methods described. I might add that every one of the methods in use has been successful in some respects. However, one thing is most important in any systematic method of appraisal and personnel development—it creates an awareness of the problem in the minds of the senior executives, directs their thinking, and gives the junior people greater confidence that their hard work, imagination, and success will not pass unnoticed by those who have the power to make promotions.

To my mind, the details of any system of management development are less important; the important thing is to have *some* system in proper operation, receiving frequent attention from the head of the firm himself. But let me be more specific on some of the areas of management development and our experiences with them.

DELEGATION

It is through having specific responsibility and an opportunity of making decisions that the best and most-rapid development of higher personnel occurs. In this respect, a decentralized operation such as ours has many advantages. We have no less than 73 people making the most important management decisions all the time. In addition, those in direct contact with them see them at work, making such decisions, and consulting on problems. They see them thinking of how to seek out and grasp business opportunities. They, too, tend to see the over-all picture, and their horizon grows. This kind of observation begins in the third and fourth echelons, where people are usually rather far removed from both specific responsibility and from the opportunity to make real decisions on their own.

Companies that are centralized in one geographical location face the natural tendency of having most important decisions constantly channeled back to the most senior people available. In order to assure the proper development of higher personnel through the all-important experience of decision making, it becomes necessary to decentralize internally. This step is very difficult to take and is a condition that is even more difficult to maintain.

PRINCIPLES OF PROMOTION

We operate on the principle of promotion from within. All our senior executives are men who have spent the major part of their careers in our organization. There are many factors to be weighed when promotions are made. To complicate matters, sentiment often also becomes involved. Whatever one does, somebody is going to feel hurt. However, we have found that if an appointment is well made on merit, the problems of the hurt feelings dissolve more rapidly, and at the same time everyone benefits, for the capable man brings the whole enterprise or department to a greater prosperity that all can enjoy. At the same time, the capable younger newcomers have been carefully observing the selection process in action, drawing their own conclusions from the viewpoint of their own future careers.

With us, promotion from within can take on a very wide scope indeed, and I would like to see in operation a true—that is, world-wide—promotional system. We have no preferred nationality, and it would be ideal if selection could indeed be on a world-wide basis for at least every executive position. It is unfortunate that difficulties of language, local restrictions, and traditions of family life still make this ideal unattainable. Nevertheless, we already have companies where the ten top executives are each of a different nationality or racial origin, and where harmony and cooperation are excellent.

There have been promotions in Bata of Indians to Canada, of Canadians to India, Pakistanis to the Congo, Nigerians to England, Dutchmen to Bolivia, Chileans to Mexico, Peruvians to Brazil—assuring a more rapid and merit-based movement. I am confident that as communications and understanding improve, so will the opportunities of international upward movement of higher personnel—all to the benefit of the people concerned and of the enterprises in which they work.

RECRUITMENT

To be able to assure the development of people inside an organization, one must first make certain that enough of the right kind of people are coming in. Many wonderful books have been written on the types of people who are desirable and about recruiting, testing, and selecting them. I find it extremely difficult to generalize, for conditions vary so much from country to country. My American and British friends know how hard it is to get first-class university graduates. On the other hand, our Indian company advertised recently for one of their training programs and received over 15,000 applications from such men. Some 500 applicants were interviewed, and 21 were engaged.

In most parts of the world, more and more young men with brainpower and ambition are able to continue their studies even though their parents may be poor. Thus, on the one hand, the educational system is playing a greater part in preparing young people for responsible positions; on the other hand, the chances of finding people of executive potential amongst the manual workers and office boys seem to be diminishing. But it would be a great mistake to look for future business leaders only among university graduates. The often hidden or sleeping potentials that can be awakened in a man with modest education should not be underestimated, and such men should be given opportunities to fill in their educational gaps even at a later stage in life. My recommendation would be to have a carefully developed system of recruitment of people for all types of employment, for one never knows from what seed that beautiful plant of executive ability and business acumen will develop.

DEVELOPMENT THROUGH RESPONSIBILITY

Our best experience in developing the talents of potentially sound people has been in giving them specific responsibility as early as possible. It has also helped when this task was as far away from the company's head office as possible.

A young man of 25, after some years of work in positions such as salesman and then merchandiser, is sent to Dahomey on the West Coast of Africa to open ten shoe stores or to the Congo to manage a district with 15 stores and a wholesale operation. If he succeeds, he is almost ready, after some management course, to run a good-sized enterprise on his own. We have done this on many occasions with a considerable degree of success.

My only regret is that even we do not have enough openings that give young men opportunities for independent thought and action. It fills me with sorrow to think how many young men of potential have atrophied in routine positions either because no openings existed at the right time, or because through inadequate appraisal methods some short-sighted executive had been able to keep a young man too long on routine and uninspiring tasks.

TALENT INVENTORY

This means that a constant inventory of talent needs to be maintained, and the potentially strong seedlings well watered and well fertilized. One of the decisions to be made is what kind of man deserves such special attention. Here I would like to refer you to a book by Crawford Greenewalt, "The Uncommon Man," which so well describes how people's unsuspected qualities blossom if given the right kind of stimulus, usually through promotion to a position of responsibility.

I believe also that general experience shows that the easy, quick, and soft way of developing executives too often results in failure. It is the difficult and challenging tasks that develop the fine inherent qualities in the men who are genuine executive material with the right kind of character, ability, and vitality. These are the tasks that reveal those who are incapable and weak, but who may possess an ingratiating manner.

We try to find the challenging tasks for those we believe to be the right young men. We create opportunities for self-improvement by organizing internal courses and by sponsoring attendance at external courses and conferences.

In Holland, France, England, and Chile, we operate, in cooperation with the local educational authorities, residential colleges giving a three-year course. In these we try to combine work with continuing education. The students are successful secondary school graduates and our aim is to broaden their education while they are acquiring a knowledge of practical work and even, in some instances, holding positions of gradually increasing responsibility. As time goes on, such graduates may be sent to other outside institutions, and several have finally attended even the Harvard Advanced Management Program.

Knowledge of the business is, in my mind, only a part of the requirement of a good executive today. He needs a sound personal business philosophy and a code of ethics. This can be acquired primarily as a result of the example of his seniors.

NEW ROLES FOR BUSINESS AND ITS EXECUTIVES

Today a business enterprise has responsibilities to its community, its nation, and indeed to all of mankind. This responsibility can be discharged only if the executives have developed a close attachment to the enterprise in which they work and consider their association of a permanent nature and are willing to attune their efforts to the company's policies, or to influence the company to modify its policies to conform more to their own businesslike and ethical thinking. Business is faced not only with normal competition but also with competition of a political nature. This again consists of competition not only from merchandising by state enterprises operating for political ends, but also of political competition that is directed toward the elimination of business and free enterprise. Thus the business and industrial community needs a strong, positive philosophy of service, and the future executives need an inspired example of leadership.

*The day has long since gone when a busi-
nessman can limit his thinking to the problems peculiar to the enterprise with which
he is associated. He has now a broader stage
for his activities, a greater challenge against
which to exercise his intellect. His duty to
himself, to his business, and to his nation
demands that he think about his country's
problems in the broadest possible terms. He
can and must participate as a willing and
effective partner in the leadership of his
country.*

NEW RESPONSIBILITIES

By Crawford H. Greenewalt *

Within the span of a single century, the agrarian economy that
once prevailed in all nations has been superseded in the more
advanced countries by a system relying primarily upon industry.
We have, in fact, a term which we apply to those nations in
which industry has not become well established: we call them
the undeveloped areas. It is perfectly clear that the strength and
vitality of any country in the world today—its prosperity, its security, and its general welfare—are in direct proportion to the
strength and vitality of its industrial establishment.

A century ago the production of food was the preoccupation
of the entire community. Of the population at large, nine out of
ten adult males of all ages, plus a substantial share of all children
able to walk, were engaged in agriculture, aided at harvest time

* President, E. I. du Pont de Nemours & Co.; member, President's Commission on National Goals, President's Committee on Higher Education;
Business Council. (Mr. Greenewalt was unable to attend. His address was read
by Lammot du Pont Copeland, vice president, executive committee, E. I.
du Pont de Nemours & Co.)

by a large proportion of the feminine contingent. All other community needs had to be met by the small number who could be spared from the demanding task of meeting the bare necessities of life.

There was little exchange of services as we know that process today. Very frequently each man had to be his own cobbler, his own blacksmith, and his own barber. The medical, legal, educational, and spiritual needs were left to a handful of individuals who were probably the only educated persons in the community.

In striking contrast, an examination of our modern societies reveals that our needs for food can be met by a small fraction of our population. Perhaps the most significant milestone in modern history was the day, not long in the past, when the number of persons engaged in business first exceeded those engaged in agriculture.

Today perhaps four out of five members of the work force in our more modern societies are directly engaged in one way or another in industrial activity. Indeed, all citizens are influenced by the health and prosperity of our business system, either as consumers, stockholders, or as suppliers of services to industrial employees.

BUSINESS PROGRESS CONCERNS EVERYONE

For it is the business and industrial wherewithal that furnishes to every branch of society the means to achieve its ends. It is the state of business and industrial health that determines whether we shall have high living standards or low, and when the vigor of the business system is impaired, the unpleasant results become epidemic throughout the community. Nor can any element of society find immunity: it is business progress that nourishes both lawyer and client, doctor and patient, buyer and seller, the jailer and the jailed.

Business and industry are sometimes challenged for representing materialistic values that are regarded as incompatible with the loftier aims of mankind. Such viewpoints are of course illusions. The fact is that social progress is impossible without the enabling reality which is provided by industrial advance. Indifference to or acceptance of human suffering is the by-product of want, not of plenty. It is the Eskimo, whose affluence is the chance blessing of wind and weather, who condemns his aging parent to death on the ice; it is in the jungle that human life has its lowest value.

Modern societies set higher goals and the development of our business institutions, many of them very large, is the direct outgrowth of our aspirations. As needs have become more complex, larger and larger organizations have become necessary to cope with the problems—technical and financial—involved in present-day production. And an ever-larger share of the total economy has come to rest on the foundation stones of these organizations.

A century ago, when organizational needs were much simpler, any given business institution might have disappeared from the scene without undue effects upon others. Today, the failure of some large unit within the business sphere would have disastrous repercussions to the economy as a whole, for modern society is not made up of isolated and independent elements; it is, rather, a tightly interwoven and integrated network, in which the weakness of any part will swiftly be communicated to the whole.

A NEW OBLIGATION—A NEW OPPORTUNITY

Clearly, businessmen and the industries over which they preside have come to provide the foundation for national progress and national prosperity. It is in these circumstances that business leadership finds a new obligation and a new opportunity.

The pattern for discharging this responsibility may be found, I think, within the workings of our own organizations. As executives, we know that we can be effective only as we can reconcile, consolidate, and compromise the various talents and viewpoints under our direction to the end that each makes the largest possible contribution to the business. So if we can consider our organizations, for the moment, as small models of society in general, we can see that the greatest strength and efficiency can be attained in much the same way—by seeing to it that each of the many elements comprising our modern society contributes effectively to the nation's social and political progress.

It is a fundamental in the philosophy of any democratic society that all groups and all individuals participate in its councils, for no institution can long endure if the general franchise is assumed by any single group to the exclusion of others. It follows then that business leadership everywhere must take an active and constructive position toward the functioning of society as a whole. This is at once a responsibility and an opportunity.

All too often, I am afraid, we in the business community have been remiss in this respect. In our attitude toward government, for example, we have been inclined to take a negative position, characterized more by opposition to social change than by a thoughtful and cooperative consideration of broad national problems. Too often have business people complained about what "those fellows" in Washington, in Paris, in Bonn, or in Tokyo were doing to them, rather than concerning themselves with whether what was being done was right—and making certain that "those fellows," in Washington, in Paris, in Bonn, or in Tokyo, had enough information on which to base a sound conclusion.

REPRESENTATION IS NOT ENOUGH

For too long a time, too, I fear that business leadership has permitted itself to be "represented," either through its various associations or by third parties. Neither method, in my opinion, is adequate. The responsibilities of the general welfare, like the responsibilities of parenthood, cannot safely be delegated to others. Literature from Julius Caesar to Miles Standish is replete with warnings about the uncomfortable consequences of trying to resolve our obligations by emissary.

If the balance is to be preserved in our free societies, business leadership must lend the full weight of its experience and its resources to the solution of national problems. If it does not accept the obligation, it loses its right to protest if its interests are disregarded.

One of the most regrettable of modern tendencies, I think, has been the formation of mutually exclusive groups among those concerned with business and those concerned with government, dealing with each other at arm's length. If the growth of the corporation has bred a professional class of business managers, the growth of government seems to be breeding a professional class of administrators. All too often, I am afraid, we have seen the two arrayed one against the other in attitudes of mutual distrust and suspicion. Even more unfortunately, we have observed on either side a sublime indifference to the attitudes, viewpoints, and problems of the other.

There was perhaps a time when such a division was natural. Political leaders, in this country at least, have come traditionally from the ranks of the professions, and in past years politics at the national level, at least, represented a substantial share of our educated people.

Today, in sharp contrast, both business and government draw their leaders from the same pool of talent, and the educational backgrounds of the two, allowing for scientific specialization, are not dissimilar. Men who enter the business field are not conspicuously different, by temperament, by inclination, or by motivation, from those who engage in any of the professions, including government.

THERE SHOULD BE NO GULF

It is therefore absurd that any gulf should develop with business and government on opposite sides. Business leadership has special contributions to make, based on its broad experience in human relationships. I think the time has come for us to come forth, to speak up, and to seek not the basis of contention but the basis of common purpose. And common purpose can be found most readily in common understanding.

In seeking this mutual area of comprehension, business and businessmen need to define their responsibilities in a broader dimension. They cannot stand aloof or indifferent to the public need in the serene conviction that the obligation for this service lies elsewhere. It is insufficient to conclude that it is the job of the public official to officiate and the job of the businessman to do business. The fact is that each can be effective only to the extent that he understands the role of the other.

A BROADER PERSPECTIVE AND DUTY

The individual business leader may find it difficult to recognize the connection between his own concerns and the broader purposes of society. He is trained to think in terms of the specific and to allow the general to take its own course. I suggest that all of us who qualify as business leaders should let our vision command a broader perspective of the world in which we live—a world in which private decisions can have important public consequences, and public decisions may have private consequences of catastrophic importance.

This responsibility must be reflected in the example we give to our own businesses and to society generally. I think there can be no question about the fact that ethical standards in the business world must be counted an important factor in the attainment of popular approval. Lapses from grace when laid at the doorstep of a business institution cannot fail to do damage to the entire business structure. Further, with business occupying such an important place in the national effort of all countries, the entire nation suffers when some breach of ethics is revealed. Such matters are no longer private in either their application or their effect. They become a stain on the flag of one's own nation, an embarrassment to its friends, an aid and comfort to its enemies.

The thesis I have tried to develop here is in reality very simple and very obvious. Perhaps I can summarize it in this way:

Any nation's prosperity is directly related to the health, vigor, and vitality of its industrial establishment. The growth in size and complexity of industrial units has drawn to positions of business leadership men of highest competence and intellectual capacity. Hence political thought in a nation's governmental councils is clearly inadequate if it does not embrace and include a business viewpoint in the decision-making process.

The responsibility of business leadership is clear. The day has long since gone when a businessman can limit his thinking to the problems peculiar to the enterprise with which he is associated. He has now a broader stage for his activities, a greater challenge against which to exercise his intellect. His duty to himself, to his business, and to his nation demands that he think about his country's problems in the broadest possible terms. He can and must participate as a willing and effective partner in the leadership of his country.

Business leadership will recognize that decision-making is a privilege which can be exercised only to the extent that it promotes the ends of all society. If the responsibilities are not discharged to the public satisfaction, we may be sure that the privilege will be withdrawn.

There is much encouragement in the fact that business has become increasingly aware of its enlarged horizons. This gathering is in itself a recognition of new purposes. The times afford us an obligation and an opportunity. I am sure that both can be met with honor, with satisfaction, and with the pride that goes with solid achievement.

1. *Business and Public Policy*

Because businessmen and industrialists in the developing countries have not given much attention to our public relations, we are misunderstood. Some overzealous critics even accuse us of being "enemies of the people." And it is not only the businessmen of the developing countries who have failed to promote good public relations. In the well-developed and economically advanced countries their record in this respect is no better.

BUSINESS: ENEMY OR CITIZEN?

By Mohamed Aly Rangoonwala *

At a reception in a Far Eastern country a few months ago I got into discussion with a prominent local newspaperman about the high level of prices in that country. While discussing the issue I explained to him that as production increased, the prices would automatically come down.

He seemed, however, to have very definite views on the subject and said: "The businessmen will never behave. They are enemies of the people."

This was not the first time I had heard businessmen accused of some crime or the other. But his remarks left a deep impression upon me. I have often recalled that discussion and reflected on the role of the business community in the affairs of nations, the

* Chairman, Burma Oil Mills, Pakistan; former president, the Pakistan National Committee; chairman of Mohamed Aly & Co., Dodge & Seymour Industries, Frontier Industries, and others; member of the Advisory Committee to the Ministry of Commerce (1957–60), Council of Industries, Panel on Credit Facilities & Fiscal Concession, Ministry of Industries, and Taxation Enquiry Committee, Government of Pakistan; director in several companies.

281

contributions it has made toward the development of national economies, and its alleged evils.

Here was an educated and intelligent man who, by virtue of the demands of his profession, was required to have a proper appreciation of the events of national and international life. And yet he charges that businessmen are enemies of the people. The significance of his remark lies in the fact that this journalist-friend, probably unconsciously and without realizing its serious implications, had divided the country's people in two distinct groups—the businessmen and the people. And having made that distinction, he asserted that the businessmen were the enemies of the people.

This was not a stray remark heard at a party in a far-flung city of the Far East. I am sure that at some time or other similar statements have been made in different countries and different climates. Could there be anything more disastrous, from our viewpoint, than such remarks which, while separating the businessman from the people, actually represent him as being opposed to the welfare of the people? I think this remark is typical of a general feeling that we, the members of the business and industrial communities, have generated either through our actions or lack of them.

WHY BUSINESS IS MISUNDERSTOOD

The chief reason for such an impression is that private enterprise has made little effort to play its proper role in shaping public opinion and in educating the people about the contributions of private enterprise in the affairs of nations. We have been too busy planning new business ventures and preparing the blueprints of new mills and factories. While doing this we have not realized that earning the understanding of our fellow-nationals is as important as getting big contracts, licenses, or securing the necessary capital for our ventures. It may even be more important.

The contributions of private enterprise to the economic development of the world cannot be denied. In the developing countries, where businessmen and industrialists are constantly under fire, sometimes for circumstances and developments beyond their control, private enterprise can feel proud of its contribution to economic development. But because we have not given much attention to our public relations, we are misunderstood. As a result some overzealous critics, like my journalist-friend, accuse us of being "enemies of the people." And it is not only the businessmen of the developing countries who have failed in their duty to promote good public relations. In the well-developed and economically advanced countries their record in this respect is no better.

On several occasions I have discussed American economic aid to foreign countries with businessmen in the United States. These friends tell me that they and others in America are quite conscious of the fact that American aid funds in many cases have not been properly utilized. They also seem to be aware that certain countries that have managed to secure aid through blackmail and constant use of unholy pressures have been using American economic aid for aggressive preparations against other countries that are allies of the United States. They are convinced that the aid funds would have been better utilized if private enterprise had been invited to participate actively in the programs. Yet these people say they cannot do anything about it. It appears that private enterprise in America has not been successful in convincing the country's public about its viewpoint. If this is true in America, the situation in other countries can well be imagined.

BETTER PUBLIC RELATIONS NEEDED

The promotion of public relations, therefore, appears to me to be a very important and vital need to which private enterprise in various countries will do well to devote its attention. We owe it not only to ourselves, but also to the people at large, to put into motion mechanisms that will keep the people properly informed about the role of private enterprise. This function can be taken up at the international level by such organizations as the International Chamber of Commerce, at national levels by the country's trade and industrial chambers and associations, and even by individual businessmen and industrialists. I have no doubt that in this task, cooperation will come from the sponsors of this conference—the National Industrial Conference Board and Stanford Research Institute. Such public relations work is necessary to make the people aware of the responsibilities as well as privileges of the businessmen and industrialists. It will also help explain to the public the role that private enterprise plays and the contribution that it makes to the programs of national development. Such a close liaison with the public will help us gain their understanding and sympathy. With this public support, private enterprise will be able to discuss issues and problems with governments from a stronger position.

BETTER PUBLIC RELATIONS PLUS ACTION

But more public relations will not be enough to build good will for private enterprise. Public relations efforts must be backed by solid actions to show that private enterprise is interested not only in making profits from economic ventures but also in nation-building activities. To prove that we are interested in making our contribution to the social welfare of the nation a very wide field of action is open to us. There is the whole range of activity in education, health, and development of healthy traditions of cultural, social, and political life. By participating in these activities and by making our contribution toward their promotion, we can prove that we are an important and proud section of the population and are far from being "enemies of the people."

Unfortunately, not much attention is yet being paid by businessmen and industrialists to these fields. True, there are quite a few who can feel justly proud of their contributions, but the number of such enterprising and farsighted people is small. The need for such activity has yet to receive general recognition, especially in the developing countries. The sooner the need for it is realized, the better it will be for the future of private enterprise in the world.

Besides the contribution that private enterprise may make in various social fields, attention must also be paid to certain matters within trade and industry. For instance, we must always endeavor to improve the quality and standard of our products, keep their prices at a reasonable level, take steps to meet all reasonable demands of the workers, and provide them with the necessary amenities. Such measures, though having an indirect impact, will also help to raise the prestige of private enterprise and create good will among the public.

GOVERNMENT–BUSINESS COOPERATION

In any free society the roles of government and the business community are complementary, and it is essential that there should be understanding and cooperation between the two. No government, however strong it may be, is capable alone of executing all the programs for a country's development. The assistance and cooperation of the business community is essential in the successful implementation of any programs of development—economic, social, or cultural. Similarly, businessmen cannot prosper without support and understanding from both government and the public.

In many countries there are joint bodies of government and business where problems of common interest are discussed. National policies are formulated, altered, and revised in the light of these discussions. It will contribute to a greater understanding between the government and business if the scope of such joint discussions and consultations could be expanded and enlarged. Their value and ultimate impact will be enhanced if representatives of the general public also participate. Their association will help them to consider themselves as a part of the machinery deciding public policies. In Pakistan, Advisory Councils for different fields of industry and business have been formed. Even the President of Pakistan has been having regular meetings with the leaders of business and industry. Through these measures some effective steps have been taken to stabilize the country's economy.

WHAT NEEDS TO BE DONE

I believe that if the business community wants to be secure it should make every effort to get its members elected to legislatures and other elected bodies in the country. I consider this necessary, because the presence of our representatives in the legislative bodies will ensure a proper presentation of our views. Otherwise our interests and those of our nations will suffer by default. It is essential that we should consider what we must do to achieve our objectives of economic development and social welfare.

Unity in our ranks is a prerequisite. It is unfortunate that in most of the countries this unity does not exist, and the business and industrial community has yet to travel a long way toward the goal of international unity and international cooperation. All efforts should be directed toward the healthy organization of chambers of trade and industry in various countries of the world, toward the achievement of international unity and cooperation among members of world trade and industry, and toward the preparation of a united front on issues affecting private enterprise.

We should prepare a Code of Ethics. This Code should determine and govern the actions and behavior of private enterprise in relation to the public it aims to serve. We have many shortcomings, and we have quite a few irresponsible elements in our ranks. We shall have to do something about the situation if we desire to achieve the moral standards that are inherent in the role assigned to us in the affairs of the world.

Today we are faced with a challenge of the gravest character. Private enterprise will undoubtedly be destroyed unless we reassess our position, realize our shortcomings, take stock of our resources, and prepare to meet the task of serving humanity. We claim to serve humanity in the same way as any social worker or devoted and honest politician will. But unless we reorientate our outlook and use our intelligence, experience, know-how and resources toward this goal, we will forfeit the right to be respected members of society.

In the developing countries, private enterprise is prepared to do its best in making this world a better place to live in. We will not lag behind in any efforts to improve the condition of mankind. Our cooperation and our willingness are there. We hope that our "elders"—the developed countries of the free world—will give us the desired leadership.

The free enterprise system is a prerequisite for real political freedom. It is by no mere chance that this system has developed simultaneously with political democracy. Democracy and free enterprise are two different aspects of a single social status, just as a planned economy and bureaucratic dictatorship are also two aspects of a different single status.

PRESERVING THE FREE ENTERPRISE CONCEPT

By Hans Hohn *

The concern of this conference, in my opinion, is not merely to point out where we stand today but, far more important, to proclaim in a convincing manner the role that free enterprise must play in the future.

Today we find that free enterprise is under constant pressure, and its supporters are in a posture of perpetual defense against the advocates of government intervention, socialism, nationalization, tariff barriers, trade restrictions, and so on.

Our minds and efforts should be devoted to securing such rec-

* Member of the governing board, Osterreichische Stickstoffwerke; chairman of Austro-Chematom Kernbrennstoff; member of the executive committee of Reaktor Interessengemeinschaft and a board member of Danubia Petrochemie, Schmidtstahlwerke, and Oberosterreichesche Ferngas. Dr. Hohn, professor at the Technical University of Vienna, is president of the Society for Natural Science and Technology, a councillor of the Federal Chamber of Commerce, Industrial Section, and a member of the board of the Federation of Austrian Industrialists, and of the Society for Industrial Chemistry. His paper was read by Dr. Mautner von Markof, president of Brauerei Schwechat (Austria).

ognition of free enterprise in the world as is necessary to lead it forth again from its defensive position. To that end, it is necessary that we who proclaim ourselves convinced disciples of free enterprise shall give it that recognition which it deserves. Unfortunately, free enterprise has, as a consequence of the terrible devastation and dire results of World War II, lost for the time being its power to convince and to gain the confidence of the people. This confidence must be restored. It is not only the institution of free enterprise that must be given new recognition, but the conviction must again be developed that *only* free enterprise can release the forces necessary to avert the threat of dictatorship in the world.

WE MUST BE CONVINCING

The concept must be a most convincing one. It must be convincing for those people who are today wavering, and wondering whether, in view of the economic offensive of the East, the West should also strive for a planned economy. They overlook the fact that in the free economy the *Market* achieves a plan that even the boldest economic planner doesn't dream of. While there are certainly many people who are convinced of the importance of free enterprise, it is nevertheless worthwhile, in my opinion, also to stir them up, to direct their attention to the importance of preserving and extending free enterprise, and to make them realize the urgency of working and fighting for it.

Let me go further and challenge each one of us to give some thought to what he has done up to now to preserve the values of free enterprise, and to obtain for it the respect that is its due. Shouldn't many of us consider whether it would not be better to battle it out with competitors in the market than it would be to call upon government for help and have the battle decided in our favor by protectionist means?

This, of course, requires courage and a readiness to sacrifice and accept risks. But our forefathers also showed courage when they left Europe and opened up a new continent—America. We are going to need this same courage in opening up the newly developing regions of the world. The market is the best guiding mechanism, and cannot be replaced by even the most cleverly devised economic plan.

In political discussion the most obvious and understandable planning of any business or trade policy is often mistaken for the planning of a managed economy. Every one of us has had to establish in advance, and with the utmost care, his business policy. Here in the U. S., especially, long-range planning of company policies has reached a point that can hardly be surpassed. This takes place, however, always under the assumption that the market decides which products will be sold. It is exactly here that the dilemma of the planned economies of the East is gradually becoming apparent.

PLANNED ECONOMIES FAIL THE CONSUMER

So long as the East was building up and expanding an almost exclusively capital-goods industry, the planned economy system functioned after a fashion. During the last few years, however, the consumption-oriented branches of the economy there have been given somewhat more of a chance to develop than heretofore. And now the planned economy is breaking down. It is too unwieldy. It is having very limited success in effecting a rise in living standards.

The planned economy countries are now trying—I refer here to Yugoslavia as an example—to introduce the market in some form or other into their system as a regulating device. However, and I believe the audience concurs in my opinion, there is no substitute for the market and, moreover, no possibility of building it into a planned economy system.

The market chooses. It represents an automatic performance control on every enterprise, and passes judgment on whether the decisions of the enterpriser were right or not. The market presumes freedom of decision and independence of the individual enterpriser. But these are not compatible with a planned economy system. It is characteristic of the planned economy system that the free enterpriser is replaced by a planning official.

Free enterprise is the best system for a highly developed consumption-oriented economy. It has the highest degree of efficiency and creates the highest living standards. Like every system, it has its shortcomings. It tends to encourage a practical materialism, for example. It misleads us, therefore, into thinking largely in terms of money and property values. I have no doubt, however, that we will succeed in overcoming these and other defects of our system. We must simply want seriously and consciously to do so. I would remind you that we have already succeeded on the whole in mastering the susceptibility of our system to economic crises. From the standpoint of both economic theory and economic practice, we are in a position to avoid major crises. If we do not always succeed, it is because large groups of people are not always ready to accept the consequences of the acquired knowledge. It is for this very reason that we must rise to the challenge of improving our already good system even more. But the mere willingness to do so is not enough.

COMPETITION MUST BE SAFEGUARDED AND EXTENDED

For this, the following is also required: We know that free competition provides a stimulus to efficiency, a stimulus that is lacking in the planned economy system. Therefore, if we wish to preserve and extend our superiority, we must try by every means possible to preserve this free competition. This effort cannot be restricted to the individual national economies. It is even more necessary to bring about a real and effective international competition, and to remove all obstacles that stand in the way of this.

I have said that the free enterprise system is economically and technically the best system for a highly developed, consumption-oriented economy. But it is also politically the best system. This is the fact that we should, distinctly and emphatically, call to the attention of the whole world, over and over again. Freedom of decision and independence of the individual enterprise, which are integral parts of our system, bring about an extensive decentralization of economic power. This means that our system is so constructed as to make bureaucratic concentration of economic power difficult, if not impossible. On the contrary, bureaucratic centralization of economic power is inescapably bound up with the planned economy system.

DEMOCRACY AND FREE ENTERPRISE A SINGLE CONCEPT

From the identity of economic and political power, it can be concluded that the free enterprise system is a prerequisite for real political freedom. It is by no mere chance that this system has developed simultaneously with political democracy. Democracy and free enterprise are two different aspects of a single social status, just as a planned economy and bureaucratic dictatorship are also two aspects of a different single status.

This circumstance, to my mind irrefutable and convincing, is hidden under an abundance of slogans and emotions. We should commit all our energies and influence to help bring about an awakening of this point of view in our own countries, in the still-developing nations and, last but not least, even behind the Iron Curtain.

I attach special significance to this point, perhaps because everywhere in Europe we can observe a sort of "cold socialization" taking place. Almost imperceptibly in the various countries the regulatory influence of the market is being replaced by government intervention. The economic power of the state is constantly increasing.

At the same time, regard for the moral and political values of personal independence and self-sufficiency, as well as for private property, is declining more and more. The government is charged with more and more responsibility and resources, and the individual becomes more and more a social dependent, a minor, and, in the end, a being unfit for freedom. I do not mean to say that this is a situation already reached, but rather a tendency that is clearly discernible.

We should regard this tendency as a serious danger. It is useless to talk about freedom if one is not determined, at the decisive point, to accept the consequences of his conviction, and be completely resolved to fight for the independence and self-sufficiency of the individual and for individual free enterprise.

This seems to me the more important because modern technical development and the great tasks that we see placed before us throughout the world make a strong government necessary. It is, however, a matter of balance. And this balance, it seems to me, has already been gravely disturbed in many countries.

A specific example of cooperation between government and the business community in providing a good "climate" for economic progress. The word, or concept, is not easy to define, but Mr. Thygesen supplies one worthy of study: "the general long-term conditions—political, social, and economic— conducive to the successful operation of a private business, and the pursuit by the government of sound economic and financial policies."

PROVIDING A GOOD CLIMATE FOR BUSINESS

By I. C. Thygesen *

The business life of any country depends to a marked degree on the political institutions of that country and on the policy that is actually pursued. At the same time, business is substantially influencing the political, social, and cultural life of a country. Actually it is a case of reciprocity and not of sharply divided sections.

This is abundantly confirmed by history. The men who left Europe some centuries ago and settled in America wanted to be free. As was natural, their urge for political freedom was also reflected in the economic system they created. Democracy led to free enterprise—and this state of affairs has existed ever since. In my country, too, similar examples of the interaction between politics and economy may be found.

* President, Federation of Danish Industries. Mr. Thygesen was unable to attend. His talk was read by A. B. Bendix, managing director, United Paper Mills, Denmark, and vice-president, Federation of Danish Industries.

In the Soviet Union and in other dictatorship countries, on the other hand, we see how political coercion pervades the economy. There is no denying that an extensive planned economy may lead to great results in the fields of technology and production. Such results are, however, as a rule restricted to special sectors of production that are deliberately and at all costs furthered at the expense of others. This is clearly illustrated by the apparent difference between the range of consumer goods offered the peoples of the free world and those of the Soviet Union.

During recent years, the problems of the technically and economically less-developed countries have become of great interest. The principal needs of these new countries are capital, know-how, and education. So far, the governments of most of these countries have had a pronounced political conviction that the initiative is primarily a State affair. The necessary capital is to a large extent imported by the governments, and this capital comes from international funds, or in the form of foreign government aid.

At the congress held by the International Chamber of Commerce in Copenhagen in May, 1961, these problems were discussed in detail. The basis was a study prepared by the United Nations under the title of: "Report on the Promotion of the International Flow of Private Capital." According to this report there is "an increasingly receptive attitude towards private foreign investment among capital-importing countries." But some of these countries still regard private capital as merely the second-best method of financing.

This is in contrast to the views held by private enterprise. The following statement was adopted by the International Chamber of Commerce at its Copenhagen congress:

Cooperation and trust between government and private enterprise is essential. Private enterprise needs strong, stable government to provide the economic and legal framework within which it can create, achieve, and make its maximum contribution to an improved standard of living. Government needs the initiative, skills, and experience of private enterprise to meet the rising tide of expectations; moreover, business profits supply its most valuable source of revenue. In guiding the economy, government should encourage and stimulate private enterprise—not inhibit individual initiative.

PREREQUISITE FOR PROGRESS

One of the most important prerequisites for economic and technical progress and expansion is the over-all climate, that is, "the general long-term conditions, political, social and economic, conducive to the successful operation of a private business, and the pursuit by the government of sound economic and financial policies." These words apply equally to the developed countries and to the countries that are now trying to catch up in the economic and technical development.

Industry in my country has repeatedly emphasized corresponding views to the Danish Government, Parliament, and the general public. "The climate" is the main thing. At the same time, Danish industry recognizes that society and the State have a right to adopt various measures in order to regulate economic life.

COLLABORATION BETWEEN GOVERNMENT AND INDUSTRY

For many years our industrial organizations have collaborated with the authorities in these fields. We believe this to be the best for business and society. I should like to mention a few examples of such collaboration. Because of foreign exchange difficulties, Denmark had to resort to quantitative import restrictions for many years which, of course, limited free enterprise. Realizing the necessity for such controlling measures, the Danish organizations assisted in the administration as objective, advisory bodies. We believed this to be sensible, and the results were better for business in general than if the regulation of imports had been left exclusively to the government. I should like to add that almost all these restrictions have now been eliminated.

As you well know, Denmark is a member of the EFTA. The consequences of joining this large European market were given careful consideration prior to the political decision of accession. The industrial organizations took part in these deliberations. Now the Danish Government has announced that if the United Kingdom were to join the Common Market, Denmark would presumably follow suit. This will entail new investigations and deliberations of many problems of importance to our trade and industries. Business will, quite naturally, be called upon to contribute toward the solution of these problems.

I should like to mention a few additional examples of fruitful cooperation between government and business in Denmark in recent years. A committee, in which business played an important part, prepared an extension of the export credit system. New rules for tax-free depreciation and for investment funds were likewise proposed by a committee in which business was represented.

In these two instances it was substantially the views of business that were implemented by legislation. While contrary views may be decisive in other cases, we believe it to be of value for industry and other sectors to present their views partly during the preparation of new bills, partly during the readings in Parliament of important bills.

I would characterize the form of collaboration between government and business in Denmark as a "frame" economy. It is the task of legislature to provide a framework for the economic life, but business must fill it out. There are some politicians who want to go a step further. They would have the government play a more active part, such as offering aid to investment. The Federation of Danish Industries is convinced that government loans and credits for investment in private concerns should be granted only in exceptional cases. The great demand for public investment in a modern community (roads, public utilities, research and educational institutions) also suggests that governments should refrain from direct investment in private business.

Capital is scarce in Denmark, and at times it has been difficult to raise enough for the investments that are needed to secure a continued industrial expansion. For this purpose, private saving is much to be preferred to government grants. A couple of years ago business made a considerable effort in this field by establishing an investment institute for industry and handicrafts. Industry, insurance, banking, and other interests collaborated closely in this institute, thus giving a palpable proof of the effectiveness of free enterprise. Another possibility of creating good will for private enterprise is the establishment of investment trusts, through which the man in the street will have an opportunity to invest his savings. In Denmark, however, we are still far behind the U. S. in this field.

WHERE PRIVATE ENTERPRISERS HAVE FAILED

In Europe, at least, it is a fact that those who favor active intervention on part of the State in the economic life meet with easy approval in wide circles. It is often difficult for those who advocate free enterprise to convince the general public that a system of private economy will secure more effectively a high rate of employment, maximum production, and a high standard of living. We have probably neglected to spread the necessary information on these matters to a wider public. A more determined public-relations activity may presumably be useful.

A more active political effort, by encouraging business men to run for Parliament and other public bodies, may also strengthen free enterprise. In Denmark, however, it is difficult to persuade active business men to take up such political tasks which are, admittedly, extremely time-consuming. Nevertheless, I believe that in the future it will be necessary to work for a more ample representation of business in Parliament. Finally, satisfactory human relations and a good "climate" in private concerns are of fundamental importance.

Business, it is true, is no goal in itself. Human life has many other aspects to offer the individual who lives in a democratic state. But an effective economic system forms the basis of most other human activity. Thanks to modern science, technology, organization, and free enterprise, the peoples of the West have been given much better conditions than at any other time in history. This has supported the confidence in our democratic institutions which, in turn, guarantee the maintenance of free enterprise.

We must now try to utilize this experience for the benefit of the enormous population in the less-developed countries.

Australia has had more than a century of experience with the ups and downs of a producer of "primaries." A plea is made here for the development of industry in countries that face similar problems.

INDUSTRY-GOVERNMENT COOPERATION IN AUSTRALIA

By G. G. Foletta *

Having watched my country develop with a minimum of control since the turn of the century, when the former six British Crown Colonies became one self-governing economic unit, my experience suggests that developing economies face seemingly insurmountable problems. I believe that with tolerance, better understanding, and growing world enlightenment, these problems will be progressively overcome. Australia's record shows that the fulfilment of the individual's desire for self-expression will be better safeguarded in a society whose citizens are subject only to laws of their own making, and not to the controls of an educated or any other elite.

The Australian economy is politically and ideologically based on Great Britain. Today, as always, public policy is considerably

* Chairman, Prestige Ltd. (textiles); fellow, Australian Institute of Management; past president, Australian Industries Development Association.

influenced by business interests. To illustrate the need of an enlightened approach by the better-educated minority and business leaders, I draw briefly on my still-developing country's history. I do this because I am convinced that a growing sense of responsibility for human relationships has been the major factor in banishing the poverty associated with our earlier history.

BEGINNINGS

When mainly unwanted people, including convicts and their keepers—the first settlers—arrived in Australia during 1788, they found a few primitive people inhabiting a huge continent—mostly arid desert, with a wilderness covering its relatively small arable area. Opportunity and support by British financial interests encouraged other men to seek freedom and fortune in Australia. What had been little more than one big prison farm was subdivided into large, privately owned pastoral holdings. Then the "Gold Rush"! And one and a quarter million people by the middle 1860's. The gold boom temporarily put an end to poverty in Victoria, where more than half of Australia's then population resided; but when gold became scarce, poverty and even destitution very soon became the lot of a rapidly growing army of unemployed.

A little secondary industry was established to relieve unemployment. However, little progress was made before the opportunity for further exploitation of pastoral resources attracted an increasing flow of money from Great Britain, and because profitable utilization of these resources demanded ready availability of the cheap labor which secondary industry was absorbing. Financial and importing interests supported the then elite, thus enabling consumption needs to be imported and labor was diverted to the expansion of primaries.

Unemployment was relieved in Australia, and also in Britain by enabling her to obtain wool at low prices for her industries in exchange for exports. This was quite a commendable pattern from an Old World standpoint, and it was also in Australia's best interests while her population remained sufficiently low.

BOOM AND BUST

A booming wool industry, new discoveries of gold and other metals, increasing land values, and ample employment obscured the need for a better-balanced economy. There was an orgy of speculation and undreamt-of prosperity. But when prices of our exports fell seriously the false prosperity collapsed. The majority of our banks closed. This boom broke in the early 90's, and having few industries we were left with unprecedented unemployment and poverty, and with an already strong Labor Movement that was spreading Marxian theories.

Then came the Commonwealth of Australia. In succession, we obtained tariff protection for industry, a few new industries, further exploitation of mineral resources, steady growth in pastoral and primary production, the Commonwealth Court of Conciliation and Arbitration, and a basic wage for workers. There was a considerable expansion of public enterprise, mainly in utilities and for these, the Old World called us "Socialists."

When this needed enterprise had reduced unemployment sufficiently to quieten unrest, policy vacillated between that influenced by shortsighted, self-interested free traders and the then-called protectionist policy of, maybe, equally self-interested workingmen and industrialists. These men were later to prove more enlightened when the next quarter century added relatively little to living standards and maintained a far-too-high level of unemployment. However, loan money from Great Britain, although unduly high and embarrassing, enabled the economy to gather ample "Preconditions" for what Rostow terms a "take-off." Among them were private and public capital formation with some new secondary industries which, lacking adequate support, had considerable excess capacity.

During the world recession of the 30's, Australia's economic structure was still based mainly on the export of primaries; the economy lacked so much balance that the troubles she encountered are evidenced by these indicators: huge international indebtedness—British loans no longer available—42.5% of income from exports (average over four years) needed to meet overseas obligations—no money for even essential imports—unemployment averaging 25% for four years, to peak at 29%.

Again, poverty and hardship and fear of repercussions enabled the new radical government to overcome precedent and adopt policies aimed at obtaining a better balance within the economy, including positive support for the rapid development of secondary industry.

Although this considerable expansion of needed industry added to the "Preconditions," Australia had not staged a "take-off," in line with Rostow's doctrine. There had been insufficient foresight to prevent public reaction when, believing the requirements to promote further secondary industry had been met, sympathy swung toward primary producers, many of whom were poverty stricken.

IMPERIAL PREFERENCE

The government then negotiated the Ottawa Agreement of 1932, and although heralded by both Australia and Great Britain as a triumph of statesmanship, it was that Agreement which was to become the most effective control ever exercised by overseas interests on Australia's industrial development. To the credit of its negotiators, Ottawa gave some badly needed assistance to primary producers but, lacking sufficient experience and vision, Australia failed to foresee the troubles inherent in that Agreement.

By granting terms that enabled Britain to control the amount of tariff accorded to secondary industry, she was soon to find it was Britain, and not Australia, who controlled the development of secondary industry. Nor could her negotiators then know that the small specific preferences Australia obtained over primary products would prove both grossly inequitable and unduly embarrassing to Australia's subsequent attempts to sell her products in other world markets.

Although Australian entrepreneurs, without any assistance from the seriously reduced tariffs, did establish very considerable secondary industry during and immediately after World War II, it was the protection supplied by extreme world short-supply and exorbitant prices for imports which, in spite of Ottawa and

GATT, then enabled Australia to achieve full employment, and to provide for a high annual intake of migrants. Favorable terms of trade, when wool prices boomed, played their part at first. The major factor, however, was the full use of labor resources, with the aid of secondary industry—that is, there was a balanced economy.

For the first time in Commonwealth history there was no poverty, and living standards were achieved which, for the lower income groups, are not exceeded even in U.S. What is highly important to Australia is this—consideration for the needs of her people generally has so strengthened the desire for the retention of the freedoms inherent in private enterprise that, although the Left Wing of the Labor Movement still gives lip-service to Marxian theories, it has so little public support that Australia now lacks what every government needs—a strong Opposition.

That both Britain and Australia, as well as other countries who enjoyed Australia's trade, would have been better off without either Ottawa or GATT is clearly seen from this record.

The world depression seriously reduced Australia's imports for the first few years of the decade prior to World War II. Although Australia signed Ottawa during 1932, the restrictions of that Agreement had so retarded Australia's development that predepression levels of Britain's exports to Australia had not been regained seven years later (i.e., the beginning of the war). However, when our economy achieved industrial balance after the war, exports from Britain, at constant prices based on 1958/59 price levels, registered an increase of 119.7% between the immediate prewar decade and the ten years prior to 1959/60. (Total world exports to Australia, similarly valued, increased by 98.2%.)

THEN GATT

Surely Old World business interests, which devised and negotiated GATT should, by now, have learnt from similar examples that it would have proved far more profitable had they put as much effort into devising ways and means of helping the underdeveloped nations to help themselves.

Wisdom dictates that, instead of retarding their efforts, as does GATT, whose aim is to retain the status quo, it would be far more profitable to assist needy societies with encouragement and understanding.

Although an altruistic approach to its duties and responsibilities to society may be too much to expect from the business community, any approach which is ethical, even if it is no more than enlightened self-interest, would constitute a powerful, yet peaceful, offensive with which to offset the alluring promises that simply cannot be fulfilled by Communism.

It is full stomachs and improved living standards that give enlightened people the strength and determination to stand firm and fight, if necessary, to retain their freedoms. It is "delivering the goods"—not promising them—or atom bombs—that will win the cold war!

I could well be asked how Australia, which again lacks adequate industrial protection, is maintaining full employment and high living standards. The answer is: she is not, temporarily, but she soon will when she learns what the par is for that hole, and makes it—by traditional means.

Having seen the dangers inherent in GATT, and having learned that her seriously adverse terms of trade resulted largely from inflation fanned by eight years of import licensing, Australia has almost completely abandoned this genesis of a controlled economy. She is now "tuning up" to stage a "take-off" in line with Rostow's doctrine.

I trust this brief history will show that it is far more profitable for developed economies to encourage and assist industrial expansion in the underdeveloped nations than to try to bind the world with such an inequitable trade system as GATT. This approach would remove those unethical controls of that system, which encourage the control-minded elite to take over in so many societies, to the distinct disadvantage of all the world's people who are striving to save the freedoms inherent in private enterprise democracy.

We have a duty to influence government by expressing, indeed pressing, our viewpoint and opinions, but no right to shape or control policy. A democracy gives the absolute right to all interests to press their views, but recoils from the concept that a sectional interest should try to capture the government.

INFLUENCING PUBLIC POLICY IN BRITAIN

By Sir Norman Kipping *

In our day, no effort is required from the business world itself to make sure that the policies of the developed countries of the West will reflect the objective of business prosperity. A high level of domestic and international trade, high levels of employment, investment in the developing countries, international systems for the support of currencies in temporary difficulties, the development of larger markets, and the progressive removal of barriers to trade—all these things are as much the essential busi-

---

* Director general, Federation of British Industries; chairman, British Overseas Fairs. Sir Norman has held various positions with the Government of Great Britain, including head of the Regional Division, Ministry of Production, and under-secretary, Board of Trade. He headed the United Kingdom delegation to the Nigerian Industrial Development Conference. He is a member of the National Production Advisory Council on Industry, Western Hemisphere Exports Council, Export Council for Europe, British Productivity Council, and the Advisory Council on Middle East Trade.

ness of governments today as are defense and education. There is no question of business having difficulty in persuading governments to give consideration to its opinions; rather do governments seek out those opinions. They are concerned to equip themselves with the soundest advice they can get.

TO WHAT EXTENT IS BUSINESS AN ENTITY?

What, then, is "business opinion"? But what is "business"? This term is more widely used in North America than in Europe. It appears to connote an amalgam of those engaged in the management of trade and commerce, including banking, insurance, shipping, and distribution. It excludes farmers. It must follow that "business opinion" coming from such diverse, and sometimes conflicting, interests will amount to a reflection of trends of thought or a general climate of business sentiment. It is unlikely to be clear-cut even on general issues. It may be a signpost or a weather vane, but not a yardstick.

In Britain, we speak more of "industrial opinion" and "city opinion," but the world of shipping is of such importance to us that it, too, has developed a separate voice, expressed through our Chamber of Shipping. We rarely find the need to try to combine these voices in the form of a single "business opinion." In fact, we would be very sceptical about the usefulness of trying to do so.

But this is not to say that sectional opinions held in Britain cannot often usefully be combined or contrasted with similar sectional opinions held in other countries, and for this purpose we value our association with the International Chamber of Commerce.

FOMULATING COLLECTIVE OPINION

If it is important to governments to receive sound business advice, and equally important to business to see that they get it, it must follow that the methods of formulating the advice should be deliberate and responsible. It may be sound for governments to listen with attention to the opinions of exceptional individuals (and they will naturally always do so whether it is sound or not), but this does not replace the desirability of formulating and expressing collective opinion wherever this can be done.

How practicable that is varies from country to country. In Britain and most European countries, geographical compactness makes it possible to collect together frequently (and even at very short notice) the leaders in any side of business activity. Urgent problems or government requests for advice can thus be thoroughly dealt with. In North America, distance has made this impracticable, though jet travel may bring about a change; consequently, discussions between businessmen with kindred interests have tended to take place at relatively infrequent conventions, a situation that lends itself less conveniently to a continuing process of consultation and representation.

The last 50 years have seen the formation of a number of employers' organizations as a countermove to the organization of labor in trade unions.

Also during the same period and particularly in the last 20 years trade associations have come into being covering virtually the whole of industry. Originally, many but by no means all of these were born to administer intercompany agreements concerning prices or distribution. The ending of almost all such agreements following "restrictive practices" legislation has not led to the general disbanding of the trade associations, for in the last 20 years they have developed a usefulness to their members in other ways. This period has seen a very marked growth in the interest taken by government in industrial and commercial affairs, and every trade and branch of industry needs to possess a mechanism for meeting and discussing its own special problems, first within itself, and secondly with government.

In the United Kingdom, the bulk of these trade associations belong to the Federation of British Industries. Those dealing with "labor matters" belong also to the British Employers Confederation. This makes it entirely practical as a continuing process for the Federation, through the whole system of trade associations, to organize the study of current economic or commercial situations, and to mobilize—and to some extent to lead—what may fairly be called "industrial opinion" on matters of moment.

The work is done with a sense of responsibility, and the Federation of British Industries has elected as its presidents (for two-year periods of office) industrial leaders of the very highest caliber. The opinions it expresses to government undoubtedly carry great weight.

The individual trade associations are autonomous, and would not stand for any interference from a national body. But they are glad to come together with similar bodies from other branches of industry on matters of common concern.

LIMITATIONS OF COLLECTIVE REPRESENTATION

Whatever form of collective organization a country may have developed for individual trades, or all trades, or even for all "business," to what extent and in what ways are those organizations able—or entitled—to influence governments, or to "shape public policy"? I would say that we have a duty to influence it by expressing, indeed pressing, our viewpoint and opinions, but no right to shape or control policy. A democracy gives the absolute right to all interests to press their views, but recoils from the concept that a sectional interest should try to capture the government. Neither the electorate nor the legislature generally may have the specialized knowledge to reach informed conclusions, but there is always resentment if it appears that government has fixed things with sectional interests, and is treating the legislature as a rubber stamp.

Nevertheless, the sectional interests possess a degree of knowledge of their own trades which neither government, nor legislature, nor the public can possess. This justification for making known the facts is their special contribution to the forming of policy. In Britain, industrial interests normally prefer to make their representations to Ministers and their departments. It is rare for industries to seek to have "tame" Members of Parliament (though the trade unions do). The Federation of British Industries has no pressure group in the House of Commons. This preference for dealing with the executive leads to the fact that organizations maintain a nonparty political position. Our trade organizations do not contribute to party funds, nor encourage their members to do so (though some individual companies do) nor engage in party-political propaganda.

Perhaps this outlook has its cause in the circumstances of government in Britain. Our (substantially) two-party system depends on strict party control. The government of the day must be highly sensitive to currents of feeling among its supporters in Parliament, but when it feels it has evolved a generally acceptable policy, then party discipline, together with party loyalties, take charge. Thus the Federation of British Industries, though it may have friends in Parliament, has no pressure group; such a group would be ineffective in case of a collision with the government and the bulk of its party.

This consideration is reinforced by another. The legislature, though often involved in much detail in the process of legislation, is bound to leave an immense mass of subsidiary decision-making to the executive. The execution of public policy, which in Britain today touches the industrialist at so many points, rests in many hands, from Minister down to comparatively junior civil servants. These are the people with whom the bulk of our problems must be discussed, for they, not the legislature, have the task of solving them. Even where we disagree with the broad policies of the government of the day, we in practice retain our links with those who administer them. Though circumstances are conceivable in which divisions of view go so deep as to cut industry off from government, the chances of so uncharacteristic a development seem at the moment to be small.

We oppose policies, not parties.

2. Financing Corporate Growth

France has faced many special difficulties in providing financial help for her smaller enterprises. The successful measures adopted have arisen from the cooperation of the public authorities, the industries, and the organized regions, on the one hand, and the banks and credit establishments, on the other. This has been done without paralyzing the flexibility of private initiative or destroying the advantages of a market economy.

HELPING THE SMALLER COMPANY

By Henri Deroy *

The financing of small and medium-sized concerns has posed grave problems in France. During the greater part of the 19th century such enterprises, normally family-owned, were financed mainly through the savings of their proprietors and by loans given on a personal basis by local bankers. Local bankers gradually disappeared, being taken more and more into credit establishments with headquarters in Paris. Little by little this loosened the personal ties existing between the smaller company and its banker just at a time when investment needs were growing. It was also at a time when the capacity of the family to save was

* Vice-chairman, Banque de Paris et des Pays-Bas; chairman, Cie Générale Industrielle pour la France et L'Étranger; vice-chairman, Cie Internationale des Wagons-Lits and Banque de Syrie et du Liban; director of Banque de 'Algérie, Banque Ottomane, De Wendel et Cie, Banque Française et Italienne pour l'Amerique du Sud, Raffineries de St.-Louis, ELECTROBEL (Brussels), and INVEST (Milan). M. Deroy was director general, Ministry of Finance (1930–45); governor, Crédit Foncier de France (1945–55). He is a director of the Bank for International Settlements.

309

being reduced by an increasingly heavy burden of personal taxation, by a change in habits and manner of living among the lower middle classes and shop owners and, above all, by the depreciation in the value of money caused by the two great wars. Thus it is natural that solutions were sought to this problem during the two periods of reconstruction which followed the two wars.

LOANS OF *CREDIT NATIONAL*

The *Credit National* was created in 1919 with private capital but was encouraged and controlled by the State. It was kept busy at first by the settlements owed those who had suffered war damages. Rather rapidly it became an industrial development bank granting long-term equipment loans to industrial or commerical enterprises. Its resources came essentially from the issuance of bonds to the public or to large institutional investors. At the end of 1960, the total amount of loans in force came to $600 million.

In special cases—motion picture industry, hotels, industries agreeing to move out of Paris to the provinces or to try out new techniques, etc.—loans are made for the account and risk of the State by the *Credit National,* or by specialized establishments such as the *Credit National Hotelier.*

The resources made available to industry by these means have occasionally been insufficient because the *Credit National* had difficulty in selling enough of its own bonds to the public. Moreover, having all loan applications examined by officials in Paris entailed delays and misunderstandings in the examination of files.

BRANCH BANK FINANCING

On both these accounts it appeared useful to bring together all banks whose branches are spread throughout the country for the purpose of granting at least medium-term, if not long-term, loans to facilitate the purchase of new capital equipment. These credits, granted by the banks under their own responsibility, give rise to the issuance of short-term paper renewable for a maximum of five years and discounted by the *Credit National* in the amount and for the period desired by the lender. The *Credit National* itself may rediscount this paper to the *Caisse des Depots et Consignations* and, as a last resort, to the *Banque de France.*

Operations of this nature, begun on a rather small scale before the last war, were greatly extended immediately following the war, and fiscal reforms have been carried out in order to make credits of this type less burdensome (the present rate is 5.80%). At the end of 1960 the total amount of these credits in force amounted to about $1.3 billion.

INDUSTRY GROUPS

Medium-term credit played an important role in postwar reconstruction and in carrying out the Monnet Plan, but the development of credit also contributed to the inflationary tendencies of that period. As soon as a certain savings capacity again existed, attention was quickly paid to easing the access of concerns to the financial market for the sale of stocks and bonds. The new formula was the creation of professional groups that borrow money for a certain number of companies, each of which guarantees its share of the loan. The operations of these groups, notably the coal, electrical machinery, shipbuilding, and machinery industries and the department and large, low-price stores have substantially assisted in this type of financing.

These various measures, although perfectly suited to the needs of the larger companies, could not by themselves solve the particular problems of the small and medium-sized businesses.

The *Credit National,* for its own loans, and the banks, for the medium-term credits for which they assume all the risks, naturally demanded guarantees. Many small or medium-sized concerns could not meet these guarantee requirements. Also, the dispersion throughout the country of small and medium-sized concerns made the contacts necessary for the loan applications and clearances difficult in many cases.

A strong effort was made to remedy these defects by setting up within the framework of various industrial and professional fields a system of mutual guarantee of loans by organizing new institutions on a regional basis.

MUTUAL GUARANTEE GROUPS

The system is based on the creation of one or more mutual guarantee societies for a single occupation, industry, or profession. By becoming guarantors of the repayment of medium-term credits, they make it possible to obtain the endorsement of the *Caisse Nationale des Marches de l'État,* a public institution created in 1936. In its turn, this endorsement permits the intervention of the *Credit National.*

The mechanics of the guarantee call for depositing with the mutual guarantee society a fraction of the loan (4% to 6%), which remains immobilized until the loan is repaid. This formula, which was put into operation immediately following the last war, has had great success, and was helped by the network of the *Banques Populaires.*

Nearly 70 mutual guarantee organizations have been created, and the total amount of loan authorizations granted has attained nearly $700 million, with an extremely low percentage of recourse to the guarantee mechanism.

REGIONAL DEVELOPMENT ASSOCIATIONS

The postwar industrial expansion quickly revealed the need for a better balance between the various regions of the country in order to avoid an excessive concentration of new investments in the regions that were already highly developed. It was also necessary to bring the means of financing closer to the headquarters of the small and medium-sized concerns.

Legislation for this purpose was necessary. A law was passed that provided for the establishment of regional development associations. Capital for these groups is furnished mainly by banks and other credit institutions. State assistance is provided through the guarantee of dividends and official auditing services. These associations offer help either by long-term loans or by taking minority stock participations. In this way concerns of a family nature have been able to remedy their lack of sufficient funds in relation to necessary investments without losing control of the business. Regional development associations can, at the end of a few years, sell back to the interested parties the shares of stock to which they had subscribed.

About 15 regional development associations have been created during the past five years. Their degree of activity and results have varied according to local conditions encountered and to the capability of their managers. Nonetheless, it can be said that, especially in the last two years, the experiment has been a success. It has been possible for several of these associations to issue collective bonds within their own region. The income from these sales has been shared by many concerns that would not by themselves have been able to gain access to the market.

PROMOTIONAL ASSOCIATIONS

Regional development associations, being closer to middle-sized concerns, have been able in many cases to advise the latter on how to increase business in existing lines or to convert to new ones. In most cases, however, they have not been able to go beyond the bounds of the financial field and give truly technical advice.

This is why associations intended to "aid businessmen in problems concerning both their financial structure and their technical and commercial situation within their industry" have been set up under the double sponsorship of the banks and professional organizations. This movement is only in its beginning stages, but the example of the TEFICA et SOFIMECA association for the machinery industries will surely be followed by others.

The adaptation of the medium-sized concerns to the new needs of the economy and to the changes within their industry or their own line of activity will be further eased by the very recent creation of the SODIP association. The purpose of this association is to give advice on all of the technical and financial problems of the concern.

All these efforts have been facilitated by the possibility, since 1954, of recourse to productivity loans financed by State funds to cover the expenses involved in the reorganization of an enterprise or the material costs that are expressly appropriated to increase productivity.

SUCCESS THROUGH COOPERATION AND FLEXIBILITY

It should be emphasized that these measures have arisen from the cooperation of the public authorities, the industries, and the organized regions on the one hand, and the banks and credit establishments on the other. This is true no matter whether the latter belong to the public, semipublic, or private sectors.

Operation of the development plan without recourse to over-rigid regimentation marks a step toward what has been called a "consultative economy." The State, by granting tax advantages in a large number of sectors and encouraging supplementary facilities for the granting of credit by public or semipublic organizations, has assisted the success of the development plan without paralyzing the flexibility of private initiative or destroying the advantages of a market economy.

It would be fitting to add that the success of all these measures would have been both less significant and slower in developing had France not joined the Common Market. The need for adaptation in order to survive under completely new conditions of competition has forced a number of company chiefs, either independently or in collaboration with their colleagues, into decisions which they would otherwise have been reluctant to take.

*Money in irresponsible or dishonest hands
can and does do more harm than good. It
leads to misuse of valuable land, buildings,
plant, machinery, and raw materials. It leads
also to misuse of the energies of human beings, to misery and poverty and to the lowering of men's opinion of the whole social
system in which such events can take place.
This is equally true of state-owned and of
privately owned enterprise. It is useless to
plan any scheme for aiding development
unless satisfactory arrangements have been
made to select and maintain good management.*

RISK INVESTMENT WITHOUT
OWNERSHIP CONTROL

By Sir Nutcombe Hume *

My experience, both in the private and public sector, has been
largely in the field of financing and in overcoming the difficulties
of providing risk capital without also taking voting control of
the undertaking financed—not only in highly industrialized
countries but also in underdeveloped areas. My organization,
The Charterhouse Industrial Development Company, was formed
in 1934. Since that time we have provided capital for more than
100 industrial and commercial companies in Great Britain, Australia, and Canada. That was in the private sector.

* Chairman, The Charterhouse Group Limited, United Kingdom; director
of several business and financial firms in Canada and Great Britain; former
director, deputy chairman, and chairman of Colonial Development Corporation, and currently chairman of The Charterhouse Group Canada, S. Japhet
& Co., Alenco, Associated British Maltsters, Associated Book Publishers, Cur-
rys, National Film Finance, and Yeoman Investment Trust Ltd. Sir Nutcombe
is governor of the English-Speaking Union, and member of the Grand Council, Federation of British Industries.

In 1948 the British Government invited me to become one of the first directors of the Colonial Development Corporation—an organization with funds wholly provided by the British Parliament. Its activities cover the whole of the British Colonial Empire as it was in 1948, but many parts of which are now independent members of the British Commonwealth of Nations. In this pioneering scheme we did, of course, make some bad mistakes. We paid the penalty of having started with too much money and too little experience and an urge to do things quickly. But today the CDC can look back on 13 years of endeavor with some degree of pride. The Corporation has financed more than 100 schemes in 27 different countries. It can now produce a balance sheet that shows a profit not only in terms of money, but also in terms of that far more valuable international currency—progress and human welfare. Indeed, of all the many inspiring words in President Kennedy's Inaugural Address, none struck a more answering chord in the organizations with which I am connected than his call to forge against poverty and the common enemies of man—"a grand and global alliance that can assure a more fruitful life for all mankind."

It is a fundamental fact that the progress that has already taken place has not been due wholly, or indeed primarily, to the provision of investment capital but to the honesty and purpose of the men on the spot and the intelligence and singlemindedness of leaders in the investment sector. It is fashionable to decry our predecessors in the Victorian age, but it was the great entrepreneurs and adventurers of those days who opened up great areas where there are thriving nations today.

EVEN MORE THAN MONEY—MEN

More possibly than ever before, the provision of adequate money presents a big enough problem, but there is an even greater challenge—the provision of the men to make an honest and intelligent use of that money. The selection of such men as borrowers calls for real judgment in the financial field. The more remote in distance, the more difficult it is to provide. The intelligent and honest use of money in all forms of investment makes this the paramount demand. Management must be in the hands of men of integrity, and if you cannot find such men with skill and understanding as well, it is better by far to make no investment at all. For money in irresponsible or dishonest hands can and does do more harm than good. It leads to misuse of valuable land, buildings, plant, machinery, and raw materials. It leads also to misuse of the energies of human beings, to misery and poverty and to the lowering of men's opinion of the whole social system in which such events can take place. This is equally true of state-owned and of privately owned enterprise. It is useless to plan any scheme for aiding development unless satisfactory arrangements have been made to select and maintain good management.

How then is this to be done, especially in a distant country, or when the financial partner does not have the legal right to control the enterprise?

We do not insist on a majority equity shareholding, which carries the voting control. Policy at Charterhouse is to put up money mainly in the form of loan or preferred share capital but always with a minority holding in the common stock or equity capital. This gives us a share in future growth of profits and assets, and it also engenders a feeling of partnership and a true community of interest between those who provide the money and those who provide the management. Except for investments in public utility undertakings, or where an acceptable guarantee is given, a participation in the equity is essential because the result of a bad investment nearly always leads to the loss of the prior charge as well as the equity capital. As compensation there must therefore come from the successes something more than mere interest and capital repayment. In all appropriate cases, the CDC also takes an equity participation and this has proved very satisfactory. It is worth noting that the International Finance Corporation, at first prohibited from taking equity participations, has recently sought powers to do so.

Our philosophy is this. If the financier really wants to get the best out of management—and by this I mean proved, honest management—he must give that management the feeling that it is trusted, and that if it is successful it will enjoy the lion's share of earnings.

It is true, of course, that where big companies are concerned, management and ownership (which carries the right to profits) are nowadays seldom in the same hands. But with the type of medium-sized developing business to which our methods of financial treatment are best suited, it is surprising how often ownership and management are in fact largely in the same family. Ownership of the equity of any business, however, does not concern me at the moment. I am concerned now with the methods which I have found to be workable and practical in exercising a degree of control that will safeguard an investment in a minority of the common stock.

A DEGREE OF CONTROL

Initially, it is of course vital to be certain as far as possible that the business to be financed is a real business, soundly conceived and founded, that present management is in capable and honest hands and that there is capable management potential to follow on. But having become satisfied on these vital points, it is unwise and indeed unhelpful if machinery is not established for keeping a close watch on the progress of the business.

Despite the fact that Charterhouse is a minority equity holder, it demands, as a condition of subscribing capital, the right to exercise control over: (1) capital expenditure beyond a defined limit at any one time; (2) the exercise of borrowing powers beyond a defined limit; and (3) appointment of senior management and upward changes in senior management remuneration.

We invariably stipulate that we shall have a representative on the board of directors, and it is through him that these controls are exercised. It is of the utmost importance that the man who represents the financier on the board be not only knowledgeable but of a personality that encourages friendship and willing consultation. A strong reason for seeking these qualities in the nominee who provides the link between management and financier is because the three controls I have just listed can really be effective only if the financier is consulted in advance. The remedies open to him if the management fails to observe those controls and presents him with the *fait accompli* may do more harm to the business than even the original breach of the agreement.

These methods differ materially from those used by banks engaged in conventional banking, which have their own remedies through the security they take. In the case I am seeking to describe, the underlying objective is to provide risk capital alongside the entrepreneur and, in so doing, to increase and not to use up part of his creditworthiness as a banker or other creditor assesses it.

PROBLEMS IN THE UNDERDEVELOPED COUNTRY

Making a success of this work in another country, particularly in an underdeveloped country, involves far greater and more varied problems. There is greater difficulty in the original choice of investment and subsequent management. In addition there are such questions as land tenure, local legislation governing trading corporations, and restrictions on movement of capital or dividends. These difficulties are challenges that must be accepted; they must not be made reasons for refusing to provide the needed capital.

Since World War I, private capital has not been available for these areas in sufficient quantities. In the interwar years there can be no doubt that economic development in, say, Africa, was much retarded because there were no other sources to supplement the flow of private capital. Since 1945, however, there has been a much greater awareness by governments, especially those of the United States and Great Britain, of the necessity to provide capital for underdeveloped countries. A number of agencies for doing so have been established, of which the International Bank for Reconstruction and Development is the outstanding example. But there are and must always be many other such agencies, and in the case of most of them a whole host of new problems arise when a government is involved. It is seldom easy to blend sound commercial practice with a degree of political control over the money.

DECENTRALIZED FINANCING

This brings me to my experiences under the Colonial Development Corporation which, as already stated, is wholly financed from public funds in Britain. From a small headquarters in London its work is decentralized into six regions, each under the management of a controller carefully selected for his business ability. The regional offices are in turn staffed by a few individuals hand-picked for their general and specialized business knowledge. This organization suffices when individual projects are large and can be expected to attract adequate management, which in most cases is expatriate at the start. But when the relatively small undertaking is to be financed, quite different considerations apply. Determination of the basic viability of the business calls in itself for detailed local knowledge, as does also the selection of local as opposed to expatriate management. Above all it calls for proper supervision of the project after it has been mounted. This can only be done by an organization beyond the regional office system to which I have referred.

The best solution so far devised to meet this problem is a local development corporation, so capitalized and managed as to maximize the urge of all concerned to make it a success. To that end the local government, local banks and other capitalist bodies should be participants in its capital; but it goes without saying that the greatest need is to clothe it with the right management. Initially, this will have to be entrusted to one man who combines with all the other needed attributes—integrity, financial knowledge, judgment, and an agreeable personality—a real ability to train management in both the development corporation itself and in the enterprises it finances. Such men are difficult to find.

These are the principles and some of the methods that I believe should be adopted by those who have responsibility for financing new projects, particularly in underdeveloped countries. In this way, we who are in the investment field can best help to implement the President's pledge to "those people in the huts and villages of half the world, struggling to break the bonds of misery."

It is well for us to remember that this great country of America was once an uncleared and undeveloped area. And it was men and management rather than money that worked the miracles of the last century. Of those days, Walt Whitman wrote: "Have you your pistols? Have you your sharp-edged axes? O Pioneers—O Pioneers."

Today, bulldozers have taken the place of the sharp-edged axes and the pistols have gone, but the pioneers of the financial world have still to find their proper targets and to use their limited ammunition with economy and to maximum effect.

At least one of the keys to Japan's phenomenal recovery is what Mr. Satoh calls "the popular propensity for capital accumulation." Commercial banks, starting from scratch after the war, have borne an excessive burden in financing industry. The author hopes for more diversification in financing methods.

COMMERCIAL BANKING IN JAPAN

By Kiichiro Satoh *

There are two schools of thought about the extent to which commercial banks may finance so-called risk enterprises. Let us take the case of a certain enterprising businessman who asked the president of a bank for a loan, taking with him the blueprint of a "promising" new project. The president refused, on the ground that the particular project was in an experimental stage and not economically established. The same businessman, however, could receive a loan from another bank whose president believed the loan was warranted on the ground of extending a helping hand to any highly promising project after careful investigation. Suppose this businessman succeeded in his new project. Should the second bank be proud of its foresight? Or should the conscientious management of a modern bank refuse to share in the risk

* Chairman, The Mitsui Bank; chairman of the Board of Counsellors of the Japanese National Railway from 1949–54, and financial director of the Japan Federation of Employers Association since 1950. Mr. Satoh is director of Mitsui Petro-Chemical Industry Co., and has been vice-president of the Federation of Economic Organizations since 1948.

because the project is simply "promising?" I believe the answer lies between these two verdicts.

I need not explain in detail how the "Zaibatsu" (industrial combinations) developed in prewar Japan. They were few in number, but very powerful. Most of them, besides being scrupulous in going after self-interest, could afford at the same time to take responsibility for serving the economic development of the country. Before World War II, these Zaibatsu played an important role in solving the problem under review. New projects that were risky and demanding large capital were generally started and financed by Zaibatsu interests. At the same time, financial institutions that were an important part of the vast business combine of the Zaibatsu enjoyed a high degree of public confidence. Thus, the major part of what people saved found its way to these affiliated banks in the form of deposits, especially as time-deposits. Under the guarantee of the Zaibatsu, banks were able to supply funds to develop enterprises without bearing unwarranted risks in doing so. It was by such a process that the formula of what we call "indirect investment" by private investors in industry was born.

It may be of interest to you to know that the rate of capital formation in Japan in 1938 already stood as high as 24%, as compared with 8% in the United States, 10% in the United Kingdom, and 19% in Germany.

POSTWAR CHANGES

One of the most noteworthy changes in the Japanese economic structure after World War II was the impoverishment of these Zaibatsu as a result of the very heavy capital levy imposed on them during the Occupation period, and their eventual dissolution. There was also the abrogation of the war indemnity clause, provided by the government to enable commercial banks to finance the armament industries. Most of the banks were therefore forced to start from scratch by issuing new share capital to a public that was also impoverished by the war.

It was the government coffer that eventually benefited. In 1949, the yen was fixed at ¥360 to a dollar, a curtailment to one-ninetieth of the prewar value. In consequence, the interest on government bonds was reduced to an insignificant item in the national budget. What worried us most at that time was the fear that the public's incentive to save would be lost, because of the sharp depreciation of the currency. For instance, anyone who bought a prewar insurance policy with the thought of providing for their rainy days found with resentment that it was not worth even a year's premium in its purchasing power at maturity.

After World War II the Japanese economy made its fresh start under such unfavorable circumstances. Fortunately, the public's confidence in the banking system had not been lost, although most of the big banks sustained heavy blows. At the same time, the stability of the currency in Japan, established as early as 1949, did much to encourage savings.

From 1949 up to the present, the government budget has continued either to be balanced or to show a surplus. No government bonds have had to be issued except for conversion. The only governmental operations that have competed with private business were the issuance of corporate bonds under government guarantee by quasi-governmental agencies, such as the Japanese National Railways, the Nippon Telegraph & Telephone Public Corporation, and other public organizations, amounting in the aggregate to $1.1 billion in value. Spurred by the high level of economic activity, over-the-estimate surpluses of revenue in the national budget have been sizable each year. That in fiscal 1960, for instance, reached $0.9 billion, or some 20% more than the original government estimate. In addition, private funds were channeled to the Trust Fund of the Ministry of Finance through postal savings, postal life insurance, and other governmental operations.

ENCOURAGEMENT TO SAVE

During the postwar period various positive measures were taken to encourage depositors, in view of the imperative need for indirect investment to accomplish economic rehabilitation. Bank deposits were exempted from the income tax for a few years, and the rate of interest on the one-year time deposit was placed at

6% until 1960 (it is now set at a little less than 5% after taxes). Thus, during the period from 1949 through the end of 1960, bank deposits increased 11-fold from $2.2 billion to $24.6 billion. Of this increase, time deposits accounted for some 55%. Meanwhile, the total amount of bank resources grew from $2.8 billion to $36.0 billion. On the operative side of these resources, the amount of government and government-guaranteed bonds in the portfolio accounted for only 5% of the total. At present, the ratio of bank loans to bank deposits has reached a high level of 92%, reflecting a heavy demand for money by expanding businesses. It is noteworthy that the ratio of external liabilities in the total amount of capital employed by Japanese industry and commerce rose from 40% in the prewar period to 60% soon after the war, and to 70% in recent years. In other words, it vividly demonstrated that the external liabilities of private businesses would taper off when the government finance is in need of borrowing, whereas the demand for funds by the private sector would tend to increase when the national budget stays in the black.

BANKS AS SECURITY BUYERS

Generally speaking, the equity capital formation by Japanese industrial corporations is still inadequate as compared with the prewar level. Soon after the end of the war, many companies needed to increase their equity capital, but because of the lack of investors, institutional as well as individual, banks had to come into the market as substantial buyers of securities, although with reluctance. Recently the sale of shares to the general public has become more active, paralleling the growth of investment trusts. The market value of shares held by these investment trusts is estimated at some $1.7 billion, or 11% of the total value of shares outstanding. However, those shares held by banks are considered no less than those of the investment trusts in current value, judging by the amount of dividends being received by all banks. This is an inevitable state of affairs in Japan because of the "helping hand" that Japanese banks have been called upon to extend to enterprises after the dissolution of the Zaibatsu.

The same has been true of corporate bonds. Since World War

II commercial banks in Japan have been prohibited from under-writing issues of corporate bonds. As the funds available to the bond market are markedly restricted, however, banks are eventually required to buy the major part of new issues. Of the total amount of corporate bonds outstanding, valued at $1.9 billion, banks are now in possession of some 66%. Banks that act as trustees of bond issues are naturally considered well informed of the credit standing of the bond-issuing companies. Therefore, although the banks are not legally responsible for the ultimate fate of the bond for which they acted as trustee, there have been some instances in which banks continued payment to the bond holders when the issuing corporations were in financial trouble.

In conclusion, I may say that since World War II commercial banks in Japan have continued to play a cardinal role in supplying industrial capital through three major channels—stocks, corporate bonds, and loans. I would not venture to predict what their future will be. However, I hope that positive efforts will be made to alleviate the excessive postwar burden on them through greater diversification of financing methods, and that more dependence will be placed on life insurance companies, investment trusts, and other institutional investors, particularly in the long-term investment market. Whatever those efforts may be, they should not, for the sake of an academic concept, discourage the popular propensity for capital accumulation that is so essential for the growing Japanese economy.

*It is becoming increasingly clear that the
new enterprise can grow only if it ploughs
back the greater part of its profits. This is a
"must" up to the time that the company has
become big enough to have access to the
open capital market. . . . We must once again
make self-financing easy for such companies
by allowing them to retain in the business
all or the major part of their profits.*

GROWTH THROUGH AUTO-FINANCING

By Fernand J. Collin *

In most industrialized countries the independent small and
medium-sized companies are responsible for a substantial part
of industrial and commercial activity.

Such small businesses are the main reservoir of managerial talent available to large commercial and industrial firms. The success
and the rapid growth of a small enterprise is the surest proof of
the value of its chief. This natural selection is the best way of
discovering managerial talent. No wonder, therefore, that some
mergers have been mainly aimed at securing the managerial
talent existing in a small enterprise.

* Chairman, Kredietbank, Belgium; professor at the University of Louvain
since 1927; chairman, Benelux Committee; chairman, Imperial Products,
Belgian Association of Investment Funds, and Utrecht-Allerlei Risico's; vice
chairman, Banque Diamantaire Anversoise; director, Gevaert Photo Products,
Assurantie Belgische Boerenbond; member, managing committee of Institut
de Réescompte et de Garantie; General Council of the Belgian Savings Bank,
and Beirat Deutsche Schiffahrtsbank (Bremen); vice-president, Business Managers' Training Center.

These are among the many reasons why the financing of such small and medium-sized firms is a significant problem. And it is a difficult problem. In order to grow, these firms need adequate means. How are they to get the capital they need?

CREDIT IS SELDOM THE ANSWER

It is not a question of credit; in most industrialized countries there is plenty of credit available, although it is not always cheap. But often credit is not the real solution of these financial problems. The credit given to a firm should not exceed certain limits. Large credits assume adequate guaranties, which are not generally available. Moreover a loan must be repaid. As long as annual repayments of principal do not exceed the annual depreciation of assets allowed for tax purposes, there is no great problem, if sizable profits are made.

But the repayment of a debt alone is not necessarily a strengthening of the business. If it does not exceed depreciation in the value of fixed assets, no real progress is made. High debts are a heavy load. For many firms they have been the main cause of ruin.

Medium and long-term loans alone cannot solve the problem of growth of most small and medium-size businesses. They undoubtedly need a less-expensive form of financing.

NOR IS FINDING CAPITAL

What they require is not so much an increase in loans as additional capital and surplus. No interest is due on these and they need not be repaid at a fixed time.

But where is the independent enterprise to obtain such additional capital? Generally not from outside sources; they do not have access to the capital market and, if such an operation were possible, it would be far too expensive.

Small and medium-size firms frequently are one-man or family businesses. Independence is something very important to them. Therefore, when they are prosperous their owners are not prepared to accept outside capital if it means losing their independence. But at the same time they are extremely vulnerable. When their leader disappears there is generally no ready replacement. Managerial talent is not always inherited. Consequently, capital is not readily available nor is it always eagerly desired.

Instead, many a successful businessman has preferred to practice economic Malthusianism in order to avoid losing his autonomy; not finding a satisfactory solution to the financial problems that have arisen from rapid growth, he prefers to slow down the expansion of his company.

For him, no other solution is in sight. Private partners are difficult to find, and if they can be discovered their terms may be unacceptable. It is quite usual to impose, as a condition for the bringing in of new capital, that the new participant, or a member of his family, be appointed a manager or a director. He has to be well paid for his services, the quality of which may sometimes be questionable. The price so paid for capital is very high indeed.

SELF-FINANCING

Thus it is clear that a small independent enterprise has no other solution to its financial problems than to save and to practice self-financing. Credit can be of temporary assistance, but no real progress can be made unless the small firm makes profits and ploughs most of them back. For the great majority of small and medium-size enterprises, this self-financing is not only a virtue, it is a necessity.

It is evident that the public authorities are not at all aware of this fact. Governments sometimes make great efforts to attract new industries. They are prepared to give important advantages, such as free building sites, subsidies, loans at reduced interest rates, reduced taxes over a certain number of years, etc. But would it not be a far simpler solution to favor the self-financing of small and medium-sized enterprises? Would this not be the best way to promote a natural selection of the most valuable initiatives and of the best-qualified business leaders?

Only a prosperous company is able to save. Its success and its profits are the most convincing proof of the value of its services and of the quality of its management. Such success is in itself ample justification of governmental favor. In addition, this method is the best way to avoid the suspicion that special advantages may be due to political favor or other pernicious influences.

The history of the industrial revolution of the 19th century is a striking confirmation of this thesis. Before World War I, the building of an industrial empire by more than one talented businessman was possible only because at that time self-financing was not hampered by a steeply progressive system of taxation. Before 1910, an income tax was simply unknown in many countries. Where this tax existed, as in England, its impact on earnings was small. Enterprises that made sizable profits during those years could grow rapidly by using them for new investments in building and equipment.

If we look into the price lists of the main stock exchanges, we see that a considerable number of the corporations whose shares are listed had a very modest beginning, either as one-man or family businesses. Proof of this fact can be found in such concerns as Ford, Woolworth, and du Pont de Nemours in the U.S.; Kuhlmann, Schneider and Peugeot in France; Lever, Vickers, and Guinness in England; Cockerill, Solvay, and Gevaert in Belgium; Krupp, Thyssen, and Bayer in Germany.

There is nothing astonishing about them. Yet industries whose prospects are such as to appeal to the public from their very beginning are exceptional indeed. Progress in our economies will as a rule be made in the tertiary sector. New ventures will be much less in the field of heavy industry; they will generally start in the sector of services, which are more and more required in an affluent society. Thus, it is becoming increasingly clear that the new enterprise can grow only if it ploughs back the greater part of its profits. This is a "must" up to the time that the company has become big enough to have access to the open capital market.

One often hears the complaint that the free economy has lost some of its old dynamic growth, that management has little imagination and no daring, and that as a result not enough new jobs are created. This is generally the argument used to defend industrial initiatives by the State.

ENCOURAGING SELF-FINANCING

But we should not forget that this problem itself is government-made. If the financing of the smaller independent enterprise is growing more difficult every day, this is due to a large extent to the steady increase of direct taxation, and this is the main cause of the drying up of capital investment.

I do not propose the abolition of direct taxation, because the times are not yet ripe for such a radical reform. It may well be that in the end this will be the only way to give a new impetus to our free economy, just as this measure seems to be required even in the Communist economy to reward good management. At this moment a less drastic remedy might bring about a great improvement.

If we seriously want to promote the growth of the most promising new enterprises, we must once again make self-financing easy for such companies by allowing them to retain in the business all or the major part of their profits.

The advantages of such fiscal exemption cannot be denied. No administrative inquiry could yield any better solution. The investments rendered possible by such a measure would be, in all probability, economically justified. In any case they would certainly promote the expansion of a profitable enterprise.

The sacrifice made by the State would probably not be very great if it were limited to the smaller companies. The fiscal administration would be freed from many difficult and complicated investigations, whose cost might well be higher than their yield. But even if this were not true, it would be worth while to make the experiment, because it would show to what extent direct taxation, especially a very steep scale of direct taxation, is a damper on private initiative.

If we want the advantages of a free economy, and they are great and numerous, we should not hamper the growth of new ventures. On the contrary we should see to it that those who take such an initiative get their well-deserved reward. At the same time this may be the best way to secure full employment in a free and expanding economy.

3. Technology and Growth

One should never forget that it is the technical side that causes the unforeseen costs. Only the engineers can see all sides of a technical problem. It is therefore advisable to make them lay down beforehand what is the precise object of the work, what kind of technical operations are necessary, what materials, what special apparatus and so on are needed. If you do not know these things, your estimate will not help you very much.

BUDGETING FOR RESEARCH AND DEVELOPMENT

By Hans C. Boden *

An ordinary industrial company has a manufacturing program that is carried out in its factories. It also has to take account of its competitors, who are constantly trying to improve their current products and to create new ones. So the company is obliged to improve its own products and to develop new ones as well.

This work may be done either in the ordinary design departments or in special departments that do nothing else. Minor improvements of a particular model are generally made in the design departments, and their costs are budgeted as ordinary manufacturing expenses.

* Chairman, Allgemeine Elektricitäts-Gesellschaft; president, International Chamber of Commerce; chairman, Olympia Werke, Osram, Elektrofinanz, Papierfabrik, Rosenthal-Isolatorem, Telefunken, and Lloyd Dynamowerke; board member of Esso, Deutsche Werft, Hamburgische Elektricitats-Werke, Mannesmann, Dresdner Bank, and Hochtief. Dr. Boden is chairman of the Export Commission of the Federation of German Industries.

On the other hand, the work done in a special development department is "development" and is budgeted separately. Its scope can vary greatly. If it is an engineering problem, the first question to ask is: What exactly is the work involved?

If a new model is desired, a lot depends on whether the materials to be used are already available and whether the technical methods to be applied are familiar. In such cases it is generally possible to estimate the expected costs with reasonable accuracy. "Reasonable" means that the efforts will lead to the desired result after a reasonable time and a reasonable consumption of the different materials. You will generally arrive at such a solution if the new model does not differ too much from the existing one. The more it differs, the less accurate your estimate becomes. And if you have to use new materials and to apply new methods, your costs are likely to rise to quite unforeseeable heights.

CONTROLLING TECHNICAL WORK

My first point is this: *You can budget properly for development only if and to the extent that it is possible to control the technical side of the work.*

Even if you cannot budget accurately for the work, it may be possible to make a rough guess at the costs. The ability to make such estimates is an important part of the know-how of a company. But one should bear in mind that occasionally even the best guesses may be far off the mark. In particular, one should never forget that it is the technical side that causes the unforeseen costs. Only the engineers can see all sides of a technical problem. It is therefore advisable to make them lay down beforehand what is the precise object of the work, what kind of technical operations are necessary, what materials, what special apparatus, machine tools, and so on, are needed. If you do not know these things, your estimate will not help you very much.

If the work on a development project is spread over a long period, it is advisable to introduce interim checks at regular intervals. Engineers and scientists prefer not to be disturbed while working on a project. However, they should not consider it an unbearable inconvenience if the people who pay for the work inquire from time to time about its progress. It is helpful for them, also, to make a report on their work from time to time. It should be recognized, however, that you cannot produce inventions with the same regularity as you can loaves of bread. As point 2, I would suggest: *Have the progress of a development project controlled by a qualified engineer or scientist.* But do not be impatient.

The next step in passing from development to research comes when you find that you cannot get the new materials you need. You may feel that you should try to develop this new material yourself. In practice, this means in most cases that you would be forced to enter a different field. Estimate with the greatest caution the costs of such a venture and then double them. Even then your guess will probably not be sufficient. Remember that here you have no know-how at your disposal. In almost every case it will be cheaper to pay a pretty high sum to a company that works in this field and possesses the know-how to do the work for you.

A similar situation arises if entirely new methods are needed. For this purpose special research groups have to be created. The further removed from your present work such research is, the more difficult it will be to estimate its costs, even roughly. You may obtain a result fairly quickly or you may not obtain one at all. Besides, even if you do eventually obtain it, somebody else may have got there before you.

A RESEARCH INSTITUTE AND ITS COST

The acme of research is represented by a company-financed research institute, where a number of scientists may freely do research work on subjects in the company's field that they consider important.

Here you can assess fairly well the anticipated costs. You know that they will be high. And you will have to provide for these costs for a considerable length of time. The minimum, I would say, is ten years. Also, the institute must have a minimum size, which depends on the general line to be pursued. But considering the fact that modern research in any field cannot be one-sided, you will have to have quite a number of scientists. I dare say that if you want to provide for a real scientific research institute for ten years you must expect to spend at least some $25 million during that period. And what will be the result of this expenditure?

Nobody can tell exactly what new inventions will come out of it. In this respect a research institute bears some resemblance to a racing stable. In the one you hope for a winner of the Derby, in the other for a winner of the Nobel Prize. But how often do you really get one?

You may have to be content with minor scientific progress and with the publicity value of the institute's publications on particular scientific topics.

If properly staffed and maintained, however, such an institute gives your company scientific standing. That, in itself, may be a sufficient compensation for your expenditure. So we might say, as point 3: *A research institute should be complete in its way and of a long-term nature.* If you want to have one budget for a total expenditure covering a long period (not less than ten years), do not count on cash returns.

But the picture would not be complete if we look only at these various efforts in the field of development and research as isolated events. As I have tried to show, each effort has its particular rules and offers a particular return. But all of them together have an additional importance.

A modern industrial company must be dynamic or it will soon lose its position. This applies especially to the technical field. Of course the company must also be active in the field of marketing, and it must make the best use of progress in the field of office organization. But these efforts will lead nowhere if the quality and the price of the technical goods which the company produces cannot be maintained in the top flight of the industry.

If you want to remain among the leaders of your industry, you have to make continual improvements in your program. And you can achieve this only if you devote the bulk of your energies to technical development and research. Of course, you must make sure that your expenditure in this field does not exceed the eventual total benefits you may desire from the results of your efforts. You must also keep your total efforts well within the financial means of your company. But you should also bear in mind that all the people in your company must be kept fully aware of the necessity for technical progress. The existence of a general research institute may contribute considerably to such a spirit of awareness. That's why one should not be content to let such an institute work in a watertight compartment, but should be brought into contact with all the engineers of the company. The purpose of this is not so much to inform them about details of the work going on in the institute, but to spread the scientific approach even to the technical problems that may arise in day-to-day operations. Which leads to point 4: *Awareness of the necessity for development and research and the spirit of scientific approach to all technical problems should be cultivated throughout the company.* It may be considered as an additional return on the expenditure for research and development.

I have tried to show how and to what extent a company should cultivate development and research, how it can be controlled and budgeted for, and how far the costs involved can at least be limited in planning the total expenditure of the corporation. To a large extent—sometimes to a very large extent—the returns from such expenditure depend on what seems to be luck.

HOW TO SEEK INVENTIONS

What you really want are inventions. And there is an element of the artist in every inventor. Of course you need scientific knowledge—the best you can get. But knowledge alone does not produce the results you desire. You need the fellows who, on the basis of the best information available, are able to arrive at really new solutions. If you succeed in picking the right people, you may get the right returns. And you not only have to pick them—and maybe educate and train them afterwards—you also have to treat them properly, to give them the proper environment needed for this kind of work. This does not mean that you have to leave them entirely to themselves. They rather want to have the feeling that you care for them and for their work. Whatever control is exercised should be part of the care for the man and his work. So the last, point 5, would be: *Take all the trouble you can to pick the right engineers and scientists and give them the proper care!* But remember: For all successful development and research you still need that little bit of luck. The chances for luck are the better, the more carefully you prepare the way for it.

I have been able to give you only a few general considerations. Each industry offers different conditions and each company has a different mentality. These factors have to be considered. Please do not take what I have said as more than it is meant to be: a few general observations on a very complicated subject, but one that certainly deserves to be studied closely.

*What are the attributes with which technical
assistance to the young nations must be invested? It can only be temporary. Naked
colonialism should not be replaced by economic colonialism; the benefactor must
therefore be ready either to withdraw at a
given moment, or to be forced out.... Technical assistance should take the shape of
pure science and Technical Technology at
every stage, but with the definite prospect
of desirable economic benefit to the new
nation, and to the eventual withdrawal of
the benefactor.*

THE TWO TECHNOLOGIES

By Maurice J. Ponte *

   The economic development of those nations called "civilized,"
in the modern sense of the word, originates in the technologies
of energy production and transmission. These are characteristic
of the 19th century, during the first half of which the steam
engine and electrical machines appeared.
   It must be emphasized, however, that the basic principles—
causes or effects of research—are not necessarily bestowed on the
most technologically advanced. Admittedly, we are a long way
from the period when Faraday discovered induction with the
aid of a piece of wire, a battery, and a compass-needle. The re-

   * Chairman, Compagnie Générale de Telegraphie Sans Fil; chairman of
the Consultative Committee to the Prime Minister on Scientific and Technological Research in 1959 and 1960; member of the Scientific Council to the
High Commission on Atomic Energy and of the Planning Commission, Council on Instruction, National Institute for Nuclear Science and Technology.
M. Ponte is a member of the Development Council of the École Nationale
Superieure des Télécommunications and the École Nationale Superieure
d'Électricité.

search worker uses the technological facilities available at the time. But he is not enslaved by them, and one may even ask whether an accumulation of such facilities does not render research less fertile. This point is particularly important when considering the future role to be played by the underdeveloped nations in the growth of human knowledge.

TWO FORMS OF TECHNOLOGY

It is possible to distinguish two characteristic technological groups, bearing in mind, of course, the obvious limitations of such a simplification. Certain technologies are interwoven in such a way that their development is inevitably linked with technical progress in general. This we shall call *Technical Technology*. Examples of this kind of technology are abundant. When Sainte-Claire-Deville separated aluminum by electrolysis, the metal was considered a curiosity. The technology of its preparation was developed as a result of a demand created by other technologies calling for light metals. The requirements of jet-engines, of electric components, of atomic energy have inevitably resulted in extremely varied developments in metals, ceramics, and plastics. Technical Technology is a structure based on a wide range of scientific research. It has a logical framework, arbitrarily laid down, from which will come the technologies of the future, spurred by requirements as yet unforeseen.

On the other hand, we find technologies that have been developed to satisfy the requirements of a market, notably those concerned with mass-production. This we will call *Commercial Technology*. Here, too, many examples may be found. The automobile industry is probably the most significant of these, but one may also mention the large-scale plastics industry. It should be noted that, in contrast to Technical Technology, the stimulus of Commercial Technology is the requirement of the commercial market—sometimes artificially created by persuading the consumer of the necessity of the new product. It stems from Technical Technology but is aimed at increasing the quantity and reducing the cost of its products.

TECHNOLOGY UNDER CAPITALISM AND SOCIALISM

At this stage we should examine the interaction of technology and economic structure, and the way in which they condition each other's growth. Here, again, I shall simplify by dividing modern economic systems into two groups: capitalist and Socialist.

Capitalism presupposes free competition between enterprises created by capital investment calling for profit returns that must be as high and as quickly obtained as possible. In a Socialist system, the individual works to a common end which is the aim of the mass; finance is a means like any other to be used within an imposed general plan of development from which no one is allowed to deviate—in theory, at least. Technical considerations alone (again, in theory) are taken into account when establishing the Plan, and any modifications to it derive from the results achieved and the development of technology.

This statement alone clearly shows that modern economic structures do not fall into such well-defined divisions. State intervention is becoming increasingly important within all modern capitalist structures, and Socialism itself has deviated in respect of remuneration and property.

It now appears that Commercial Technology is the inheritance of capitalism. Since competition is free, the amount of capital invested in a given enterprise is such as to permit the capture of a market at a price that is as low and as profitable as possible. The associated technology is adapted to this end and draws on the best resources, both material and human.

In certain enterprises of our time it has been found that if research costs *one,* technological development costs *ten,* and mass-production costs a *hundred.* Commercial Technology is included in this hundred. Competition gives rise to the simultaneous development of several sources of production of the same thing, which results in a division of technological facilities and, to some extent, to waste. On the other hand, competition implies technical competition also, which speeds up technological development—with such a system there is no time to "wait and see."

Opposed to this, Socialist systems can develop Technical Technology on a sounder, more direct basis according to a logical plan, since the problem of competition does not exist. Even in the case of something that is to become an everyday product there is no need to carry its development to the point where it can stand competition from another, similar product. As a result, a large proportion of the "hundred" may be economized—particularly in human resources—to be employed to the benefit of the Technical Technology.

Are we to say then that capitalism is associated with Commercial Technology and Socialism with Technical Technology? Things are not so simple. Commercial Technology calls on Technical Technology and spurs it on. One of the final aims of the Socialist system is to bring utility goods to the consumer. The difference between the two systems is in the nature of an inversion of the importance of the two technologies. In a capitalist system, science and Technical Technology certainly exist, but they may be retarded if the needs of Commercial Technology draw off the limited available human resources with a priority determined by price considerations.

If we recall the figures already given for the cost of development within a competitive commercial system, we see that Commercial Technology absorbs a far greater proportion of the available resources than the other. As a result, for equal scientific and technical populations, the priority accorded to Technical Technology in a Socialist system will lead to an acceleration of development that will be greater than that of the capitalist system.

Even with modest beginnings the Socialist system may thus reach a higher level of per-unit technical achievement—a difference that cannot fail to accentuate with time. This accounts for the results obtained by Soviet technology in the domain of nuclear energy, and one may suggest that the existence of more than 60 million television receivers in the U.S. may be responsible for the Soviet lead in human space flights. At the same time, this is made possible only by limiting the volume and quality of products made available to the masses.

TECHNOLOGY IN THE U.S.

How are technological problems posed in the various nations throughout the world at the present time? We can only take a few examples.

The United States has the highest level of economic development; income per capita is the highest in the world and, if the standard of living is expressed in terms of the number of commodities made available to the individual, this also is the highest in the world. This tremendous expansion springs in the first instance from the spirit of enterprise of the people of this nation that has led to the development of widely varied techniques with a minimum of delay following their conception. It is a striking success for a Commercial Technology that has been able to develop continuously without massive destruction due to wars.

The present state of technological expansion in the U.S. calls also for the following remarks: As we have seen, different technologies are interwoven. In a country as highly evolved as the U.S., any one product calls for a ramified and widespread set of technologies down to the smallest component parts. The result of this is a technological framework that forms a structural whole found only in the U.S. Thus, American technology can be "exported" to a lesser-developed country only if the latter is prepared to rely on the U.S. for the supply of basic materials or semifinished product.

Such a highly developed technology is necessarily rigid, and its development may not be rushed. Mass production is aimed at satisfying a sufficiently large market, as a consequence of which the enormous resources required can only be brought into action relatively slowly. It is also possible in the development of a new technique to make the mistake of accumulating too soon a mass of technical resources that can be paid for only by undue price increases. This probably explains the loss of much of the transistor market in the U.S. to the Japanese.

Finally, the sheer size of modern technical resources in the U.S. has led first to economic and then to political consequences. The U.S. certainly holds all records for the formation of trusts leading to gigantic private concerns whose individual turnovers may be of the same order of magnitude as the French national budget. This state of affairs has led the American Government to legislative measures such as the Antitrust laws, which again shows how technological expansion may lead, even in the U.S., to deviations from a "purely" capitalist system.

TECHNOLOGY IN FRANCE

Let us take France as an example of a country of "average" development, as compared with the U.S. France's economic development over about the last 130 years has been influenced by a wider variety of factors. Science and technology have played a fundamental part, but in a localized sense one finds certain areas that have remained more or less in eclipse. Lack of essential raw materials and, until recent years, of certain sources of power, put a brake on expansion. In the political field, the Socialist viewpoint has had its effect. Finally, France suffered the terrible drain on human lives caused by World War I and the despoilment and mass destruction of World War II. All these factors have combined to produce an economy that is characterized by a certain balance between Technical Technology and Commercial Technology, and also between the various economic principles. Public services such as gas, electricity, rail transport, coal supply, etc., are in the hands of the government.

These services have a high technological development. The railways are the fastest in the world, and the Électricité de France has a research and development organization of international standing. The principal problems of our day, such as that of atomic energy, are also the concern of State organizations. In the field of telecommunications, all the various services are State-controlled, and technological development is advanced although expansion is limited by credit restrictions.

As a consequence of the French mentality and culture and, it must be admitted, a certain repugnance on the part of the consumer in France for anything that is new, French technology is for the main part Technical Technology, with its attendant successes and perils. The successes are of technical origin, a typical example being in the fields of the prospecting for oil, where the Institut Français du Pétrole has perfected methods that reduce prospecting time to a fifth or a tenth. The same organization is on the way to profoundly modifying the basic chemistry involved in the use of natural fuels. France's economic expansion is the subject of a "Plan," under the direction of the Prime Minister, and in which scientific and technical research find their place.

The development of technologies in France, particularly from the technical point of view, has generally indicated that they could and should be aimed at a larger market than France alone. A similar problem exists in other European countries and technological development should logically lead to organizations or treaties that overcome national barriers. I might mention the Iron and Steel Community and the Common Market. Such supranational developments are thus the consequences of technological development.

TECHNOLOGY IN THE "NEW NATIONS"

What will be the role of technology in the expansion of the underdeveloped countries? What kind of technology will be required by such technical assistance as may be forthcoming?

It would be better to term these countries "Young Nations." A young nation is a young organism endowed with a power that it wishes to exercise speedily and in as spectacular a manner as possible. It seeks to demonstrate its might to others, but above all to itself.

Its leaders must find a national objective calculated to endue the masses with enthusiasm and cause them to share in a global task. The objective of "raising the standard of living" in the American sense, for example, thus has no meaning. Certain individuals may be tempted by automobiles, refrigerators, or televisions sets, but this cannot provide an immediate and inspiring prospect for youth, which longs to join in a common effort.

It follows from these considerations that young nations will tend to make a clean start, neglecting their existing assets and attaching themselves to the most advanced science and technology. Indeed, science and technology offer fields for the youthful exercise of national talent, but above all they offer a means of contributing to other nations a share in a world achievement.

It is very clear also that young nations will naturally tend to be attracted by Technological Technology of the most advanced kind, and thus by Socialism which, besides, offers them the philosophy of the direct placing of technical achievements at the disposal of the masses. At their present stage of development, these nations are quite prepared to wait for results.

WHAT KIND OF TECHNICAL ASSISTANCE?

What are the attributes with which technical assistance to the young nations must be invested? It can only be temporary. Naked colonialism should not be replaced by economic colonialism; the benefactor must therefore be ready either to withdraw at a given moment, or to be forced out. The beneficiary wants to be able to join in the project, and very possibly the benefactor will himself derive advantage from this. These considerations are of general application, and hold good for others besides the young nations.

Purely financial aid is to be avoided: it will be hard to win the youth of a young nation to the ideal of working to repay interest on foreign capital, even when this improves the standard of living. Equally out of the question is assistance in the form of luxury goods, as this also is a modern form of colonialism. To repeat, then, technical assistance should take the shape of pure science and Technical Technology at every stage: education, technical training, general technological arrangements, but with the definite prospect of desirable economic benefit to the new nation, and to the eventual withdrawal of the benefactor.

SOME COMPARISONS

We have agreed that while technology is an essential driving force of modern expansion, it can take more than one form. Technological Technology develops by logical necessity as one technique comes to imply another. Derivative products are developed to a variable extent, assured of production under optimum conditions by Commercial Technology, which springs from the Technical Technology which it directs into given channels, while leaving other avenues of progress in the shade.

Technology is dominated by definite aims generated by the economic milieu in which it develops: it is possible either to devote the maximum resources to technology in the expectation that results will later make possible a mass development of products or, on the other hand, to make the best use of results in the wake of existing demand.

In the first instance, expansion is technical from the outset while consumption is curbed: in this way, spectacular technical results may be obtained. The future can be forecast by reliance upon a strong basis in technology, even though its realization is remote. In the second case, the standard of living rises steadily.

It is the first method that is likely to attract underdeveloped countries because they are convinced of their ability to contribute to global advance, and also because it allows them freedom to develop their own economies for themselves, without waiting for a rise in their currently low standard of living.

SOME QUESTIONS

Now let me pose a few questions for your consideration. Is it possible for countries with high standards of living to continue with their policies of economic freedom? Can they continue to devote so much of their means to disorderly development?

We have arrived at the hour of decision. I have said that we are already no longer an altogether free economy. Should we not be compelled by the ultimate prospect of an irresistible tide of superior products, looming as the outcome of Technological Technology, to adopt an increasingly directed economic system here and now?

Bearing in mind the magnitude of the human potential that modern Technological Technology requires, what size of economic unit is called for? Present experience suggests that in order to be capable of maintaining modern technology, a group must contain some 200 million individuals: the U.S., the U.S.S.R., the Common Market. Will this be sufficient for the future? And if, as is probable, larger groups are needed, will not the existing ones be forced to amalgamate in their turn, if they are not to be dominated by ethnic groups, like the Chinese, who seem to be rapidly absorbing the most modern technologies?

These are points that I leave for your reflection, having shown that while expansion is certainly based on technology, the outcome of this expansion will not be merely technical in character.

Whether encouraged or discouraged by the numberless individual policies and actions of their different governments, businessmen under many flags have worked hard and successfully at the job which is theirs alone —to find more and more useful work to do, to provide employment, and to produce the cash profit that supports both people and governments.

NATIONAL POLICY AND TECHNOLOGICAL INVESTMENT

By Malcolm P. Ferguson *

National policy is not necessarily either government policy or the actions of government, although it is easy to assume that they are one and the same. I believe it is instructive to see how our national policy affecting the subject we are discussing has developed, how it has been translated into government policy and action, and what the effects have been.

The national policy of the United States really antedated its government. In the debates over the writing of our Constitution, late in the 18th century, wise men laid the foundations of policy for a new government. They examined with care and deliberation the fundamentals that appeared to them to be sound and of overriding importance. They drew on their experience in our turbulent colonial period and borrowed much from the experience of the older countries, as well.

* President, Bendix Corp.; director, U.S. Rubber Co., National Bank of Detroit, Michigan Bell Telephone Co.

It was not accidental, therefore, that the national policy which emerged contained basic provisions and guarantees that promised the most encouragement to, and the least interference with, the rights, energies and ambitions of individual men and women.

More specifically, they designed the framework to meet the requirements of growing industry, and what we would now call technological investment. Equal status under law, rights of private property, sanctity of contract, recognition of the obligation of governmental debt, sound currency, tariff-free commerce between the new states, a patent system, and other practical matters were simply and directly embedded in the national policy that they handed down to us.

FUNDAMENTAL POLICIES TO ENCOURAGE INVESTMENT

Wise national policy generated technological investment by encouraging the three fundamental ingredients that are required for it and the growth of a national economy. I believe it is worthwhile to list them and note what was done with them.

First, *the creativeness, the ambition, and the self-interest of the individual:* The patent system was fundamental, but so also was the national climate—open, free, giving every man a chance to succeed or to fail. Incentives and the fruits of success were big and once harvested largely belonged to the earner.

Second, *education and training:* Even before our federal union was formed, the Congress of our Confederation initiated the policy of granting lands and money to the states for public education.

The third ingredient is *capital:* Many policies fostered the growth of capital—low tax rates, vigorous use of private credit, much of it from abroad and, particularly, the maintenance of the government's credit and a sound currency. It was achieved, I may say, through some perilous crises. The element of risk, however, was great, and both the gains and the losses were great also.

These three ingredients are just as indispensable today, and where national policy has paid proper attention to them the results have been predictably good. Even the Communists stress incentives, education, and the purposeful use of capital.

CHANGES NEEDED, CHANGES MADE

These conclusions have to be qualified, however, because the opportunity to build great industrial empires under a favorable national policy and a favorable government climate can produce, and in fact did produce in this country, certain excesses. Some of the most acquisitive industrialists engaged in practices that had the effect of throttling competition. But the public became alarmed by some of their methods and this resentment crystallized into a national policy of antitrust legislation.

In this country antitrust policy has had a powerful effect, though it began as a defensive measure against abuses. It has definitely fostered competition—the law of life in American industry. Under the changed conditions technological investment became almost the essential element in the competitive battle. By reducing costs and introducing innovations and added values, such investments gave price and product-appeal leverage to those who made them first. But the backward competitors were quickly driven to similar investment for their own survival. I am convinced that no single element of United States policy has equaled the maintenance of vigorous competition in its effect on technological investment.

This American competitive philosophy played its part in another trend which has also stimulated such investment. With its focus on low costs, intense competition had a tendency to restrain wages. The rise of organized labor was the inevitable response and it gained the support of national policy implemented by the Wagner Act. As a result labor costs have gone up, but this, too, has forced investment in technical advances to maintain competitive strength.

These major developments in national policy—the result of years of growing agitation for greater justice to competitors, to labor, to investors, and to consumers—actually accelerated investment in technology. The ultimate beneficiary was the nation as a whole through the spectacular rise in productivity, a sharp rise in the standard of living, and improvement in the goods and services offered to the public.

An important, though more oblique effect, resulted from the adoption of the principle of the graduated income tax in 1913. We can hardly believe now that, as pointed out by Frederick Lewis Allen in his book, *The Great Change,* wealth was then accumulating in a few hands at an amazing rate. Over the years the working of taxes did much to create the great middle class with its volume of purchasing power. And this, in turn, stimulated investment.

The crash of 1929 and the Great Depression raised grave doubts about some of our national policies. Then policy changed and was reflected in legislation that prevented speculative abuses and regulated our financial markets. Again, the American people authorized and wholeheartedly endorsed corrective action.

A LESSON FROM DEPRESSION

Yet, as the 30's dragged on, we learned a lesson worth keeping constantly in mind when debating national policy. It is expressed in a homely way, "The government cannot push with a rope." Government can effectively implement national policy *but it cannot force prosperity.*

In the eight years between 1933 and 1940, the New Deal Government here ran deficits of about $3 billion a year, more than doubling the national debt in the process. But as late as 1939, a decade after the crash, we still had 9,480,000 unemployed, which was 17.2% of our labor force.

In addition, statistics show that in contrast with the recovery of many of your countries, virtually no net capital was added to the United States economy during the decade of the 30's.

What is the explanation? No one can say with certainty, and opinions violently disagree. But this much is certain. At no time in this country's history was the businessman, the industrialist, and the capitalist so outspokenly attacked.

The outbreak of war in Europe changed the entire situation, but it is probable that our economic system would have slowly recovered if peace had continued. Certainly no one would argue the desirability of a war to invigorate an economic system. But it is a fact that World War II strongly stimulated technological invention and investment.

The postwar consumer buying demand and subsequent effort to sustain it prompts me to emphasize the growing role that instalment credit plays in our economy. In this country we recognize the necessity of mass production to provide goods and also employment. We have also developed mass distribution. But neither of these fundamental forces in our society can be sustained, we believe, without sound installment purchasing, which has been described by one of our leading merchants, Walter Hoving, as "post-consumption saving." Here again, national policy has an indirect effect on technological growth.

AN UNSOLVED PROBLEM

We do face a problem today that is inhibiting technological investment, and illustrates the gap between national policy and governmental action that sometimes occurs. This is the problem of depreciation policy, where our national policy is quite rigid, and is in fact outmoded. Our basic policies are 25 years old and, in the judgment of many, need overhauling.

The irony is this: one can sense the sentiment of national policy in the fact that both of our political parties in their 1960 platforms recognized the seriousness of the problem and promised to take corrective action. But it is still to come, and the United States stands in sharp contrast with many of your nations which have dealt with depreciation policy both realistically and helpfully.

GOVERNMENT AND TECHNOLOGY

A new and most powerful effect of national policy on technological investment arises from the active role of government in financing research and development. In 1950 our Department of Defense expended for R & D a total of $245 million. In 1960 expenditures reached $4.2 billion. More significant, even, is this comparison. The cost of all research and development in the United States in 1945 was estimated at $1.8 billion, of which the government financed the lesser part, $800 million. But in 1959 the total was $12 billion and the government's share was $7.2 billion.

The trend is upward and will continue to be. More and more weight is with government as technology grows in the conquest of space, in communications, in atomic energy, weather, and other fields. And this raises many problems. There are violent disagreements among businessmen over the tendency that government-sponsored programs in these fields may lead to government operation and ownership. One of the problems to which I refer grows from the government's tendency to sponsor research in nonprofit educational and specially created institutions, as compared with their being performed in the facilities and laboratories of private industry. More serious is the view strongly expressed by some that inventions made in the course of performing government-financed R & D contracts should become the sole property of the government and not of the individual or company in private industry.

PATENT PROTECTION IS VITAL

At this point I will express in the briefest terms my conviction that patent protection is absolutely vital to the advance of our technology. Since the patent office was established, close to 3 million patents have been granted. The majority never proved of profit either to the investor or to society, but great commercial successes have been built on patent protection.

I must say that as a businessman called upon to approve very large sums for research and engineering in my own company, I cannot visualize many such investments being made if there were no hope of a patent-protected return.

It may appear to some that in these tense days of the cold war and military technology, we must relegate to secondary importance many developments, even those profound in their effect, that influence technical investment in the private sectors of our economy. I do not accept this view. The strength of the free world is, in fact, economic, and accounts for its military and political weight in the current struggle. And it is this economic and social strength that must be preserved and in fact deliberately fostered. In this light, it is not merely relevant but extremely important that we do understand fully the facts of our present situation, and the very real implications of trends that are certain to affect technological investment in the future.

TO THE CREDIT OF BUSINESS MANAGEMENT

I will state boldly that the most significant fact of all is that business management in free countries has performed since World War II a miracle in achieving economic and social progress. I assign the credit to management for reasons that to me are clear and compelling. Skilled and cooperative labor was, of course, necessary. Capital was necessary. But it is certain that management alone is responsible for the organization of all the necessary resources, and it is the success or failure of management which determines whether the organization will prosper or fail. Companies have disappeared which had loyal and skilled workers, which had access to capital; yet they failed because management was not equal to its responsibility.

Whether encouraged by or discouraged by the numberless individual policies and actions of their different governments, businessmen under many flags have worked hard and successfully at the job which is theirs alone—to find more and more useful work to do, to provide employment, and to produce the cash profit that supports both people and governments.

Broad international patent exchange agreements between various nations have in the past greatly benefited their technological interchange of ideas and developments. The ECA programs and the numerous technical agencies of the United Nations have added to our over-all technical growth, but I would emphasize that national policy of the future must be stimulated toward further such efforts and plans. Similarly, there is the matter of technical investment by private enterprise of one country in that of another country. National policy of our countries will play a major part in encouraging such future programs and personally I hope that such policies will be aggressively pursued.

IN SUMMARY

First, we know what *has* happened. So we can trace—as I have attempted to do—the forces that develop within a nation, the policies established for dealing with them, and the results of these policies. We may interpret them differently, but the facts we cannot change. In other words the test of experience is in most cases the most valid one we have.

Secondly, I had to ask myself which of the guidelines of the past are valid today; and, also, which are not valid. And, of course, to try to understand why this is so. For example, the development in this country that I have sketched for you took place under a stable government in a community with a high rate of literacy, and with a broad base of enterprise, even though it was practically all in small units at the beginning. In contrast, technological advance is today not only passionately desired, but is taking place in many areas of the world where governments are new, where literacy is not high, and where there are few if any commercial and industrial units as a base for expansion.

Thirdly, government has grown steadily in size; it plays an increasingly active role not only as regulator and policeman, but as creator and customer. My own opinion is that government has a tendency, therefore, to exaggerate its paternity for all the progress we have made. Forgetting that industrial and technological advance have until recently been the province of private groups operating within the bounds of national policy, extremists argue today that only government can adequately plan and achieve further progress in the future.

I do not believe that initiative, competition, and the willingness to risk are qualities to be found in government in the same degree that they are found in the private sector of an economy. And because I believe they are necessary for technological advance, I continue to believe that the fundamentals about which I have been talking are just as good for tomorrow as they were yesterday.

The problem—and we cannot escape it, because it creates the blackest headlines in our daily newspapers—is the problem of dealing with human nature so that our energies are organized for the progress of individual men and women throughout the world, rather than being dissipated in political antagonism and bitterness. It is the quiet but powerful leadership of men such as you who can play the greatest role in charting the future course of the system which has achieved so much, and for which the potential is so great.

Historically and psychologically there are arguments for starting the development of a nonadvanced country by a number of peak activities in the field of modern technology and industry. It is a fact that working with atomic energy or in airplane plants is far more attractive and far more able to capture the enthusiasm of youth than being taught hygiene or history.

PREREQUISITES TO TECHNOLOGICAL PROGRESS

By Gunnar Randers *

There are different views concerning how and when to introduce advanced technology in a less-advanced country, even if most people realize that a standard of living like that of the Western world requires the use of modern industrial techniques. It is not unusual for specialists who have visited the less-advanced areas to conclude that a great number of purely social efforts must have priority before any modern industry or technology can be profitably introduced.

We have, for example, the usual calculations showing that im-

* Director, Norwegian Institute for Atomic Energy; chief scientist, Norwegian Defense Research Establishment (1946–48); chairman, Norwegian Atomic Energy Council, Atomic Energy Institute (1948); special adviser on atomic energy to the Secretary General of the United Nations (1954–56); adviser to the Director General, International Atomic Energy Agency (1958–59); governor, International Atomic Energy Agency (1960). Mr. Randers was vice-president of the European Atomic Energy Society from 1954 to 1958. His paper was read by Rolf Oestbye, president of Norsk Hydro-Elektrisk Kvaelstof.

provements in living standards by any reasonable rate of expansion in the industrial field would be offset by the rate of population increase. The immediate reaction is to maintain that the problem of birth control must be solved before even thinking of industrial expansion.

And there is the observation that so much sickness and filth exists that priority must be given to developing social hygiene and improved living habits in order to avoid such deplorable conditions. Finally, there is the experience of hopelessness in trying to run complicated machinery without trained personnel. This experience indicates strongly the priority of education.

It is not unusual, therefore, to hear the opinion that there is a list of overriding priorities like birth control, hygiene, and education in the greater part of the world that obviously could keep assistance programs busy for 50 years to come. Only after having solved these pressing problems, it is argued, would it make sense to introduce modern industrial techniques and research and development into less-developed areas.

FALLACIOUS ARGUMENTS

These arguments are dangerous, because they tend to stop a very important part of international assistance work. They are also fallacious. The fallacy stems from the fact that the Western world uses its own judgment of what it considers reasonable today, without paying any attention to the history of the Western civilization itself. Western civilization did not start with birth control, hygiene, and education in order to go on to applied technology. It is more true to say that the opposite was the evolution. It is also impossible to imagine a society brought up to the best standards of hygiene and education without the basic industrial production to support the economy of the nation.

Not only historically, but also psychologically there are arguments for starting the development of a nonadvanced country by a number of peak activities in the field of modern technology and industry. Psychologically it is a fact that working with atomic energy or in airplane plants is far more attractive and far more able to capture the enthusiasm of youth than being taught hygiene or history. The important thing is to create the atmosphere and enthusiasm for hard, coordinated work in a nation, because then the development necessary to keep the work going spreads by itself of necessity, like a chain reaction. If you have an automobile factory, you will soon have the machinists, the electricians, assembly and other workers appearing. On the other hand it is difficult to build up this group of specialists by promises of automobile factories in the far future. It is from this point of view that atomic energy might, in spite of all the doubts raised, be one of the most important catalysts for a rapid technical development in less-advanced countries.

*Foreign aid and strong internal efforts are
both required if the "lagging" country is to
make technical progress. Different modes of
living and cultures must also be taken into
account in giving foreign aid.*

STIMULATING TECHNOLOGICAL
DEVELOPMENT

By K. Y. King *

After World War II, the United States engaged in a unanimously applauded program of extensive economic aid to lagging
and war-crippled countries. However, the scope of this aid has
thus far been confined mainly to loans, grants, and commercial
procurement. Less emphasis has been placed on the technical
side. While economic help is more or less of a first-aid nature,
technical assistance is more fundamental and creative. Proper
guidance and technical assistance from scientifically progressive
countries like the U.S. will stimulate the lagging countries to become scientifically and technically conscious and facilitate their
technical and industrial development. In this way they can ultimately achieve economic stability.

* President, Chinese Petroleum Company. Mr. King was unable to attend.
His talk was read by J. C. Huang, managing director, Cyanamid Taiwan
Corporation, Taipei.

Among the means of technical aid I would consider technical teams, assisting in the basic training of local people, helping establish technological institutes, granting traineeships for advanced study abroad, and providing basic scientific and research equipment.

INTERNAL DEVELOPMENT PROGRAMS

The lagging countries themselves should undertake long-range programs to match outside aid for industrial and technical development. First of all, adequate and competent technical personnel are required for carrying out such programs. Basic training for such personnel should be given in colleges and universities, with emphasis on both pure and practical sciences. Government and industry can help broaden the scope of research by sponsoring and financing research and technical development projects in colleges and universities. Such undertakings are mutually beneficial. Technical forces for different fields may be built up gradually through proper scientific education. To provide advanced training for technical personnel, government and industry may help by encouraging and sponsoring study abroad by qualified science and engineering graduates.

Equally important is a healthy working environment for research and technical personnel. Government should encourage and subsidize the establishment of research institutes, and these should be provided with the necessary facilities. Technical libraries should be kept up-to-date with books, journals, and technical literature. The research and technical working forces should be properly compensated with reasonable salary and other facilities sufficient for a decent living. Furthermore, all contributions or achievements made by research or technical personnel should be appropriately rewarded.

NATIONAL POLICY AND TECHNICAL INVESTMENT

National policy plays an important part in the growth of technology, especially in lagging countries where major industries are government-owned or under government guidance and subsidy.

Inasmuch as the growth of technology is a prerequisite to the growth of industry, it is important that investment for research and technological improvement be given equal emphasis with other capital investment in industry.

In countries that are well aware of the significance of research to industrial growth, many companies budget a fixed portion of their income for investment in research and development. This is not always the case in lagging countries where industries are still young and are reluctant or ignorant of the benefits. Under such circumstances the government could help encourage technological investment by exempting or reducing the tax on income that is allocated to research and development. Government-owned or controlled industries should be allowed to retain an appropriate part of their income or profit for this purpose.

A fundamental means of encouraging research and development, of course, would be the establishment of government-owned or government-subsidized research institutes. Their activities should include research projects both for pure scientific advancement and for applied technological development, such as those called for by many industries. Government might also sponsor research through universities.

RESPONSIBLITY FOR RESEARCH

Industry and research are inseparable. They should coexist and progress hand-in-hand. Industry, as the immediate beneficiary of research, should carry out its own research. Universities are responsible for providing basic training to research and technical personnel. Without proper basic training, it is impossible to build up and maintain a technical force of qualified scientists and engineers indispensable to carrying out research and technological developments. Universities are like cradles where research personnel are nourished and grown, and where fundamental research activities are initiated. Inasmuch as research is a prerequisite for achieving scientific progress and the industrialization of a country, government should not overlook any opportunity of cultivating it. It should promote it through subsidies and favorable national policies.

A NOTE ON FOREIGN AID

Despite the fact that East and West have come to know each other better, it is still very difficult for the people of one country to change their philosophy and adopt immediately a basically different one. This has been the main factor weakening the effect of foreign aid. If the country giving aid can modify its program to a certain extent so that the country receiving it can utilize the aid more in line with its own mode of life, I am sure a more fruitful result can be expected.

Furthermore, there is always a sharp contrast in the standard of living of those administering the distribution of aid in a lagging country and the native receivers. I have always admired the missionaries who, while preaching in foreign countries, can actually live with the local people. If this missionary spirit can also prevail in aid programs, it will certainly help to reduce the biased feeling among the local people that tends to frustrate cooperation. The U.S. Government's program of sending Peace Corps representatives to aid foreign countries undoubtedly aims at spreading such missionary spirit to all its aiding activities.

4. Long-range Corporate Planning: Case Studies

We insist on first determining where we are, then where we want to be, when we wish to arrive at that point, and what it takes to get there in the time allowed. Finally, in our kind of business, we feel that all planning should start with the product manufactured, or the service rendered.

WORTHINGTON CORPORATION

By Walther H. Feldmann *

My company, Worthington, is a world-wide corporation selling about $250 million worth of products a year. We manufacture these products in 20 domestic plants, and in 12 foreign plants located in 10 foreign countries, and we have foreign representatives in most of the countries in the free world. These products are essentially heavy capital goods with one exception, which is home heating and air conditioning. All the others are heavy capital goods such as commercial and industrial air-conditioning and refrigeration equipment, liquid pumps, air and gas compressors, diesel and gas engines, steam turbines and gears, electric motors and generators and controls, pneumatically operated valves, instruments, and controls, steam condensers, deairater water heaters and ejectors, mechanical power transmissions, air-operated tools, concrete-construction equipment, and liquid meters.

Our products require a long development period. They are

* President, Worthington Corp.; president, Electrical Machinery Co. Ltd. (Canada); director, American Management Association.

highly engineered. In our case they happen to be divided about equally between pre-engineered shelf goods or inventory products, and custom-designed, manufactured-to-order products. We have a relatively high labor content, both direct and indirect. Our sales are to industry and government. Our total available volume is not materially affected by price levels, and I mention that in contrast to many of your domestic appliance products, Dr. Otten, where the price level has a great influence on the extent of your market. We experience severe domestic competition, and also severe foreign competition in world markets but not yet in our domestic markets.

A BASE FOR PLANNING

We have some convictions on which we base our planning efforts, which will enable you to understand some of the things we do and which, I hope, may give you some useful suggestions. We think it is important to differentiate between "crystal balling," which is our American slang for wild guessing, and forecasting, which we can call scientific guessing, and planning, which is a commitment for future action. I am indebted to Larry Appley, President of the American Management Association, for his excellent statement in this connection. He said, "The establishment of long-range objectives does not insure their attainment. A forecast is not a statement of what is going to happen. A projection of past results into the future does not portray the future. *Something has to be done about it.*"

Another conviction we have is that long-range plans must be living documents, and I assure you that they will be when they are a determination of action. They are obviously subject to change under changing conditions. We believe that when we do not change for the better, time will change for the worse, and so it is necessary to plan. I am indebted to Mr. Appley again for an expression that we like: "Good management *makes* things happen; it doesn't simply react to what does happen."

Our philosophy with respect to research and development is based on the policy, "Tell us what is needed and we will invent it"; in other words, we follow the marketing research concept rather than invention on an intuitive or inspirational basis. We try greatly to avoid defending yesterday. Rather, we insist on first determining where we are, then where we want to be, when we wish to arrive at that point, and what it takes to get there in the time allowed. And finally, in our kind of business, we feel that all planning should start with the product manufactured, or the service rendered.

Now, as to the history and scope of long-range planning in Worthington, I think I'd better read you a couple of items from our corporate objectives. Some of our people call these the "ten commandments." Our feeling is that if you are to set a course it is necessary to have some general philosophy.

First, it is our objective "to conduct a successful, diversified manufacturing business in products and services that will contribute importantly to better living for people throughout the world." Second, it is our aim "to grow both by development from within and through acquisitions of kindred products for kindred markets where our knowledge, resources, skills, and experience will enable us to make a sound contribution." Those objectives keep us from getting on our horse and riding off in all directions at once.

For some years now we have been making five-year plans. The first year is our budget for the coming year, worked out in complete detail. Each year we project one year further out and drop one year. These five-year plans are prepared in booklet form and are presented to our top staff and operating line people by our various divisions, of which we have sixteen. We review these plans in considerable detail with the top management of local divisions.

We have made some improvements over our early efforts. I think at first we did too much "crystal balling" or forecasting on a historically oriented basis. We extrapolated from the past and did not establish enough commitments to specific actions. I assure you that we make commitments now. We also became involved in too much detail in planning the second, third, and fourth years. One of our real problems is to keep the magnitude of this planning down to the point where our managers will not be frustrated, and will not be overwhelmed with the volume of it. We do not feel that the detail for the second, third, and fourth years is too important. We do think the first year must be completely defined, and the fifth year target must also be well defined.

EMPHASIS ON PRODUCT

We do not go into too much detail any more with respect to the required facilities, manpower, finances, etc. But we give much more detailed attention to our products, because without good products in our type of business there is no need for all these other items. With good products we feel we will have time enough to do the necessary planning for manpower, finances, and facilities. We put a great deal of emphasis on product planning. We attempt to determine the strengths and weaknesses of each one of our product groupings. This is done by our marketing people, separately by our engineering people, and separately again by our manufacturing people. All our existing product groups must be rated in this way. Our marketing people rate them with respect to price competitiveness, sales features, completeness of the line and market penetration. Our engineers analyze them for design features, performance, and reliability. Our manufacturing people analyze them from the standpoint of cost of production and quality assurance. We also record the number of years since the last major redesign of the product, the year of the last market survey, and the estimated life remaining in the product. We do all this for what we call first-generation products, which are the products in current production and offered for sale.

LOOKING FURTHER AHEAD

We also analyze the second-generation products, which are the products actually in development, with scheduled dates of release, and which will make our existing products obsolete. Then we will go further and give some attention to what we call third-generation products. These are the products that will replace the products that haven't been introduced yet. In this last area our consideration is largely limited to the research and development that must precede the designing of a product.

We also consider at this time new products that we are not now making, but which are kindred products and for kindred markets. We consider them only when we feel we can make a contribution in engineering, in manufacturing, or in marketing, and we set up certain criteria to guide each division in its evaluation of these products.

About 80% of our planning is in the product area, because we believe our products are our life blood, our birthright, our reason for existence. Now with the future competitive ability of each product group defined, we then ask the men to spend the remaining 20% of their time estimating the usual things—billings, costs, profits, facility additions, research and development needs, cash flow, financing needs, personnel needs, inventory of jobs versus inventory of people, and marketing programs. This is done without great exactness for the second and subsequent years in order to minimize the work load.

What does Worthington expect from its planning effort? We expect it to provide a challenge, that it hold the interest and stretch the abilities of our best people. We hope it provides the assurance of an improving competitive position. It gives us a firm position for one year. It gives us a five-year target and a trend between the first year and the fifth year. It gives us a much better knowledge of our customers' needs and desires, because our divisions must go to the customers to find out what will be needed in the future. And this, I think, is quite important. It produces an emphasis on the long range to offset the inherent pressures on the short range. Many of us in America use the return on investment as a measure of performance. But that has one great disadvantage, as it encourages managers to strive for a better showing short range, at the expense of the long range. Our five-year planning gives an emphasis to the long-range picture that we think is essential.

ROLE OF THE CHIEF EXECUTIVE

I have been asked to comment on my role as chief executive of the company in this planning effort. I consider it necessary first to establish the policy, and then to provide a good climate. In our company we have no problem of interest on the part of the participants. The only thing we have to watch out for is to minimize their work load so that they don't become frustrated and overwhelmed. And I think it is necessary for the chief executive to participate actively in this planning effort. Then, of course, he must commend and reward good performance in both plans and accomplishments.

ON GETTING SUPPORT

How do we achieve company-wide support? First, I think it is wise to sell the need for an improved situation. When General Lucius Clay went into Continental Can, he said, "It is my job to instill a spirit of dignified dissatisfaction with the way things are done." Now we try to get a spirit of dissatisfaction with the many things that go on at Worthington that are not done well. Then we must persuade our people to help in the long-range plan and convince them of what it will mean to them as an individual, as a division manager, and for the company as a whole. We feel that our divisional planning must be done by the line people, as opposed to staff people, both for realism and also for future commitment to the program. So our division general managers, and their functional department heads are the people who develop these plans. We use our staff people only to develop procedures so that we have a correlation between the various divisions. In order to achieve company-wide support I think it is necessary to keep planning in proper focus. Everybody should understand that it is a tool to help achieve results that we all want, and not a means in itself.

In concluding, I would stress two things. First, planning is a commitment for future action. If it is not, then I am afraid your future plans will not be achieved. Secondly, if planning is vigorously followed by a management group, that group will make the desired things happen, and not just react to what does happen.

I have no faith in a plan drawn up by a team of theorists. Planning is not statistical extrapolation. Within the limits of the directives from the management, every executive must set his own objectives. He can believe in such ends, and fight for them.

N. V. PHILIPS

*By P. F. S. Otten **

I have taken a particular interest in the practical side of long-range planning in my capacity as president of the Philips concern. It is a concern with a very special character of its own, not only because it has undergone such a remarkably rapid growth in the past decades but also because it has a very small home market and therefore conducts most of its activities outside the home country. It does this by means of dozens of sales organizations, operating independently throughout the world. These are often combined with production organizations which cooperate in a federative relationship. It is a concern, moreover, which comprises thirteen industrial divisions, each of which is, to a large extent, vertically integrated.

In the course of the years I have become more and more convinced that there is—or, at least, that there ought to be—a very

* President, Board of Directors, Philips Industries, Netherlands. Mr. Otten is also a director of Rotterdamsche Bank, and serves on the Board of Control of the Dutch Educational Institute for Industrial Life.

close relation between two elements of the task we have in common, that is, between management and planning. It is a relationship that applies to a greater degree to Philips, I think, owing to the special character of this enterprise.

In many countries an important part of the total economic activity is carried on by an extremely small proportion of all the enterprises. In addition to a very large number of small and medium-sized enterprises, a limited number of very large and often highly integrated concerns are operating. It is within these large organizations that an important evolution has taken place. When I say that our task is to manage the enterprise, then that is not incorrect—but it is incomplete. What has happened is that the mature, large-scale enterprise has outgrown the stage in which it could be managed by one man who was predestined for the task by his intuitive, inventive, and organizing endowments. Genius is no longer a prerequisite for a managerial function. For the initial period of growth of an enterprise, a manager endowed with genius may well be a prime requisite. My predecessor, Anton Philips, was such a man, and you all know a number of names: Rockefeller, Carnegie, Nobel, Renault, Ford—and there are others. In the present stage of development of their creations not only would they no longer feel at home, but really they would no longer fit into these organizations. In industry and commerce the accent has largely shifted from solitary leadership to teamwork, from rigid central management to federalism, from intuition to systematic, scientific thinking.

"SOCIAL CAPITALISM"

Another change, of even greater significance than this evolution in management, is the new form of capitalism that is now in the process of development. In my opinion, it is and must be our most effective weapon in our universal struggle with that other system of which Karl Marx is called the spiritual father. I should like to call it "social capitalism." I believe it may be regarded as a triumph of free Western thinking that it was possible for this new form to develop spontaneously.

I am of the opinion that—at all events in Europe—present-day capitalism is becoming more and more conscious of its responsibilities toward the interests of the community. This is not because of softheartedness but because of the realization that in the long run no member of any community can evade those responsibilities without placing himself outside that community. No longer is it the pursuit of maximum profit that governs our actions; it is the pursuit of continuity. Our aim now is continuity in the conduct of business, which of course creates the necessity for continuity not only in the rewarding of capital, but also in the opportunities for employment and sound personnel relations, in good contact with customers, and so on. Pursuing this line of reasoning, our enterprises are becoming institutional.

That this is no hollow phrase—at any rate in the case of Philips —may be shown by what is stated in the second clause of our articles of association—that the primary aim of the enterprise is to ensure opportunities for long-term employment. I would repeat that this evolution in capitalist thinking is not a symptom of senility but, on the contrary, a proof of vitality. It is the consequence of well-understood self-interest. The entrepreneur has become conscious of his social responsibilities with regard to the welfare of the employee, but he has also come to realize that the consumer is none other than the employee without his overalls. So there can be said to be an important shifting of the accent in the conception of the task of the entrepreneur. It is a shifting which leads to an untold intensification of the manager's task, for it makes the effect of our decisions much greater and accordingly increases the necessity for a correct foundation for those decisions.

MANAGEMENT BY OBJECTIVES

Accordingly, modern management can no longer permit itself to make do with the vague indication of desires for the future— with wishful thinking. Its outlook is now characterized by the expression "Management by Objectives." The modern entrepreneur sets himself well-defined, achievable objectives and sees to it that they are attained. Long in advance he must consider the development of the technical, the economic, and the social climate and must take all foreseeable structural changes into account in his policy. He will also constantly have to ask himself how and to what extent the enterprise, in its turn, influences its surroundings. In other words, he will ask himself how great the effect of his policy (and of that of his competitors and other fellow entrepreneurs) is on the development of that climate.

ECONOMIC CYCLES LESS IMPORTANT

It will perhaps surprise you that apparently I do not attach any value to influences of economic cycles. I do, of course. But I am sure that those influences will become less and less important.

The fact is that many governments are gradually coming to pursue a wiser and more circumspect economic policy. There is an increasingly fruitful cooperation between these governments and industry and commerce, not least of all on account of the more constructive attitude of the employers' and employees' organizations—in Europe, at any rate. We see a growing understanding of economic cycles on the part of the leaders of the large labor parties, which can exercise a moderating influence on the reactions of the masses. We see a growing realization on the part of the entrepreneurs of the necessity for well-thought-out long-term policy on a scientific basis. And there is an increasing inclination on the part of the large entrepreneurs to solve problems jointly.

All these factors will, I am convinced, help to lessen the violence of economic fluctuations. We may perhaps even cherish the hope that phenomena such as world-wide crises and slumps, of a severity such as we remember from the 1930's, will once and for all become things of the past and that reversals in economic conditions will be of a much less drastic nature.

THE NATURE OF SCIENTIFIC MANAGEMENT

If we can agree about the task of the entrepreneur and about his growing social function, then I think we are also in agreement about the need for scientific management. This, however, also implies an ever-higher degree of delegation. The problems of management are becoming more and more extensive and more and more intricate. The handling of the modern methodologies is more and more becoming the work of specialists. Even where there is extreme efficiency of the division of labor at the top, the management as such will hardly ever again be able to work out the essential problems completely. These problems must be analyzed, made "ripe" for decisions, and submitted to the management at any desired moment. When assessing them, the management will have to confine itself to fundamental decisions. The organization of the enterprise will accordingly have to be adjusted to a system that can provide the required information at the right moment. The entire *preparation* and frequently even the *initiative* of each management decision will have to be extensively delegated.

Once such a decision has been made, it must no longer, in principle, be a daily preoccupation of the management to determine how the decision made is to be carried out so as to result in the intended effect. The more farreaching the decision made, the more time its implementation will take and the more the dynamics of modern society will be in a position to influence both the measures adopted and the climate. In other words, at the moment of the decision it will be necessary to anticipate, as far as possible, the effects—during the whole period of enforcement—of the interplay of free forces on the enterprise. Since such anticipation can never be complete, there will also have to be a system permitting of continual corrections where anticipation was inadequate. Moreover, the management will have to be relieved of preoccupation with the realization of the decisions, and this entails a high degree of delegation of the *implementation* as well.

At Philips we have found an excellent means of solving these problems—by long-range planning. Obviously the system employed is entirely adapted to the particular structure of our concern. Far be it from me, therefore, to present this Philips system to you as the only good one. Nor is there any point in wearying you with a detailed description of the whole mechanism. I merely hope that our philosophy in respect of this subject may provide you with some useful ideas.

SOME PRINCIPLES

I shall begin by considering with you some principles underlying our system. As the first principle, or, rather, as our first fundamental law, I should like to put this to you: *The planning* (essential aid to the management of an enterprise) *must be a mental attitude—a continuous, uninterrupted thought process.*

A policy is not a basic decision that one can have engraved in the façade of one's office; a policy is an organism—*a policy must grow.* Our objectives and the directly resultant measures to be adopted must continuously be confronted with: (a) the measures already taken; (b) the effect of those measures; and (c) the behavior of the surroundings.

It has never become clear to me how there can possibly be enterprises that draw up a plan for, say, five years, confine themselves during those five years to the unemotional comparison of forecast and reality and then, when that period has elapsed, prepare a new plan. Planning of this kind contributes in no way at all toward the support of policy and management decisions. It fulfills no real function. In order to fulfill that function properly, a plan must be *regularly* reviewed and readjusted; it must be continually filed and polished. It must live. That can be achieved in only one way: by creating decision moments.

Accordingly, my second fundamental law reads as follows: *Compel those whom you have made responsible for carrying out the plans to discuss them with you from time to time.* By this means compel them regularly to take stock of the state of progress, of the suitability of the plan for the current situation, in the form which it has at a given moment.

In addition, see that you are constantly kept informed of the state of affairs, in order to be able to judge whether, and to what extent, the policy must be adjusted. The intensive preparation of those discussions, necessary to prevent them from running to marathon length, forces the executives to go into the problems over and over again.

The alternative is that if you only lay down the requirement that the plans be reviewed regularly, without discussing them fully with the persons concerned, these reviews will come to be regarded as a very annoying hunger for paper on the part of a planning office. For this reason it is also necessary for every phase of the realization of the fixed objectives to be laid down in set

tasks, so that everyone knows his part in the total performance—
so that the optimum effect can be attained. If every plan ends in
a series of budgets relating to investment, production, sales, costs
and profitability, the follow-up given to each one will ensure
that those with whom you cannot speak regularly likewise feel
committed to their tasks.

The point is not only that our decisions are carried out in the
spirit in which they are made, but also that these decisions are
supported by data emerging from the factories and offices. We are
concerned here with a problem of communication in two directions. We must be certain that the directives penetrate to the
levels at which they are put into effect, but we must also keep
ourselves informed of the way in which they are implemented.
Hence there is a large degree of interdependence between the
various levels of the enterprise.

I have no faith in a plan drawn up by a team of theorists. Planning is not statistical extrapolation. Within the limits of the
directives from the management, every executive must set his
own objectives. He can believe in such ends, and fight for them.
Moreover, in all the departments of an enterprise an incredibly
large amount of essential information is available. The only way
to make this information of benefit to the policy of the enterprise
is to *absorb everyone,* from president to salesman, *in the system
of planning.*

This seems to be an overstatement. I can assure you that it is
done at Philips and that we are very satisfied with it. Accordingly, you may safely regard this as my third fundamental law:
Make your plans by starting at the bottom. Make sure that your
directives penetrate to the lowest level and make use of the
knowledge available at this level. The man is perhaps not aware
of it, but you often obtain the most valuable information with
regard to the market from the man at the front, from the reports
of the traveling salesman.

HOW PLANNING WORKS AT PHILIPS

It is obvious that in our case, as elsewhere, the necessity for the
managing team to confine themselves to essentials has led us to

delegate an important part of our authority. We have placed the product policy, for example, in the hands of our *industrial divisions*. The products for which these divisions are responsible differ widely at Philips and include electronic and electrotechnical products. They extend from midget lamps to town-lighting systems, from memory cores to synchrocyclotrons, from pocket radio sets to radio transmitting stations. We have carried that delegation through to very great lengths, with the result that to some extent the industrial divisions are even each other's competitors. Naturally this requires top management to concern itself with the coordination of its policies. In addition, we have delegated our geographical policy to our *national organizations*.

Since these two policy lines, product policy and regional policy, may intersect, regular attuning is necessary. The whole planning game, then, rests on the policy discussions. These take place regularly, though not at set intervals, both with the industrial divisions and with the local organizations. As far as the former are concerned, the field of commercial activities is marked out. On the basis of product trend forecasts covering periods of up to ten years, our activities are roughly defined. At the industrial division level these ideas are then worked our further, in concrete terms. The resultant directives are afterwards passed on to the national organizations and from there to the sales-manager level. In the case of the second kind of meetings, those with the managements of local organizations, the over-all development of the activities within a country is discussed in the light of the product policies and against the background of the whole economy of such a country.

In all these discussions, current plans play a very important part. These are the "moments" to which I referred in my second fundamental law. But they are not confined to this level. At lower levels, as well, talks of this kind take place—such as those between the local managements and the product sales managers.

The directives issued on the basis of the policy discussions must now be given a definite form. For this purpose, four-year plans are prepared annually in the national organizations. Within the frame of the guiding lines given by the local management, these plans are built up, and the knowledge of all the levels is incorporated. In the first instance they are built up as market and sales forecasts.

Just as in the case of the product-trend forecasts, intensive use of the market-research methodology is made here, both locally and in the industrial divisions, both in the form of field research and in that of desk research and statistical analysis. The object of all this is to ensure that a picture of the market and market share is obtained which is as clear and objective as possible. We attach a very great deal of value to modern research methods. Because we are so highly integrated, the sales forecast has to be as reliable as can possibly be achieved with the most up-to-date aids. This does not alter the fact that they remain aids. Ultimately, the targets are set by those responsible for their attainment—by the sales people and not by the methodology specialists.

After the sales plans for the coming four years have been drawn up, the entire industrial activity is accordingly worked out carefully, in all its details. This is a process that is made more difficult because, along with our industrial integration, there is also a far-reaching international division of labor.

PROFITABILITY FORECASTS

This working-out in industrial activity is followed by the calculation of all quantities in money and by the differentiation of all the data in terms of investment and financing, of turnover and costs, of liquidity and profitability. This profitability forecast is definitely not claimed to be a reliable prediction of the expected profit. Because of the regular reviewing of the plans this does not matter so much. It is important above all because it finally emerges in the elaboration of the plans as the resultant of all the task-setting factors included in the calculation: production costs, sales costs, selling-prices, etc. And especially important, too, is the confrontation of this resultant with the roughly estimated possible profit considered when the policy was determined. These fully developed plans, then, must be the precipitate of the permanent consultation between industrial division and national organization.

A final readjustment is therefore necessary. This affords an opportunity to take recent information into account and to ascertain whether all the component parts fit into the over-all policy.

The influence of the time factor on the preparation of these four-year plans is also important. It is a well-known fact that where the period separating us from the moment of realization of our ultimate aim is a long one, our knowledge of the situation that will exist at the time of that realization is limited, whereas our flexibility, our range of possible choices, is extensive. As the moment of realization approaches, our knowledge increases and our flexibility decreases.

In accordance with this, the fourth year of each plan is the least detailed, whereas the first year is in full detail; hence this first year must be regarded as the operational plan, which needs only to be anchored in working budgets. The fourth year is still entirely of a strategic nature and the resultant budgets are confined to investment budgets concerning long-term projects. Since a new four-year plan is made every year ("the revolving system"), the plan for any given year successively passes through all the stages of strategy, via tactics to operational orders, and in each succeeding stage the internal and external influences that have made themselves felt in the intermediate period can then be taken into account. As soon as the plan for the first year has been accepted as a task and its realization begins, the so-called short-term planning (the daily "housekeeping" with means and their utilization) commences, both commercial and technical, both social and financial.

You will, of course, have been able to note that in the system described here my three fundamental laws—continuous processing and touching-up of the plans, full discussion at intervals and regular review, and starting at the bottom—are all accorded their full value.

Fairness compels me to add that the carrying-out of this system does not yet approach the ideal in every detail, even though we have now had many years of experience, but I can say that we are very satisfied with it. It is no exaggeration to say that the results we have so far achieved, notably in respect of organization but also with regard to the mutual spirit of cooperation which this system undoubtedly stimulates, may be called noteworthy, though these results are perhaps difficult to evaluate in terms of money.

I hope that I have made two things clear: First, that all our actions must be well-thought-out long in advance and that, in addition, we must operate a system of planning which is adapted to foresee and consider all the consequences of our actions; secondly, that we must realize that we are not primarily competitors, but rather fellow passengers in the ultraswift space ship of our Western economy. We are fellow passengers whose main object must be to reach our destination together and in a state of well-being—in other words, we must become more and more aware that it is of vital importance to us to harmonize our philosophies more than in the past.

Despite the importance which we attach to long-range planning, we must realize that it can fulfill its task in the service of industrial management only if we know and accept its limitations. Only with such knowledge can we master industrial planning as an instrument instead of being dominated by it.

THE THYSSEN GROUP

By Hans-Gunther Sohl *

The fact that industrial planning gained such an early foothold in the United States may be explained by the special economic conditions of this continent. Its vast and uniform economic area forced the entrepreneur from the very beginning of industrial development to think in terms of the future and to plan accordingly.

In Europe, the situation was fundamentally different. During the period of its industrial development, it was divided into many nations constituting self-contained economies separated from each other by a multitude of trade barriers. In such narrow and clearly defined markets of limited capacity and purchasing power, management could get along with day-to-day decisions. Up to the most recent years, there was not a complete lack of planning—

* President, board of management, August Thyssen-Hütte Aktiengesellschaft; chairman or director of a score of West German enterprises; member, advisory committee, European Coal and Steel Community; chairman, Iron and Steel Industries Federation.

for business has at all times been planned action towards a definite goal—but a deep-rooted tendency to rely largely on experience and intuition in the conduct and promotion of enterprises.

The economic situation of the recent past also shows a marked difference between our two continents. During the first years after World War II the paramount task of the European entrepreneur was to rebuild his productive equipment and to get it started again. Everywhere there was such a pent-up consumer's demand that for years the goods were literally snatched from the manufacturer's hands, a market situation that was certainly not conducive to long-range planning. During the same period the supply of goods became more and more abundant and diversified in America and competition grew in intensity, with the result that large enterprises could prosper and expand only by having recourse to systematic and improved methods of planning.

EUROPE'S STEPS TOWARD PLANNING

It was only when a buyer's market developed in the Old World that a general climate was created that was more favorable to thinking in terms of the future. In my opinion it is of decisive importance for this more recent trend that for about the last ten years Europe has been moving toward the creation of larger markets. This tendency started in 1953 with the Common Market for Coal and Steel. There followed in 1958 the European Economic Community extending the Common Market to all branches of economic activity. It will probably experience a noteworthy expansion through Great Britain's membership together, it is hoped, with other European countries. This development is now creating for Europe, too, economic conditions which are similar to those in America and which will increasingly render large-scale industrial planning indispensable.

For the time being there will remain certain differences in the degree of what might be called the "willingness to plan." This can be partly explained by the fact that the necessity of long-range planning still varies greatly from industry to industry and from continent to continent. Moreover, for many a businessman the word "planning" has a nasty connotation with an economic system which is abhorrent to all of us. I would say, however, that free enterprise planning is necessary to avoid planning on a State level, which would mean a planned economy of Socialistic tinge. It is our task as managers to take the initiative in all planning, and we have to teach our assistants on all levels to think in terms of planning so as to enable them to supply reliable data on which we can base our decisions.

PLANNING AND ACTION

What results do we expect of planning? To use one common denominator, planning is an instrument in the hands of business administration to narrow down the uncertainties of the future. But planning, however perfect it may be, is no substitute for executive decisions. On the contrary, planning presupposes a will for creative action that is not satisfied to accept developments passively. The chief executive sets the goals and his planning division then evaluates different possibilities of development and prepares different alternatives on approaching these objectives. In that sense planning actually promotes executive initiative by writing down, so to speak, future possibilities of development to their present value with the help of a careful data analysis.

Planning compels us to look beyond the confines of our own enterprise and to examine all external possibilities of development of our particular industry within national as well as in the international perspective. Thus prognoses of the probable overall economic trend and analyses of political and social tendencies serve the further preparation of industrial planning. They are supplemented by forecasts of factors peculiar to the industry concerned, of products and their scope of application, of possible substitutes, etc. As a result, the framework is set for determining the goals and objectives that appear attainable on the basis of these analyses. Finally, any long-range planning requires short and medium-term programs which afford continuous control of the actual business operations and which are indispensable for the current re-examination of long-range planning goals.

PLANNING IN IRON AND STEEL

I come from the iron and steel industry, one of the few industries whose products, despite increasing specialization and existing differences in quality, are standard products that can be manufactured all over the world by the same processes, in the same dimensions, and with the same analyses. Such an industry naturally gives rise to particularly keen competition, all the more so as the steel industry is experiencing a rapid and world-wide growth. International groups of experts anticipate that more than 600 million metric tons of crude steel per year will be produced in the world by the middle of the 70's, as compared with the present output of about 300 million tons.

It is obvious that we can only keep up with this accelerated pace in the world steel industry and with increasing international competition if we endeavor to achieve a technical and economic optimum in developing our enterprises. For this reason more and more importance must be attached to planning. This applies in particular to the procurement of raw materials, where our predominant requirements of iron ore force us to look decades ahead on a world-wide scale; for raw materials represent within the cost structure of our European steel mills almost half of our total costs and are thus by far the largest single item.

Competition, which is particularly keen in the steel industry, compels us perhaps more so than other industries to include external factors in our planning. We follow with great interest forecasts of the general development of the world steel industry, such as those prepared by the ECA from time to time. The last study of this kind was published in 1959 and dealt with the development of the world steel economy until the middle of the 70's. Similarly, the High Authority of the European Community of Coal and Steel supplies current forecasts by which we can orient our planning. In addition to short-term estimates of demand and production, the High Authority also publishes for the area of the Coal and Steel Community so-called "General Goals and Objectives," containing forecasts for a number of years. A forthcoming study of this kind deals with the probable development until 1965. Supplementing these official studies, prognoses of the future development of our industry are being regularly worked out by the German steel industry. It may interest you to learn that the German steel industry maintains an Institute for Business Administration, which serves our steel companies as a platform on which to discuss questions of industrial planning and to exchange and compare cost figures and other internal production data. It also stimulates our planning work, at short term for measures of rationalization, and at long range for investment projects.

THYSSEN'S TEN-YEAR PLANS

Let me add a few words on what the enterprises of the Thyssen Group do in the field of planning. You must keep in mind that our first task after war, dismantling, and decartelization was the reconstruction of our works. Our company was not reconstituted until 1953. In the field of industrial planning, therefore, we have not had many years of experience, although we benefited from the experience gained by our predecessor companies. On the other hand, as an enterprise still in the process of reconstruction we are particularly interested in the problems of planning. By now we have reached the point where our planning extends to periods of up to ten years. Moreover, at least once a year we prepare an over-all medium-term plan in which the partial plans of the sales, production, finance, and accounting departments are co-ordinated. It serves us as a basis for current decisions.

As to our long-range planning, we fully realize that the completeness of the forecast diminishes in proportion to the length of the period covered and that such a plan is only a rough guide. As a supplement to medium-term planning, however, the long-range plan is of definite value provided it is carefully prepared and applied with flexibility. It provides useful information as to sales, costs, returns, depreciation, credit possibilities, and other relevant data concerning the long-range development. In the course of time long-range planning is improved as more reliable data become available on the basis of current short and medium-term plans.

Planning as we carry it out has certainly proven an efficient instrument of orientation. Nevertheless, much remains to be done in this field. You know that the introduction of electronic computer systems has considerably facilitated the application to planning. You also know what progress has been made in the field of operations research not only in America, but also in Great Britain and other countries. In the Thyssen Group, we have set up a small operations research section to collect experience in this field and to methodically feel our way toward the major tasks. Results have been rather encouraging.

It is only natural that planning cannot fully develop its advantages in the first stage of its application; it is like wine, improving with age. Similarly, the value of planning improves from year to year as organization and market perspectives grow and cooperation of the people concerned becomes closer and closer and more dependable, resulting in a greater adaptability of the enterprise as a whole.

Despite the importance which we attach to long-range planning, we must realize that it can fulfill its task in the service of industrial management only if we know and accept its limitations. Only with such knowledge can we master industrial planning as an instrument instead of being dominated by it. Even the best planning cannot solve the uncertainties of the future. Therefore, plans must not be rigid nor must they become the maxim of executive action. This very postulate distinguishes our industrial planning from a State-planned economy which, having no other aim than to fulfill the plan, plays havoc with any willingness on the part of the entrepreneur to assume risks.

Whether for political or economic reasons, actual business operations may skip the predetermined tracks and improvisation may become necessary. In such a situation it is the man who counts and his readiness to fill the gap. We of the Thyssen Group are therefore of the opinion that the creative forces can best be developed if responsibility is delegated to the widest possible extent. The organization of our Group is decentralized and the managers of our subsidiaries enjoy a great amount of independence in operating and developing their plants, but always subject to the ultimate goal we have set for the entire Group.

5. The Multinational Company

*For global companies, profit no longer can
be the sole motive, important as it must always remain. While management can never
discount its obligations to shareholders of
a parent company, it must recognize that
those obligations can be fulfilled best by
industrialists who are also sensitive to the
motives of nationals of foreign countries.*

WHY EXPAND OVERSEAS?

By Sven T. Aberg *

My remarks will be limited to an account of the experience
of the multinational company with which I am most familiar—
the Ericsson Company—and to the presentation of some principles derived from that experience.

First, it should be noted that Ericsson produces and sells capital
goods in the telecommunications field, which is highly technical.
The life of our products is often twenty-five to thirty years, or
longer. The service problem is an integral part of our activity.
Our customers are largely governments or other public agencies
with virtual monopolies in their respective areas. Our sales are
based mainly on technical presentations of a complex type.
Production and selling are actually only part of the economic

* President, L. M. Ericsson Telephone Company; chairman of some half-
dozen companies in the Ericsson complex in Sweden, and board member of
associated companies in France, Italy, and the United States. Mr. Aberg is
chairman of the Swedish Association of Electrical Industries, and board member of the Federation of Swedish Industries and of the General Export Association of Sweden.

function we perform. What we offer basically is a telecommunications "package" that includes a detailed analysis of telephone needs in a particular area, including economic planning, design, construction, and installation of complete systems and, in some cases, suggested tariff schedules. Prospects for this package are entire nations, as well as municipal and regional administrations. All this means that the problems we face differ from those encountered by companies producing for, and selling to, the general public through conventional merchandising approaches.

EARLY MOTIVATIONS

When Ericsson first expanded beyond the borders of Sweden at the turn of the century, the motive was quite simple. Through good design and high quality, our products had found ready acceptance in many parts of the world and we responded to the opportunity to move more goods overseas, although a sales organization and sales efforts in the modern sense were then unknown.

Product acceptance was soon followed by demands for local manufacturing of those products in important markets. In Russia, for example, this pressure was so heavy that an Ericsson factory was established in St. Petersburg as early as 1897. The problem there was typical of many that were to develop in other areas in the future. If we did not choose to manufacture locally, we risked losing our position in the market. It is worth noting, incidentally, that our first foreign manufacturing venture was in what would today be termed a rather "underdeveloped" country.

We established a number of overseas factories during the first part of the century. In the same period, we began to acquire a number of telephone operating franchises in foreign countries, although we were to reverse our policy in this field in later years. Our files and records of the early days of foreign expansion make fascinating reading for a modern executive. And one of the striking facts is that there are so few references to the instability of foreign currencies. It was not until tension began to mount before World War I that the problems of devaluation and of frozen funds, both so well known to businessmen today, became significant.

World War I interrupted our expansion abroad. But during the period between the two great wars additional subsidiaries, both manufacturing and sales companies, were established in a dozen countries. Many operating franchises were also acquired. After World War II a large number of sales companies and manufacturing facilities were established overseas.

PRODUCT QUALITY AND ACCEPTANCE BASIS

If there is one distinguishing feature of our continuing foreign expansion, it has been the fact that product quality and product acceptance have created the conditions in which the profit motivation could be applied realistically. Our primary motivation has been pride in the caliber of our research, designing, technical ability, production efficiency, and reasonable prices. This has been, and is today, the one factor responsible for our development as a multinational company. And I am certain the same factor is responsible for the growth of other successful companies of this type.

Product acceptance in a foreign country can, as we have seen, create its own problems. The agents or the sales companies of a multinational company almost inevitably demand that local manufacturing or assembly facilities be established. This pressure may be supported by local governmental policies and reinforced by such factors as increased tariff rates, exchange restrictions, or the freezing of profits. Management is faced with the crucial decision whether to manufacture overseas or lose a valuable market.

In effect, management must reconcile the expectations of its sales people with the technical problems faced by production experts. The latter understandably are concerned by the difficulties involved in trying to manufacture complex technical products in a foreign country on a smaller scale and still at a reasonable profit.

FINANCING OVERSEAS EXPANSION

In studying these problems, we soon learned that a new manufacturing venture beyond our borders almost always means that the parent company has to carry an additional financial burden for a period of years. This is particularly true in developing countries where political considerations or the desire for national industries frequently outweigh rational economic thinking.

Assuming that management is prepared to accept the extra burden, it has to face the specific problem of how to finance the new enterprise. Two main approaches are available. One is to finance the whole undertaking with funds created or obtained by the parent company. The other is to seek participation by capital in the country in question, either through public offerings of securities or through cooperation with already established industrial enterprises. We have tried both.

In the telecommunications business, owing to the acute shortage of risk capital, expansion in developing countries normally means providing the whole investment yourself. A private investor in most developing countries, particularly those with strong inflationary trends, seldom finds investment attractive in an industry like ours, with its very long-range projects. His capital flows to other fields offering quicker yields. We have, however, arranged successful financing through participation by local interests in a number of well-developed industrial countries. In such cases, cooperation with local industrial and technical leadership can offer attractive results.

These decisions with regard to investment—where funds are to be obtained and how much capital is needed—are among the most crucial to be taken by the management of a multinational company. Many risks must be weighed: nonconvertibility of currencies, freezing of dividends and royalty payments, possible expropriation without adequate compensation, the hazard of losses from revolutions or wars, and many others.

CONCESSIONS AND PROMISES

During the postwar period we have repeatedly seen laws enacted to attract foreign investments to new manufacturing enterprises. The benefits commonly promised include tax relief during an initial period, reduced tariffs on machinery imports, and guarantees covering the transfer of dividends and royalties, and the repatriation of capital.

We have generally attached little importance to such promises. Close analysis of the actual value of such concessions often discloses offsetting limitations that hamper, rather than encourage, productive effort. At best, these so-called incentives have been minor factors in determining the course of our overseas expansion. Perhaps we recall too well how quickly the economic climate for long-range investments, particularly in developing countries, can change through the imposition of new rules.

It is a mistake, we believe, to base programs of foreign expansion on so-called inducements or concessions. The only sound basis for such programs must be the existence of an established market, or the conviction that a market for a company's products can be established with long-range prospects for competitively priced merchandise. Profit motivation based on sound management principles should not be subordinated to politically inspired concessions.

NEW FACTORS, NEW MOTIVATIONS

Our strong motivation to acquire franchises has been destroyed by new factors in the picture. What once seemed a logical way to expand is no longer attractive. The unfortunate economic fact today is that it is no longer possible for a multinational company to operate foreign utility franchises efficiently, much less profitably, overseas. Operating companies have an insatiable appetite for increased financing and this appetite must be fed if service is to be maintained at reasonable standards. In our experience, even when an agreed rate structure was based on the gold standard, we discovered that local political and economic factors made it impossible to adjust rates as needed to permit sound development of a foreign franchise.

If, however, we failed to expand the system, it was inevitably argued that we had failed to live up to our part of the franchise contract, thereby justifying withdrawal of the franchise by the local authorities. The question of proper compensation was always a delicate one. Frequently long-term bonds of questionable value were offered in payment. And even where franchises were retained for long periods of time, many ways to harass the foreign company could be, and were, discovered.

Accordingly, about twenty-five years ago, we drew up what we call the "golden rule" for running foreign public utilities. This rule states very simply: "Whoever has the authority to establish rates should own the company."

PROSPECTS FOR INTERNATIONAL AGREEMENT

It is regrettable that this situation has developed. There is still an enormous demand for new telephone services. Staggering amounts of capital, much of which could be provided by multinational companies under proper circumstances, are needed. But it is clear that we are not going to see that type of investment by private companies until we get watertight international agreements protecting foreign long-term investments, of the type described by Dr. Herman Abs at San Francisco in 1957.

Since that time, the need for such agreements has been discussed repeatedly by governmental and private organizations such as the International Chamber of Commerce, and many others. The principles required in such protection plans are well known and were stated clearly at the 1960 meeting of the Chamber in Karachi.

Even if an international convention of this nature should become a reality, it will probably not be enough to promote the necessary international capital flow toward the developing countries. The deeply rooted distrust of the political and economic stability of many developing countries is a strong barrier. The capital-seeking countries must wholeheartedly, and through specific action, accept the principle that allowing credits and attracting investments should be handled as business propositions and not as gifts.

The distrust is somewhat relieved through bilateral agreement on government levels. The best assurance would be, however, to have any such convention strengthened through a practical working system such as that offered in the proposed Investment Guaranty Corporation. An international guarantee of this kind would do more than anything else to promote the flow of capital and stimulate private enterprise to establish new enterprises in developing countries. Here I might add that there always remains the risk that the debtor, knowing that the seller is insured, may take lightly his duty to pay.

Perhaps mention should also be made of the fact that in some cases foreign capital investment is not welcome, mainly for political reasons. To many objective observers, it would appear impossible to reconcile the desire for industrial development, particularly in a country where local capital is totally inadequate, with a policy of not allowing foreign investment on a business-like basis.

DUAL RESPONSIBILITIES

From what has been said so far, it may appear that the incentive to expand stems mainly from outside attraction and that expansion has been the result of an inevitable cycle of events. There may be a good deal of truth in such an assumption. However, the dynamic forces inherent in all progressive companies are logically directed toward growth and expansion. In our case, as a company with roots in a small country which depends on exports to develop its economy, it is a national duty to expand beyond national borders. This means that management has to assume a multinational responsibility, partly to the economy and progress of the home country and partly to the countries where the new operations are located. This dual responsibility may not have been accentuated in the past, but today and in the future this concept will be a necessity if a multinational company is to prosper. Consequently, in evaluating the pros and cons of foreign expansion management must include this added responsibility as a factor of the equation.

Besides the motives stated, there are others in our particular case which make it imperative to expand as a multinational company. Our chosen field, telecommunications, is highly technical and huge amounts of money for research are needed. A substantial volume of business is therefore a necessity to support expenditures for research and development. We have found it unwise to try to diversify into other fields, because of the limited home market and the necessity for large production runs. Furthermore, one has to operate at a certain level in order to compete effectively for large national contracts in our field.

For us, the answer to these problems lay in geographical diversification as a necessity more dominating than the profit motive. With diversification into many countries, some of our over-all risks were diluted. In well-developed countries such risks were less apparent. But in many of those markets our chances of securing the telephone administrations as customers were nonexistent, since local enterprises have virtual monopolies. Our geographical expansion was, therefore, to a great extent directed to the developing countries.

The solutions we have found may very well be quite different from those encountered by firms operating in a huge home market such as the United States, where product diversification seems a more logical answer when expansion is considered.

SEARCH FOR TALENT

This review of our experiences would be incomplete if I did not discuss the very important aspect of personnel. I mentioned what we call our multinational responsibility. This extends in a very high degree to the personnel involved. We have to look for talent everywhere, including the developing countries. Managerial and engineering staff is in short supply even in highly developed countries, and in Sweden we also have our "crisis of management." In the developing countries the shortage is extremely acute and any expansion of activities to those countries has to be coordinated with a training program on all levels.

I mentioned in the beginning, however, that our products had an unusually long life and that we felt a responsibility for their functioning far beyond the years of service common in other industries. Service of equipment must in any case, and particularly in ours, be based on local personnel, and for us training becomes a matter of success or failure. In addition to the usual methods, I should like to mention the maintenance conferences sponsored by Ericsson in Stockholm each spring. All aspects of maintaining complete telecommunications systems are discussed. The conferences are attended by staff members invited from many parts of the world that use our equipment and systems. We have a three-year system of rotation. This year, for example, the attendance was predominantly from Europe and the East. The language used was English. Last year attendance came from the Western Hemisphere and both English and Spanish were used.

We believe that these maintenance conferences symbolize the new responsibilities that must motivate modern multinational companies if they are to expand in an orderly, profitable manner in today's world markets.

Not enough has been said, perhaps, about responsibility as a motivator in its own right. A deep sense of responsibility for quality of product, for dependable service, and for ethical dealings in the market place account for much of the progress made by outstanding multinational organizations.

In the final analysis, global companies must determine their own motivations. And it is my belief, based on our experience, that profit no longer can be the sole motivator, important as it must always remain. While management can never discount its obligations to shareholders of a parent company, it must recognize that those obligations can be fulfilled best by industrialists who are also sensitive to the motivations of nationals of foreign countries.

GUIDING PRINCIPLES

There are eight guiding principles underlying Ericsson operations in foreign countries. Many of them, we believe, may be applicable to other companies:

1. We try to provide opportunities for local investment participation, wherever practicable.

2. We believe in giving nationals of a host country a share in policy-making within our subsidiaries, commensurate with their responsibilities and investment.

3. We try to offer qualified local nationals employment opportunities at all operating levels. We want to train local people to be more productive laborers, technicians, engineers, and managers.

4. We insist that our own people give more than lip service to local customs and cultures. We want them to learn not only the language but also the history and aspirations of the host country.

5. We believe in strengthening a local economy by demonstrating our ability to provide services, technical resources, or goods not previously available in the area.

6. We do not try to do too much too soon. We recognize the value of modesty, restraint, and patience in business dealings overseas.

7. We believe that the best way to demonstrate the viability and superiority of the free enterprise system is to assume a fair share of risk in any foreign enterprise, and distribute a fair share of profits or other benefits.

8. Finally, we believe that flexibility is a practical operating principle for a multinational company. We do not try to impose our management methods and procedures on others simply because they work for us.

Businessmen, local politicians, world statesmen—everyone, in fact—share a common dream of a world at peace in which full employment can become a productive reality, rather than a by-product of war. I believe that managements of multinational companies have unique opportunities to contribute toward reaching this high objective.

In concluding I would like to paraphrase the words of a senator of ancient Rome. It was Pompey who said that "Navigare necesse est, vivere non est." For "navigare," let me substitute the word "expandere." Navigation demands experience and skill, plus the ability to cope successfully with unforeseeable hazards. So, too, does expansion in foreign countries.

A position must be taken and held without camouflage, where free, independent enterprise shows what it is and what it stands for, and demonstrates that its qualities have nothing to fear in comparison with those which are opposed to it. The multinational companies must also be in the forefront of the battle of ideas and must prove that their object of earning a proper return on the capital which they have invested is in no degree against the hopes, aspirations, and ideals of any free man.

FACING POLITICAL REALITIES

By Enrico Bignami *

I need spend little time in discussing with you the political background of the operations of a multinational company in North America or in Western Europe. The political difficulties in these countries are such as any large organization must expect to meet in its operations. But these difficulties are alleviated by the fact that in the West the large, multinational company is generally recognized and accepted as an intrinsic part of, and contribution to, the capitalist economy.

Nevertheless, in recent years we have seen two diametrically opposed factors at work in the political climate of the Western World. The creation of larger economic, commercial and—to some extent—political areas, has been accompanied by a renewal of nationalism with important effects on economic life. In some cases there has been a growing prejudice against the multinational

---

* Managing director, Nestlé Alimentana Company, Switzerland; member of the board of trustees, IMEDE (Management Development Institute), Lausanne, and a director of Unilac Inc.

company, which has been taken as a symbol of monopoly and of financial power. Even within the larger economic areas to which I have referred, there is a contradiction. On the one hand, there is a philosophy of theoretical liberalism in respect of the desirability of free competition, free movement of labor and capital, and so on. On the other hand, there is a growing tendency toward a new type of controlled economy, especially where agriculture is concerned. We are thus in the presence of two sets of contradictory forces—nationalism gaining strength from internationalism, whicn in its turn stimulates both liberalism and controlled socialism.

OBSTACLES—"NATURAL" AND "ARTIFICIAL"

In the developing or newly independent countries, the attitude of governments is nationalistic to a far higher degree than in the West. To what may be called the "natural" obstacles—such as climate, distance, language, customs, education and social outlook—which form the natural substratum on which all multinational companies must operate, are added the everchanging "artificial" obstacles which all expansion on an international scale must face. There are different degrees of political and social evolution. There are different levels of national amour propre. There is the necessity (real or imagined) for the protection of national "special" interests, a protection which often takes the form of legislation specifying the use of so-much-percent of national raw materials or so-much-percent of national labor. There is compulsory direction of production and of trade outside the local market. There are restrictions on the number of outside employees, experts, managers, and even directors. Finally, there is fairly widespread legislation on the financial structure of local companies, governing the participation of State or local private capital.

Legislation of this kind, which springs from the idea of protecting a country's basic assets, plus in some cases strategic interests, has during the last forty years been combined with a large number of regulations connected with the monetary problem and the need of many countries to control their ex-

change. For the outsider the result has been that he must sometimes ask permission to buy ground. He must have specific con-
sent to invest his money. He must use all his skill to bring local
men into his business immediately and at different levels. He
must adapt his operations and his financial policy to any partners
he may have in spite of the fact that their interests may not be
convergent with his; for example, the multinational company
may have a policy of rapid amortization, while its local partners
may look for rapid remuneration on their holding. Or the company may think that mounting inflation requires a changed
dividend policy providing for increased dividends and transfers,
while the partners may not understand or agree and would prefer
autofinancing. Last but not least, the multinational company's
lifeblood depends on the easy transferability of its earnings from
all parts of the world, and—with or without wars and political
upheavals—this can give rise to difficulties.

Must we sit idly by and watch the results of many years of
effort and investment taken from us as a result of this new and
entirely comprehensible nationalism? Is there not a constructive
policy which we can follow either as individual companies or
as a group with similar interests?

WITHDRAWAL IS NOT THE ANSWER

As a preliminary, I would like to make one point that seems
to me to be of major importance. There will be those who say
that nobody asked us to develop our trading activities in overseas
countries, that we have had a not unprofitable period in those
countries for many years, and that if we do not like present conditions it is entirely within our power to withdraw—or, of course,
to refrain from fresh ventures. In today's conditions this is not
the truth, or even the half-truth which it may appear to be at
first hearing.

The motivating force leading to expansion into nonindustrial
countries was not, and is not, only the search for immediate profit,
but also the determination to have access to the natural resources
and the large markets of these countries in advance of competition. To be first in the field was, and still is, an inestimable ad-

vantage. Twenty-five years ago, to withdraw would have meant no more than the loss of both profits and advantage; today, withdrawal by Western-based multinational companies would be tantamount to admitting the failure of some tenets—only a few but they are important—of the free world's philosophy, and this would inevitably be followed by the domination of the economy by some form of controlled economy.

This leads to the thought that—in theory at any rate—multinational companies operating under difficulties in new, independent countries should be entitled to the support and help of the Western countries in which they originate. In many countries, companies of this sort are acting as a stabilizing force both economically and politically. To remain has been made unattractive and unprofitable, with the possibility of complete nationalization always in the background; to withdraw would mean leaving a vacuum into which the Communist powers would eagerly insert themselves, without the possibility of intervention from the West. One would think that it would be worthwhile for Western governments to encourage the multinational company to stay— perhaps by means of an arrangement lasting for a definite number of years, under which taxation would be modified in respect to certain operations.

THEORY VS. PRACTICE

You will notice that I prefaced my remarks on this point with the qualification that this is what should happen in theory. Practical politics are, I fear, very different. Theoretically, the soundest way for a multinational company to operate overseas, and the most economical in the long run, would probably be to minimize its investments, to maximize the transfer of local profits (where these exist) and to keep local participation to a minimum. This is a cold and pessimistic way of regarding the problem, and it is, of course, completely contradictory to the aspects of Western and world policy which I have already touched upon. Perhaps it is a practical policy only when the operations of the multinational company in the country concerned are small, and thus go to some extent unnoticed by the government. As soon as operations get above a certain size, the local government will, in my view, take very careful note of the policy being followed and the company will not escape the ever-increasing forces of nationalism.

What, then, can be done? Overseas companies in many parts of the world are hostages to fortune and appear to be exposed to forces of opinion and legislation which are liable to make their continued operation unattractive, or even impossible. In some cases there has been legislation aimed at restricting operations of foreign companies. These restrictions have—as I have pointed out—included the stipulation that such companies must employ locally a large proportion of nationals at all levels; this has been done in many cases, I fear, somewhat grudgingly and to comply with legislation rather than in the belief that it is a desirable thing to do.

TRAINING A LOCAL ELITE

The necessity to employ more and more local managers will undoubtedly increase, but it is in these men that the future lies commercially, economically and, above all, politically. Multinational companies have what amounts to a choice of the best brains and ability available in a new country. They can pay high salaries and can offer conditions of service which are very attractive to the type of man they are looking for. This is a man who does not condemn the foreigner or the foreign company simply because it is foreign, and who is moderate enough in his views to recognize that his country needs above all the economic cooperation and impartial collaboration of foreigners in a world where economic nationalism is out-of-date. He is a man who does not resort to the repetition of nationalistic slogans in the belief that these will solve his country's problems: he is a man who sees beyond the immediate present, and after careful thought has recognized that in the long term the West has more to offer than the rest of the world.

These are the men who must be found, recruited, trained, and given status and position which will begin to make them as influential in the public affairs of their country as are the politicians. Overseas travel and contacts with their colleagues in the other local companies of the multinational organization, and above all, enthusiastic encouragement from the center, must play a most important part in the training of these men for management. They must be made to see the international nature of the concern for which they work, and the vital part which international trade must play in the future of their countries.

It seems to me not impossible that the head offices of the comparatively small number of major multinational companies which exist should cooperate in such training of potential senior executives from new countries, and that training courses should be held locally—say, in some part of Asia or Africa—to which such men would come from a number of different multinational companies for general instruction in, and discussion of, topics of international interest. But, above all, everything in the training and career planned for such men must contribute towards increasing their prestige with their own people. The companies should be more ready to convince them and their fellow nationals that the future of such companies in their countries is in their hands.

A constantly growing number of men of this kind, properly treated, properly trained, and in close and constant touch with their colleagues in the service of the other multinational companies in the country concerned, could do much to counteract the chauvinistic tides of opinion which lead to the climate of trade restriction with which we are all familiar.

SHARING THE ELITE

In the new countries, just as in the Western countries two centuries ago, it is not—and will not for some time be—possible for leading locally born businessmen to dissociate themselves from national affairs. In their desire to recruit the best available brains, the multinational companies must not deprive public life of strong recruits, and should encourage the development of a civic sense and the entry of their trained managers into the political arena. Any other policy would lead to an intellectual anaemia in public life, and thus to a breakdown of effective government. As I see it, the multinational company operating in these countries should, through a liberal staff policy, collaborate directly and indirectly in the creation of the new local elite. If they do not train this elite, there are schools behind the Iron Curtain that will be happy to do so.

If multinational companies do not release their staffs when they are wanted, then they may find that they have the managers, but the other side has the ministers. For the Western-trained, locally born manager of the future, the feeling that he is giving a useful service to the community and to the country will not be enough. Ways must be found to make him in addition a convinced and confident leader of ideas and a prominent local citizen.

URGENT NEED FOR PRICE STABILITY

There is one other subject on which I would like to touch because I believe that it goes to the heart of many of our political relations with the new countries. It is a subject which can be very complex, and I have no intention of doing more than sketch it in broad outline.

Many developing countries depend for almost the entire strength of their economy on the export of primary raw materials. In spite of a number of most ingenious and partly effective international marketing schemes, the prices they receive for these raw materials vary considerably. A large harvest of a given crop may mean a considerable drop in prices that will shake the foundations of the local economy. Such a drop can mean—and has in the past meant—a difference in income to the producing country many times greater than all the financial assistance provided to its government by the Western powers or by the international agencies.

The creation of a genuine price stability for these crops and products, at a level which might well be significantly above the true market price as established by the laws of supply and demand, would certainly be a greatly more effective and more logical way of assisting the economies, and thus the governments of the new countries, than the gifts now granted by the Western governments on request and at times of crisis. The multinational companies, who are in many cases the principal purchasers of the materials to which I refer, have an important part to play in introducing this kind of logic.

ETHICAL VALUES MUST GO ABROAD, TOO

Finally, I would urge that, in facing the increasingly delicate political problems which are inherent in its activity, the multinational company must remain true to itself and to the ethical values that have enabled it to grow to its position in the world. It must not be tempted to believe that there is one set of business ethics for operations in the West and a different set for operations elsewhere.

I have tried to give a few ideas on how the multinational company should behave in circumstances where reason shows that one cannot go against the stream, and logic shows that one cannot go with it. This situation will be met successfully only if the people concerned continue to appreciate—and persuade others to appreciate—that successful enterprises, whether they be commercial or political, always depend on the identity of interest of those involved. In the past perhaps too little has been done to persuade the governments and peoples of many countries in which we operate that in the long term this identity exists between their interests and ours. To find ways and means of convincing the other half of the world of this fact is perhaps the most important task which lies before the multinational company.

TO SUMMARIZE

1. The time is past when a company operating in a foreign country anywhere in the world can think only of relatively immediate profit. Today, and in the future, it must constantly have in mind also the political context of its operations.

2. A prime duty of the large multinational company operating in a developing country is to train locally born people for management positions and, in the course of such training, to imbue the heritage of freedom of individuals and of enterprises.

3. The multinational company must be prepared for its trained local staff to play a part in national affairs in the country con-

cerned: that is to say, in spite of its soundness, the idea of business and only business must be abandoned.

4. There should be no attempt to influence political matters through pressure groups, but only through the creation of genuine local opinion.

5. The multinational company should use its influence and strength to assist in the establishment of stable world prices for local products of new countries.

WHY BE ASHAMED?

Above all, the multinational company in a new country must do these things openly and proudly. Why should we be ashamed of a system which produces surplus food for the hungry of the world, rather than one which produces famine and want?

There must be no attempt to sail under false colors, nor to pay lip service to ideas to which Western enterprise is fundamentally opposed. A position must be taken and held without camouflage, where free, independent enterprise shows what it is and what it stands for, and demonstrates that its qualities have nothing to fear in comparison with those which are opposed to it. The multinational companies must also be in the forefront of the battle of ideas and must prove that their object of earning a proper return on the capital which they have invested is in no degree incompatible with the hopes, aspirations and ideals of any free man.

*It is only by personal contact that mutual
confidence can be built up. Without it, and
relying solely on letters, cables, and the telephone, you will very soon arrive at a situation in which the center is convinced that all
the people on the circumference are morons,
while the operating units have an unshakable conviction that the center is staffed exclusively by malevolent ogres.*

LOCAL AUTONOMY AND CENTRAL CONTROL

By Paul Rykens *

There is a certain amount of overlapping between my paper
and that of Mr. Lattman, who will follow me. I am glad to add
that there does not seem to be any contradiction, but I want to
point out a certain difference in the nature of the two businesses
on which we have based our objectives. Mr. Lattman's company,
Massey-Ferguson, mainly manufactures highly technical durable
goods, whereas Unilever is an agglomeration of businesses with
factories spread over more than 50 countries, factories which
practically without exception produce consumer goods with a

* Chairman, Middle East Industrial Development Projects Corporation
(MIDEC), Netherlands; advisory director and former chairman of the board
of Unilever, and is chairman or director of various banks and industrial com-
panies in the Netherlands. Dr. Rykens is chairman of the Anglo-Dutch Trade
Council; member of the Board of Governors of the Rotterdam School of Eco-
nomics, Netherlands Economic Institute, Netherlands Institute for the Middle
East and Netherlands Institute for the Near East, and is treasurer of the
Fondation Européene de la Culture.

quick turnover. This means that our commercial subsidiary companies and the factories producing for these selling companies are probably more self-contained in each national economy than in the case of Massey-Ferguson. Exports from most of our national units are an exception and each national organization is geared to the requirements of the country concerned. These various considerations provided in Unilever are even a stronger argument in favor of decentralization than in most of the multinational companies, and therefore support the general principles put forward by Mr. Lattman.

Running a business is very largely a matter of making decisions, and that is why the prime tests of its efficiency are speed of decision and quality of decision. In other words, the basic problem is to get decisions that are *good enough* and *fast enough*. A decision that is academically perfect is likely to be reached too slowly; a decision taken at lightning speed is likely to be less than perfect.

This battle between speed of decision and quality of decision has a particular impact on, and brings particular problems to, a big multinational business working through subsidiaries spread over the face of the world. Such is the business with which I was connected for so many years and, on the basis that an ounce of practice is worth many times that weight of theory, my remarks today are based on my business experience of balancing the center against the circumference.

THE DANGER OF EXTREMES

The theoretical extremes of choices are, at one end of the scale, to reserve all decisions for the center and, at the other, to delegate complete power to the units on the periphery. The first course, complete centralization, stultifies your operating units and rapidly results in their being staffed by nonentities. It sacrifices the advantage of having men on the spot who know local conditions and soon leads to an arthritic slowness of action, as the central management is overwhelmed with problems awaiting decision.

To go to the opposite extreme and delegate full autonomy to the local units reduces the central headquarters to the status, at best, of the headquarters of an investment trust. No longer are all parts of the business seen in relation to each other, nor are decisions taken in the light of what is for the greatest good of the greatest number.

There is a tendency to dissipate the strength which results from central financial reserves. You lose the benefits which the operating units would otherwise derive from the specialist advisory and service departments which can be built up at the central headquarters to a degree far beyond the resources of any one of the individual units.

Since to go to either extreme is to sacrifice certain obvious advantages, one must inquire whether there is a middle way, a mixture of central control and local autonomy, by which one can have as far as possible the best of both worlds. The proportions in which these two ingredients are mixed—the exact point at which the balance is struck—will probably vary from business to business, according to its nature. So far as my experience is concerned, I think it true to say that the bias should be on the side of local autonomy. We set such store by the advantages of speed of decision, of having local problems solved by the man on the spot with the local knowledge, of allowing initiative and ability to develop unhampered by checks and frustrations from above, that we have tried to keep control from the center down to a minimum. If it was ever proposed to add to the existing controls, the burden of proof would, I fancy, always rest upon those who wanted more controls to show that they were needed, rather than upon the units to show that they were unnecessary. A friend of mine better versed than I in English literature when discussing the subject of my address said that we should not lay ourselves open to Goneril's devestating remark about her father, King Lear:

> "... idle old man,
> That still would manage those authorities
> That he hath given away!"

The minimum of central control which, in our view, cannot be reduced without endangering the coherence of the organization as a whole is fourfold.

FOUR ESSENTIAL CONTROLS

It is exercised primarily by the managing directors at head office. In a very large organization like the one I have been associated with, there are 24 managing directors. Many of the members of the board undertake a specified task, and therefore carry particular responsibilities, which are separate from those vested in the board as a whole. Under these circumstances it is essential that a few members of the board—in our case three, and referred to as the Special Committee—act as a coordinating body, and are responsible also for the preparation of policy proposals to be submitted to the full board. This Special Committee, together with the managing directors particularly responsible for the subject under consideration, in practice governs four areas: first, the annual operating plan of each unit; second, capital expenditure of each unit; third, the selection, promotion, and financial reward of top management; and fourth, the general financial policy. Let me enlarge, briefly, on each of these instruments of central control.

The *annual operating plan* is essentially a forecast of performance. It shows what a unit expects to achieve over the next twelve months in the way of sales, what achievement is likely to cost in advertising expenditure and so on, and what the profit or loss at the end of the year is expected to be. After the plan has been discussed with the management directly responsible for the group of companies to which the unit belongs, it goes to the Special Committee. Once approved, in its original form or amended, it is for the operating unit to see that it is carried out, and the management of the unit has authority to take all the short-term decisions that may be necessary, or to vary the plan within limits, to meet unforeseen emergencies. Periodic returns enable the head office to keep an eye on the actual performance of each operating unit, and if necessary to take up with the local management any deviation of importance from the annual operating plan.

The *capital expenditure budget,* also drawn up annually by each operating unit, shows what capital expenditure will be needed to put the unit's operating plan into force. It covers renewals and expansion of plant, or the buying of outside businesses, and obviously it can affect the future for much more than twelve months ahead. Its proposals are passed up to the Special Committee, and it is for the Special Committee to accept, reject, or modify. Some authority for capital expenditure is delegated, but large proposals must come before the Special Committee, which is thus able to deploy the greater part of the total resources of the business. This power is essential if the strength of the whole is to be used to the best advantage of all the parts; it is as important to the holding company as the control of central reserves is to a general directing military operations.

The *selection of top management,* their promotion, and their pay also fall within the sphere of central control. These men have the direct responsibility for running the operating units, for seizing the opportunities, and for coping with their problems. It is only if they are well chosen that the whole organization can hope to prosper.

Two of these three instruments of control are on an annual basis, but running throughout the year there is an overriding *financial control* from the center, to the extent that it keeps itself posted with up-to-the-minute information on the cash balances held in each country and can arrange their transfer from one country to another as occasion may require.

"THE MEN ON THE SPOT"

Subject, then, to these four basic controls, our aims are decentralization and delegation to the men on the spot, and this is really a basic prerequisite to speed of decision. *Quality* of decision rests primarily upon the quality of the men we pick for the top jobs in the operating units. But it can be greatly helped by the effectiveness of the advisory services that are made available by the center, the specialists in marketing, research, finance, law, and the rest.

In our organization these experts do not give orders. They can only suggest, recommend, or persuade. It is for the operating unit to decide whether or not to accept their advice. Indeed, an operating unit is not obliged to use our own advisory services at all. If it thinks it can do better by hiring an outside trade-mark expert, for example, or a tax adviser, it is free to do so. Accordingly, our advisory services have to be good; if not, they will find themselves without customers—and shortly after that, no doubt, without jobs!

The link between the central advisory departments and the operating units provides a means of keeping center and circumference in touch with each other, which is often the more effective for not being a direct chain of command between a superior and a subordinate.

Finally, I must emphasize how greatly such a system as I have outlined depends upon personal contact. This is the only way in which the men at the center and the men at the circumference can get to know each other. And so, directors of the parent company and the top people in the advisory services must visit the units on the circumference, and the top men from the units must visit the center. It is only by personal contact that mutual confidence can be built up. Without it, and relying solely on letters, cables, and the telephone, you will very soon arrive at a situation in which the center is convinced that all the people on the circumference are morons, while the operating units have an unshakeable conviction that the center is staffed exclusively by malevolent ogres.

The end of free enterprise will not come through the efforts of its critics and enemies but, if it does come it will be because of malpractices—because we are not doing our jobs. Thus the reconciliation of conflicting economic and political interests within a multinational company can become the supreme test for its management.

THE PARENT COMPANY AND LOCAL MANAGEMENT

By Walter Lattman *

Following Dr. Ryken's example, I shall describe the position of my own company on this subject. We make tractors and other farm equipment, diesel engines, and hydraulic systems. We make them in many countries of the world, and in our case, of course, the marketing is almost equally important as the designing and manufacturing.

When a company has a large part of its capital committed in substantial establishments abroad, it is appropriate to call it an international company. We have used that label. But we have switched our opinion about how to run an international company

* Group vice-president, Massey-Ferguson Ltd., Canada; director of various Massey-Ferguson subsidiaries in North America, Europe, South Africa, and India. Mr. Lattman is director of the Canadian Council of the International Chamber of Commerce; chairman of the Export Trade Committee of the Canadian Manufacturers Association; member of the Institute of Export, London, and the Executive Council of the Canadian Chamber of Commerce.

and we now call ours an international company with a multi-national philosophy. We do so because we are dealing with a number of more or less independent national units each heading to one control center which, in principle, is divorced from any direct operations responsibilities.

In order to avoid the connotation that the term control implies centralization, we call ours merely the corporate group or, the corporate management. This is the ultimate administrative authority of the organization. It is the place where the strategic decisions of policy are made in the conduct of the business, both in the country where the control center is located and outside.

We had previously operated under other forms of organization, but we finally concluded that it should be possible to reconcile the different business environments on an international scale in a manner not unlike the reconciliation of the differing situations as they exist in different regions or areas of a local market.

MAXIMUM DELEGATION OF AUTHORITY

At the same time, we had decided that it was in the best interest of the company to strive for national units, which would be substantial enough to be recognized as autonomous parts of the business communities of the countries in which they operate. We also decided that the concept of maximum delegation of authority, consistent with good coordination and control, best suited these aims. Decentralization should unleash initiative, and the problem then becomes one of how to achieve the best balance between such decentralization and the continuing need for close coordination and supervision.

In our case, we decided that all this required strong local management made up largely, wherever possible, of nationals of each country within each local operations unit. This, of course, requires the establishment of appropriate personnel policies.

GLOBAL STRATEGY

At this point, I should say something about the global strategy we adopted. This calls for globally integrated engineering and product development and a high degree of global production integration through the creation of specialized plants, either for complete products or for their major components, together with dispersed assembly plants. This concept of global design and manufacturing strives to avoid the prohibitive expense of duplicating international know-how and production equipment in many producing units, but with the help of coordinating product-development groups attached to the marketing function we strive to tailor our products from the market up, and thus take care of the many specialized local requirements.

In laying out our organization we found that, in order to reconcile the aims of the strong local groups that we intended to create with the purposes and philosophy of the corporation, the corporate management had to convince the national managements of the soundness of its basic strategy and of its long-range objectives. This is particularly difficult when you deal with one class of customers who happen to be the farmers, because of their special situation in each individual country.

Each local operations unit is primarily responsible for its local market, but the corporation gives all plants the maximum chance to participate in the world market. Marketing in countries that are not the direct concern of an operations unit is the responsibility of an international export marketing agency, which is directly responsible to corporate marketing.

The rather vigorous intercompany trade, which is a by-product of our international integration scheme, creates and maintains among the managers of the national units a certain interest in the prosperity of their colleagues. This becomes a built-in incentive, and has proved to be of considerable importance in reconciling the desires and aims of local management with those of the parent company.

I should interject here that our position as a farm equipment maker is somewhat special in that on the North American continent we have a "common market." Neither the U.S. nor Canada has a tariff on farm equipment. Here we are not tempted to apportion foreign markets to any given production unit, but a relatively high degree of intercompany trade is facilitated through the specialization of the production units.

POLICIES AND CONTROL

One of the major activities of corporate management, and an extremely important one, is the establishment of policies that assure the maximum utilization of all facilities, including capital, of the corporation while, at the same time, seeking the maximum penetration of all markets in which the company is interested.

The acceptance of such policies by the national units depends largely on two things: first, on the challenge given to the local managers to contribute to the good of the whole, taking care that limitations on their freedom of action do not stifle initiative; and second, on the fairness of the procedures which lead to the assignment of intracompany tasks and which govern the carrying out of those assignments.

As those who exercise over-all control—that is, those who are accountable to the board of the parent company—must be fully informed so that their decisions may be appropriate, we demand, of course, that the local managers report in an appropriate fashion to the central group. Reporting follows a pattern, which not only gives the central group a complete picture of the local operations and the trends within these operations but, at the same time, gives the local management practically all the information which *they* require.

After having arrived at clear definitions of basic policies and agreed on adequate definition of job responsibilities and appropriate authority, we turned to the development of an effective planning and control process, which establishes a plan of action —in our case this is not a prediction or a forecast—and a mechanism for measuring performance. This control process is the key to effective supervision. It calls, of course, for the development of proper information techniques. Control by attention to exceptions or variations from plan furnishes both the operations managers and corporate management a quick and significant appraisal.

Once a national unit has obtained approval of its program, its manager makes his day-to-day decisions without referring to higher authority. He is, indeed, quite autonomous in making such decisions, as long as he does not violate company policy. The control process is intended to show when corporate management action is required. The control process is of great assistance in reconciling a large number of conflicting interests between the company and the component national units.

Another factor in the reconciliation of potential conflicts between the corporate and the national (local) viewpoints is the importance of the global experience of the corporate management group. The business climate, as it is conditioned by work habits, thought patterns, value scales, and ways of doing business is a factor that requires much less consideration "at home" than when other countries are involved. At home, there is an almost automatic, even unconscious, adjustment to changes in those factors of the business climate, because we live with them. When other countries are concerned, a very considerable effort is required to keep abreast of the constantly changing business environment.

Experience has always been an important factor in decision making. A corporate group with multinational problems can deal with many matters, of course, merely on the basis of sound reasoning. There are, indeed, a great many areas in which fundamental or general principles can be applied. A great deal depends upon the success in which such principles have been embodied in clear policy statements. There are other areas, however, where a considerable knowledge of environmental factors is required to arrive at proper assessment. This is very much a subjective quality, one that is not measurable, but it is of great importance that each member of the corporate management group be able to relate his expert knowledge to other environments.

A CORPORATE COORDINATING COMMITTEE

In this next context, we have found a corporate coordinating committee to be extremely helpful. We insist that this group must have continuous access to information from all operations units. Its discussions, which deal with all the problems of all the activities of the multinational company, at times have quite a few of the characteristics of brainstorming sessions. I am referring here to mutual stimulation, and the resulting combinations and improvements of the proposals and suggestions presented to the group. Because they are on an equal level, all participants come to recognize the breadth of experience of their colleagues and this serves as an incentive to creative thinking and to the fixing of ideas. Fitting one's thinking to different business customs, formalities, rules and laws is, of course, always a problem in international relations.

THE IMPORTANCE OF COURTESY

To start with, it is of great importance for a multinational company, and especially for its corporate management group, to mind its manners. A firm must strive in any country to be alert to local needs and, if possible, to be about as "pro" that country as, for instance, U.S. industry is legitimately "pro-U.S."

Much has been said about the proper etiquette to be followed by corporate management of a multinational company when dealing with the reasonable aspirations of the local managers in this respect. Many human problems can be solved by doing what is courteous, but in a larger sense the main emphasis must be on adequate understanding by the corporate group of the local problems and on the achievement of a sufficiently broad understanding by the local units of the fundamental principles which top management is following.

In closing, I would like to touch on two more aspects of the problem of reconciling the conflicting economic and political aims of the corporate group and the national units.

A CORPORATE PHILOSOPHY

One of them is what I might label—I hope you won't think it too pompous—"Corporate Philosophy." In a multinational company, the local political and human problems (including local nationalism), the local fiscal problems, must become the direct concern of the corporate management group, because they are part of the business climate in which its supervision and control must operate.

This also leads to the consideration, intuitively or formally, of other aspects and implications of global policy, such as the interdependence of the Western economies and the dilemma which faces the emerging countries. At a given point in our more philosophical debates and contemplations, free enterprisers are led to take a position in relation to two other economic concepts: State Socialism and Communism. Such discussions can easily become beclouded by considerations of political allegiances and by parochial viewpoints, whether they be nationalistic or merely regional. It is now axiomatic to say that the free enterprise system should be judged and should be justified by its benefits for the average consumer, and not by what it does for the entrepreneur, except in the way of incentive. The degree of freedom of competition and the many concepts of what constitutes fair competition are important facets of this problem. They are also important among the many things that make up the business climate of each country. Each country acts in this field according to its history and its state of evolution—or sophistication.

A clear understanding of these problems by all concerned then becomes an important part of any attempt to solve the problems created by potentially or apparently conflicting interests of the parent company and those of its component national units.

Basically, free enterprise accepts the proposition that competition is the only safeguard against the abuses of the power the free enterprise system can give to certain individuals and groups. Reasonable laws and rules, and reasonable administration of such laws and rules, insuring reasonably free competition in all fields are then essential, because they insure the continuation of the whole system for the benefit of the consumer. A part of the expertise of managers of multinational companies is to understand these devices in their different national contexts.

Finally, there is what we call the dilemma facing the emerging countries. Whether we like it or not, the support of Peronism or Castroism (and many other isms) comes from masses whose standard of living is pitifully low. As nations we have committed ourselves to foreign aid in many forms, and one important result must be the creation of conditions (sanitation, education, job training, providing equipment, and so on), which will bring better remuneration for the efforts of the individuals of these masses.

How well we do this job is, perhaps, the key to the survival of our free world, and the participation of the units of a multinational company in relatively evolved countries in aid of the less-developed ones is a phase that we must consider very seriously.

The end of free enterprise will not come through the efforts of its critics and enemies but, if it does come it will be because of malpractices—because we are not doing our jobs. Thus the reconciliation of conflicting economic and political interests within a multinational company can become the supreme test for its management.

IV

Challenge from Four Continents

In too many parts of the world, men today show too much willingness to put their freedom up for sale, to put a price on the treasure that has always been priceless. When men anywhere begin to tolerate the thought that the surrender of liberty may be a bearable thing—whether because they fear the tyrant's threats or because they believe his promises—then it is not improper, it is not unbecomingly emotional, to restate in the strongest terms a commitment to the preservation of freedom.

HENRY C. ALEXANDER

The ideology that we use in obtaining economic development and prosperity is more your concern than ours. . . . We are concerned with acquiring prosperity, with the wiping out of disease, with the elimination of tyranny, with increasing the standards of living and the earning power of our people. I repeat—the concern with ideology is yours, not ours.

PLAIN TALK FROM AN AFRICAN

By A. Romeo Horton *

One of the reasons why I decided to speak on such short notice is my belief that the participants in this conference—leaders of free enterprise—seem to be seriously interested in the developing countries and their problems. And if that be true, it would be most unfortunate for you if you did not get some idea of the point of view of the African peoples regarding development, free enterprise, private enterprise, and such matters.

Africa has been regarded as the Dark Continent. It can't be any darker than historians have described it. The countries in Africa are considered and called undeveloped countries, or by some persons who wish to be more polite, developing economies. But, the important thing here is that we can't go backward—we must go

---

* President, Bank of Liberia; assistant economic advisor to the President of Liberia; delegate to Economic Commission for Africa; chairman, Conference of African Businessmen.

forward. And in Africa we are determined to do just that. However, you as businessmen seem to be rushing for our markets, for our resources. Each day we have potential concessionaires coming to Liberia trying to get mineral concessions, lumber concessions, and other concessions. You seem to be anxious to have our resources, to enjoy our wealth, and there seems to be a tremendous interest in Africa today expressed through your newspapers, your radio, and through yourselves when we speak to you personally. Your governments—I know this to be a fact—are interested in getting our vote at various international conferences. But let it be clearly understood that our markets, our resources, our votes, our alliance from today on will only be obtained by negotiation and by agreement of both parties. The period of gunboat diplomacy has ended. The period of cannon diplomacy is gone. We will meet with you. We will discuss these problems, you indicating your interests and desires, we indicating our terms, and reaching agreement.

AFTER INDEPENDENCE

Many countries in Africa have obtained their political independence. They have obtained their independence themselves—some through bloodshed, some through sheer determination, will power, and courage. Years ago there were two independent countries in Africa—Ethiopia and Liberia. Then the North African countries obtained their independence. The record shows now that as a result of what happened in 1960 and this year, 1961, there are about 27 countries in Africa that are enjoying sovereignty.

What these nations are looking forward to now is economic development. They are determined to obtain economic development and they have assured themselves that they *will* in the same manner that they obtained political independence—by courage, struggle, and hard work. The ideology that we use in obtaining economic development and prosperity is more your concern than ours. We are not concerned about ideologies—whether they be that of the East or the West or the North or the South. We are concerned with acquiring prosperity, with the wiping out of disease, with the elimination of tyranny, with increasing the standards of living and the earning power of our people. I repeat—the concern with ideology is yours, not ours.

NEED FOR MUTUAL UNDERSTANDING

I propose, then, that it is in your interest to comprehend completely our ambitions, our needs, our desires, and our approaches to these subjects. I propose even further that it is also in your interest that we understand that you, as the promoters of private enterprise, have clear, honest, and honorable motives. You know that many peoples in Africa still associate private enterprise and corporations with colonialism—with imperialism and with such horrifying things as those. It is therefore important that you make it possible for us to understand your motives in coming into Africa. You must convince us that you are only interested in projects that are of mutual benefit to the Africans and yourselves.

There are people in Africa—most of the people in Africa, I dare say—who believe strongly in the merits of the free enterprise system and who subscribe to it. But there are others, even officials of government, who still suspect it. Therefore, the next move is not ours. It is yours. It is to have us understand you, and for you to understand us better.

PROPOSALS FOR ACTION

May I make these suggestions. The first one is that it might be a wise thing if the Stanford Research Institute, or the National Industrial Conference Board, or the Policy Board of this Conference, would hold in Africa a regional conference, similar to this one. On a smaller scale, however. This would bring African businessmen together. They would learn your motives and your interests. You would learn of our desires, our ambitions, and our needs. It would also make it possible to establish valuable and lasting business connections. As a result of such a conference, a bureau or an office could be established in Africa that would keep us aware of the possibilities and opportunities that you offer as private enterprise, in the expansion of your own business, and in the development of our economies.

Secondly, I would propose that some type of financial institution be established that can invest in or give credit to private enterprise in Africa. Many countries in Africa are members of the World Bank, and have enjoyed the facilities of the International Finance Corporation, but these are governmental institutions and operate with government capital and under government control. It seems to me that the various corporations that are interested in the developing economies, particularly in Africa, could come together and organize a financing institution that would mobilize private capital from America, Europe, and elsewhere that would serve the same purposes as the World Bank, but at a strictly private level. I consider this very, very important.

TIMID CAPITALISM

There seems to be a great fear on the part of private enterprise in going into underdeveloped countries; private enterprise seems always to be looking for guarantees and assurances from their governments or from our governments. What worries me most today is not the spread of Communism or anything about Communism. What frightens me most is the timidity and fear that is displayed by 20th century capitalism. It seems to have lost the rugged individualism of the capitalism of previous centuries. It seems, from my point of view, that free enterprisers have a kind of fear that was not present during the days of "Go West, young man," of the westward movement from Europe to this continent and from the eastern part of this continent to the western part. Everybody is looking for government guarantees. Today, you have the most developed systems of communications. You have the *Wall Street Journal* to keep you abreast of what is happening, you have a telephone system and a radio system to streamline the possibilities of communication, so that you know almost instantly what is happening in any part of the world. In those days when none of these facilities existed, people ventured, they invested heavily, they took severe risks, and they built the kind of economy you have in Europe—the kind of civilization, the kind of industries you have in this country. They took risks and took chances because they believed in themselves, they had confidence in themselves.

Do not forget that we in Africa, too, have reasons to be fearful and suspicious of you. Let us never forget that we, too, need certain guarantees from you. This business of guarantees and assurances is a two-way street. The peoples in Africa have had and are still having unholy experiences with members of the free enterprise system—with members of capitalism, and therefore they are justified in being fearful and in requiring certain guarantees from you.

URGENCIES AND DANGERS

Finally, I suggest that we overcome these fears and that we overcome them in a hurry, because we in Africa are going to get economic development and economic security. We are determined to wipe out poverty and to bring in prosperity, and we want to do this as quickly as possible. The people on the other side of this curtain you call the Iron Curtain are rushing to Africa. They are getting in there and they are getting in there fast. Speaking as a Liberian, sometimes I get very worried about our alignment, our unshakable alignment with the West and with the United States in particular. I think that Liberia should align herself with economic development. Her alliance should be tied in with the wishes and the desires and the yearnings of the people of Africa. Liberia has stuck close to the West; she has been a loyal ally of longstanding. It is therefore in our mutual interest that I make these representations to you and beg you to think about them most seriously.

Private enterprise cannot expect to be a vested interest in itself. Like any social institution, it must stand ready to be judged by the results it produces. By its nature, it is dynamic and resilient, as phenomenal developments in the U.S., United Kingdom, and West Germany show. I am sure that it will not be found wanting in the challenge it faces in the emergent countries.

PRIVATE ENTERPRISE AND INDIA'S PLANS

By G. L. Mehta *

In looking at the Indian economy, one becomes aware of a subtle change in the atmosphere, no less real because it has few external manifestations. We have not seen during the last two years any change in the broad framework within which the economy has to work. At the same time, there have been changes in the details that affect private enterprise and they account for the improvement in the atmosphere within which private enterprise works. I should like to enumerate here some of these changes, leaving it to you to evaluate their importance.

First, I would like to refer to the change in the foreign exchange situation in my country. Two years ago we were trying to work our way out of the foreign exchange crisis by appraising and reap-

* Chairman, The Industrial Credit and Investment Corporation of India; former Ambassador to the United States and Mexico. Member: National Planning Commission (1950–52); governing body, Council of Scientific and Industrial Research (1947–52); Constituent Assembly of India (1947); delegate to International Conference on Trade and Employment (1947).

426

praising the Second Plan. Today, the situation is different. I do not say we have got over our foreign exchange difficulties or that our Third Five Year Plan is less voracious of foreign exchange. But, thanks to the initiative of the World Bank and the imaginative approach of friendly Western countries—I would particularly like to single out the U. S.—we are better equipped to face the problems of the next five years.

Much of the proposed aid is, of course, on the government-to-government level and you naturally ask: "How does this help the private sector?" I would answer that it does so in many ways. First, it has enabled us to get rid of deferred-payment terms. Deferred-payment terms which private enterprise had to arrange, when foreign exchange shortage was acute, had many disadvantages, both short run and long. In the short run, it tended to shift the responsibility of obtaining foreign exchange from the government to the Indian entrepreneur and through him to the plant supplier. This necessarily restricted the freedom of action of the Indian entrepreneur—his choice of equipment was limited and his bargaining power weakened. Often he had to pay more for a piece of equipment that he did not consider the best. In the long run this reduced his ability to produce at a low cost and, therefore, his capacity to compete. And while he may hope to be protected in the home market from external competition, it acted unfairly on the Indian consumer and reduced the export capacity of an enterprise which, we are now beginning to realize, is vital for the success of our development effort.

One of the consequences of the easing of the foreign exchange situation is the greater willingness on the part of the government to give cash import licenses. The entrepreneur's choice for purchase may still be restricted, but it is to a country rather than to a company, as before. The Indian entrepreneur's path in setting up an enterprise is still not all roses, but it is not as frustrating as it used to be only three or four years back.

"UNCLOGGING" OF CAPITAL

A second development is what I might call the unclogging of the capital market in the country, as reflected in the response to new issues offered to the public. This phenomenon should be understood more clearly, both in India and abroad. It does not represent a sudden increase in the propensity to save. Nor is India unaware of sudden frenzies of speculation or transient fancy for industrial investment—we have known all this before. What distinguishes the present boom is its strength—it has now lasted almost two years. While the earlier excesses have tended to disappear, its momentum still continues to lead to oversubscription, at earthlier levels, of worthwhile issues.

Since it is not based on a wider base of saving, this trend reflects a shift in people's investment preference. It is a transformation through which all advanced economies have passed at one stage or another and one which we have possibly just reached. Such a shift, making people conversant with modes of investment in industry, has a more enduring value, whatever the temporary setbacks caused by market forces. This increasing public interest in industrial investment has eased the task of entrepreneurs in raising capital. Provided complementary resources are available, there appears to be enough scope for rapid industrial advance in the economy.

NO LACK OF ENTREPRENEURS

You will, no doubt, remind me that industrialization also requires entrepreneurship—do we have enough of it? This is one of those intangibles where economic pundits differ. I feel that, given the atmosphere, we have no lack of entrepreneurship. Industry along factory lines is more than a hundred years old in India. Our entrepreneurs ventured into such advanced lines as iron and steel manufacture and shipping in the first two decades of this century. Before World War II, India was self-sufficient—no doubt at the relatively low levels of consumption then prevailing—in cloth, sugar, cement, and jute. What was lacking was not entrepreneurship but conditions requisite for its exercise. A national government and planning have provided these.

In India, setting up an industrial enterprise is subject to licensing, and this, you may fear, may dampen entrepreneurial ardor. In fact, in the last two years, this has not been so. When scarcities began to appear on the Indian market, entrepreneurs have come forward to put up capacity in a large variety of industries. The government itself has given a relatively free rein to enterprise by giving licenses freely to projects that appeared satisfactory to it.

NEW ATTITUDE TOWARD FOREIGN CAPITAL

As to the prospects for foreign capital in India, they are subject, as is much of Indian enterprise, to the influence of the climate for investment—a climate which has turned for the better. Owing to the foreign exchange crisis, foreign enterprise is coming to be increasingly recognized as supplementing the foreign exchange resources available to the economy. The investing public has also come to associate foreign enterprise with advanced management techniques; consequently, oversubscription, to which I referred a little while ago, has been particularly heavy in cases where there is financial and technical collaboration with a good foreign company. Finally, as new and difficult lines are being taken up, foreign enterprise is seen as an important adjunct to Indian entrepreneurship.

These advantages are recognized not only by our entrepreneurs but also by our government, which has recently taken various measures to encourage the flow of foreign capital and know-how. In the last budget of the Union Government, the effective rate on royalties was reduced from 63% to 50%. The government always insists that royalty agreements be entered on taxable terms, and foreign collaborators have generally sought to obtain a certain carry-home return for supplying know-how. The revised tax rate should help to remove one of the main obstacles to the development of the trade in technique between advanced countries and India.

A second change introduced by the recent budget is the equalization of tax burden on companies that are subsidiaries of, or have minority participation in, foreign companies. This equalization has been brought about mainly by a reduction in the tax rate. I would like you to note that the opportunity to rationalize the tax structure was not used to raise the tax rates—as so often happens these days.

A third matter of interest to foreign investors is the establishment of the Indian Investment Center. Its primary function is to encourage the flow of foreign capital into India by helping prospective foreign investors in various ways—in their dealings with the government, in finding suitable Indian parties to collaborate with, in putting Indian industrialists in touch with their foreign counterparts, and by providing information on the Indian economic situation. I am almost tempted to say that the Investment Center will provide foreign investors with technical know-how—the know-how relating to problems of operating in India.

Both the receptivity of the government and the Indian entrepreneurs in relation to foreign capital and the conditions under which it can come in and operate have improved considerably in recent times. Many foreign firms—small as well as large, U. S. as well as non-U. S.—have come in during the last couple of years. In the first quarter of 1961 alone, the Government of India approved 101 technical collaboration agreements. The Investment Center is also handling a large number of inquiries for foreign participation and collaboration.

AN OPPORTUNITY FOR INSTITUTIONAL INVESTMENT

I should like to note that capital flows need not necessarily be associated with the flow of technical know-how. In the past, particularly before World War I, capital used to flow across national frontiers according to profitability. It is true that individuals may not be expected to undertake investment in companies in underdeveloped economies because they believe the political and economic risks are too great, and they may not have the necessary expertise in judging investment. But I suggest that investment institutions—insurance companies, investment trusts, and so on—should examine the possibility of such investment. These institutions have the necessary expertise to judge the long-term prospects of stocks and the necessary resources to absorb any shocks that may arise out of political and exchange risks. Such stocks have, besides higher profitability, very favorable growth prospects; such investment will also help to diversify the portfolio of the investment institutions. I feel that a small beginning can be made in this way; if it is fruitful, I believe it can be an important source of a free supply—free in the sense of not being attached to technical or other control—of foreign exchange to underdeveloped countries.

While the broad structure of economic policy in India has remained unchanged, its implementation has become more flexible and in many ways more favorable to the exercise of the private sector, both indigenous and foreign.

I would not, of course, deny that the government still has considerable power over economic policy decisions. The very scale of government operations has increased considerably under the Plans: the government invested in industry about $12 million during the First Plan period and is scheduled to invest $300 million during the Third Plan period. In many lines—iron and steel, machine tools, antibiotics, fertilizers, coal, cement—the government and the private sector operate side-by-side as competitors; in some of these, the relationship is that of buyer-and-seller.

Many fields of enterprise—a recent addition is oil—still remain closed to private enterprise. On the other hand, government has shown greater flexibility in its attitude toward participation and expansion of private enterprise in some others, for example, fertilizers and basic chemicals. If licensing has ceased to be an obstacle, it still remains an irritant to a prospective investor.

PRIVATE ENTERPRISE ON PROBATION

I should like to emphasize that in most underdeveloped economies private enterprise is on probation. In many ex-colonial countries, it has been under suspicion mainly because it was identified with the imperial power. The newly developing economies are like people in a hurry—they are keen to reach the destination as quickly as possible, irrespective of the means adopted to achieve the end.

In India much water has flowed under the bridge during the last ten years. As events have shown, government's attitude towards private enterprise has been more understanding. However, as I mentioned earlier, the government still retains in its armory a wide range of powers which, if circumstances or attitudes change, may be used.

The milieu within which private enterprise functions today is far different from that prevailing in the 18th and 19th centuries. Private enterprise is no longer taken for granted, and its justification is no longer to be measured only by the profit rate it is able to earn. Private enterprise will be judged by—and its survival will depend upon—its social utility to the economy. This casts a heavy responsibility upon those who sponsor, organize, finance, and operate it.

In the 19th century, private enterprise was able to bring about, consistent with its own objective of individual profit, rapid development of the economies, considerable improvement in the living standards of the common people, and tremendous growth in the social and cultural development of the community. These were often by-products of the growth of private enterprise in the advanced economies. These goals will need to be kept more consciously in view of the future. Private enterprise in India has not always been unconscious of these requirements. Many educational institutions in India owe their existence to the munificence of private industrialists. Even today, a considerable portion of the dividend income from the largest steel company in India goes to finance charitable purposes.

Responsibility always goes with power. The advantage of private enterprise has been to share this power and this responsibility—to bring about its wider distribution. To every individual's power—whether it be the power of ownership of means of production or of employment of individuals—there exists under private enterprise the countervailing power of another who is a competitor or a customer and, ultimately, the State, which acts as arbiter in case of conflict of interests.

Private enterprise cannot expect to be a vested interest in itself. Like any social institution, it must stand ready to be judged by the results it produces. By its nature, it is dynamic and resilient, as phenomenal developments in the U. S., in the United Kingdom, in West Germany, and other countries show. I am sure that it will not be found wanting in the challenge it faces in the emergent economies.

Although our governments will have to play a major role in the Alliance for Progress, it is to private enterprise that we must look for the real implementation of the program. Its survival is at stake. We realize this and are prepared to take an active part in the task since we cannot accept its failure and be resigned to perish. It is not only the capital we must invest, but also our work and sacrifice to obtain the betterment of our masses.

ALLIANCE FOR PROGRESS IN LATIN AMERICA

By Eugenio Mendoza *

President Kennedy, in his message of greeting to the Latin American Diplomatic Corps in March, 1961, referred to Bolivar's aspiration that the Americas should some day in liberty and glory be the greatest region in the world. The President stated that never in its long history had our hemisphere been so close to fulfilling this dream but, at the same time, so dangerously close to ending in failure.

Private enterprise in Latin America shares President Kennedy's opinion, and we believe fervently that we shall meet this challenge and conquer this danger, therefore making Bolivar's dream come true. However, before this happens we shall have to work hard and sacrifice a great deal. Above all, we shall have to create in ourselves the consciousness that to be successful we must rely

---

* President, C. A. Venezolana de Cementos; founder, president and advisor to many concerns in Venezuelan industry, finance, and trade.

primarily on our own efforts. If we do not, any economic or technical assistance from the outside will have been in vain.

Over the last 30 years the Latin American nations generally have exerted a great effort to advance their economies and improve the social conditions of their inhabitants. Some degree of industrialization has taken place in many countries and the revenue from exports of their products has increased income in most of these nations. This growth has been slow and has not followed the pace of the increase in the population, which is one of the highest for any major area in the world. The result has been an unequal and disproportionate increment of the demographic and productive elements of these societies.

AN ENORMOUS PROBLEM

Latin American countries, therefore, face the enormous problem of how to create jobs, educate, feed, and house this ever-increasing population. Progress has been achieved on the road toward industrialization, but the task is hard, and we have fallen short of our goals. Latin America also faces the danger of sharp fluctuations in the export prices of its primary products, which affect its social stability and its capacity to pursue a serious and continuous development program.

For this reason, it was recommended at Punta del Este in August, 1961, that a policy of minimum prices for raw materials be adopted, as the best and fairest method to aid our countries in their legitimate aspiration for social and economic development. In order to make such a plan workable, the people and the companies of the importing countries must accept this thesis and understand that the more Latin America receives for her products, the less will be the amount of foreign aid required. Furthermore, all the aid in the world cannot counteract the resentment which our people feel when they see diminishing prices for their products vis-à-vis the increase of prices for goods manufactured from these raw materials.

Another important contribution could be the idea expressed by Alfred C. Neal in *Foreign Affairs* for January, 1961:

The most important privilege which industrialized nations of the free world can offer to the underdeveloped countries is *one-way free trade*. This means that underdeveloped countries would be permitted to establish tariffs to encourage their own development but would be granted free trade treatment by the industrial countries. They could earn as much foreign exchange for their development as free markets permitted.

The nations in process of development need the industrial goods, the technical services, and know-how of advanced countries; and they also need, of course, markets for their primary products. On the other hand, the more industrialized and technologically advanced nations need not only the primary products but also the markets for their finished goods. Thus, any effort to try to solve our economic and social problems must take into account the necessary interrelation and interdependence of our nations. Neither the Latin American countries alone nor the United States by itself can solve the economic and social problems of the hemisphere.

The leaders of private enterprise in Latin America actively support President Kennedy's initiative to start at once the program known as "Alliance for Progress."

ONLY THROUGH MUTUAL ASSISTANCE

The governments of Latin America whose representatives signed the "Carta de Punta del Este," although conscious that each nation is best qualified to execute the programs pertinent to its own conditions, ratified the principle that the path to success lies only through the cooperative effort of all the nations of the hemisphere. Only with our mutual assistance can we hope really to create a better world for the millions of our countrymen who have known only misery and poverty. Let all the countries of America be aware that our respective national interests demand cooperation and collaboration with all the other nations as partners, and that any major contribution from one of the partners is not an act of benevolence but an act of solidarity at an international level.

The text of the "Carta de Punta del Este" is explicit when, using President Kennedy's own words, it defines as the main social problems of our countries: "Work, Home and Land, Health and School." These five words are so eloquent they need no explanation.

This vast program requires great sums of money but, more important than money will be the dedication and willingness to achieve the changes we in Latin America must bring about to make this program a success.

The United States is willing to cooperate with at least $20 billion during the next ten years, which will be supplied to the Latin American communities in the form of loans at low interest rates and with long repayment terms. Concurrently, the Latin American nations themselves will have to continue to supply even greater sums of capital to implement their part of the program.

GOVERNMENT *AND* PRIVATE ENTERPRISE

Although our governments will have to play a major role in the Alliance for Progress, it is to private enterprise that we must look for the real implementation of the program. Its survival is at stake. We realize this and are prepared to take an active part in the task since we cannot accept its failure and be resigned to perish. It is not only the capital we must invest, but also our work and sacrifice to obtain the betterment of our masses. Our presence in this program should serve as a sort of check and balance through our experience in administrative matters, giving the governments of our nations our best cooperative efforts to gain the common goal.

We are faced with a great challenge. The social responsibility and awareness which is asked of the leaders of private enterprise will complement in a very important way the program to improve the social structure of Latin America.

We realize that the fate of our civilization depends on certain changes of present conditions and that by bringing about such changes we shall have contributed to prevent the destruction of our democratic institutions. We believe that we will be successful in helping to create a better society for our hemisphere. This will be so because, in respecting the liberty of the individual and recognizing human and national dignity, we shall be answering human aspirations.

The Undersigned Delegates Endorse
and Are in Full Agreement With This Statement

Argentina
Juan Martin Allende
Anthony Blank
H. R. G. Clutterbuck
Norberto Schmajuk
Bolivia
Eduardo Saenz
Brazil
Clarence J. Dauphinot, Jr.
Gilberto J. Huber, Jr.
Chile
Agustin E. Edwards
Jorge Ross
Carlos Urenda
Colombia
Jose Gomez-Pinzon
Gabriel Restrepo
Alberto G. Samper
Alejandro Uribe
El Salvador
Francisco De Sola
Honduras
Robert Ramirez

Mexico
Felipe Garcia Carrandi
Luis Latapi
Luis G. Legorreta
Pablo Macedo
Fausto R. Miranda
Bruno Pagliai
Antonio Sacristan
Manuel Espinosa Yglesias
Peru
Carlos F. Ferreyros
Alfonso Montero
Manuel Ulloa
Puerto Rico
Jose A. Ferre
Maurice A. Ferre
Venezuela
Gustavo De LaRosa, Jr.
Eugenio Mendoza
William W. Phelps
Gustavo J. Vollmer

*We in the free world do not merchandise
fear. We do not flaunt our force, although
it is there in good and adequate measure.
We do not stress the military aspects of our
scientific achievements. We do not rely upon
threatening, bluffing, and boasting. We do
rely, as we must, upon convincing the unconvinced by making the way of freedom
work so well that others will be willing to
try it.*

FREEDOM CALLS AGAIN

By Henry C. Alexander *

The proceedings of this International Industrial Conference
have been distinguished by high quality. The speeches, the
papers, the discussions have been careful without being timid,
sound without being stodgy, deep without being dull. From hearing or reading nearly all of the addresses and papers, I am proud
to claim membership in an international fraternity that can
produce a body of opinion and insight as wise, as sophisticated,
as broad-gauged as this group is producing.

Perhaps no hard and fast conclusions have been drawn or will
be drawn, but a free exchange of ideas is taking place, problems
are being analyzed, and solutions are being suggested. The very
fact that these things are happening will surely lead to more rapid
progress toward the goals that free men seek in these times.

I shall not attempt to sum up the philosophy, the strategy,
the tactics that might emerge from the work of this conference.

* Chairman, Morgan Guaranty Trust Co.; director, Federal Reserve Bank
of New York, Johns-Manville Corp., American Viscose Corp., Standard Brands,
Inc., General Motors Corp., Discount Corp. of New York.

That task remains for other speakers on the closing day. They will be the first to insist, I am sure, that no adequate distillation is possible when the material is so rich and so diversified. This evening I will not deal with statistics—they are too soon out of date. I will not deal with mechanisms—they are for the technically expert. What I would attempt, rather, is to draw forth one thread that I believe has been woven through all the work of this week, and ask you to consider it as my theme.

HUMAN FREEDOM THE KEYSTONE

Everything that has been said in these deliberations has meaning only in a context of human freedom. Take that away and all the words are empty. Much has been spoken about helping the now-deprived peoples gain the benefits of a more abundant life; but if those benefits are sought at the cost of freedom, then the more abundant life will be not a feast but dry ashes in the mouths of the hungry.

In the welter of events that trouble the world today, threatening war of unthinkable horror, threatening the death of ideals as well as of men, we can hear freedom calling once more for advocates and defenders. As it has at the crisis points throughout history, freedom is summoning its supporters. It calls them wherever they may live and whatever may be the variations among their economic or political systems. It asks simply that there be no variation in their faith, their resolve, that the societies of free men shall not be dominated by international Communism or any other form of superstate. It demands strong wills and steadfast dedication. It exacts a pledge of life, of fortune, and of honor.

What response does it receive?

In too many parts of the world, men today show too much willingness to put their freedom up for sale, to put a price on the treasure that has always been priceless. When men anywhere begin to tolerate the thought that the surrender of liberty may be a bearable thing—whether because they fear the tyrant's threats or because they believe his promises—then it is not improper, it is not unbecomingly emotional, to restate in the strongest terms a commitment to the preservation of freedom.

Servitude must never become a tolerable concept, never an endurable price to pay for anything—certainly not for a totalitarian promise of better living, nor for a totalitarian grant of life itself. As our general chairman, Mr. McElroy, said in his opening address: "Our spirits must revolt against the police state."

The individual may wonder what his lonely efforts can accomplish. I would commend to his attention something another individual, a poet, wrote. These are the lines:

> You say the little efforts that I make
> Will do no good: they never will prevail
> To tip the hovering scale
> Where Justice hangs in balance....
> But I am prejudiced beyond debate
> In favor of my right to choose which side
> Shall feel the stubborn ounces of my weight.
>
> BONARO OVERSTREET

Enough stubborn ounces will outweigh a hundred megatons.

Yes, freedom calls again. It calls for reassurances. It calls for protection against the force of arms. It calls for an end of diplomatic blundering. It calls for economic sustenance. It calls for sharp decisions and strong action by all who would defend it.

In our military response, we really have no choice. Since brigands are about, threatening death and destruction, we in the free world must maintain in constant readiness a collective military strength adequate not only to deter but to defend. While we resolutely explore the possibilities of disarmament, we must do nothing to weaken the position from which we explore. The cost of our military burden is a cruel drain on resources that might be doing great work to enrich human life, but the first claim on all our resources must be the means of defending life and keeping it free. We may be frightened of war and all its indescribable horrors, but we must never be frightened at the cost of being strong enough to prevent it, or to win it.

SELF-DETERMINATION—BUT ALSO SELF-DISCIPLINE

However diligently we maintain our military might as free nations, our collective strength will be diluted if we allow political bickering and blundering to divide us. We have tortured our common cause with too much of this. To cite but one example, my own country has time and again confounded its allies and comforted its enemies by mistaken application of the historic American ideal of self-determination. We have been too quick to identify events of the 20th century with our own history of the 18th. The spell of historic tradition is so strong in us that our sense of discrimination is sometimes too weak. We have turned against our allies and unwittingly aided the work of Moscow-serving provocateurs, all the while believing we were invoking the spirit of 1776. In the process, we have helped force the premature birth of a number of nations and helped start them on the almost certain road to a subjection far worse than the one they left.

Self-determination, yes; but surely no advocate of freedom should veto, or abstain from voting on, the simple proposition that self-determination must be accompanied by capacity for self-discipline.

We in the free world should stop practicing a diplomacy that exasperates our friends and helps our enemies. Freedom cannot flourish and flower in such cold and blustery weather. My country has tortured the alliance, but so have others. The friends of freedom have indulged too much in the luxury of quarrels and disagreements over issues that are secondary to the main issue that unites them. But can we not have at least a greater degree of unity because of the urgency of the common threat against us? Too often the freedom bloc is paralyzed by indecision, not because there is any disagreement about our common basic goals, but because we fret and fuss too much about the niceties of diplomatic procedures.

WE MUST DEMONSTRATE AND CONVINCE

While defending freedom in the military and political realms, we must nurture and sustain it in the economic realm. In this pragmatic age, we must prove by demonstration that a free society can give its people greater material and social benefits than can any totalitarian regime. Some people and some nations are not convinced that it can. They suspect that a directed economy offers a quicker and easier way to progress. Theoretical arguments will not impress them. Neither will name-calling and labeling. The term "private enterprise" has no special appeal for them, nor has the term "Socialism" any special terror.

These are times of rising expectations, times of population explosion, times in which any established order may be questioned, times when nations are choosing ways and means for achieving the greatest economic and social progress in the shortest time. In the older and more highly developed countries in the free world, the choice is largely among kinds of modification and adaptation, without departure from the basic concepts of freedom and liberty. In the newer, developing countries, the choice is more fundamental. Shall it be the totalitarian way with its promise of efficiency through direction and control? Or the democratic way with its sometimes difficult and confusing methods and contradictions, but with its base set deep in a foundation of freedom?

Unfortunately, the choice is never presented that plainly. The Soviet promise of a better life more quickly achieved is accompanied by boasts of overwhelming military power, demonstrations of great scientific advancements, and the threat, implicit or explicit, of destruction for all those who thwart its will or reject its way. The soft hand of promise backed by the hard fist of power—a one-two punch that can carry persuasion.

We in the free world do not merchandise fear. We do not flaunt our force, although it is there in good and adequate measure. We do not stress the military aspects of our scientific achievements. We do not rely upon threatening, bluffing, and boasting. We do rely, as we must, upon convincing the unconvinced by making the way of freedom work so well that others will be willing to try it.

WE CANNOT COMPETE IN IRRESPONSIBLE PROMISES

The Soviets are pressing the battle hard, not alone on the military and propaganda front but in their mounting campaign of economic warfare. On this front, we can plainly outdo them in achievements, although we can be no match for them in making irresponsible promises. One of our sharpest weapons should be an increased flow of trade and investment among the friendly and uncommitted nations of the free world. We should not hope to preclude the Soviets from all trade with the non-Communist world, but we must not let that world, or any significant part of it, become so dependent upon Soviet materials and markets as to be subject to Soviet domination. Economic dependence means political dependence. Against that possibility, we must further strengthen the ties of trade and economic interaction among all the non-Communist nations.

To that end, a number of the highly developed countries have for some time sponsored programs designed to stimulate economic development in the less-advanced countries. The results have been less than we have hoped for. They have been less than we must achieve. In this area second-rate performance by the free world is not merely unacceptable; it is inexcusable. If we are inept at propaganda, naive at intrigue, unsure in the business of bluffing, these are shortcomings we can explain. But there are no valid explanations for the fact that our economic assistance has not been more effective.

Professor Galbraith had some fun with his fellow liberals recently by observing that their stock recommendation for curing any defect in foreign aid is to increase the amount spent by about 25%. I will stay out of the argument over how much the United States should be devoting to economic assistance, and certainly will not presume to suggest to any other nation how much it should be devoting.

WE SEEK NEW WAYS TO HELP

Of something else I am certain. Improved techniques are needed. The suggestion is often made that economic assistance ought to be funneled through some multinational or supranational agency because the recipient countries would like it better that way. I am not at all sure they would like it any better that way; I think they would like it best if it produced more impressive results more quickly in their own economies, regardless of the channels through which it comes.

For other reasons, however, we ought to be exploring ways to bring the aid programs of the free-world countries into a sharper, more unified focus. In the first place, coordination would make it easier to agree on a basis for sharing the financial burden of aid. Second, by providing a broader base, it would help iron out the ups and downs in any individual country's ability to provide funds. Thus, programs could be started with a greater assurance of continuity and stability. Third, and perhaps most important, the diverse economic strengths and skills of the free nations would be mobilized toward a common purpose, where up until now they have been scattered and diffused.

In the whole realm of economic affairs in the free world, whether in competition with the Soviets, in trade among the free nations, in investment in, or aid to, the underdeveloped areas, private enterprise has an important role to play, a large contribution to make. I know of no government outside the Iron Curtain that rejects the usefulness of private enterprise in principle.

LIMITATIONS ON ENTERPRISE

But in the present day, private enterprise finds limitations upon what it can do or will be permitted to do. Governments, especially in the developing countries, have preempted sectors of economic activity. Sometimes this is a matter of necessity as well as of policy. At the earliest stages of development, until the minimum framework for economic activity has been established, there is really little scope for private capital. Its opportunity to work, and to risk, comes a bit later.

There has been much discussion in this conference of the relationship between private and public capital as factors in the developing countries. I believe the consensus is in general agreement with Sir Oliver Franks' admonition that it will not serve the cause of private enterprise to oppose all government activity in the just-emerging economies. The day is past when any businessman can believe the best government is a weak, an idle, or a passive one—either in old countries or new, rich or poor. The tasks of defense and diplomacy are too great to be entrusted to weak governments. These perilous times call for able hands, guided by clear minds and stout hearts.

But businessmen rightly ask: where is the line to be drawn in the economic realm? And it is never too early to ask that question. If there is to be a place in a nation for private enterprise, not merely to exist but to grow, then that place must be provided in the basic structure. It must be provided at the very start.

SOME "MUSTS" FOR ENTERPRISE

Within such a framework so provided, private enterprise must do its job well. It must be successful; it must make a profit. If it fails for long to do that, it will be able to do little else. It must be productive of a widely shared prosperity and, as much as the politician, have a wise concern for human welfare and human progress. It must continue to strive for the kind of economic advancement that will nurture and sustain freedom and justice throughout our societies. Private enterprise cannot live where men are not free and where justice does not prevail.

The times are grim and men's hearts, I fear, are tired. This century has had too much of war, too much of big and tangled issues. After the destruction wrought by two world struggles, with a world-wide depression between, the nations that suffered most are now enjoying the contrast of great prosperity. They have earned it by sacrifices and hard work. But there is a danger that they may become preoccupied with prosperity, may let it divert attention from the hard challenge that a tireless enemy keeps pressing.

The peoples of the free world have not yet found in peacetime the effective expression of their unified purpose. Their resources, material and moral, have not yet been added up to a single-purposed sum. If they were, the total would stand beyond the risk of an attack on any front, beyond even the fear of it.

We have made progress in the direction of such a fusion by creating a number of international organizations. These bodies have been discussed at length during this conference. They are much in the minds of all who are concerned with making more effective the free world's mighty potential.

These organizations, and those that may succeed or supplement them, lend form to our collective defense of freedom. But, we must not neglect the spirit of that defense. For it is the spirit, dedicated without reservation to preserving our highest human values, that must bring us and hold us together in a great cause. While we keep high our strength in megatons and all the other terrifying denominators of modern physical might, let us never forget the importance, the power, of those stubborn ounces of our moral and spiritual weight.

Summation

The world is turbulent, potentially explosive because it is caught up in several
concurrent revolutions—political, social
and economic and, underlying all these,
scientific. Enormous energies have been
released—not only by science but also by
humanity itself. Anxieties stem from and
are nourished by the uncertainties as to
how these energies will be applied. The
reverberations that accompany these environmental changes affect all aspects of
life and force us beyond mere tinkering
—to fundamental rethinking of principles and attitudes.

J. E. WALLACE STERLING

We can brood on our troubles, our short-
comings, our errors—and brood ourselves
into inaction and depression. Positive ac-
tion, on the other hand, enables us to put
our anxieties in perspective and to do some-
thing about them.

SUMMATION

By J. E. Wallace Sterling *

No summary—certainly not mine—can do justice to what has
been said and thought at this conference. What I shall present
to you this morning, is in the nature of themes that have run
through the variety of topics covered and some notes that have
been accented.

Repeatedly the week's presentations and discussions have struck
a note of urgency—"grim urgency," Mr. McCloy called it. He
said, "There may very well be no industrial problems to worry
about, if we do not look up from our concentration on production and marketing problems and start thinking right away as
to how we are to solve the greater issues with which the world
is now faced. . . ."

Contributing to this same sense of urgency are the frustrations
of negotiating with a powerful, menacing, and unreliable enemy;

* President, Stanford University; chairman, Stanford Research Institute;
member, Advisory Board, Office of Naval Research; member, U. S. Advisory
Commission on Higher Education.

but basic to the urgency is the rapidity and fundamental character of change. The world is turbulent, potentially explosive because it is caught up in several concurrent revolutions—political, social and economic and, underlying all these, scientific. Enormous energies have been released—not only by science but also by humanity itself. Anxieties stem from and are nourished by the uncertainties as to how these energies will be applied. The reverberations that accompany these environmental changes affect all aspects of life and force us beyond mere tinkering—to fundamental rethinking of principles and attitudes. It is significant that the distinguished chemist who is the Deputy Director of the European Productivity Agency of OECD chose as the subject of his paper "Developing Human Resources." This is our problem and for that development old pills and platitudes just won't do.

Perhaps unexpressed, but nevertheless latent, is a real difference within this conference between the representatives of business in the developed countries and those in the less-developed. The latter feel keenly that the time is very short, much too short for leisurely discussion leading to the formulation of tidy, ideal plans. For them disruptive revolution is already knocking at the door. For them, the impact of Soviet propaganda on their hungry and ignorant masses is real and immediate. They are on the side of the free world, many of them—but they feel rather strongly that unless business and governments in the developed countries can act, and that rather quickly and with boldness, they will become victims of Soviet inroads and revolution.

There can be no doubt that the note of urgency has reverberated throughout this whole conference.

PAST ACHIEVEMENTS

Urgency accents the need for action. But there is also the fact that much has been done; it is simply that we have not done enough. Mr. Gainsbrugh made this clear as he reviewed the record of economic growth in the 20th century. So there was also a theme of past achievements.

The older nations of the free world have indeed broken

through many inhibitions. They have helped to bring new States into being and have put resources of men and money at the disposal of these newer States; they have sought to organize a partnership among the more and the less-developed peoples of the free world; they have continued to seek peace through negotiations with the Soviet bloc in the face of inconsistency and betrayal. They have kept the channels of trade fairly well open, cleared away many quantitative restrictions which clogged them, and clung rather tenaciously to the principle of competitive trading equality on which the success of future trade expansion would appear to depend. Currencies have been kept fairly stable and payments cleared.

These are not inconsiderable achievements. And let us not exaggerate the success of our enemies. They make mistakes, too. But such encouragement should not dissipate into complacency, because much remains to be done and there are ominous developments calling for earlier, if not immediate attention. Among them, these facts: (1) much national production goes for defense; (2) the gap in economic growth between the rich and poor countries does not close, but widens; and (3) population increase is out of control. With the mere statement of such problems one hears again the note of urgency.

SELF-DISCIPLINE

Another theme ran through the conference. I venture to identify it as an appeal for self-discipline. This was evident in discussions about the ethical standards of business practices and conduct; it was evident in the logic of Dr. Abs' argument that a nation should strive to limit its imports to those it can pay for. It was evident in the urgings of several, not least of all Mr. Edgar Kaiser, that we cast aside old labels and outworn nomenclature that impede clear vision of the dynamic realities of the present. It was eloquently evident in Sir Oliver Franks' summons to us to think through and apply the basic principles of freedom and enterprise which we accept and profess to champion.

Let there be no misunderstanding: This challenge to rethink the means by which these accepted principles may be effectively applied amid the turbulence of rapid environmental change has about it the same sense of urgency which has permeated the conference.

When we repeat 19th century cliches about Socialism and private enterprise, we are not dealing with reality—we are refusing to accept the universe; we are in fact echoing the controversy begun by Karl Marx and we are thinking in his terms, terms which by our own achievements we have done so much to discredit. Self discipline in conduct, in economy, and in clear thinking about present reality—this, I suggest, was another recurrent theme of the conference.

HUMAN RESOURCES

Another theme concerned Human Resources. This theme has many and important variations. One such variation has to do with the dramatic and ominous population increase, an increase which puts a drag on economic growth, which stands in the way of higher standards of living, which thwarts rising aspirations, and which invites a perpetuation of conditions in which Soviet promises and propaganda have strong appeal. The most knowledgeable and serious students of the population problem—several of whom have spoken at the conference—insist that the failure to solve this problem is to abet conditions which produce war. For solution, they turn to science for some simple effective contraceptive; but they turn also to the need for changed attitudes in which taboos and religious prejudice will have no place.

Another variation of the theme of Human Resources has to do with education and training, and the utilization of those thus educated and trained. This variation of the theme has manifold applications. It applies to considerations of how industry and commerce may be provided with leadership, how such leadership can be identified and advanced; it applies to conditions in the newer nations where the paucity of trained and educated personnel is poignantly acute; it applies to needs for able personnel in government positions, whether elective or appointive; it applies, it would seem to me, at any point one chooses to touch.

But it is noteworthy that despite the imperatives of urgency, one of the conditions of effective training and education is time. It is recognition of this condition that prompted Dr. King to suggest the need for a "Human Resource Strategy." He was specific in suggesting "the establishment of national and regional strategies for the development of human resources of the highest quality appropriate to future economic expansion needs, considered as part of a national investment policy and planned ... in advance." And he was specific in calling for a "much-deeper knowledge of the influence of education, science, and human skills on economic growth. ... ."

Still another variation on the theme of Human Resources is one related to the second point made by Dr. King—namely, research. The need for more knowledge was accented and reaccented —not least of all in discussions affecting business organization and operation.

I should also add as another identifiable variation on the Human Resources theme, the matter of attitudes. Again and again in the prepared addresses and in the informal discussions there was mention of attitudes. Inherent was the assumption that attitudes of mind and spirit were educable, that they could be cultivated and matured, and that the need for this was critically important.

INTERDEPENDENCE

Still another theme had to do with interdependence. Interdependence of public and private enterprise within a given country, interdependence of nations in a region and in the free world community. Interdependence thus stipulated invites, if it does not require, a concert of action—cooperation in the production and use of new knowledge, cooperation in the administration of concerted efforts to foster economic growth.

MONETARY PROBLEMS

Another theme is perhaps less a theme than an omnipresent, operating preoccupation—as one would expect it to be for leaders of business and industry. The most immediate and vexing problem confronting the conference had to do with the structure of world trade and related matters of monetary exchange and stability. All of this was effectually emphasized by Sir Oliver Franks and later, in practical detail, by M. Royer. This problem is interwoven with problems of aid, of investment abroad, and with the most effective use of capital, the supply of which is not commensurate with the need.

In this broad context, due recognition was given to the increasing effectiveness of international agencies like the World Bank, and to national institutions such as Export-Import Bank, and to institutions intermediate between the international and the national. Many suggested improvements were advanced. They included: International insurance against political credit risks, or tax incentives within the investing country as at least a partial substitute for insurance against political risks. Also suggested was the tapping of institutional finances, such as pension and insurance funds for investment abroad.

The list of such suggestions is long and I would not enumerate them here, even if I could. But there is the rather dramatic one by Dr. Ebtehaj that the administration of aid to the less-developed countries should be in the hands of an international agency, well staffed to perform its task. Such a multilateral, nonnational administration of aid would be effective, he suggests, in rooting out corruption, in advancing needed reforms, in applying aid as and where needed, and in avoiding identification of a given nation with a government that is crooked and incompetent.

As against such a suggestion, there were words of caution about the dangers inherent in shifting basic responsibilities on to the shoulders of international civil servants, in inviting the creation of a supernational bureaucracy. Such a caution was implicit in the strong argument of Dr. Abs that a prerequisite for effective cooperation among nations is that each nation should put its house in good order.

There was repeated emphasis on the importance of the human, organizing factor in development. This was stressed by Sir Leslie Rowan and echoed by speakers from Hong Kong and elsewhere. And it is the case that there is critical need for effective managerial personnel. But it is also the case that whole communities have to be reoriented toward the demands and requirements of a technical rather than a traditional society, and that this orientation must be undertaken during this rapidly moving revolution of rising expectations.

NEED FOR ACTION

Underlying the understandable preoccupation with these matters of trade, payments, investments, and managerial skills, there is another. It is, of course, the contest with the Soviet Bloc—particularly as this contest may affect the destiny of the newer nations. As Sir Oliver Franks put it: We must be able to offer the developing peoples a more attractive partnership than the Communists can offer. And in such a partnership, it should be remembered, the developed nations will need to open their door to imports from the developing nations. Trade, you recall, complements aid.

In particular, we of the more developed countries must take more seriously the problem of commodity prices which weighs so heavily on the raw material-producing countries. It is not a large problem to us, but for them it is the most important of all economic questions. There is really not much use bewailing the fact or possibility that new nations have achieved nationhood more or less unprepared for its responsibilities. We can brood on our troubles, our shortcomings, our errors—and brood ourselves into inaction and depression. Positive action, on the other hand, enables us to put our anxieties in perspective and to do something about them. It was significant, I thought, that despite the frustrations he has endured, Mr. McCloy ended his remarks with a call to action and a reassurance that if we put our minds to organizing a free world, we shall have nothing to fear. Sir Oliver laid down the same challenge.

I am grateful to Mr. Alexander for everything he said, but particularly for his insistent reminder that each of us has a "stubborn ounce of moral and spiritual weight" to place in the balance of this world-wide contest. The fact is that we have a new world in the making—a trading world, an interdependent, cooperative world and, please heaven, a free world.

ORGANIZATION OF THE INTERNATIONAL INDUSTRIAL CONFERENCE, 1961

GENERAL CHAIRMAN OF THE CONFERENCE: NEIL H. MCELROY,
Chairman of the Board,
The Procter & Gamble
Company

POLICY BOARD

CHAIRMAN: J. E. WALLACE STERLING, President, Stanford University

S. D. BECHTEL
Chairman of the Board
Bechtel Corporation
S. CLARK BEISE
President
Bank of America NT & SA
JAMES B. BLACK
Chairman of the Board
Pacific Gas and Electric Company
ROGER M. BLOUGH
Chairman, Board of Directors
United States Steel Corporation
E. FINLEY CARTER
President
Stanford Research Institute
STEWART P. COLEMAN
Former Vice President
Standard Oil Company (New
Jersey)
R. G. FOLLIS
Chairman of the Board
Standard Oil Company of Cali-
fornia

JOSEPH A. GRAZIER
President
American Radiator & Standard
Sanitary Corporation
EDGAR F. KAISER
President
Kaiser Industries Corporation
W. W. OVERTON, JR.
President
W. W. Overton & Company
JOHN S. SINCLAIR
President
National Industrial Conference
Board
GARDINER SYMONDS
Chairman of the Board
Tennessee Gas Transmission
Company
ALAN H. TEMPLE
Vice Chairman
The First National City Bank of
New York

INTERNATIONAL ADVISORY COUNCIL

CHAIRMAN: HAROLD BOESCHENSTEIN,
*President, Owens-Corning Fiberglas Corporation
(U.S.A.)*

DR. HERMAN J. ABS
*Managing Director
Deutsche Bank AG (Germany)*
M. BANK-ANTHONY
*Chairman
Borini Prono & Co. (Nigeria)*
LÉON A. BEKAERT
*Managing Director
Trefileries Léon Bekaert s.p.r.l.
(Belgium)*
DR. WALTER E. BOVERI
*Chairman
Brown Boveri & Cie. (Switzerland)*
EMILE BUSTANI
*Chairman of the Board and President
The Contracting and Trading
Company (Lebanon)*
SIR SIK-NIN CHAU
*Chairman
The Hong Kong Chinese Bank,
Limited (Hong Kong)*
A. M. DASAAD
*President-Director
Dasaad Musin Concern (Indonesia)*
DR. JORGE S. DE MELLO
*President
Companhia União Fabril (Portugal)*
MARCEL A. DEMONQUE
*President
Ciments Lafarge (France)*
EILIF DUE
*Chairman
Christiania Bank og Kreditkasse
(Norway)*

ABOL HASSAN EBTEHAJ
*Chairman and President
Iranians' Bank (Iran)*
DR. CARLOS J. ECHAVARRIA M.
*President
Compania Colombiana de
Tejidos, S.A. (Colombia)*
AGUSTIN E. EDWARDS
*Chairman of the Board
Empresa El Mercurio (Chile)*
RESID SERIF EGELI
*General Manager
Industrial Development Bank of
Turkey*
AMIRALI H. FANCY
*Chairman
Fancies Investments Limited
(Pakistan)*
SIR JAMES FLETCHER
*Chairman
Fletcher Holdings Ltd. (New
Zealand)*
DR. ALBERTO GAINZA PAZ
*Director
La Prensa (Argentina)*
TAIZO ISHIZAKA
*Chairman of the Board
Tokyo Shibaura Electric Company, Ltd. (Japan)*
K. Y. KING
*President
Chinese Petroleum Corporation
(Republic of China)*
VISCOUNT KNOLLYS
*Chairman
Vickers Ltd. (United Kingdom)*

HIPÓLITO LARRABURE PRICE
General Manager
  Banco Central de Reserva del
    Perú (Peru)
LUÍS G. LEGORRETA
Chairman of the Board
  Banco Nacional de México, S.A.
    (Mexico)
JUAN LLADO SANCHEZ-BLANCO
Executive Managing Director
  Banco Urquijo (Spain)
DR. FRANZ MAYER-GUNTHOF
Chairman
  A. G. Vöslauer Kammgarn-fabrik
    (Austria)
EUGENIO MENDOZA
Chairman
  C.A. Venezolana de Cementos
    (Venezuela)
HARRY F. OPPENHEIMER
Chairman
  Anglo American Corporation of
    South Africa Ltd. (Union of
    South Africa)
P. F. S. OTTEN
President
  N. V. Philips' Gloeilampenfa-
    brieken (The Netherlands)
MOGENS PAGH
Managing Director
  The East Asiatic Co. Ltd.
    (Denmark)
COLONEL W. ERIC PHILLIPS
Chairman of the Board
  Massey-Ferguson Limited
    (Canada)
LYELL B. ROBINSON (*deceased*
  July '61)
Chairman

  Consolidated Zinc Proprietary
    Limited (Australia)
FILEMON C. RODRIGUEZ
President
  Engineering and Development
    Corporation of the Philippines
    (Philippines)
DR. MOHAMED A. SELIM
Managing Director
  General Petroleum Co. (United
    Arab Republic)
ALBERTO SOARES DE SAMPAIO
President
  Refinaria e Exploração de Pe-
    troleo "União" S.A. (Brazil)
J. R. D. TATA
Chairman
  Tata Industries (Private) Limited
    (India)
ALEXANDER G. TSATSOS
President
  Industrial Development Corpora-
    tion, S.A. (Greece)
HON. PUEY UNGPHAKORN
Governor
  Bank of Thailand (Thailand)
PROF. VITTORIO VALLETTA
Chairman and Managing Director
  FIAT, S.p.A. (Italy)
JUUSO W. WALDEN
Managing Director
  United Paper Mills, Ltd. (Fin-
    land)
DR. MARCUS WALLENBERG
Vice Chairman
  Stockholms Enskilda Bank
    (Sweden)

UNITED STATES ADVISORY COUNCIL

CHAIRMAN: HENRY C. ALEXANDER,
*Chairman of the Board, Morgan Guaranty Trust
Company of New York*

WILLIAM M. ALLEN
*President
  Boeing Airplane Company*
STANLEY C. ALLYN
*Chairman of the Board
  The National Cash Register Company*
DR. ARNOLD O. BECKMAN
*Chairman and President
  Beckman Instruments, Inc.*
ALBERT K. CHAPMAN
*Vice Chairman
  Eastman Kodak Company*
GENERAL LUCIUS D. CLAY
*Chairman of the Board
  Continental Can Company, Inc.*
JOHN T. CONNOR
*President
  Merck & Co., Inc.*
PAUL L. DAVIES
*Chairman of the Board
  Food Machinery and Chemical
  Corporation*
FREDERIC G. DONNER
*Chairman of the Board
  General Motors Corporation*
DONALD W. DOUGLAS, SR.
*Chairman of the Board
  Douglas Aircraft Company, Inc.*
HENRY FORD II
*Chairman of the Board
  Ford Motor Company*
CARL J. GILBERT
*Chairman of the Board
  The Gillette Company*
HENRY J. HEINZ II
*Chairman of the Board
  H. J. Heinz Company*

ARTHUR B. HOMER
*Chairman of the Board
  Bethlehem Steel Corporation*
FREDERICK R. KAPPEL
*President
  American Telephone & Telegraph Company*
J. WARD KEENER
*President
  The B. F. Goodrich Company*
CHARLES H. KELLSTADT
*Chairman of the Board
  Sears, Roebuck & Co.*
AUGUSTUS C. LONG
*Chairman of the Board
  Texaco, Inc.*
HENRY R. LUCE
*Editor-in-Chief
  TIME Incorporated*
THOMAS B. MCCABE
*President
  Scott Paper Company*
JOHN J. MCCLOY
*Counsel
  Milbank, Tweed, Hope & Hadley*
DONALD C. MCGRAW
*President
  McGraw-Hill Publishing Company, Inc.*
CHARLES G. MORTIMER
*Chairman
  General Foods Corporation*
HENRY T. MUDD
*President
  Cyprus Mines Corporation*
MALCOLM MUIR
*Chairman of the Executive
Committee
  Newsweek*

CARROL M. SHANKS
WILLIAM C. STOLK
Chairman
  American Can Company
CHARLES S. THOMAS
President
  The Irvine Company
EDWIN J. THOMAS
Chairman of the Board
  Goodyear Tire & Rubber Company

JUAN T. TRIPPE
President
  Pan American World Airways
THOMAS J. WATSON, JR.
Chairman of the Board
  International Business Machines
  Corporation
FREDERICK K. WEYERHAEUSER
Chairman of the Board
  Weyerhaeuser Company
WILLIAM R. WHITEFORD
Chairman of the Board
  Gulf Oil Corporation

SPONSORING ORGANIZATIONS

National Industrial Conference Board, 460 Park Avenue, New York 22, N. Y.
  CHAIRMAN: HAROLD H. HELM, Chairman, Chemical Bank New York Trust Company, New York City
  PRESIDENT: JOHN S. SINCLAIR

Stanford Research Institute, Menlo Park, California
  CHAIRMAN, BOARD OF DIRECTORS: DR. J. E. WALLACE STERLING, President, Stanford University
  PRESIDENT: E. FINLEY CARTER

CONFERENCE DIRECTORATE

From National Industrial Conference Board: STUART R. CLARKSON, Co-Chairman; CLYDE L. ROGERS, Co-Chairman, Program Committee; JOSEPH L. NAAR, Co-Director of Public Information.

From Stanford Research Institute: WELDON B. GIBSON, Co-Chairman; ROBERT L. WOODCOCK, Executive Secretary of the Conference; GORDON H. PARKER, Deputy Executive Secretary; FRANCES O. BOHLEY, Assistant Executive Secretary; EDWARD S. PRENTICE, Co-Chairman, Program Committee; DAVID C. FULTON, Co-Director of Public Information; JEAN BURNET.

CHAIRMEN OF CONFERENCE SESSIONS

LIEUTENANT-GENERAL HAJI IFTIKHAR AHMAD
Chairman
  Pakistan Industrial Development Corporation (Pakistan)
HENRY C. ALEXANDER
Chairman of the Board

  Morgan Guaranty Trust Company of New York
MOHAMAD ALI
Chairman
  Pakistan Industrial Credit and Investment Corp. Ltd. (Pakistan)

DOUGLAS W. AMBRIDGE
President
  Abitibi Power & Paper Company,
  Limited (Canada)
DR. SALVADOR ARANETA
Chairman of the Board
  Republic Flour Mills
  (Philippines)
STEPHEN D. BECHTEL
Chairman of the Board
  Bechtel Corporation
ANTHONY BLANK
President and Managing Director
  Anthony Blank & Company S.A.
  (Argentina)
ROGER M. BLOUGH
Chairman, Board of Directors
  United States Steel Corporation
HAROLD BOESCHENSTEIN
President
  Owens-Corning Fiberglas
  Corporation
WILLIAM T. BRADY
Chairman
  Corn Products Company
H. M. VAN MOURIK BROEKMAN
President
  Royal Dutch Salt Industry
  (The Netherlands)
TORE BROWALDH
President
  Svenska Handelsbanken
  (Sweden)
EMILE BUSTANI
Chairman and President
  The Contracting and Trading
  Company (Lebanon)
E. FINLEY CARTER
President
  Stanford Research Institute
A. M. M. MURUGAPPA CHETTIAR
Managing Director
  Tube Investments of India, Ltd.
  (India)

NORTON CLAPP
President
  Weyerhaeuser Company
H. R. G. CLUTTERBUCK
Managing Director
  S.I.A.M. di Tella Ltda. (Argentina)
JOHN T. CONNOR
President
  Merck & Co., Inc.
CLARENCE J. DAUPHINOT, JR.
President
  Deltec S.A. (Brazil)
GENERAL WILLIAM H. DRAPER, JR.
Partner
  Draper, Gaither & Anderson
MARRINER S. ECCLES
Chairman of the Board
  First Security Corporation
AGUSTIN E. EDWARDS
Chairman of the Board
  Empresa El Mercurio (Chile)
A. J. ENGEL
President
  Algemene Kunstzijde Unie, N.V.
  (The Netherlands)
ROBERT L. GARNER
President
  International Finance Corporation
JACQUES GEORGES-PICOT
Chairman of the Board and Managing Director
  Cie. Financière de Suez (France)
CARL J. GILBERT
Chairman
  The Gillette Company
G. ARNOLD HART
President
  Bank of Montreal (Canada)
HENRY T. HEALD
President
  The Ford Foundation

HAROLD HOLMES HELM
Chairman of the Board
  Chemical Bank New York Trust
  Company
WILLIAM A. HEWITT
President
  Deere & Company
WALTER HOCHSCHILD
Chairman, Board of Directors
  American Metal Climax, Inc.
PAUL G. HOFFMAN
Managing Director
  United Nations Special Fund
LOGAN T. JOHNSTON
President
  Armco Steel Corporation
C. F. KEARTON
Managing Director
  Courtaulds, Limited (England)
FRANCIS KETTANEH
Senior Partner
  F. A. Kettaneh and Kettaneh
  Frères (Lebanon)
TOM KILLEFER
First Vice President and Vice Chairman
  Export-Import Bank of Washington
DR. C. A. KLAASSE
Managing Director
  Amsterdamsche Bank N.V. (The
  Netherlands)
THE VISCOUNT KNOLLYS
Chairman
  Vickers Limited (England)
HARALD KNUDTZON
General Manager
  Den Danske Landsmandsbank
  (Denmark)
BARON LAMBERT
Senior Partner
  Banque Lambert (Belgium)
HERBERT H. LANK
President

Du Pont of Canada Limited
  (Canada)
HIPÓLITO LARRABURE PRICE
General Manager
  Banco Central de Reserva del
  Perú (Peru)
LUÍS G. LEGORRETA
Chairman of the Board
  Banco Nacional de México, S.A.
  (Mexico)
EDWARD D. LOUGHNEY
President
  British American Oil Company,
  Ltd. (Canada)
MAXWELL W. MACKENZIE
President
  Chemcell Limited (Canada)
WARREN D. MCDONALD
Chairman
  McDonald Industries Limited
  (Australia)
NEIL H. MCELROY
Chairman, Board of Directors
  The Procter & Gamble Company
JOHAN MELANDER
Managing Director
  Den norske Creditbank (Norway)
MAERSK MC-KINNEY MŒLLER
Partner
  A. P. Mœller (Denmark)
COLEMAN MORTON
Executive Vice President
  Capital Research and Management Company
LLOYD K. NEIDLINGER
Executive Director
  United States Council of the International Chamber of Commerce, Inc.
J. WILSON NEWMAN
Chairman of the Board
  Dun & Bradstreet, Inc.
DINO OLIVETTI
Vice President
  Ing. C. Olivetti & C., S.p.A. (Italy)

ANDREW N. OVERBY
Vice President
  The First Boston Corporation
W. W. OVERTON, JR.
Chairman of the Board
  W. W. Overton & Co.
DAVID PACKARD
President
  Hewlett-Packard Company
MARCEL A. PALMARO
General Partner
  Lehman Bros.
DR. AURELIO PECCEI
Managing Director
  ITALCONSULT (Italy)
DONALD C. POWER
Chairman
  General Telephone & Electronics
  Corporation
ROBERT W. PURCELL
Chairman of the Board
  International Basic Economy
  Corporation
B. C. J. RICHARDS
Governor
  Bank of Rhodesia and Nyasaland
  (S. Rhodesia)
DAVID ROCKEFELLER
President
  The Chase Manhattan Bank
VICTOR E. ROCKHILL
President
  Chase International Investment
  Corporation
HUGH N. SAUNDERS
Deputy Managing Director
  The Rio Tinto Company,
  Limited (England)
JOHN S. SINCLAIR
President
  National Industrial Conference
  Board, Inc.
ALLAN SPROUL
Former President

Federal Reserve Bank of New
  York
J. E. WALLACE STERLING
President
  Stanford University
WILLIAM C. STOLK
Chairman of the Board
  American Can Company
GARDINER SYMONDS
Chairman of the Board
  Tennessee Gas Transmission
  Company
JESSE W. TAPP
Chairman, Board of Directors
  Bank of America NT & SA
ALAN H. TEMPLE
Vice Chairman
  First National City Bank of New
  York
ALEXANDER G. TSATSOS
Chairman and Managing Director
  Industrial Development Corpora-
  tion, S.A. (Greece)
ANTHONY WILLIAM TUKE
Chairman
  Barclays Bank Ltd. (England)
WILLIAM O. TWAITS
President
  Imperial Oil Limited (Canada)
JUUSO W. WALDEN
Chairman and Managing Director
  United Paper Mills, Ltd. (Fin-
  land)
ARTHUR K. WATSON
President
  IBM World Trade Corporation
CHARLES REGINALD WHEELER
President
  British Iron & Steel Federation
  (England)
CHARLES M. WHITE
Honorary Chairman
  Republic Steel Corporation